Preaching
That
Built
a
Great
Church

EVE-2

$3.95

JOHN R. RICE

Preaching That Built a Great Church

Sword of the Lord Publishers
Murfreesboro, Tennessee

7444

Printed in the United States of America

TABLE OF CONTENTS

INTRODUCTION:
The Story of the Church

In July, 1932, I began an independent revival campaign in the open air on a vacant lot at 10th and Story Streets in Dallas. I had been in full-time work as an evangelist since 1926. I had first held many two-week revival campaigns in churches, principally Southern Baptist churches, and then began large independent campaigns without any local church sponsorship in cities and towns in Texas and Oklahoma. These resulted in vigorous new churches in Decatur, Sherman, Waxahachie and other Texas cities. Those campaigns sometimes ran as long as ten or twelve weeks, time enough to win hundreds of converts, organize a thriving church and help them in building a tabernacle and sometimes in calling a full-time pastor.

For two years I felt burdened, felt that God would lead me to Dallas for the purpose of starting an independent, fundamental Baptist church.

In Dallas, without any organized sponsorship, we rented a vacant lot for $5.00 a week, printed some handbills and gave them out from house to house, had services in the open air, raised a little money, built some more benches. After some weeks a new church was organized with a clear-cut, fundamental statement of faith, charter members agreeing to membership if this evangelist would remain as pastor of the church.

First, we met in the open air, then in a rented furniture building. We bought a lot and began construction of a great brick tabernacle, 90' x 145'. Within a year there were more than 300 members. The membership grew steadily through the seven and a half years of my pastorate to some 1700 members and converts went to dozens of other churches throughout the Dallas metropolitan area.

In one six-months' period—from June 25, 1933, to December 25—we had recorded 1,005 professions of faith. In another three-months' period there were recorded 250 professions of faith. So about 7,000 people claimed Christ under this ministry in our seven years, and many hundreds of them were baptized.

Besides the growth of this strong congregation in what was first called the Fundamentalist Baptist Tabernacle, thousands of the converts went to many churches throughout the area. It was not unusual to have people attending from fifteen or twenty miles away, and necessarily and perhaps properly, many, many of these soon found churches nearer at hand where they could take their families regularly.

When the Fundamentalist Baptist Tabernacle of Dallas began, there was not another independent Baptist church in the whole Dallas area; when I resigned in early 1940, there were fifteen or eighteen such churches and most of them, and many other churches, had as their principal workers and officials, people who were won to Christ in our services.

Naturally There Were Many Difficulties

It is true that there is nothing too hard for God, and Jesus said, "All things are possible to him that believeth" (Mark 9:23). But it is only fair to name some of the difficulties which had discouraged many and had some part, perhaps, in the failure of other attempts to build such an independent, fundamental Baptist church in Dallas.

1. The powerful, popular, predominant and well-earned loyalty of a Southern Baptist people made an independent Baptist church unpopular.

Dallas had a concentration of Southern Baptists. One out of every six men, women and children in the Dallas area was a member of a Southern Baptist church. Dr. George W. Truett was pastor of the First Baptist Church, the largest Baptist church in the world. We started our open-air services and built the Fundamentalist Baptist Tabernacle within two blocks of the second largest church in the area, Cliff Temple Baptist Church, with possibly the second largest attendance of any Baptist church in the world.

Southern Baptist leaders were fundamentally sound and evangelistic. The people could hardly believe that modernism had crept into certain universities, colleges and seminaries of Southern Baptists. Denominational loyalty was well taught by greatly trusted, noble Christian leaders such as Dr. George W. Truett, Dr. L. R. Scarborough and others.

In the nature of the case, some churches openly breaking with the Southern Baptist Convention were thought to be queer, rather fanatical and possibly heretical. And there was great indignation against any one who preached as I did, that Christians ought not give undesignated funds to a great general program which partly supported modernistic teachers, as well as a host of good missionaries.

2. The problem was complicated also by the Frank Norris issue, then at its peak. Dr. J. Frank Norris of Fort Worth had made a bold fight for the fundamentals of the faith but had been turned out of the county association and the Convention. He did a great work in standing for the fundamentals of the faith but his methods were not always commendable, his statements not always reliable. So widespread distrust of Dr. Norris left an odium on other independent Baptists who openly opposed modernism.

Three and a half years after the church began in Dallas, Dr. Norris began an open, scandalous attack on this preacher and his church, and the growth of the church necessarily depended on simply pressing the Bible plan of a local New Testament church with soul winning the main issue, plain, sharp Bible preaching and absolute loyalty to the fundamentals of the faith, and committed to reaching common people by the thousands with the Gospel.

The church eventually, in order to disassociate itself in the minds of the public with Dr. Norris, changed its name to Galilean Baptist Church but continued steadfast with the same statement of faith, the same type of preaching, promotion and soul winning with which it had begun.

3. We had the problem of starting from scratch, with no money, no financial support, no organized backing. It was in the heart of the depression in 1932. The people who attended the revival services and were drawn toward the new church were very largely poor people. At least half of them were on relief. Many of those who had jobs did only common labor. A few came who had been misfits in other churches, as is always the case in a new church. Some others came with strong convictions and who felt a need for the kind of church we would build, with emphasis on evangelism, with strong defense of the faith, with an all-out attack on modernism and worldliness, using no Sunday school literature but the Bible. But the church membership was largely made up of the converts we won to Christ and those to whom we taught the Bible and trained to be soul winners.

We bought a large two-story house and lot. We tore down the building and there built the big tabernacle. We had to pay cash for every carload of brick, every load of lumber. Much of the work on the building was done by volunteer labor, and the good ladies brought lunch for everybody at noon week after week, month after month, and we raised what money we could for other things. We entered the tabernacle at first with wood shavings on the floor. We maintained an active soul-winning work, along with the enormous labor of building, of raising money and supervising the work. I personally bought every bit of the material. An architect gave the plans, after we had outlined to him what we wanted. Many felt it was an amazing and blessed thing that God helped us build that large building for cash, in the midst of depression, with poor people.

4. We did not have the help of an adequate church staff. The people were poor. I had no regular salary, and my income included whatever people put in the envelope and marked for the pastor or the offerings from my revival campaigns and preaching outside the church. Our living and our giving were sacrificial. Part of the time we had a music director for our 80-voice choir, congregational and solo work. Part of the time we had an associate pastor to fill the pulpit when I was away and to help in the visitation.

This book is titled *The Preaching That Built a Great Church*, because the great amount of visitation and soul-winning work done with the people was not on a paid basis but inspired and led by the preaching and teaching of the pastor.

5. It should be considered also that my ministry in Dallas had to share time with many other activities. I was and am an evangelist. During those years in Dallas I held revival campaigns; a citywide campaign five weeks in Binghamton, New York, an extended campaign in Englewood, Colorado; one in Whittier, California; weeks in Chicago; a tent campaign in Waterloo, Iowa; a tabernacle campaign in Springfield, Missouri; a large independent campaign in Gainesville, Texas; revival efforts in Kilgore, Wichita Falls, Bridgeport, Texas, and elsewhere.

The last twelve months I served as pastor of this church I was gone eighteen Sundays and an even larger proportion of the week days I was preaching in outside engagements.

I had a two weeks' debate with a Church of Christ preacher, with large attendance from Oklahoma and Texas.

Besides that, my written ministry was extensive. Some years before Dr. W. B. Riley, Dr. T. T. Shields and Dr. J. Frank Norris had planned to have Sunday school lessons through the entire Bible and had asked me to prepare notes on those lessons. It took five years, including the first years at Dallas, with a lesson prepared every week.

The weekly SWORD OF THE LORD began September 28, 1934, and took much labor.

During that time I had books published—*The Soul Winner's Fire* published by Moody Press; *Jewish Persecution and Bible Prophecies* published by Fundamental Publishers; a book of sermons published by Zondervan; the book on prophecy, widely sold—*The Coming Kingdom of Christ* in hard binding.

In the midst of many, many difficulties we must give God the glory that He graciously blessed in the saving of thousands of souls and the building up of many, many Christians through the limited ministry of this unworthy servant.

You Will Note That the Sermons Published Here Are Typical of Many Others

Here we give twenty-nine sermons which were taken down in shorthand and published in early issues of THE SWORD OF THE LORD. You will note the sermons here on the *Great East Texas School Tragedy*, on *The Kidnaping and Murder of the Little Matson Boy*, on *The Abdication of King Edward of England*. Not recorded here is a sermon I preached on "How Max Baer Lost the Heavyweight Crown." He trained on beer! I preached on lewdness at the Texas Centennial at Dallas, on gambling at the race track. I preached on the modern movies and on the unequal yoke and bloody oaths of the lodges.

It is noted that I preached many sermons on doctrine. I preached on salvation by grace, on the security of the believer, on the power of the Holy Spirit, on Christ's premillennial second coming, on literal fire in Hell, on the verbal inspiration and scientific accuracy of the Scriptures. On many subjects dealt with in the sermons, I dictated carefully and meticulously the messages and they are published elsewhere.

But here are sermons taken down in shorthand by two expert, devoted and faithful Christian women, Misses Lola Bradshaw and Viola Walden, my secretaries.

I think it is also noticeable that whatever was the subject, there was an earnest appeal to sinners and we regularly expected to see and did see people claiming Christ as Saviour in the Sunday morning and Sunday night services, whatever the subject. My old teacher, Dr. L. R. Scarborough, who was then president of Southwestern Seminary, used to say, "Any end of the Gospel is good just so it is the hot end." By which he meant that a fervent zeal of heart and Holy Spirit power would have some effect on everybody who heard the message whether it be addressed to Christians or lost people.

I take great joy in the fact that in the midst of a heavy building program, in the midst of enormous labors, all the details and administration of the church, outside revivals, regular radio preaching, a tremendous two-weeks' debate with a Church of Christ preacher where attendance came from over the state and beyond—in the midst of all this, we were enabled to press the claims of Christ continually and see people turn to Christ and claim Him!

The sermons are rough and colloquial. In the nature of the case they would be, taken down word for word under the heat of a burning heart, pressing always for decisions. It is notable that among the conversions were some of the harder and abandoned sinners. I suppose I baptized more than 100 confirmed drunkards who had been saved in the work at Dallas besides other hundreds saved and going to other churches.

Now, as I have read over these sermons, there has been a tremendous warming of my heart. First, to remember that God in mercy blessed us. And second, because of the Scripture truths that burned in my heart then and came tumbling out in a flood of compassion and concern. Those truths still burn in my heart.

It is my earnest prayer that many a man will find encouragement to go out and build New Testament churches. We started from scratch, with no preceding organization, no organized backing. But so what? So did every preacher in apostolic times who started out to win souls and build new churches!

Oh, and if God in loving mercy will set holy fires burning in ten thousand hearts as they read these messages, we will rejoice and thank Him!

John R. Rice
1974   Murfreesboro, Tennessee

I. DISCIPLESHIP AND DEDICATED LIFE

1—Jesus and Peter

(Sermon preached June 14, 1936, at the Tabernacle; stenographically reported)

PRAYER: Our dear Father, we pray that our lives may count for Thee. Now people come with their burdens, some with sorrows, some carelessly indifferent. But bless every heart here this morning through Thy Word. And Thou, dear Jesus, suffering and betrayed, denied and forsaken; Thou Jesus, who prays for us and loves us and will not let us go, bless us this morning through the preaching of the Word and through the sweet songs. Hold on to us this morning by Thy grace. Amen.

In Luke, chapter 22, we will begin with verse 31; then in the same chapter we will read some other verses. We are accustomed to bringing our Bibles to the services and looking on.

> *And the Lord said, Simon, Simon, behold, Satan hath desired to have you, that he may sift you as wheat:*
>
> *But I have prayed for thee, that thy faith fail not: and when thou art converted, strengthen thy brethren.*
>
> *And he said unto him, Lord, I am ready to go with thee, both into prison, and to death.*
>
> *And he said, I tell thee, Peter, the cock shall not crow this day, before that thou shalt thrice deny that thou knowest me.* —Vss. 31-34.

And now skip to verse 54.

> *Then took they him, and led him, and brought him into the high priest's house. And Peter followed afar off.*
>
> *And when they had kindled a fire in the midst of the hall, and were set down together, Peter sat down among them.*

But a certain maid beheld him as he sat by the fire, and earnestly looked upon him, and said, This man was also with him.

And he denied him, saying, Woman, I know him not.

And after a little while another saw him, and said, Thou art also of them. And Peter said, Man, I am not.

And about the space of one hour after another confidently affirmed, saying, Of a truth this fellow also was with them: for he is a Galilaean.

And Peter said, Man, I know not what thou sayest. And immediately, while he yet spake, the cock crew.

And there Matthew adds the words that he cursed and swore and said, "I know not the man."

And the Lord turned, and looked upon Peter. And Peter remembered the word of the Lord, how he had said unto him, Before the cock crow, thou shalt deny me thrice.

And Peter went out, and wept bitterly.—Vss. 54-62.

Now there are those who say that Christians never sin. There are those who say Christ saves us from sin and therefore if you are really a child of God, you will never do anything very bad. There are those who say that if one is born again he will never curse or get drunk or commit adultery. They are wrong, utterly wrong.

Simon Peter was a truly converted man, born again, yet here he denied that he even knew Jesus. The Scripture says that he cursed and swore. He was guilty of cowardice, lying, was unfaithful, disloyal; was guilty of outright cursing and blasphemy. Peter was guilty of as bad a sin as a Christian could be, I suppose. It was a terrible sin.

I. Really Born-Again Christians May Get Drunk, Curse, or Deny Christ

You will not gain anything for Christ and Christianity if you always take up for Christians. Many people are truly born again, and yet they do very wicked things. I am sorry that they do, but they do. You will give more glory to Christ if you admit it. The blood of Christ is enough not only to save a man but to help him live a victorious Christian life. That is true, but it doesn't do a new convert any good to tell him he is out of temptation and will never more have trouble from the Devil. Old Peter had plenty of trouble after he was saved.

It is a bad thing that this world is against Jesus Christ. Oh, it is too bad for sinners to turn down the Saviour and drive away the Holy Spirit and grieve Him and not hear the Gospel! But it must be worse in the sight of God. And the results are infinitely worse when children of God are unfaithful.

Of the ten virgins, five were wise and five were foolish; yet they *all* slumbered and slept. I am sure the Bridegroom was more concerned about the wise who had the oil and yet went to sleep. It is powerless Christians, not wicked unbelievers alone, who curse a country and block revivals.

Oh, Peter did wrong. I want to discuss the case of Peter and help you if I can. Here Peter committed terrible sin. If Peter did, you may, too. You are no better, no wiser. You don't pray any more, you do not read the Bible any more, you do not love Christ any better than did Simon Peter. If he sinned, then you may commit the same kind of sin.

I want everybody here to know that there is no limit to the terrible depths of sin you may fall into after you are saved except, you cannot commit the unpardonable sin. That is the only sin as far as I recall that you cannot commit if you are saved.

A lost man can get drunk; so can a Christian. Noah did, and Lot did. A lost man can curse and blaspheme; a Christian can, too. Peter did. I know some other people who did, too. A lost man can commit adultery as did David and Samson; so can a deacon or preacher. Born-again ones may commit any kind of sin in the world. You had better pray and watch your step, watch your heart! Watch and pray, or you are likely to fall into bad sin—even if you are a Christian. Peter did.

II. Peter Lost Out by Not Praying

What did Peter do that led him into this terrible sin? In the first place, Peter slept and didn't pray. You have read the case of Peter when he was with Jesus in the Garden of Gethsemane. Already Jesus had warned the disciples, and Peter particularly. But when it came time to pray, Peter slept. He said, "I am sleepy and tired."

There are many times when you ought to pray when sleepy. You say, "But I have to get my sleep." You had better get your prayers answered and victory over Satan first. Peter got into trouble because he slept instead of praying.

Anybody who wants to live straight and not get drunk nor fall into adultery and not deny Christ will have to spend a good deal of time praying. I hope you will make a definite engagement with the Lord every day. If you could pray at the same time every day, perhaps that would be better. At least you ought to have some time in secret prayer every day, a private consultation alone with God every day. I find that when I don't do that or when I postpone it until afternoon, I often fall into sin, and I don't get as much work done. A Christian will most likely deny Jesus somewhere during the day if he forgets to pray.

> Ere you left your room this morning,
>   Did you think to pray?
> In the name of Christ our Saviour,
> Did you sue for loving favor,
>   As a shield today?
>
> When you met with great temptation,
>   Did you think to pray?
> By His dying love and merit,
> Did you claim the Holy Spirit
>   As your guide and stay?
>
> When your heart was filled with anger,
>   Did you think to pray?
> Did you plead for grace, my brother,
> That you might forgive another
>   Who had crossed your way?
>
> When sore trials came upon you,
>   Did you think to pray?
> When your soul was bowed in sorrow,
> Balm of Gilead did you borrow,
>   At the gates of day?

> Oh, how praying rests the weary!
> Prayer will change the night to day;
> So in sorrow and in gladness,
> Don't forget to pray.

If you hadn't thought to pray as you started out the day, you will fall into temptation. Peter sinned and lost his power, joy and courage and committed a terrible sin because he failed to pray. A Christian cannot succeed and not pray. A Christian cannot whip the Devil unless he prays. Someone has said,

> "The Devil trembles when he sees
> The weakest saint upon his knees."

If a saint really prays with sincere devotion and contrite heart, the Devil may well tremble, because he can't get the man who holds on to God in prayer. Peter sinned by not praying.

How much do you pray? Do you pray fifteen minutes a day? Most of us don't. Do you pray five minutes a day? Most of us do not. Three minutes? No, most of us don't spend that much time in honest, real, secret prayer to God, begging Him for help in time of need and for strength in time of temptations.

God help us to pray! If you want to whip the Devil, you must pray. If you want to please God and if you want to have strength for temptations, you must pray. Those who fail to pray through may deny Christ, as did Peter.

III. Peter Was Weak Enough to Deny Christ Because He Did Not Know His Bible

Another thing: Peter fell into sin because he didn't understand about the crucifixion and resurrection. It will not take many Scriptures to show you. Here is an amazing thing. Every time Jesus mentioned His crucifixion, the disciples were astonished. One time Peter had plainly said, "Lord, this shall not be for You. No, You are not going to die. We can't let You be crucified." Jesus turned and said, "Get thee behind me, Satan: thou art an offence unto me." He said, "Peter, you are on the Devil's side about this. The Devil is trying to keep Me from going to the cross, and is trying to get Me to detour around the crucifixion. That is what he has been telling Me all the time." So

Jesus said to Peter what He had said to Satan, "Get thee behind me, Satan: thou art an offence unto me."

In Luke 18:31-34, we find this Scripture:

> *Then he took unto him the twelve, and said unto them, Behold, we go up to Jerusalem, and all things that are written by the prophets concerning the Son of man shall be accomplished.*
>
> *For he shall be delivered unto the Gentiles, and shall be mocked, and spitefully entreated, and spitted on:*
>
> *And they shall scourge him, and put him to death: and the third day he shall rise again.*
>
> *And they understood none of these things: and this saying was hid from them, neither knew they the things which were spoken.*

They did not understand the Old Testament teaching that Jesus would be tried, crucified, and rise again.

Every time Jesus mentioned going to the cross, being buried and the third day that He would rise again, they didn't understand about it. They didn't understand about His death, and didn't understand about His resurrection. Until Jesus came into the Upper Room, they didn't believe Him. Then they thought He was a ghost until He said, "Here I am. See My hands, with the nail scars. Put your finger there and thrust your hand in My side. Do not be faithless, but believing." Not until then did they understand the Scripture about the resurrection.

Peter fell into sin and denied Christ because he hadn't learned the Word of God as he ought. Because they came to the time when the world turned against Jesus and He was now ready to be crucified, and thought, "Jesus has failed and the Gospel has failed and we are ruined!" Peter just didn't understand it, and didn't know what to do. He didn't know how it would turn out because he hadn't studied and prayed over the Word of God as he should have.

Those two walked down the road to Emmaus that day sadly talking. When Jesus came along they didn't know Him. Jesus asked, "What are you talking about? Why are you so sad?"

They said, "Well, there was a man named Jesus of Nazareth, a prophet, and we thought it was He who should have redeemed Israel, but now He is dead!"

Jesus said, "O fools and slow of heart to believe all that the prophets have spoken. Ought not Christ to have suffered these things and to have entered into his glory?" And He opened up the books of Moses and the Psalms and the prophets and taught them case after case and Scripture after Scripture and proved that Jesus had to die and had to rise again the third day so that His blood could pay for sinners.

Had Peter learned that back yonder, he wouldn't have committed that terrible sin. He wouldn't have been discouraged. When you get discouraged you are likely to fall into sin.

Somebody says, "I am so blue boday." You had better get out of your blues and get into the pink. When you are blue, the Devil is on your trail.

This is the way of this physical body. There is normally a slight alkaline chemical reaction in the body. If that body doesn't have enough exercise or if you eat too much meat, fat and sugar and not enough vegetables and fruit, then you get an acid condition. Then the stomach, the elimination and other things are not right, so any kind of infection prospers. Any time your body gets sour by an acid condition, then there will be throat trouble, enlarged tonsils, constipation, kidney trouble or some other ailment. The doctors have found that if it is just trouble in the toes, it is often caused by an acid condition.

So when you get blue and discouraged and disheartened and down in the mouth, it gives the Devil a good chance to attack you. I know men can whip the liquor lust and the drink habit—until they get down in the mouth and discouraged and feel that they don't have any friends. When a man's wife scolds him and isn't happy around him, then he goes out and says, "I will just have a glass of beer to pick me up." Then the first thing he knows he is drunk and back again in the old habit and in the gutter of sin.

Peter wouldn't have been discouraged and downhearted and

defeated had he said ahead of time when Judas came and placed the shameful kiss on the face of Jesus, "It is sad, but He is going to die, and His blood will be poured out and it will pay for my sins. But I will see Him rise again. I will see Him ascend."

Peter would never have denied Jesus had he known this ahead of time. Peter wouldn't have been whipped that day. Peter did wrong. Peter did not study the Bible. He didn't learn the Bible. Had Peter known the Bible, he wouldn't have fallen into that terrible sin.

No wonder David said, "Thy word have I hid in mine heart that I might not sin against thee." If you don't learn the Bible, if you don't hide it in your heart and store it away in your heart, like precious treasures, you are going to fall into some terrible sin. The only safeguard for a child of God is holding on by prayer and then hiding the Word of God in your heart. What I mean is this: John 15:7 says, "If ye abide in me [through the Holy Spirit's leadership], and my words abide in you [the Bible], ye shall ask what ye will [in prayer], and it shall be done unto you." That is constant prosperity, constant safeguarding, constantly winning the fight every day through the Bible and prayer. Peter missed those two.

My friends, do not neglect the Word of God. Sin will keep you from the Bible or the Bible will keep you from sin. The man who goes on in sin and enjoys sin and holds on to it, will have no taste for this Book.

There is something bad wrong with the Christian when the Bible is dry to him, when he takes this Holy Book, this Book written by the Holy Spirit, words of God written by men, and reads about redemption, about salvation, about God's love and the romance of creation and a thousand mysteries and glories of the world to come; and it is dry to you! Brother, you have been doing something you oughn't to do. Something is wrong in your life or that Book would be sweet, fresh, fascinating and lovely beyond compare. You get this! The Word of God is a safeguard against sin.

Many a Christian starts out but he has a little persecution; or a soul winner starts out to win sinners and people talk a little sharply or insult you and you get discouraged and quit. What is wrong? You didn't read your Bible. If you had read your Bible, you would have expected that ahead of time, and would have said, "I know they despised Jesus and they will despise me, too, but He said He would be with me." If you had read your Bible, you would know that the Bible says, "Blessed are ye, when men shall revile you, and persecute you, and shall say all manner of evil against you falsely, for my sake. Rejoice, and be exceeding glad: for great is your reward in heaven: for so persecuted they the prophets which were before you." If you knew your Bible, you could say, "Thank God, He is going to bless and help me! I will go on and do more for the Lord."

You will fail without the Bible. Peter failed and fell into sin because he didn't know God's plan. Satan came to Peter—the Devil took him by surprise—and Peter said, "It is my own life." So Peter told the shameful lie, cursed and swore and tried to get out of the accusation of being a Christian. He broke his own heart and the heart of Christ. Peter became the pattern for all backsliders, the most shameful picture of a child of God. Satan was able to get him to act that way because he didn't know the Bible.

If you do not know your Bible and do not have it on your heart—the spiritual interpretation—and hate sin, the Devil will whip you. You can't beat the Devil without the Word of God.

The Lord Jesus Christ was our example on this matter. One time He went out into the wilderness to be tempted of the Devil. He was led of the Spirit to be tempted. He was our example. He was filled with the Spirit. We may be filled with the Spirit. The same way our Lord whipped the Devil, we may whip the Devil. Some think Jesus had advantages that we don't have. No, He didn't. He was weak when He went to be tempted. He fasted forty days so He would be weak as any man.

If you do not watch you will be down in the mouth and commit some terrible sin. If your heart is not glad, the Devil takes advantage of that. Another: If you have trouble in the home, you may go off and get drunk. The Devil will take advantage of every trouble or weakness.

Somebody mistreats you; perhaps you mash your finger. You never intended to say anything wrong, but when you mashed your finger hard the Devil said, "This is a good time to get mad." You may not say anything out loud, but the Devil takes advantage of everything that comes along.

Jesus said, "I will give the Devil every advantage over Me, and yet defeat him. I will, so that no weak sinner can say I had a better chance than he." So Jesus went forty days and nights without a bite to eat, then when the Spirit led Him out to face the Devil, Jesus defeated him with the Word of God!

This thing I praise God for. He is a wonderful Saviour. He put Himself in my place and met the Devil and said, "I will not use a single weapon but what John Rice can use, too." When Satan said, "Take these rocks and make bread," Jesus said, "In the first place, John Rice could not make bread out of rock and I am not going to either. In the second place, I cannot give way to the Devil, even about bread. I have to whip him the same way John Rice can whip him." So Jesus said, "It is written, Man shall not live by bread alone but by every word that proceedeth out of the mouth of the Lord shall man live." And Jesus said, "If the Devil ever bothers John Rice about something to eat, John Rice can use the same Scripture."

Then the Devil came along and said, "Here is another thing. I will give You all the kingdoms of this earth if You will bow down and worship me one time." Jesus had a Bible answer to that. He turned to Satan and said, "It is written, Thou shalt love the Lord thy God and him only shalt thou serve."

And so with the other temptation about falling off the pinnacle of the Temple. The Devil told Him that the angels would bear Him up lest He dash His foot against a stone. Jesus answered, "Thou shalt not tempt the Lord thy God." He answered Satan by Scripture; so can you. When Jesus whipped the Devil, He whipped him with this Word of God.

IV. Had Peter Understood Isaiah 53 and Psalm 22, He Would Never Have Denied Christ

Had Peter known the Word of God as he sat out there that

night, he would not have denied Jesus. He would have looked on with a broken heart, to be sure, but he could have said in his heart, "Now I am going to see the 53rd chapter of Isaiah fulfilled, and the 50th, too, where it says, 'I gave my back to the smiters, and my cheeks to them that plucked off the hair: I hid not my face from shame and spitting.' Now I am going to see Him taken out and led to the cross and crucified!"

Had Peter known the Bible, he would have been moved with compassion and tears but he would have been as bold as a lion and could have said, "Now I am going to see Him bear His cross, and I am going to hear Him pray the prayer of the 22nd Psalm, 'Eli, Eli, lama sabachthani? that is, My God, my God, why hast thou forsaken me?' I am going to see Him put down into the grave and I am going to see Him come up again triumphant over death, Hell and the grave!"

Had Peter known that, he wouldn't have sinned that time. Peter, had you just fed yourself on the Word of God! There is no bread that can give strength for temptation like the Word of God. Feed on the Word! It will keep you from sin.

Peter made a mistake by not understanding those things. Whenever Jesus spoke of His death and resurrection, the disciples said, "We don't understand it." None of the disciples did. Peter made a mistake by not praying and reading the Bible.

V. What Bad Company Costs

Peter also had the weakness of bad company. My friends, you say, "Well, there is danger in there." Peter too said, "There is danger in there if I go with Jesus, if I just walk right in where He is being tried."

That may be so. I frankly admit to you sometimes if you are close enough to Jesus you will suffer for it. You had as well face that.

I will give you the other side of it. Just as certain as you run with the Devil's crowd, you will suffer for it. You will suffer more by running with the Devil's crowd. Yes, you will!

Somebody says, "There is so much to give up if I come out and out for Jesus." It is nothing like what you will have to give up if you don't!

Somebody says, "Brother Rice, it costs something to be a Christian." It costs more to serve the Devil and take the Devil's wages, for the wages of sin is death.

I am sure Simon Peter lost more. I am sure as he looked back many and many a time he said, "If I had it to do over. . . ! I wish I could take it back that I denied Him and cursed and swore and said I did not know Him. I wish I could take it back. But, oh, it is written down for uncounted millions to read!" If Peter could only take it back! But he couldn't!

Tradition says when they took Peter out to crucify him, he said, "Don't nail me that way. I am not fit to die like Jesus died. I am not worthy. I denied Jesus. Turn me head down and nail me to the cross like that. I denied Jesus!"

That is part of the cost of bad company.

VI. "Burn This Hand First"

When they were going to burn Archbishop Cranmer of England at the stake because he held on to the Bible and to the Protestant religion, in the reign of Mary, with his hand he wrote a retraction: "I will take it back. The Catholic Articles are correct. My books are contrary to the Bible." Later on his conscience smote him, and after awhile he said, "I can't do it! I am going back and say I still believe it all—salvation by the blood and not by the church."

They tied him to the post, piled grass and brush around him, and after awhile with glee somebody set fire to it. As the fire burned around him, he held his hand up over the flames and said, "I want this hand to burn first, the hand that signed the retraction, the one that wrote I didn't believe the Bible. I want to burn that first."

Peter never got away from what it cost him to get away from Jesus. It will cost something to stand out and out for Jesus. It cost me the classmates at Baylor University who used to call on me to preach the Commencement sermons in their high schools. It has cost me friends. Oh, but I wouldn't trade what I got for it!

Peter said, "Well, I am afraid it will cost me something if I claim to be His disciple."

My friends, bad company will cost you more than anything can cost you for running with Jesus. Oh, the danger of bad company! I hope you will teach your children the danger of bad company. I never get tired of telling you. Bad company! Bad company!

If your boy plays with a little boy who uses bad language, teach your child to stay away from him or others who use bad language, who smoke, drink beer, talk about the preacher and are against the Bible. Shun them. Brother Roberts, you are in as much danger as your boy, and I am in as much danger as my little girls. Nobody is safe. Peter was not safe—that iron apostle, the rock, Simon Peter. He was not safe when in bad company.

Peter did wrong. Doubtless he said, "Everything is gone! What is going to happen? Nobody will observe me." So he sat down outside with the soldiers. He listened to their ribald jokes, their cursing. Then somebody came along and found him. Taken unawares, Peter denied Jesus. In bad company.

Here is the danger of bad company. If Simon Peter could have said, "I am out and out for the Lord, I am all the way across for the Lord," he would have been all right.

VII. The Traitor Inside the Gate—Inbred Sin

Every man here has an inbred traitor inside the gate. It is sin inside. The wicked nature inside you will betray you, Brother Houpt. If you get in with the Devil's crowd, if you run with the Devil's crowd, that traitor will unlock the door and let them in. Inbred sin! "The heart is deceitful above all things, and desperately wicked."

Simon Peter sinned in going in there with those wicked soldiers. He had been as bold as a lion before this time, but the first thing he knew the sinful nature inside had betrayed him. He wouldn't believe it, himself. He didn't intend to do it. He himself didn't know he would do it until he heard himself cursing and swearing.

Oh, Jesus turned and looked at him and the rooster crowed. Then Peter realized how he had sinned! He didn't mean to, he didn't want to, but he was betrayed by the sin inside.

When you run with bad company, there is a traitor in your own breast that will lead you to your ruin. I beg you, don't run with the Devil's crowd. Have no part with them. If you do, the first thing you know, something wicked inside will find friends there and you will learn to enjoy it. No man can run with the Devil's crowd without betraying Jesus Christ. No man can find pleasure with the Devil's crowd without betraying the Lord Jesus Christ. There is a sinner inside the gate that will betray you—your own inbred sin.

Peter denied Jesus because he was running with the wrong crowd. Had he gone in there and said at first, "I am one of His disciples. If you are going to kill Him, kill me, too," the temptation would have been over.

A new convert often says, "I know what my temptation is going to be—the crowd I run with." I will tell you how to face that. Tell them, "I have found Jesus." Go with the light of Heaven on your face and make a beeline to the hardest one and say, "I have been saved, and I want you to come and take Jesus as your Saviour." Take the Bible with you out there and tell them of the love of God. And the next time you are out, testify for Jesus Christ and say, "I am looking for you Sunday night. I want you to be on the front seat to hear my preacher."

Take your Bible with you every time you go, and talk about the Bible, and you will have no trouble with bad company. They will give you up, Brother, if you get red-hot for Jesus Christ. They will either leave you alone or come with you to serve the Lord Jesus Christ.

This halfway business for Jesus gets you in trouble. You say, "I am a Christian, but I am no fanatic." Not being a fanatic is what gets you in trouble. A real fanatic for Jesus Christ has a safeguard. People say about me, "John Rice is sort of a fanatic." But they never say, "Come on, Brother Rice, and take a drink from my bottle." It is worth being called a fanatic to have that!

It is very rare that anybody ever offers me a cigarette; and to be sure they don't offer it the second time! That is one safeguard you have by being a fanatic, Brother. I thank God for that!

Extreme! Radical! You can save yourself a lot of trouble by

being radical, by being an extremist, a fool for Christ. If Simon Peter had been radical and right in there by the warm side of Jesus Christ trying to win somebody, he wouldn't have gotten into this trouble.

Brother, you will get in bad trouble if you run with the Devil's crowd. If you run with bad company, you will find there is a traitor inside—your own inbred sin. You had better crucify and mortify that fellow inside and put him to public shame and come out and out for Jesus. Then you won't be tempted to fall into sin and deny Jesus Christ.

VIII. Peter Fell Under the Enslavement of an Old Habit—Cursing

Here is another thing: the enslavement of an old habit. Sin, sin, sin! If people really knew! How the Devil gets people to do wrong! He is a deceiver and by nature a liar and the father of liars. Oh, how does Satan do it? By deceit. No wonder God hates a lying tongue. The Devil was the first liar. No wonder that outside the Holy City and outside of Heaven the Scripture says will be liars, whoremongers, etc. The Devil himself is a liar. The Devil got Peter to sin by deceiving him, by lying and enslavement.

If you would but realize what sin will do and what it costs to tell a lie, you would not do it. If you would but realize what it costs to steal, you wouldn't steal. If you would but realize what it costs to drink, you wouldn't drink.

A sinner who turns down Jesus is deceived. A man wouldn't do it if he would but realize where it is leading him. He is fooled. The Devil must lead him. The prodigal boy never would have gone into the far country and wasted his substance with riotous living had he not been deceived. He didn't know it would lead him to the hogpen. And when "he came to himself," he got up and went home like he ought to have done.

Back in the years when horny-hand Peter was a fisherman by the side of the Sea of Galilee, day after day pulling in the fish, he never thought a little cursing would hurt him. Oh, Simon Peter, if you but knew that those lips that you trained to curse;

if you but knew when Jesus was on trial for His life; if you had but known that you would curse and swear and deny Him, you wouldn't be cursing out there!

Sin will betray you. You let sin get a hold, and then in the trials of your life, it will betray you. You may say, "I can drink a little now, then I can quit it." Maybe you can, but you won't stay quit. You give in the first time of weakness. A man says, "I think it is all right to drink a little before you are married." Then one of these days after you are married, and when the boys say, "Let's go out for a little good time," you drink a little, then the old habit and lust for it will return and you are gone!

Poor old Simon Peter was just going back to his old habit. Do you think this is the first time Simon Peter ever cursed? Do you think it is the first time he ever swore? Oh, no! Listen, yonder is a man out by the sea coast. He hangs his net on a shag and lets out a string of oaths.

Do you think that old nature died when Simon Peter was converted? No. He is still wearing the same pants. There are two men wearing the same clothes. But that old blaspheming curser has been there all the time. The only safe way is never to begin doing something you do not want to do in a crisis.

Anybody who ever cursed will have it come to mind a thousand times. You will wish it never did. A Christian curse? Yes. It will come into your mind a thousand times when you wouldn't, for any amount of money, have it possess your heart.

A man hears a dirty yarn or tells a dirty story. But one day when you have married the sweetest girl you ever knew and have little children who love you and look up to you, and you long to be pure and good; when you start to win souls and wish you were worthy to carry the Gospel message in such a poor earthen vessel, it will come back with the crashing ruin of an old evil, enslaving habit, like it came back on Peter in the time of temptation.

You had better beware of the thing you tied on back yonder. It will still be tied on now. When you are trying to safeguard your testimony, you had better beware, and stay close to Jesus because you have sown some seed back there that you will be reaping in the time of the hardest temptation. Beware of the enslaving habits!

IX. Which Was Greater Shame: Betrayed by Judas or Denied by Peter?

Oh, that was bad when Jesus was betrayed by His enemy. But can you imagine any kiss ever burning like the kiss of Judas when he came and said, "I will show you where He is. The one I kiss will be Jesus"! And when he came to kiss Him and Jesus said, "Hail, friend," and Judas kissed Him on the cheek,—do you suppose any kiss ever burned like that kiss did! I wonder? How do you suppose Judas felt when his unholy lips touched the face of the pure Son of God? Can you imagine the pollution and shame? Jesus loved him and called him "friend." He did not rebuke Judas. He didn't shame or scorn him. Can you imagine the pollution that Jesus felt?

I do not think any pure girl who was ever seized by a ruffian and violated ever felt the shame that Jesus, the Holy One, must have felt when Judas, the betrayer and enemy, came and kissed His face and betrayed Him. And then He was taken yonder and condemned and wicked men mocked Him and spit in His face and drove the nails in His hands.

Oh, this world! What a terrible heart the sinner has! The Devil's people helped to crucify Jesus. That was bad. When Jesus turned and Judas kissed Him on the cheek and Jesus said not a word, I can't believe that was one-half as burning and wicked as when Jesus saw Simon Peter yonder and heard him say, "I don't know Him. I don't even know the Man. I tell you, blankety-blank, I don't even know Him!"

Someone says, "Surely you are with Him; you are a Galilean."

"No, I don't even know Him!"

And the third time, lo! a rooster crowed! Startled, he looked at Jesus and Jesus looked at him. Jesus didn't say a thing. I don't know whether the Son of God could be struck speechless. When they put on that crown of thorns and pressed it down, I don't think that hurt Jesus as much as to have this disciple whom He loved and prayed for, out there cursing and swearing. I don't think so.

When they sat down and mocked Him—this wicked world—and said, "Come down from the cross; come on down; if You are the Son of God as You say, save Yourself then"—do you think that hurt nearly as much as the shame when His own blood-bought children, His own disciples who had slept in the same bed with Him and had eaten from the same loaf and John lay his head on Jesus' bosom, when they all had forsaken Him and Simon Peter had cursed and swore and denied Him? I think the thing that hurts the heart of God most is when His own children turn away and deny Him.

Betrayed in the house of His friends! Denied by His own—those bought by His blood!

X. Jesus Loved Peter Still!

The suffering Jesus, betrayed, condemned, denied and forsaken!

There are two or three things I want to mention about Jesus. I have preached this morning to my own heart. It has been like a whip falling on my own back. Everything I have said this far has hurt and pained. But I come to another part. It is good for us sinning Christians.

Someone asks, "Do you think sinners will get to Heaven?" That is the only kind of folks who will get there. But sin will be taken out then. You say, "Do Christians sin?" That is the only kind of Christians there are.

What kind of a Saviour do we have? A Saviour who loves us still. He still loved Peter.

When somebody said, "Oh, how I love Jesus," Mr. Wyzenbeek said we ought to sing, "Oh, how we *ought* to love Jesus!" That is the way I feel this morning.

Do you love the Lord? Well, I do. My life may sometimes deny it, my life may contradict it, but I do love Him. Yet, oh, I fear, so little! I ought to love Him more.

I asked an old man, "Do you love the Lord?" He said, "Oh, not nearly as much as I ought to," as if it were a good excuse why he couldn't claim to be a Christian. I am in the same boat. I don't love Him nearly as much as I ought to. But my being saved and my safety and security are not dependent on my loving Jesus but on His loving me. And He loves me still!

I asked a man, "Do you love the Lord?" His answer was, "Yes, but I know something a lot better." I was a good deal surprised and about ready to rebuke him, when he said, "He loves me!"

My dear brother, Jesus loved Peter. That is strange, but He loved him.

XI. Jesus Prayed for Peter

Jesus prayed for Peter. I told you awhile ago that you need to keep on praying. Praying is a safeguard. It keeps you from doing wrong. That is right, but my salvation doesn't depend on my praying but on Jesus' praying. Someone says, "If you quit praying, you will lose out." No, if *Jesus* quits praying, I will lose out. He is at the right hand of the Father praying for me, interceding for me. And He sends the Holy Spirit down to teach me how to pray, and the Holy Spirit prays for me with groanings that cannot be uttered.

Jesus had said to Simon Peter, "You are going to deny Me three times before the rooster crows in the morning."

Peter said, "I am not! Everybody else may, but I won't."

"But Peter, I have prayed for thee that thy faith fail not. The Devil desires to have you to sift you as wheat. You may think you are gone, but I have prayed for you."

Peter did think he was gone. Peter never thought he would any more be a preacher. Peter never dreamed he would at Pentecost preach and see three thousand saved. Peter thought, "I have lost my reputation. Christians no more will have confidence in me. Jesus won't have any thing to do with me any more."

But Jesus said, "Peter, I have prayed for you. I know how the old Devil is going to shake you. He will shake out some of your pride and bragging that you are better than the other disciples. But I have prayed for you that your faith fail not."

Thank God for the love of Jesus that forgives us and that never lets us go! "I have prayed for you."

A mother prays for her boy. After he is saved, I have seen her shout and praise God up and down the aisle and say, "I have prayed for him ever since he was born!" That is a long time to pray. That is faithfulness in prayer. I have seen a wife get up again and again and say, "I have prayed for my husband thirty years; now my prayers are answered!" That is a long time to pray. That is faithfulness in prayer.

But thank God, for these nineteen hundred years the Lord Jesus has remembered me, loved me, and He has never let me slip, never let me go. He has held on. God has answered His prayer.

Not every mother's prayer is answered. But Jesus' prayer is answered. And He has prayed for me, and I am kept. The Devil can't get me. He shakes me. He shakes out all my pride and all my self-reliance. He shakes all the things out of my pockets. The Lord can get good out of the Devil's works.

Sometimes God even makes the wrath of men to praise Him. But the Devil can't get me out of reach of the prayers of Jesus. "I have prayed for thee."

I am thankful that I have a High Priest praying for me, One who has entered into the vail, into the holy place, to the Shekinah glory! I have an anchor sure and steadfast. My friends, I thank God for the prayer of Jesus!

"Brother Rice, aren't you afraid one of these days you will fall so far you cannot get back?" I have fallen many times. "The steps of a good man are ordered by the Lord: and he delighteth in his way. Though he fall, he shall not be utterly cast down: for the Lord upholdeth him with his hand." The Lord Jesus is praying for me. And I am kept, I am preserved by His prayers; Jesus, whose prayers are always answered, as in the case of Peter. Jesus loved him and warned him. God prays for us, then He warns him.

You don't have to sin. When you do, that is your fault. Someone asks me if I believe in sinless perfection. I believe in it but I don't practice it. Nobody else does but Jesus. I could do right about some particular thing, but I don't. I am just too mean. I want to. Why don't I do right? I don't know, unless it is the wickedness within me. This much I know: After He warns me and after He tells me, He still loves me and still prays for me and still keeps me. Oh, love that will not let me go!

XII. Jesus Warns, Loves, Prays for, Then Holds on!

First, Jesus loves you, then He warns you and prays for you. And what else? Then He holds on to you. The song says, "Hold to God's Unchanging Hand." That is all right as far as it goes. You ought to pray and trust. But as far as your safety is concerned, it ought to be the other way. *God holds on to you!* How can I hold on when my hand is not unchanging? I am too weak to hold on, but He is the unchanging God, and He holds on.

When Peter was warned, when Peter was prayed for, when he denied Jesus and when Jesus turned and looked on him in that last night, do you suppose it was in anger? Did Jesus say, "I told you, I warned you that you would fall into sin. Why didn't you listen? You didn't pray, you didn't read your Bible when I tried to teach it to you! You got in bad company; now you have done what I told you that you would do!"?

Was there anger in the eye of Jesus when He, the persecuted, mistreated, despised and denied, turned those sad eyes on Peter? What was in that look of Jesus?

When you get out and do wrong, God is looking at you. Christ is looking at you. What is in that look?

Sinning Christian, listen to me! You loud-talking, quick-tempered, critical, hot-headed Christians, the Lord Jesus Christ is looking at you when you sin! What is in His mind? Grief, I think is there. Anger? No, I don't think so—maybe in some sense. Reproach? Some. Scorn? Does He say, "I am through with you! I have tried and tried, and you have promised and promised; but now I am through with you"? No! No!

What is in that look? I will tell you what was in that look when Peter had denied Him three times because he didn't pray and didn't study His Bible. It was a love that would never let go! That is what was in that look. Jesus turned and looked and with infinite compassion said, "Peter, I am sorry. You hurt Me but I love you. I am praying for you. You are My sheep and I will not let you go. You are Mine!"

What was in that look? "Oh, I will not let you go. I warned you and prayed for you, and the Devil can't get you. You are Mine. I will not let you go!"

When Jesus stood that day with the crown of thorns on His head and with that spittle on His face, condemned to die, yet He took time to look at Peter with love and compassion and forgiveness. And Peter went away with a broken heart. He couldn't get away from the love of Christ! Holding on!

Jesus rose from the dead after awhile and said, "Mary, I want you to carry a message for Me. Go tell all My disciples—Matthew, John, the whole bunch—that I want them to meet Me in Galilee. And tell Peter especially. Go tell My disciples AND PETER." Peter didn't think he would be counted as one of the disciples any longer. He thought, "Judas is no more counted with the disciples. He betrayed Jesus and then went out and hanged himself. Neither am I fit to be in that crowd." So Peter may have thought.

A man is a member of this church. He came here after being many years a drunkard. He was wonderfully saved. The night I baptized him, he said, "Until seven weeks ago, I have been drunk for twenty-five years!" He came here, we loved him, he gave his testimony.

Then one day he drank some beer, and he has not felt like coming back. He is so ashamed. He ought to be ashamed. But my heart goes out in love to him, and I want him. He has done no worse than Peter did. He has done no worse than I have done and you have done. We ought not let people like that go. Jesus didn't.

So when Jesus arose from the dead, He said, "Tell My disciples *and Peter! I want Peter in that crowd! He is Mine! I will not let him go! He is Mine! Peter is Mine!*"

XIII. Jesus Knew the Love of Peter and Made Him Tell It

Later on when they went out fishing, Peter said, "I am going fishing. I see now I can't live a Christian life. I just can't make it. Who is going with me?"

The others said, "We also go with thee."

Jesus in His resurrected body came on the seashore, got some sticks, built a fire and called to them: "Children, have you any meat?"

They looked up and saw Jesus and said, "No, this fishing business is not what it is cracked up to be." (It never is when you are away from God.) "We haven't got a fish, not one in this world!"

Oh, backslider, you say, "I am going back to the Devil's ways." Well, you will find it a bitter old path, and you will say, "I don't know what I ever got out of this before I was saved. I can't see what it was."

Simon Peter was out fishing. Jesus said, "Let down the net on the other side." They said, "We have been fishing all night and have caught nothing, but we will try it anyway." And they got the net full. John, who was quick of spiritual discernment, said, "That's Jesus!"

When Peter looked around and saw Him, he said, "I've got enough of this fishing business!" He had been running away thinking he was unworthy. He felt it and knew it. He thought, "If I had a good chance, I would go and tell Jesus I love Him. I would tell Him I am sorry." Peter said, "I am done with fishing! Give me that coat!" So he jumped in the sea and said, "Boats are not fast enough for me!" He got out and swam to the shore.

When Jesus said, "Bring Me some fish," Peter said, "Let me do it." So he brings some fish for Jesus. Jesus cooked it for them. They sat down and ate. He didn't scold Peter. Peter sat there on needles and pins, so ashamed to speak to Jesus about it! Jesus said, "He is Mine. I bought him. I paid for him. I have prayed for him. I will not let him lose out. I will not turn him loose. He wants to tell Me that he loves Me. I will make it so he will."

So Jesus says, "Peter, do you love Me more than these?"

Peter said, "I am ashamed now to brag, but Thou knowest all things. Thou knowest that I love Thee."

"Then why don't you get busy working for Me?"

"I didn't believe I could. I thought an old cursing man like me was ruined from any preaching."

"Peter, lovest thou Me?"

"Lord, thou knowest all things. Thou knowest that I love Thee."

Jesus told him three times to get busy. Then He told Peter, "I have not thrown you away. I haven't turned you loose from preaching. I haven't turned you out of the ministry. I haven't taken away your ordination papers. I haven't let you be tricked out of winning souls. Get busy, Peter."

Old Peter says, "I am going to do it!" And the next time you see old Simon Peter, he is on a stepladder down on the corner of Main and Commerce in Jerusalem preaching the Gospel!

Oh, my friends, He will not let you go!

Peter had been warned, yet he denied Him and sinned against Him, but Jesus loved him and turned and looked at him. Peter went out and wept bitterly.

You have wept many times over sins. Remember He sees you and hears you when you deny Him. But, thank God, He sees you when you weep and repent. Nobody else can see your broken heart and your shame, but He sees that, too, when you go away and weep bitterly. And He will not let you go!

Oh, troubled backslider and dishonored Christian, you have lived a sorry life and have done so little, but He loves you still and prays for you still. He knows your broken heart. He loves you still and He will not let you go.

Come today and say, "Lord, thou knowest all things, thou knowest that I love Thee." And He will say, "Get busy. There is work to do. I am still for you. I haven't thrown you away. You have thrown yourself away, but I won't throw you away."

Oh, love that will not let me go! Mr. Stroh will sing a verse or so of that song with me. Oh, the love that will not turn you loose! Why don't you say, "I am His and I will serve Him"?

> O Love that will not let me go,
> I rest my weary soul in Thee;
> I give Thee back the life I owe,
> That in Thine ocean depths its flow
> May richer, fuller be.

I want to sing that last verse, too, with Mr. Stroh.

O Cross that liftest up my head,
I dare not ask to hide from Thee;
I lay in dust life's glory dead,
And from the ground there blossoms red
Life that shall endless be.

It takes a cross to go with Jesus; but it is worse if you don't go with Him. Oh, I hope you will not shun the cross, will not deny the Lord Jesus. When you sin, you can say, "Lord, Thou knowest I still love Thee."

PRAYER: Our dear Father, teach us this morning that You love us and will not let us go. Oh, help us to know that You seek us and pray and woo us back. O Lord, these who have been out of service and not winning souls and who are disappointed and shamed because of sin, let them come and lay everything down, as did Simon Peter, who was prayed for and forgiven and blessed again!

Save today any lost person who may be here. Let any who ought to, come for membership. Bless any backslider who ought to come and confess his backsliding. For Jesus' sake. Amen.

2—The Absolute Essentials of a Successful Christian Life

(Sermon preached Sunday morning, August 27, 1939, Dallas, Texas. Stenographically reported.)

I come this morning to speak to you on what I think is a very important subject: *The Absolute Essentials of a Successful Christian Life.*

Christians should succeed. There are a number of Scriptures which indicate that a Christian should be full of joy, victorious, and that everything he puts his hand to ought to be successful. Paul said in Philippians 4:13:

> *I can do all things through Christ which strengtheneth me.*

That means success for a Christian. Here is another good Scripture in the 1st Psalm, verses 1 through 3:

> *Blessed is the man that walketh not in the counsel of the ungodly, nor standeth in the way of sinners, nor sitteth in the seat of the scornful.*
>
> *But his delight is in the law of the Lord; and in his law doth he meditate day and night.*
>
> *And he shall be like a tree planted by the rivers of water, that bringeth forth his fruit in his season; his leaf also shall not wither; and whatsoever he doeth shall prosper.*

One of the strangest, most all-inclusive sentences in the Bible is that a man who follows certain requirements will prosper in everything he does, that he can certainly expect full prosperity.

Here is another. In John 16:24, Jesus said:

> *Hitherto have ye asked nothing in my name: ask, and*

ye shall receive, that your joy may be full.

God wants a Christian to be full of joy because he gets what he wants, because he gets all he asks for, because he gets his prayers answered.

The same thing is told in John 15:7:

If ye abide in me, and my words abide in you, ye shall ask what ye will, and it shall be done unto you.

A Christian can have what he wants when he is in the will of God, when the Word of God is abiding in him and he is abiding in Christ.

Again, Psalm 37:4 says:

Delight thyself also in the Lord; and he shall give thee the desires of thine heart.

A Christian can prosper. He can have what he goes after. His work can be blessed, his prayers can be answered, his heart can be happy, his family can be cared for, his business can turn out successful. That is the plain promise of the Word of God.

Here is another promise for success. In the 1st chapter of Joshua the angel of God appeared to Joshua and said, "You come on and enter into the land of Canaan, and as I was with Moses, so I will be with thee." And then he said:

Only be thou strong and very courageous, that thou mayest observe to do according to all the law, which Moses my servant commanded thee: turn not from it to the right hand or to the left, that thou mayest prosper whithersoever thou goest.

This book of the law shall not depart out of thy mouth; but thou shalt meditate therein day and night, that thou mayest observe to do according to all that is written therein: for then thou shalt make thy way prosperous, and then thou shalt have good success.—Vss. 7,8.

I know human prosperity does not necessarily indicate spiritual prosperity. But Christian prosperity certainly involves material things as well as spiritual things. I want to lay on your hearts some things about this that are absolute essentials to success in Christian living.

WHAT IS SUCCESSFUL CHRISTIAN LIVING?

I think I had better define *Christian success*. What do I mean when I say I want to be a successful Christian? First, happiness. A Christian ought to be happy. A long-faced Christian, one who isn't happy in the Lord, one who has no joy, is a mighty poor signboard for Christ. If you can't be happy, surely you can't recommend Christ. A Christian ought to be happy.

Acts 8 says that down in Samaria where Philip went and preached the Gospel, "there was great joy in that city." And you find at Pentecost, after the power of God came upon the Christians and many were saved, they "did eat their meat with gladness and singleness of heart, Praising God, and having favour with all the people."

A Christian ought to be happy, and Jesus said that is one reason to pray:

Ask, and ye shall receive, that your joy may be full.

There are many such promises throughout the Bible.

Rejoice in the Lord alway: and again I say, Rejoice.—Phil. 4:4.

Be careful for nothing; but in every thing by prayer and supplication with thanksgiving let your requests be made known unto God. And the peace of God, which passeth all understanding, shall keep your hearts and minds through Christ Jesus.—Phil. 4:6,7.

A Christian ought to be happy. You are not a successful Christian if you are bowed down with sorrows, burdens and care.

Another test of a Christian's prosperity is: Do you get your prayers answered? To be a happy and successful Christian would necessarily involve getting not what you sometimes think you need, but what you really need you can get. Prayer is more than just asking. Prayer is more than just adoration. Prayer is not only talking to God, but real prayer is getting things from God. Prayer is going to God and getting what you need. You are not a successful Christian if day by day you cannot get what you need.

Suppose there is a depression on and here I am a child of God. Next door to me lives a child of the Devil. He is out of work, and I am out of work. He doesn't know what to do. He is under the circumstances and bowed down by the depression and sorrow, and he can't get a job. I am a Christian. I tell my next-door neighbor that God answers prayer. But He doesn't answer mine for a job. I can't get work, and I can't pay my bills. I am defeated and downcast just like my unsaved neighbor. If so, I certainly am not a successful Christian.

If a Christian can't get his prayers answered, he is not a prosperous Christian.

I do not mean that Christians are sure to have everything they want, but what we really need, we have a right to get. And if we are right with God and learn the secret of prosperity, we can. I say, Christians surely ought to learn how to be prosperous and get their prayers answered.

Here is another necessary mark of a successful Christian life. If you are going to be a prosperous Christian, you must be a soul-winning Christian. Do you believe that a real Christian—one who is successful, his Christianity makes his heart happy all the day and gives him victory over his problems and supplies all his needs—cannot convince a single soul that there is something to it?

Mr. Patton, if you are the right kind of a Christian and it works for you, if your Christianity is successful, somebody else will catch it. Your brother who lives next door will say, "I wish I had what Tom Patton has." You will be able to win somebody else to Christ and to have the same joy and same victories over sin and the same blessings you have.

A really successful Christian will have to be a soul winner. If you are not, you are not doing what Jesus said. "Follow me, and I will make you fishers of men" (Matt. 4:19); He said, "Let him that heareth say, Come" (Rev. 22:17). The Scripture says about New Testament Christians, "Therefore they that were scattered abroad went every where preaching the word" (Acts 8:4). And saved people in the Bible who were happy Christians were soul-winning Christians.

No matter how much you pray, or how many times you go to church, or how many prayers you get answered, if you are not a soul winner, you are a failure. You are not doing the main thing that God wants a Christian to do.

Jesus said, "Follow me, and I will make you fishers of men." If you walk after Christ, you will be a soul winner. You are not successful, you are not really following Christ, if you do not win souls. Your Christianity is a failure if you do not win somebody to Christ.

You say, "I pay the preacher to win souls." Yes, I know, but you are still not a successful Christian unless you yourself win souls.

There is a real standard, a high standard of daily blessedness and spiritual prosperity that every Christian can obtain. I will show you from the Word of God how you may have it.

Fourth, a spiritual Christian can do some good work for God and that work will be blessed and will continue and grow and prosper. A prosperous Christian will have a job for God and will do that job and be blessed in it. "Whatsoever he doeth shall prosper," the Lord plainly promises. Look at I Corinthians, chapter 12:

> *Now there are diversities of gifts, but the same Spirit . . . For to one is given by the Spirit the word of wisdom; to another the word of knowledge by the same Spirit. . . .*—Vss. 4,8.

And then I Corinthians 12:7,

> *But the manifestation of the Spirit is given to every man to profit withal.*

God wants every Christian not only to have the Spirit inside but some working of the Spirit. God has a work for everyone to do, I mean something else besides soul winning. It may be teaching a Sunday school class, or being head of a department, or running a mission. Maybe it is leading a choir, or being pastor of a church. But God has some work in which the Spirit of God can show Himself and bless and prosper every Christian.

New Testament Christianity does not anticipate seat-warming Christians. Christianity which consists of "go to church and sing when the others sing, rise when they rise, sit when they sit, put a quarter in the collection plate," Christianity is not prosperous nor successful. That kind of deadbeat riding instead of pulling, that kind of being a load instead of a team, is not prosperous Christianity.

There is something for you to do. It may not be leadership, some official position. God does not necessarily want everybody on the ship to be captain. But He wants everybody to be a full-fledged seaman. There is some work for you to do for Christ. Start out to find your job. You are not a successful Christian if you do not have something to do for Christ. I would say, "This is my job, and I will learn to do it."

Years ago my Uncle George N. Rice of Gainesville, Texas, who has gone to Heaven, said to his pastor, "I wish there was something I could do. I feel so useless."

"There is one thing you can do," the preacher said. "I like to shake your hand. I know how you love people."

It was amazing how everybody loved Uncle George. Let me illustrate.

When my father's first wife died, he left two children with his brother, my Uncle George, and he reared Jimmie, my older sister. All the youngsters in town piled into his big house. Half the town pretty soon called him "Uncle George."

I went to see him before his death, and there came in a middle-aged woman. She stooped over his bed and kissed him, and said, "How are you, Uncle?" though she wasn't kin to him. She was a former member of a fine big class of 100 girls he had had in Sunday school. She had been kissing Uncle George all her life, and when he was seventy years old and sick, she came in and kissed him.

I was at his house for dinner one day and an old fellow came by with a load of wood. Uncle George bought the wood from him, though he didn't need it, and made the man get down off his wagon and tie his horses and come into that nice dining room with its beautiful silverware, and the gleaming white linen cloth. He brought that man in with his overalls and sat him down at the table. Aunt Gertrude had everything as fine as could be. He would bring in any chicken peddler to eat dinner with him. He didn't just give them some food in the kitchen, he brought them to the dining table with the family. Everybody loved Uncle George. This is the point I started to make—everybody loved him.

He said, "I wish I could do something for the Lord."

The preacher said, "You can. There is one thing you can do. You love people. Get out in the vestibule and shake hands with everybody that comes in the door, then shake hands with everybody that goes out."

And my Uncle George did. Soon he was teaching a class of 100 young women. Later he was partially paralyzed and everywhere he went he had to be in a wheelchair. They would set that chair in the vestibule by the door, and it got to be a custom that hardly anybody used the other doors at all. Everybody went in one door and they would file by and shake hands with Uncle George as they went out.

Now God wants every Christian to have a job and fill that job happily, successfully, prosperously. If you do not do it, you are a seat-warming Christian, a parasite, growing without any roots.

A prosperous Christian, then, will have happiness in his heart, will get his prayers answered, will win some souls, and have a job to do for God. But how will he do it? What are the absolute essentials of success in the Christian life?

I. A Working Knowledge of the Bible

So the first essential for success in the Christian life is a working knowledge of the Bible. No Christian can be a good Christian without the Bible. This thing has been on my heart ever since I had my Sunday school class down at the park. You people have been stuffed and stuffed, very much like the way they fatten ducks for Christmas. They put a duck in a narrow cage and feed him and feed him, and a few days before Christmas time they nail down between the duck's web feet some broadheaded tacks and fasten the duck's feet down to the floor on each side, and all he has to do is to stand there. They then feed him and he eats until he becomes fatter and fatter. He can't lose any of it by exercise for he is nailed down. Then when it seems he cannot eat any more, they take a broom handle and put some food in his mouth and cram it down.

And that is like some people. You are nailed here and you sit around with indigestion. You don't digest your food. All this hearing and no doing is not good for a Christian.

A lot of you people have sat under my ministry, have been in my Sunday school class week in and week out, month in and month out for years, and you can't quote ten verses in the Bible! You are just common parasites. You don't mean business for God. You are insincere. You haven't taken it to heart. You have sat under the light and basked and turned it away like rain on a duck's back. If you do not learn more about the Bible, God is going to cast you away. You won't have your prayers answered. People will have no confidence in your religion. You will never get a soul saved.

I know if you are right with God you can learn something about the Bible. If you don't remember it as you used to, then just work harder. You have said, "I can't do it." You can do other things that you want to do. And you can have a working knowledge of the Bible if you try. The main reason is that you don't even read it. And the reason you don't read it is because you are not interested.

Anybody can read four chapters a day and read the Bible through in a year's time. That is mighty little, and no Christian ought to be willing for a year to go by without reading the Bible through at least once. You can read it through in a year by reading fifteen to thirty minutes a day. You could read four chapters in the Psalms in ten minutes. But with an average of not over thirty minutes a day you can read the Bible through in less than a year, by reading four chapters a day. Or by reading three chapters a day and five on Sunday you can read it through in a year. You read the newspapers more than that. You gab about your neighbors more than that.

If you really read your Bible, and read it with an open heart, you will absorb some of it. Any Christian who reads the Bible and marks the verses that are a blessing to him, and then goes back where he marked them and reads them over again, will soon know them, and have them in his heart. Memorizing isn't so hard. We say we know them by heart. The reason you don't know the Scriptures by heart is because you haven't taken them to heart. Anybody can learn some of the Bible if he works at it. I say, you can have a working knowledge of the Word of God.

You have to know some of the promises to have happiness. You cannot understand and live on top of this world and its sorrows and the problems you meet, unless you have a knowledge of the Word of God.

I thank God for Romans 8:28. If there comes a time, after I have sweated and worked and prayed and given until my family went without and used secondhand furniture, I see the fruit of my tears and prayers go up in flames, then I will need Romans 8:28. Thank God, I have it and I know it and can quote it. And in the blackest night I will know it still. I have it in my heart. After I have toiled and toiled and prayed and sweated and then see no fruit of my labor, I can go back to Matthew 28:20 where the Lord Jesus said, "Lo, I am with you alway."

In Matthew, chapter 28, verses 19 and 20, the Lord said:

> *Go ye therefore, and teach all nations, baptizing them in the name of the Father, and of the Son, and of the Holy Ghost:*
> *Teaching them to observe all things whatsoever I have commanded you: and, lo, I am with you alway, even unto the end of the world.*

You may feel your work is in vain. You may not see any outward manifestation, but you have Christ's promise that He is with you! You are going to have to know the promises of the Bible to have happiness and contentment and a sense of victory.

How blessed the Bible is, and how blessed it has been to me! Many is the time when I have turned and read:

> *Hast thou not known? hast thou not heard, that the everlasting God, the Lord, the Creator of the ends of the earth, fainteth not, neither is weary?*

I get tired. This past week I have been driving to Kilgore, Texas, and preaching three times a day. Last Wednesday I spoke four times. I drove back to Kilgore Thursday and drove back again here Friday night and got in bed at 1:30 Saturday morning. I want to preach and thank God that I can. Yet the work is hard. But thank God I can say:

> *Hast thou not known? hast thou not heard, that the everlasting God, the Lord, the Creator of the ends of the earth, fainteth not, neither is weary? there is no searching of his understanding.*
>
> *He giveth power to the faint; and to them that have no might he increaseth strength.*
>
> *Even the youths shall faint and be weary, and the young men shall utterly fall:*
>
> *But they that wait upon the Lord shall renew their strength; they shall mount up with wings as eagles; they shall run, and not be weary; and they shall walk, and not faint.*—Isa. 40:28-31.

Today I have preached on the radio and taught my class and then am preaching in this service now and will tonight preach again. Then this afternoon I must get things ready for THE SWORD OF THE LORD. After speaking twice last Wednesday night, four times in the day and driving 125 miles, I had to get copy ready for the paper and it was after midnight before I got to bed. But God renews strength. I memorize the promise, I believe it, I claim it, and God renews my strength.

Is your Bible marked at sweet promises? And do you weep over them and thank God for them? You are not a successful Christian and you cannot be happy without a working knowledge of the Bible.

I go to troubled homes. I visit people who have a boy in jail. I go into homes where somebody has had an automobile accident and a life has been snatched out. I stand and look into an open casket upon the cold features whom somebody loved. Every time I hear somebody say, "Why did this happen to me?" I know they need the Word of God. If they had the Word hidden in their hearts, they would know that God is good and that He means good by this. They could sing:

> God's way is the best way
> Though I may not see
> Why sorrows and trials
> Oft gather 'round me.
> He ever is seeking
> My gold to refine,
> I'll trust in Him always,
> My Saviour divine.

If you know the Word of God and hide it in your heart, it will be a strength in time of trouble. It will be a joy in the blackest night. It will be the voice of God when no other voice could tell you which way to go.

You need a working knowledge of the Bible. You will have to learn at least some of it. You will never be a successful Bible Christian unless you memorize parts of the Bible. At least I would get enough to help in trouble. I would memorize a lot of it. I would hide it in my heart.

Another thing. You need a working knowledge of the Bible to whip sin. There isn't any such thing as a Christian living a victorious life and winning out on the sin question except with the Word of God.

David asked this question to the Lord, "Wherewithal shall a young man cleanse his way?" Then He answered, "By taking heed thereto according to thy word." Then David wrote it down, "Thy word have I hid in mine heart, that I might not sin against thee." There is no such thing as a Christian living a life pleasing to God except he know enough of the Bible to know what pleases God.

There are some men in this church I have prayed for, and there are one or two I am getting especially anxious about on the cigarette question. I know how you can get victory over smoking, but the reason you do not is because you do not take time to get the thing whipped on the Bible basis.

I would take thirty minutes every day of my life and find Scriptures that fit my case. Then I would pray and claim the Word of God for the grace I need and for the help I need and for comfort for my heart. I would claim the Scripture and go to God in prayer and tell Him so. I would live that day without cigarettes. After a few days you would have the Devil so scared and whipped, you can leave them alone the rest of your life. You are not going to do it otherwise. The Bible has a remedy for sin.

There is more than that, blessed be God! The psalmist says, "Wherewithal shall a young man cleanse his way?" and then answers back, "By taking heed thereto according to thy word." Then he says, "Thy word have I hid in mine heart, that I might not sin against thee."

If you don't know what God's Word says, you will not know whether you are sinning or not.

When Jesus Himself wanted to whip the Devil, He picked His answer out of the Word of God. Every time the Devil tempted Him, He would answer back, "It is written." And you too can whip the Devil if you know the Word of God.

More than that: a working knowledge of the Bible is important because it is God's only way for you to serve Him. You can't win souls without the Word of God. Somebody doesn't know why he doesn't win souls. I know why. You can't win souls without the Bible. The Scripture says, "He that goeth forth and weepeth, bearing precious seed, shall doubtless come again with rejoicing, bringing his sheaves with him" (Ps. 126:6). The Bible says, "The seed is the word of God" (Luke 8:11).

Preachers may depend on illustrations, but illustrations won't do it. I think illustrations may be used by God to make clear a Scripture, but just a tender story isn't enough. Hebrews 4:12 says, "The word of God is quick, and powerful, and sharper than any twoedged sword, piercing even to the dividing asunder of soul and spirit, and of the joints and marrow, and is a discerner of the thoughts and intents of the heart."

I saw it Friday night at Kilgore. There was a great crowd. I preached to those oil workers from all over that country. When I preached on "The Great White Throne Judgment of the Unsaved Dead" and used Scripture after Scripture, I felt and I believed and I claimed and it happened. The Holy Spirit pressed it on the hearts and men were convicted. I came to one young man and asked him, "Are you a Christian?"

He said, "No."

"You ought to be," I said.

"I know it."

"Don't you want to be?"

"Yes."

"Well, come on then."

And he came openly to trust Christ and claim Him. God answered prayer and used His Word.

You will never win souls unless you learn to use the Word of God. You say that you do not know enough of the Bible. Well, I hope you know John 3:16. Get a working knowledge of John 3:16 and get the Spirit to help you use it. There is John 5:24, John 1:12, Romans 8:9, etc. A Christian is better off with just a handful of Scriptures that you know and can quote and really believe, than with a smattering of a good many. If you have a working knowledge, not a perfect knowledge, of the Bible, you can win souls, but you can't do it without knowing and using some of the Bible. God intends every fellow, if he wants to make good for God, to give attention to it.

A working knowledge of the Bible is essential also for daily guidance. You need the Bible to guide you and settle your problems of daily living.

Here is a girl who says, "Brother Rice, why is it not all right for me to wear slacks?"

Deuteronomy 22:5 says: "The woman shall not wear that which pertaineth unto a man, neither shall a man put on a woman's garment: for all that do so are abomination unto the Lord thy God."

Now if you know that one verse, you know that no woman has any business wearing slacks or shorts. If you don't know the Bible, you may go into sin. You need guidance from God.

You say, "I believe in asking the Holy Spirit to guide me." Do you really think you can come to God and say, "I really don't care about Your Word. I know You have written instructions there, but I want the Holy Spirit to show me what You want me to do"? Then do you think the Holy Spirit will do it? Not usually. The Holy Spirit works with the Bible and in cooperation with the Bible. God's Word has already told you what you ought to do about many things, and you cannot be a successful, prosperous Christian without a working knowledge of the Bible.

That would mean memorizing some of it. That would mean meditating on it day and night. I would set my life sails by the blow of the winds of the Bible.

First of all, I would read it. I would read it through at least once a year.

Then I would memorize some parts of it. The Scripture said, "Thy word have I hid in mine heart that I might not sin against thee." I would find some good promises and mark them and memorize them and say them to myself. Then after you memorize them, meditate on them. The Word of God is sweet. It is rich.

Out yonder is an old cow. She has better sense than a lot of you Christians. You have teeth above and below too, but a cow doesn't. A cow has teeth only on the lower jaw. A cow wraps her tongue around some grass, pulls it into her mouth, cuts forward with her teeth, chews it once and down it goes, then she grabs another mouthful! After she is full she will lie down in the shade of a tree. She says, "Let's see what I have here," and she brings up a mouthful and chews and chews on it. That is her cud. She is lying down in the shade to enjoy it. You know, a cow has more stomachs than you have. She has four. So she brings her food back and chews it and digests it and gets the good out of it.

Now the word "meditate" in the original language is the same word for chewing the cud. God wants you to meditate in the Bible, chew the cud in the Bible. Read it, then chew it good. Have as much sense as a cow! God wants you to meditate therein. I would form this habit. Then what I find in the Bible I would believe it and what I believe, I would practice. God will bless it to your heart.

II. Daily Prayer

Now let's see the next thing—a daily meeting with God. You cannot be a prosperous Christian without daily meeting with God, particularly for prayer.

Pray for forgiveness. The Lord Jesus said:

For if ye forgive men their trespasses, your heavenly Father will also forgive you: But if ye forgive not men their trespasses, neither will your Father forgive your trespasses.

You are already saved, but you need a daily cleansing, a daily confession of your sins, a daily wiping out and having renewed confidence and fellowship with God. You need to pray for forgiveness.

Then you need to take your burdens to God, every day "casting all your care upon him; for he careth for you."

Be careful for nothing; but in every thing by prayer and supplication with thanksgiving let your requests be made known unto God.—Phil. 4:6.

Do you know how not to have care?

You say, "Brother Rice, I have some things that are heavy. I have some burdens on me."

I know. There is no way for a Christian to go without burdens except to turn them over to the Lord. We ought to have burdens. The Bible says, "Every man shall bear his own burden," and yet He says, "Be careful for nothing." Every day take your burdens and cares and lay them all on Jesus Christ and trust Him and have a time of prayer. The best time is early in the morning. Every day meet God early in the morning and pray and get your burdens lifted, get your sins all out of the way by daily meeting with God.

What else in this daily meeting with God? Ask God what to do today. You say, "There are certain things I must do today. I must have God's wisdom." Well, ask for it, for the Scripture says:

If any of you lack wisdom, let him ask of God, that giveth to all men liberally, and upbraideth not; and it shall be given him.—James 1:5.

Every day go to God and talk with Him and ask Him to show you what to do today.

I knew one farmer in West Texas who raised corn by prayer.

Nobody raised corn around there. The reason was just now and then, about one year out of three, there was enough rain for corn. The rest of the time they just wasted the seed and the use of the land and wasted all the time and effort, so they thought it was not worth it. Now and then they had a good crop once every four or five years.

But this farmer, Mr. Wolf, planted corn. First he prayed, "Lord, shall I plant corn this year?" and if the Lord said "yes," he would go ahead and plant it and he would make a good crop.

So like this man, we need wisdom from Heaven. I say pray every day for wisdom. Ask God to prosper you. No Christian is a successful Christian, a useful Christian who does not meet God every day and have this thing settled about his sins and burdens, problems and worries. So we ought to pray through to God every day. You will not prosper without it.

What else?

III. Get Definite Christian Training and Preparation

What is the secret of a really prosperous, successful Christian life?

The third secret is a definite training for what you ought to do. Every Christian needs training. A good many Scriptures say that. For instance, in the Great Commission the Lord says, "Go and make disciples"—that is getting people saved, "baptizing them . . ." and then He said, "teaching them to observe all things whatsoever I have commanded you" (Matt. 28:19,20).

Now no Christian will observe the Bible commands except he be taught to do so. People need teaching how to live right. Look at Luke, chapter 11. The disciples came to Jesus. One said, "Lord, *teach us to pray*, as John also taught his disciples." John taught his disciples to pray. John had special classes in prayer life for his disciples and taught them how to pray. Jesus taught His disciples how to pray, and people need training even to know how to pray. They certainly need training in how to win souls. They need training about living a separated life. And no Christian will be a successful Christian who does not take some definite training.

At Kilgore the other day a man about sixty-five had just been saved. The preacher took me out to see him. When the preacher asked how he was feeling, he said he was fine. "I wonder why I ever put salvation off so long. It is wonderful to be saved, and I am saved, sure enough! A lot of people are afraid somebody will laugh at them. If any of these roughnecks laugh at me, I will knock them end for end, and I will make Christians of them," he said.

Now that new convert won't make Christians like that. He is wrong about it. He knows how to handle roughnecks. He has been out in the oil fields all his days nearly, but he must be taught another way besides that to make a Christian! You must train men if they are to win men. Just to whale away with your fist because somebody laughs at you doesn't make him into a Christian.

So no Christian is going to be a good Christian without some definite training in Christian living. There are many Scriptures which say so. Look at II Timothy 2:15:

> *Study to shew thyself approved unto God, a workman that needeth not to be ashamed, rightly dividing the word of truth.*

Most of you Christian workers are not approved of God. Most teachers do not appear unashamed, rightly dividing the Word of truth.

You ought to take training to teach a class. Some of you ought to go to a Bible Institute and the rest of you ought to take some special training about your department in Sunday school, or how to conduct jail services. You need some special supervision to teach you how to have street meetings. You need teaching as to how to win souls. Every Christian ought to work at it.

My books and pamphlets go all over America. And here are people in my church who have been here six or seven years who have never read a one of them! Book stores all over the nation sell my books, and some of you people never read them.

Not just my books, but I can't get you to pay a few cents for *How to Pray* by Torrey, or a book of sermons by Moody, or *Bible Questions Answered* by Gray, or books on the second coming by somebody else. Do you know why? You are dead upstairs. You are petrified. And you Christians will not amount to much until you read Christian literature, unless you take a study course.

You come and sit here year in and year out and hear preaching. It goes in one ear and out the other. You come to Sunday school without studying your lesson. You don't read Gospel literature. You won't read revival sermons nor Bible Studies. You do not take your Bible and check up on what I preach. When I offer the SWORD to you cheaper than I do to other people, a lot of you are not even good enough Christians to want Christian literature of any kind. You are not studying to be good workmen.

Nobody will be any good for God unless he works at it, gets some definite help anywhere he can get it, maybe just diligent, prayerful, studious reading.

Perhaps you should take a teachers' study course or correspondence courses from Moody Bible Institute. Or perhaps you ought to go off for definite training at a Christian school. According to the Bible, nobody is going to be able to observe all Jesus commanded unless somebody teaches him.

Here in the 8th chapter of Acts the Ethiopian eunuch was riding in the chariot. Probably one servant was holding an umbrella over him, another may have been driving. He was robed in rich garments. The treasurer of the nation was a man of great authority. He rides down through the desert.

A poor preacher named Philip—just a deacon—who had been having a big meeting in Samaria, comes along and says, "What are you reading?" and the eunuch told him he was reading Isaiah but didn't understand it. He was reading the 53rd chapter of Isaiah where the Scripture says, "He was led as a sheep to the slaughter and like a lamb dumb before his shearer, so opened he not his mouth," etc.

Philip said, "Understandest thou what thou readest?" The eunuch didn't say, "Nut, I wouldn't be reading it if I didn't." No, he said, "How can I, except some man should guide me?" Then Philip said, "I will teach you." So he got up beside the eunuch in the chariot and taught him. New-born Christians ought to expect to get some training and teaching.

That is the reason some of you are not successful Christians. You won't read good books. You won't take study courses. You won't go to school to get Christian training. The fact is, what I am preaching this morning are the very fundamentals of Christian living, yet you haven't taken any notes on this sermon today. You haven't marked any Scriptures. You haven't memorized any Scriptures. You haven't put down any references. It will be out of your head before you get out of the door this morning.

But I want to tell you, no Christian will ever be a successful Christian who does not say, "God helping me, I am going to take what training I need to be something for God."

That is the reason some of you teachers are not approved of God. Without work, preparation, training, you cannot be approved of Him. You don't want to study. You can't be superintendent of a department because you don't want to pay the cost. It takes work to be any good for God.

Mr. Hoover, it takes work to be a brick mason, doesn't it? It will wear your fingers down. And without training, you make a fool of yourself because you make the joints come over each other instead of lapping them. Then training and long practice is necessary to get a wall straight, plumb, level and strong. It takes training to make a bricklayer. You think that's all right; but you can be a *good Christian* without any work and training! No, you can't!

To be a schoolteacher, after one has finished high school, he goes off to college and takes special training. But you think in God's work it doesn't matter! You can teach God's Word without study of maps, or reading books, or learning, or diligent study of the Word. You think so? *It isn't so!* I tell you, if you want to serve God you have to work at it and get ready for it.

It is the same thing with personal soul winning, giving out tracts, preaching in the jail, etc. Anything worth doing is worth learning how to do well. Unless you work at it you will never learn to do it acceptably to God.

I tell you, there has been too much of this same thing all over the country. You think if you believe the Bible it is all right to be ignorant. But that isn't so. In this church we ought to settle some things this morning. We don't have a lawyer in this church. We don't have a doctor in this church. We don't have a dentist in this church. We are only seven years old. We have had only one public schoolteacher in this church. She came this summer and put her membership in the church but has now gone back to her school.

This church started out with people who didn't have training. There were hardly any musicians. My wife played the piano. When we started out, we had no trained songleader. Nobody knew how to run a department in the Sunday school. We had no trained teachers. We started out with untrained singers and untrained soul winners and untrained musicians.

About music: why don't you say, "My boy (or girl) is going to start taking music lessons. My girl can make a real good pianist." Mrs. Mayo, what about you? In all these departments we have need for more pianists. I would say, "I will get ready to play the piano."

I wonder how many of you will say, "Yes, I want to learn to do something good for God"? You can't do it without learning. How many will say, "God helping me, I am going to try to take lessons or whatever is necessary to play some instrument for God"? How many will say, "I will try to be some good in music for God"? God bless you. That is right. God bless you. You can do it. You ought to do that.

I tell you right now, I love my crowd. You know I do. In lots of ways you are the best church I ever pastored. But I don't believe it pleases God to have a church full of people who do not know how to do anything. It takes working at it to learn how. My children have a natural gift for music. They sang by the time they could talk but still had to take voice lessons from someone who can teach them. Joanna goes to the piano and picks out with one finger a tune, but that is not good enough for God. It takes training.

In order to have a fine orchestra or a great choir, you have to train for it. I mean some of you ought to go to college and get ready. Take a teacher-training course. God wants a sharper ax. If you have a good ax, let God sharpen it. Definite training. You can't be a successful Christian without learning how. You can't be a good teacher without working at it. You have to learn how to teach attractively to attract young people. You must learn how to build up the attendance of a Sunday school class.

IV. Be Filled With the Holy Spirit

If you are going to do anything for God, you must have a special anointing of the Holy Spirit. You *must* have. I would like to take time to talk about some other things, too, but I can't. For instance, if you cannot control the lust for money, if you can't learn to tithe and give offerings, you will never be a success. You must make a complete surrender of self. If you say, "My life is Yours, God; You can have it—my life, my influence and my talents." That will include tithing and giving up anything that displeases God. I can't take much time to discuss that now.

A daily self-surrender and crucifixion of self involves giving up money, giving tithes and offerings that belong to God, and then what you have left all belongs to God, too. And what you spend for yourself, spend as He directs. Maybe sometimes you ought to keep the tithe and give God the nine-tenths. In any case, put God first. Crucify self and be separate from the world. You can't be a successful Christian without it.

The last point: You must be especially anointed or you can't have power and blessing on your Christian life. You need the Holy Spirit of God. The Pentecostalists are wrong about a lot of things, but they are dead right that a Christian can have a special enduement and power of the Holy Spirit. They are wrong about tongues and they are wrong about a lot of the rolling and hollering, and some of them are wrong about claiming sinless perfection, but they are right when they say that a Christian can have and ought to have a definite empowering by the Spirit of God.

I have had it on my heart about you Sunday school teachers. If your teaching is any good, you must have God breathe on you. You can't do it otherwise. Five loaves and two fishes won't feed five thousand people and have twelve baskets left over.

Listen to me! Take a walking stick and hold it out and try to divide the Red Sea. A walking stick won't divide the Red Sea. And seven loaves and a few fishes are not enough to feed four thousand people. They just won't do it. And one man with the jaw-bone of a donkey can't go out and kill a thousand armed men. He just can't do it. None of these are possible without a miracle and God's power.

And one man, poor, weak and puny, can't take a soul away from Satan. He can't do it, and all of us together can't do it. We must have the power of God upon us. It takes a miracle. There isn't any such thing as living a prosperous, successful Christian life without an anointing from God, without day by day having the Spirit of God to breathe upon you and give you joy, power, wisdom and the witness you ought to have.

We need to come back to the thing we had in the early days of this church—when we prayed, "O, God, fill me with the Holy Spirit! Fill me with the Holy Spirit." We need to pray that again. Suppose we sing,

> Come, Holy Spirit, fill me,
> I need Thee, I seek Thee.
> Come, Holy Spirit, fill me,
> Lord, fill me with the Holy Ghost.

Oh, it takes the power of God whether you teach a Sunday school class or whether you are superintendent of a department. Some of you téachers can't find boys and girls for your classes, you say. But the Spirit of God could help you find some. If you had Him, He could. You superintendents say, "I don't know what to do about teachers when they don't do the work." But the Spirit of God can show you.

The Spirit of God can do what we can't do. If we have Him, if we are anointed with Him, we can have our problems settled. The Spirit of God can rake up some more boys. We had as well quit trying to serve God in our own poor human ways. We had as well quit trying to serve God in our own power and wisdom. All our influence together is not enough to get one sinner saved without the Spirit of God. Only God can touch his heart and save him.

All of us can't get a single prayer answered. All of us here

can't take the Word of God and put it into one heart, for the
human heart is at enmity against the Bible. Only the Spirit of
God can break that down and plant the roots there. If we don't
have an anointing, an enduement, a filling of the Spirit of God,
then all is vain. Our fathers used to sing it in country churches
long ago and I think it is true:

> Brethren, we have met to worship
> And adore the Lord our God.
> Will you pray with all your power
> While we try to preach the Word?
>
> All is vain unless the Spirit
> Of the Holy One come down,
> Brethren, pray and Holy Manna
> Will be showered all around.

Oh, that is what we need!

3—Counting the Cost

(Stenographically reported sermon preached June 4, 1939, Dallas, Texas)

The text for my message tonight will be found in Luke, chapter 14, a message which I have never preached before. The Bible is an inexhaustible Book. It is a mine, with rich veins of treasure which never run dry.

I will begin with verse 25 and read down through verse 35.

> *And there went great multitudes with him: and he turned, and said unto them,*
>
> *If any man come to me, and hate not his father, and mother, and wife, and children, and brethren, and sisters, yea, and his own life also, he cannot be my disciple.*
>
> *And whosoever doth not bear his cross, and come after me, cannot be my disciple.*
>
> *For which of you, intending to build a tower, sitteth not down first, and counteth the cost, whether he have sufficient to finish it?*
>
> *Lest haply, after he hath laid the foundation, and is not able to finish it, all that behold it begin to mock him,*
>
> *Saying, This man began to build, and was not able to finish.*
>
> *Or what king, going to make war against another king, sitteth not down first, and consulteth whether he be able with ten thousand to meet him that cometh against him with twenty thousand?*
>
> *Or else, while the other is yet a great way off, he sendeth an ambassage, and desireth conditions of peace.*
>
> *So likewise, whosoever he be of you that forsaketh not all that he hath, he cannot be my disciple.*

Salt is good: but if the salt have lost his savour, wherewith shall it be seasoned?

It is neither fit for the land, nor yet for the dunghill; but men cast it out. He that hath ears to hear, let him hear.

I. A Serious, Costly Thing to Be a Good Christian

The Lord intended there to be an enormous difference between a Christian and one who is unsaved. It is a sad thing that Christians these days live so much like unsaved people. The Lord tells us in II Timothy 3:2-5, that in this age,

. . . men shall be lovers of their own selves, covetous, boasters, proud, blasphemers, disobedient to parents, unthankful, unholy,

Without natural affection, trucebreakers, false accusers, incontinent, fierce, despisers of those that are good,

Traitors, heady, highminded, lovers of pleasures more than lovers of God;

Having a form of godliness, but denying the power thereof: from such turn away.

It is sometimes hard today to distinguish between one who says he is a Christian and one who is not. The Lord intended there to be a difference between a Christian and one of the Devil's children. He intended that there should be an enormous gulf, that they should be as much different as black and white.

The Lord says in II Corinthians the 6th chapter:

Be ye not unequally yoked together with unbelievers: for what fellowship hath righteousness with unrighteousness? and what communion hath light with darkness?

And what concord hath Christ with Belial? or what part hath he that believeth with an infidel?

And what agreement hath the temple of God with idols? for ye are the temple of the living God; as God hath said, I will dwell in them, and walk in them; and I will be their God, and they shall be my people.

Wherefore come out from among them, and be ye separate, saith the Lord, and touch not the unclean thing; and I will receive you,

And will be a Father unto you, and ye shall be my sons and daughters, saith the Lord Almighty. —Vss. 14-18.

Now God does not want Christians living like the Devil's crowd. You had as well go into this and count the cost—whether or not you want to be a Christian. In the first part of this sermon, you will think I am discouraging you. But the discouraging you are going to get, you had better get now and weigh this matter carefully and see if it is worthwhile to be a Christian. I frankly say it costs. You ought to know what is involved and face it.

It is a serious thing to say, "I am going to be a Christian." You are to have a different heart within, you are to be born again. You are even to be a different man, to have Christ living in you through the Holy Spirit. If you are not different, and if you are saved inwardly and are not saved outwardly, your life will be a constant grief and a fight, with unhappiness and dissatisfaction for yourself and for God, and your influence will be wrong through all the days of your life. Everyone should count the cost and make up his mind to get on one side of the fence or the other.

The Saviour gave this parable:

For which of you, intending to build a tower, sitteth not down first, and counteth the cost, whether he have sufficient to finish it? Lest haply, after he hath laid the foundation, and is not able to finish it, all that behold it begin to mock him, Saying, This man began to build, and was not able to finish.

If you are going to build a tabernacle, you had better sit down and count the cost. If you build a foundation and do not have enough money to go ahead with it, people will begin to say, "I told you they would never build it. They do not have enough money. They cannot do it." And people will begin to mock.

You may say, "I will be a Christian," but you do not count the cost. I want to tell you what will happen. First, a lot of people say they will be a Christian who are not, who have never been saved. That is pictured when Jesus

> . . . *spake many things unto them in parables, saying,*
> *Behold, a sower went forth to sow;*
> *And when he sowed, some seeds fell by the way side,*
> *and the fowls came and devoured them up:*
> *Some fell upon stony places, where they had not much*
> *earth: and forthwith they sprung up, because they had*
> *no deepness of earth:*
> *And when the sun was up, they were scorched; and*
> *because they had no root, they withered away.*—Matt.
> 13:3-6.

Some seed fell on stony ground but it did not take root because it did not have enough soil. They had no root in themselves. That pictures a person who has never been born again.

I say to some people, "Will you take Christ as your Saviour?" And they say yes. But they never stop to consider and weigh what they say and may not be saved at all. They may not have salvation in the heart, a turning of the whole soul to Christ. It may be just on the surface and incidental and have no meaning at all.

Not everybody who says, "Lord, Lord," is saved. Not everybody who walks down the aisle is a Christian. Not everybody who is baptized is born again. Not everybody who says, "Sure, I will be a Christian," is really saved.

As Christian workers, we had better face this thing, and face it squarely. It is a serious business, and we ought to know what it will cost. Jesus said if you lay a foundation and then are not able to build on top of that foundation, everybody will mock you.

First of all, you may not truly be saved. But if you are saved, your life is out of joint. You say, "I am saved," but you will not give up your old life. You have been born again, but you are still holding on to the same crowd and the same bad habits. You are still talking as you talked before. Inside you are one thing;

outside you are another. There is disappointment and frustration and failure all the days of your life.

Oh, my Christian friends, if you are saved you had better sit down and count the cost whether or not it really pays to be on the Lord's side. If you are lost, of course you ought to come tonight and be saved. But it ought to be "whole hog" or none, and you ought to face that and settle it out and out for Jesus Christ. And you had better settle it now, for Jesus said, "What king, going to make war against another king, sitteth not down first, and consulteth whether he be able with ten thousand to meet him that cometh against him with twenty thousand?" If he decides, "I am not able with my ten thousand men to whip those twenty thousand," then if he has any sense, he will sit down and write a message to the other king desiring peace. He might say, "I am angry, but I am not angry enough to get the whole outfit wiped out." So he sends a messenger saying, "Let us have peace." You had better send and make peace.

If you say, "Well, it costs so much to be a Christian. If I have to give up my sins and turn my back on my own way and if the Lord is supposed to be put first in my life and have a say about everything, and if I cannot have my way about anything—if it costs that much to be a Christian, then I will not be a Christian. I will declare war against Jesus Christ. I am going to live for the Devil."

But wait. The Scripture says before you do that, you had better figure whether with your puny resources you will be able to meet the enemy. Death is coming! Judgment is coming! Eternity is coming! Are you able to meet them with human strength and power? If you are not, you had better send an ambassador desiring peace. You had better say, "God, I cannot fight You. I will lose everything if I do not give myself to You."

My friend, you had better count the cost before you go to Hell.

You may say you cannot afford to give up this or that, but, brother, you may find yourself giving up everything in this world and in eternity, too—your poor soul and peace and all—giving it up for torment in an endless Hell!

That certainly is a thing to be considered. Stop and count the cost. Stop and figure what you are going to do when death comes and which side you are going to be on. If preachers would preach more on these themes, there would be more real and genuine repentance. The members of their churches do not live for God. Preachers should have such an urgency in preaching that the members of their churches would say, "I must come back to live for Christ out and out or I will have my name taken off the church roll and get my bad influence out of the way."

It is a blot on the name of any church to have church members who drink, lie, sell booze, go to picture shows, and live for the Devil. I would make up my mind which way I was going. You ought to be separate. You are going to be separate in the next world when Jesus comes. There will be a separation in the graveyard when the dead in Christ rise first. And here in this life you ought to be separate. A Christian and a sinner are not alike in their hearts, and they should not be alike outwardly. There should be a real change, a division between them.

I beg every one of you here to get off the fence, and count the cost and ask yourself the question: "Does it pay to be a Christian?"

If it does, the Saviour said, "Whosoever he be of you that forsaketh not all that he hath, he cannot be my disciple." You may have been born again, but you are not really a follower of Jesus unless you say good-bye to everything you have in this world. Can you say, "I am willing"?

Are you willing to hate father, and hate mother, and hate husband or wife, and land and everything else in this world? If you are not, you are not fit to be His disciple. If you are a Christian, you ought to go over the thing fair and square. Count the cost. Weigh it honestly. Make up your mind that if it does not pay to live for God, you will turn your back on Him. I would be out and out for God or I would be against Him. I would not be a lying hypocrite.

Some people bring a curse, shame and reproach on the cause of Christ because they claim to be Christians but live for the Devil. Don't be a lying hypocrite. Count the cost. If it pays to live for God, then set out to pay the price, whatever it may be, or get out. Do one or the other.

The Bible says you had better count the cost. If a man says, "I am going to be a Christian" and builds a foundation but no house on it, people will mock him. Too many Christians have laid a foundation but have never built anything on it. You made a start but have never done anything for God. You have been saved but have never been baptized, or were baptized but have never won a soul. You trusted the Lord but have not quit tobacco or picture shows. You are saved, but your tongue did not get saved. You are saved, but your mind is lustful and wicked. Maybe you are saved, but your pocketbook never got saved.

You are saved, but it does not make any difference in the home: there is no family altar. After you were saved, you did not change your practice at work. You are saved, but your mouth is not. You had better count the cost. Too many people have laid a foundation and have never built upon it. That is the shocking shame on the church before the world today.

But Jesus said you had better beware lest you put on your armour and start to make war against God and do not have an army with which to meet Him.

If you say, "No, sir, I am not going to be a Christian; I cannot do it; I would have to give up too much," you will find that you have to give up more if you are on the Devil's side, and your poor, damned soul besides. You had as well count the cost.

There are three things I lay before you which I want you to consider honestly and fairly. The first is: What does it cost to be a Christian? If it costs too much, I would not be a Christian. Do not let anybody tell you it does not cost something to be a real Christian. It does cost. Do not let anybody tell you that it does not matter. It does matter. And you had as well make up your mind that there are some things to quit if you are saved.

Second, we will find out what it costs *not* to be a Christian. And third, we will talk about another matter—the danger of delay.

II. What It Costs to Be Saved

What does it cost to be a Christian? What do you have to give up? First, you have to do a hard thing—confess that you are a sinner. There is no way in this world to be a Christian without first coming to face the solemn fact that you are a sinner, a Hell-deserving sinner. You ought to go to Hell, and you will go, and your own sin will take you there, if you do not do something about it. No one ever was a Christian, and no one ever will be a Christian until he comes to admit to himself and to God that he is a poor, wicked-hearted sinner who ought to go to Hell, and he must admit his sin and get it forgiven.

That costs something. That is not easy. People do not like to admit that.

I talked on a train to a Jewish rabbi from New York City. We talked about the Jewish situation, and he was interested in that. We talked about Zionism, and, of course, he was interested. When I tried to talk to him about the Jew from the standpoint of prophecy, he derided me because I believed that sort of thing. We could not find a common Bible ground. When I tried to talk to him about Abraham, Isaac, and Jacob, he was suspicious and on the defensive.

I said, "But one thing I know, and you know, too, and that is that you are a sinner. You must have a sacrifice, but you do not have any more sacrifices. There is no passover lamb, no more bullock and no more red heifer, no more morning sacrifice and evening sacrifice: there is no scapegoat, no turtle doves. You are a sinner and know it, and you have nothing to do with that sin, nobody to take it away."

His face turned red. "No, I am not a sinner."

I said, "Now I have taken you at face value, but I know that is not so, and you know it is not so. Your wife who sits beside you knows it is not so. You are a wicked sinner, and you must pay for your sins if you do not have Someone to atone for them."

She looked knowingly at him. Finally he smilingly said, "Well, all right."

Listen! Right here is where people refuse to come to God. They are not willing to admit they are poor, wicked Hell-deserving sinners who ought to go to Hell.

I warn you now, if you are not willing to admit that, then you will never be a Christian. If you are not willing to admit that, then you are damned and doomed. You will have no forgiveness in this world nor in the world to come. There is no salvation—God has none at all; the Bible offers none at all—for anybody who will not admit he is a sinner.

When John the Baptist preached, there went out to him Jerusalem and all Judaea and all the region round about Jordan, and they were baptized of him in Jordan, *confessing their sins.* If you do not admit you are a sinner and need a Saviour, you will never be saved.

The Bible says, *"There is no difference: For all have sinned, and come short of the glory of God"* (Rom. 3:22,23).

The Bible says again, *"All we like sheep have gone astray"* (Isa. 53:6).

You are a sinner. If you do not admit it, you cannot be saved. It costs something. You must humble yourself before God and admit you are a guilty sinner. That is one thing you MUST do if you are going to be a Christian. I am giving you the unpleasant side of it. You are going to Hell if you do not admit you are a sinner. It costs, but you must confess you are a sinner.

If you are going to be saved, you must do more than confess you are a sinner. You must honestly repent of your sins. Here is a fundamental reason why a lot of people will not be saved. Being baptized never did save anybody and never will. It could not save anybody. I am showing you now why no form or ceremony could possibly change the heart. God will never receive anybody for salvation until he honestly, in his deepest soul, hates sin and turns from sin. That is repentance.

Now get this straight: Repentance does not mean living a sinless life. Repentance does not mean you have quit sin, so you will never sin any more. Repentance means that in your heart you turn from sin. You hate sin. You are against it. You are guilty of it. You admit that, but you are sorry, and turn from it.

Repentance is not just sorrow for sin alone. That might be

remorse. Nearly everybody, when his sin leads to trouble, is sorry. That is not what I am talking about. This is a turning in the heart from sin. If in your heart you do not have your fill of sin, if you cannot come to the place where you can say, "O God, I am a sinner and I want to quit sin, I want to turn my back on sin, I am sorry," you cannot be saved.

Now I am saying that repentance is a real, sincere turning of the heart from sin and the love of sin. If you have not done that, you are not saved. If you do not do that, you will never be saved. That is one thing you have to face. There is not any way to hold on to sin and love the Lord. Mark you, everybody who is saved still sins. But people who are truly saved have in their hearts confessed their sins, and in their hearts have lamented them, and in their hearts have turned from them and long to be different.

I am not talking about an outward practice. The best man that ever lived, the best woman that ever lived never did live up outwardly to all God put in the heart when they were saved. Brother, in your heart you may have repented, but in your heart there is grief because you are not a better Christian.

Repentance is the turning of the heart. You can turn the heart but it takes some long while to get the life changed. "Except ye repent, ye shall all likewise perish."

Listen to me as again I say this: There is one thing that keeps people from being saved, and that is sin. I do not say if you sin you cannot be saved, but I say, as long as you keep holding on to sin and loving sin, you cannot be saved. Do you see the difference there?

I believe people who are saved do sin, but saved people are folk who turned in their hearts from sin and wanted God to forgive them and they are born again, with a new heart toward sin as well as a new heart toward God.

If you are not going to admit to God you are a sinner, and turn from it, and repent, if that is too hard for you, then you are going to Hell. If you say, "No, sir, I love sin, I will not turn it loose," and you hold on to it, then, brother, you are doomed. Nobody ever was saved, nobody ever will be saved until in the heart he repents—in the heart and not just with the lips, not just the way he lives. I do not want anybody to think that one good act can save you, or a thousand days or years of good living will save you. It will not. I say, man must in his heart repent or he cannot be saved.

Another thing it is going to cost you—you have to give up self—trust, all dependence on self, all boasting about your goodness, all relying on your goodness. There are two theories about how to get to Heaven. One is God's way, and the other is man's way. God's way is Abel's way. "By faith Abel offered unto God a more excellent sacrifice than Cain, by which he obtained witness that he was righteous, God testifying of his gifts: and by it he being dead yet speaketh" (Heb. 11:4).

That bloody sacrifice pictured a Saviour. By that Abel said, "Lord, I get out here and sweat and grow a crop, but I cannot earn favor with God." You cannot go out here and dig in the ground and get gold and silver and offer it to God and have favor with God. Abel said, "I cannot make with my own hands implements, houses, furniture, pictures or anything and give that to God. That does not buy favor with God." Rather, Abel said, "I will kill this lamb, and as that warm red blood flows onto the ground God knows I am thinking about and longing for the Lamb that God is going to send that will take away sin."

He said, "I cannot depend on this lamb's shed blood to pay for my sin. It cannot do it; but I am looking to God for the sacrifice which this pictures." That is God's way of salvation.

But man's way is Cain's way. Cain said, "No blood for me." Cain said, "I am as good as Abel. I am as good as anybody else." Cain said, "I will work and make my living by the sweat of my brow, and when I have made my good crop, I will bring the Lord some corn and tomatoes. And if He likes them, all right. If He does not like them, He can lump them. I am paying my way." But the Word of God said that God had no respect for the offering of Cain, and that God did not bless him because sin lay at the door.

My friend, before you can ever be saved, you must be willing to say, "The best I can bring in this world is not good enough.

All the good works I could do are no good, and God despises my works, and my righteousness is no better than filthy rags in His sight (Isa. 64:6). My heart is deceitful and desperately wicked (Jer. 17:9.)" You will have to say, "O God, I have to give up any thought of saving myself."

You will have to come as a pauper. You are a pauper, and you will have to admit it. If you do not come that way, you are doomed for Hell. You cannot march up to God's front door and say, "How do You do, God," and walk in and shake hands and say, "I have a favor to ask of You. I will do You a favor, and You do me a favor, and we will keep on even terms," or, "I want You to do something for me, and I will pay You for it."

No, do not think you can come to God that way. A poor, vile sinner cannot march up to God that way. You must come as a poor beggar in rags and filth and admit, "I am a poor beggar. I cannot work. I am hungry. But won't You have mercy on me and give me something?" You must come to God that way. To be a Christian, it means quit depending on yourself. It means you must quit leaning on your own righteousness and lean on the righteousness of the Lord Jesus Christ alone.

Oh, the wickedness of this world! It wants to take the crown from Jesus Christ and put it on man. The lodges do that. The Masons and others teach that if you live a good life, the great Architect of the Universe will say you have earned your way. If you hold out and live a good life, you will get there after awhile. That is not true. That is a deceit of Satan. And I warn you now, if you are ever saved, it is going to cost you this one thing—admitting, "I am not good. I am weak and sinful. I am sold to sin and if God does not have mercy on me and save me, I am gone! I have nothing to pay."

Now you say, "I do not like that." I know. The Pharisee who went up to the Temple to pray paid his tithe and lived a good life outwardly, but he would not admit he was a sinner, so he went to Hell. He did not mind paying a tithe, and that was right. He did not mind being honest, and he should have been honest. He paid his bills. He was not an adulterer, says Luke the 19th chapter. He did not mind living a clean, straight life. But he said, "God, I thank Thee I am not as other men are. I will not admit I am a sinner. I am paying my way."

But that man went down to his house and died and he went straight to Hell because he would not admit he could not save himself, and so would not trust in God. He would not depend on the atonement Christ made. When Jesus said, "It is finished," the Pharisee said, "It is not finished for me. I will work mine out."

This goes against your pride. It stops your boasting. That is one thing it is going to cost you to be saved. You will have to admit you cannot work your way to Heaven. You will have to take salvation like a beggar, take it with Jesus paying the price for you. You must be bought by the blood. You cannot save yourself.

Everybody who is saved will have to come that road. You cannot be a Christian unless you do these things. You must admit in your heart and to God that you are a sinner. I know it is hard on your pride, but you must turn your heart away from sin and hate sin.

Then you must turn away from your own self-righteousness. You cannot even trust your own goodness. You have to say, "I hate sin, but I am a sinner." Or, "I want to go to Heaven but I ought to go to Hell." You have to say, "I want to go to Heaven, but I have no ticket. If I get there, it will have to be on a pass."

That is God's way to be saved. If that is too much, then you go on to Hell. There is no other way that one can possibly come to God. The Lord says here that you will have to surrender all right to self. "If any man come to me, and hate not his father, and mother, and wife, and children, and brethren, and sisters, yea, and his own life also, he cannot be my disciple."

III. It Costs More to Be a Disciple Than to Just Be a Christian

There is a distinction between a disciple and a Christian. Judas was a disciple, a follower, but he was not a Christian. Judas was not born again. So when the Lord says here that unless a man hates father and mother, wife and children and brethren and sisters, he cannot be His disciple, He did not mean that you have to do that in order to be saved. Listen carefully now and get this distinction. You do not have to turn your heart from wife or mother and other things to be saved. But in the heart you have to turn to Christ. At least you are going to have to admit that you ought to be willing to give up father and mother and wife and children and houses and land for Him.

You may be going your own way and yet truly be saved. Every Christian does in some matters. Sometimes you may want this or that. Maybe you do want it, but you have to admit you no more have a right to your own way. When Jesus died for sinners, the sinner legally died. The sinner is now counted dead to sin. He has no right now to his own way.

I do not mean when you get saved you do everything right. But when you get saved you ought to be willing to give up any claim to your own way.

You do not have any right. You are saved the rest of your life. After you are saved, you may go on in your own way, but you cannot be happy when you do. You are not doing right and you cannot hold your head up and face God with it. I am not talking about getting saved. I am saying that when you are saved God has a claim on you every hour of the day, every minute, every second. It is silly for anybody to say, "I am born again and my sins are nailed to the cross of Christ, but I have a right to my own way." You have not! You have already sold out when you were saved.

That does not mean you will live a perfect life. I am not saying how you will live. I say, you have no right to your own way after you are saved. You say, "Although I want to be a Christian, I still want to retain the deed, all the papers on my own life. I want that still registered in my name. I still want to have all the say. I want to be the foreman, boss, the straw boss, the chairman of the board of my life." But you have no right to that after you are saved. Anyone who trusts Jesus Christ says, "I belong to Jesus Christ now. All I do that displeases Him is wicked and dishonest." A person ought to please Jesus in everything. He gives up all his rights to his own will when he is saved.

If you want your own way (everybody wants to have his own way), then you go ahead. You will find your way is not God's way. After you are saved, you should confess your way is wrong and strive to give Jesus the reins.

What else will it cost you if you are saved? You will have a constant reminder of your sins. If you are saved and you do something wrong, I will tell you what will be true. There are some important things in store when you get to be a Christian.

For instance, I was just a boy when I was saved, but when I was lost there were some things I did wrong that did not bother me. They did after I got saved.

People tell me again and again, "I am saved but I am backslidden. And, Brother Rice, I have done ten times more bad things since I have been saved than I ever did before I knew the Lord." Oh, I have been told many times, "I know after I was saved I really was lost again." "How do you know you are lost?" I would inquire. "I feel it" is the answer. "I feel worse now than before I was saved. I feel farther away from God. I feel meaner now than I ever did before."

Do you know what that really means? When you are saved, God's Holy Spirit moves in and you have a constant reminder about your sins.

Now you do not have the freedom to sin you once had. Maybe back there you used to drink and it did not bother you at all. But after you are saved, I promise you it will bother you aplenty. Spirit of God takes charge and comes into your heart and moves into your body. If you go on in sin, you are headed for trouble. You will have a reminder, an unease of conscience, when you sin. Trouble comes for a Christian who still tries to hold on to sin.

Are there Christians here who will bear me out in that? Can you say, "Yes, after I was saved, I have had more trouble with the Devil than I ever did before. I feel more guilty when I do wrong"? (Many held their hands.) When you did things wrong before you were saved, you did not think anything about it, but now it seems sinful and your conscience hurts you. You have a reminder now about sin that you did not have before.

A Christian should be willing to say, "Now I have the Spirit of God living in my body and He always tells me when I do wrong. If I will let Him, He will keep me from sin." You are not going to be happy in sin after you are saved. There is something about sin that gets bitter to a Christian. You may still sin, but it does not make you happy but rebukes you, after you are saved.

I remember a young man in Decatur, Texas, about whom I heard a good many years ago, who professed to be saved. Perhaps he was—I do not know. Someone asked him how he was getting along in his Christian life. "I have just enough religion to make me miserable," was his reply. He did not have enough to have the victory over sin and whip the Devil every day, but he had had a change in his heart so that he could not go back and enjoy sin as he used to. It was a torment to him all the time.

If you have been saved, you will not enjoy your Christian life if all the time you are slipping back into sin. You are going to have a reminder when you do wrong. If you do not want the Spirit of God to live in your body and raise an objection about your sins, then I would not get saved, because that is what happens to a Christian.

Here is another thing it costs to be a Christian. God not only reminds His children that they have sinned, but He actually punishes them. Hebrews 12:6 says, "For whom the Lord loveth he chasteneth, and scourgeth every son whom he receiveth."

Do you wonder why a wicked man can go on and live in sin, yet sleep well at night? Maybe he is a liar, a cheat, a drunkard, lustful and dishonest; yet his conscience does not bother him. He prospers in business. David said in Psalm 37:35, "I have seen the wicked in great power, and spreading himself like a green bay tree."

After a man has been saved, after God has given him light, then let him go back into sin. Will he get by with it? No. Somebody else's children may do things wrong and I do not rebuke them. But let one of my girls raise trouble in church and there is going to be a settlement. They are mine. I am accountable for them.

God too whips His own children when they sin. Don't think you, a Christian, can go on in sin without any whipping, without any punishment. When a child of God goes into sin, he gets whipped. He gets taken to the tan yard.

If you do not want that kind of discipline from God, don't trust Him. If God is going to keep you out of Hell, then all His whippings will have to be done down here. He is not going to send you to Hell if you have been saved. So He will have to whip you when you need it.

But when He gets you to Heaven, He will kiss away the tears because sin will all be over. A lost man may go on in his sin and not be punished here, but he will have to go to Hell after awhile because he did not trust Jesus Christ, and be punished there. In that case, God will leave off the whipping now, but the sinner will get it in Hell. There is no hurry for God to punish a wicked sinner. But God is going to whip His own children. It costs something to be a Christian. If you are not willing to confess your sins and admit you are a sinner in your own heart and before God, if you are not willing to repent and turn from sin, if you are not willing to quit trusting in your own good works and trust in Jesus Christ alone, if you are not willing to have the Holy Spirit come in and remind you when you sin, and if you are not willing to have God chasten you, then you cannot be a Christian. That is the blood-bought way. It costs something to be a Christian.

What else? If you are going to be a Christian, folks may look down on you. A true Christian loses some things. He loses some friends. Sometimes a person wonders what he will do about his unsaved friends since he is saved, how he will cut loose from his old crowd. Do not worry. You will have no trouble quitting them. If you stand up for Jesus like you should, and talk about the Lord to them every time you see them, they will quit you. You do not need to worry about their running after you. If you are living out and out for Jesus Christ, you will lose some friends. "All that will live godly in Christ Jesus shall suffer persecution" (II Tim. 3:12).

The world says you are a nut if you are a very active Christian. They say you have gone crazy over religion. My friends, if you are a child of God, they will hate you. This world hated Jesus Christ and it will hate you, too, if you love Jesus. It really costs something to be a Christian.

IV. What It Costs Not to Be a Christian

But I would like for you to see the other side, too. Now let us see what it costs to be on the Devil's side. Let us see what you will gain and what you will lose if you are not saved.

In the first place, I warn you, there is no peace for you. Young people, listen to me. A part of your heart seeks for pleasure, and I do not blame young people for wanting to have a good time. They are like horses on a frosty morning. How many of you have ever ridden a good blooded, spirited horse on a frosty morning—one that was kept up in a stall and fed plenty? You had to watch him then or he would buck when he would not do so any other time. Young people have young vigorous blood. You blame young people about flaming youth, but there are more flaming dads and mothers. If you had enough get-up, you would get into devilment, too.

You people who run down young folks remind me of a one-legged deacon who walked on a wooden leg. He arose in prayer meeting to testify. "One thing I never do is dance." That wooden-legged deacon did not dance! I do not blame him. But these young people do not do some things you older people do.

Young people, boys and girls, your restlessness, your looking for pleasure, is because you do not have real peace. It will show a little later. You cannot say what it is now. Now you think you will be happy when you run down this rainbow. You say, "I will build my castles." But I tell you with a heart that is tender—I have had heartaches, too. I tell you because I have had my castles tumble about me. I have tried the primrose path and it had many thorns. And sooner or later all these things which promise peace, joy, pleasure and thrill will turn to nought and you will be just like other older people—disillusioned, unhappy, with no peace. "There is no peace, saith my God, to the wicked" (Isa. 57:21).

Young people deceive themselves. Young people do not know their own hearts. They do not quite see through things. I tell you, the Devil has no happy old people, because sin never did make anybody happy.

You will not have peace if you go on in sin. One thing it will cost to stay on the Devil's side is real peace. You never will know real peace of heart outside Jesus Christ.

Another thing: if you live on the Devil's side and are never saved, it will cost you disappointment and failure. Listen, you boys and girls who are not Christians, people who are not Christians have a high standard. They say, "I am going to live right. I will be a good man," or, "I will be a clean woman. I will do thus and so." All those things you hope to do, but you will not. You are going to fail after awhile. And when you look back on your life you will see it strewn with broken dreams and plans. Disillusionment and sadness and failure will come. Later you will see all of life has been a failure. Pleasures of the world and refusing to trust Christ do not bring happiness. You may make money, but money will not bring happiness. You may get fame; you may marry the girl you wanted or the man you wanted; you may get the job you want; but life without Jesus is, at the end, barren, full of disappointment and failure.

Many people have talked to me and in countless cases have told me, "I wish I had been saved when I was young. Much of my life is gone now and there is nothing left but disappointment."

Another thing. If you are not saved, life is full of disappointments and fears. Down in the heart of everyone away from God is a haunting fear. People try to drown that fear the best they can. Why is a man an infidel? Because in his heart he has a fear of God and Hell and judgment and death until after awhile he says he has to get rid of that, so he builds up such a wall against it until he does not believe in God. He is scared. He does not want to believe in an eternity. He is afraid of meeting

God. There is not a single lost soul here but that you are afraid.

When I was a boy teaching in a country school, I spent a night in a home where there was a young man. He was one of the vilest cursers and heaviest drinkers in that community. He was loud-mouthed and guilty of all kinds of sin.

One night we were left at the house alone. To my astonishment, as soon as the rest of the family got away, this young fellow who was a loud-mouthed, drinking, cursing bully, a roughneck, a fighting man, got up and barred all the doors, putting chairs against them. I said, "What's the idea?" "You never can tell what might come along," he said. He sat there and every time he heard any kind of a noise outside, he jumped and trembled. He was scared.

Sin does not help people, sin does not bring contentment, but puts fear in the heart.

A thirteen-year-old girl I had the joy of winning to Christ said, "Now I won't be afraid to go to sleep any more."

If you are not saved, all your days you will have fear. You know it is your guilty sins that bring you remorse of conscience and make you fear. You think you can go on in sin. But it will cost you remorse of conscience if you do. You think you can go on in sin and never have to give an account. But you are going to give an account to yourself. Your own conscience will accuse you. One day you will pay for all your sin in remorse. Sin never does pay. Sin does not bring contentment.

Do you know why some people never spend an hour alone? Do you know why some people never sit down and quietly meditate but must be on the go all the time? They think they have to have a wild time. Why do they get drunk? Because they cannot face their own conscience. A guilty conscience and remorse sting them day and night.

Nobody on the Devil's side will escape that forever. Someday your conscience will catch up with you and you will see that sin does not pay. If you never are saved, as certain as there is a God, as certain as the Bible is true, as certain as death, as certain as anything God has ever told you, you are going to wake up in Hell, an eternal place of torment! Awful? Yes! But it is certain. Eternal? Yes. Away from God and begging for a drop of water to cool your tongue. I tell you, my friends, Hell is certain for unrepentant, unconverted sinners.

Now the Saviour said what man with ten thousand men is going out and jump on another fellow that has twenty thousand unless he first sits down and figures, "Can I with ten thousand men whip this fellow with twenty thousand?" If he cannot, he had better send an embassy and request peace. If you cannot face the whole question, if you do not have an answer to the question of Hell and judgment and eternity, then there is only one way out—turn from your sin to Jesus Christ. There is no other way to miss Hell but through Christ alone and His shed blood. You had better take into account the fact of Hell.

Then there is death. People are going to die. I come to tell you frankly that that is one of the things it will cost not to be a Christian.

Oh, my friends, if it means torment of conscience, if it means the breaking down of your hopes, if it means disappointments and remorse of conscience, if it means a wasted life, if it means damning others about you, if it means enslaving yourself in sin and dying without Christ, if it means Hell without relief, and judgment before the Saviour you have rejected—if it means that, is there anybody here who would say it pays to live for the Devil and die and go to Hell? Surely, surely not!

V. The Terrible Danger of Delay

I turn to another thing which I want you to consider last. Oh, the terrible danger of delay! You agree, do you not, that whatever you give up for Jesus you gain back, and more? Yes, and you gain Heaven and an eternity of blessedness besides. You can afford to lose everything down here. You and I will get to see our mother and father and other loved ones and Jesus, and will have peace and joy and perfection forever. Would it not be worth what it costs to anybody down here? I know you will agree that is true. Let me show you what danger there is in delay.

First of all, if you delay about this, you may be enslaved by

sin. I remind you that nobody ever intends to go as far in sin as
they go.

I talked to Bob Silver after he and a man named Stone had
shot down Roscoe Wilson in Fort Worth as he came from the
Majestic Theater with $5,000 in a bag. After shooting Wilson,
these two got in a Chrysler coupe and sped away. Over by the
Baptist Hospital they changed cars and got in another Chrysler
of another color. They started out toward Oklahoma. The
officers thought they had gone down toward Houston. They
combed every road looking for a certain kind of a Chrysler. As
these two hold-up men drove over into Oklahoma, they
breathed a sigh of relief. "We got away!"

Bob Silver told me, "We breathed a sigh of relief, but there
had been a rain, and a car had slipped off the highway. And
some other cars had stopped to help them out, blocking the
road. We stopped the car and got out. A deputy sheriff came
along. He had heard the broadcast, 'Look out for two fellows
from Fort Worth, Texas, in a gray Chrysler coupe.' The car we
had stolen was of a different color, but the sheriff said to us,
'Wait a minute, boys; I want to talk to you.' "

He told me that they tried to slip back in the car and get their
guns, but the sheriff pulled a gun quickly and covered them. He
found in the car the $5,000. The sheriff put handcuffs on the two
and brought them back to Fort Worth. Bob Silver said to
me—that young man whose face was pale because he had been
in solitary confinement, and whose hand was as palsied as a
man of eighty—"I turned to Stone and said, 'It is God! We can't
get away from God!' "

I tell you, my friends, Bob Silver never intended to go that
far. "I do not know what made me shoot him," he said. "I did not
mean to do it."

Nobody else ever intends to go as far in sin as they go. It
enslaves you. Somebody may have started to take a shot of dope
but nobody intended to be a slave to dope.

Second, there is the deceit of sin. Many are blinded by sin and
cannot see straight. They cannot see the truth. The Devil fools
you on everything. He tells you that you will have plenty of

time to prepare for Death. He tells you preachers are after your money. He says that church members are hypocrites. The Devil says don't go up there to the front; you can be saved some other way. Oh, the deceit of sin! There is danger in delay.

Next, there is danger of hardening of the heart. It is a terrible thing for a man to hear the Gospel and not be touched. My own heart has been stirred as I have gone over this again. Surely any one who is not saved has a hard heart. He has gone on in sin until his heart is not stirred by a Gospel message.

I have been preaching this Gospel for years, and tonight God knows if I could cry my heart out for sinners to get somebody saved, I would. I am concerned about you, and you are not. Why? Your heart is hardened and you have come to the place where you are not concerned. No kind of preaching or Bible teaching, nothing God ever does, no sweet singing, no praying mother or wife, will ever touch your hard heart any more if you do not beware! Hardening your heart! Oh, what danger that is!

There is danger also of a wasted life. But you are in danger one of these days of committing the unpardonable sin and your heart will be so hard that you can never be saved.

Here is another thing. Anybody who postpones salvation runs a terrible danger of sudden, unexpected death. It is a strange thing, is it not, about death, that people are never ready for it? We someway do not believe it is for us. We believe that somebody else is going to die, but not us. Do you expect to die very soon? No. Of course not.

When Rev. P. B. Chenault closed his message here that night, he did not expect to die so soon. Mr. Simmons, some other policeman will go to work and die who did not expect to die. In Dallas, Fort Worth or somewhere some policeman may be killed tonight. Or you may have a tragic accident on your way home after hearing this message. Is it not strange how death is always unexpected!

You and I do not expect to die. A person who is sick does not expect to die. Talk with people who have tuberculosis and they will tell you they are feeling better, where very soon they will be dead! Death is an unwelcome guest. We always try to believe it is not for us yet, that it is not our time yet. The Devil says, "You have plenty of time," but that is a lie. Do not believe him. You do not know that you have any time left at all.

If you are not saved, I warn you now there is deadly danger that your heart will be hardened or you may die unexpectedly, not ready and not prepared to meet God.

Sinner, have you counted the cost tonight? Isaiah 1:18 says, "Come now, and let us reason together, saith the Lord: though your sins be as scarlet, they shall be as white as snow; though they be red like crimson, they shall be as wool."

I have tried to reason with you. "Come now, and let us reason together," the Lord says. Are you a sinner? Do you admit it? There is mercy and forgiveness for you if you will but take it. I showed you awhile ago that you had to confess your sin. You have to see sin as it is. I said that in your heart you must turn from sin. But if in your heart you have found out how wicked sin is, how it brings ruin and blights happiness, then it is not so hard to turn from sin. The song says,

"I hate the sin that made Thee mourn,
And drove Thee from my breast."

Oh, I wish I had never sinned! I wish I was never attracted by sin.

Do not harden your heart. Have you counted the cost? Are you not willing to come to Jesus? It is not any trouble for you to say, "I will not come. I will save myself. I will not take it free." But will you say instead, "Jesus paid for my sins. I couldn't pay it. I do not have the coin to pay it with. I will trust Him to forgive me"? That is not hard.

You may say, "The world will be against me if I am a Christian." But you have the Devil and the world against you if you are not a Christian. The Devil's crowd will make you fall, but they will not help you up. When Judas Iscariot took the thirty pieces of silver, he thought he had some friends, but when he came back with an aching heart and said, "It is the price of blood! It is horrible. I can't get away from the thought of it!" they said, "See thou to that." Your friends will not help you then.

Listen! A fellow may drink up everything he has, lose his job, wife may quit him, and when he doesn't have a bit to eat, and has drunk up his last penny and his clothes are in rags—do you know who that man will come to? Will he look up the drinking crowd and have them give him something to eat? No, he will hunt up a preacher, or a good Christian. They come to me nearly every day. The drinking crowd will quit you. They go to church people when they are down and out.

Someone has said there is honor among thieves. There is not any honor among thieves. The only true Friend a sinner has is Jesus Christ, and for Jesus' sake, some people are your friends.

Have you counted the cost? Tonight if your sins are like scarlet, they can be as white as snow. If your heart is black, come to Him. He will forgive you and wash you in His blood. Have you an unease of conscience, a fear? Have haunting footsteps of remorse made bitter the nights and weary the days? God loves you, Jesus Christ died for you, and you can have peace.

Can anybody here say, "I am saved, but I find it too hard. I wish I had not gotten on the Lord's side"? No one ever said, "I am sorry I got saved." No, you will never find a soul like that! No, friends, come and let us reason together. Though your sins be as scarlet, they shall be as white as snow. Have you reasoned about it? What are you going to do about it?

If you are a Christian, I would say, "God helping me, I am going to be the best kind of a Christian I can be. I see more than ever that it pays to be a Christian. If it costs much, it is worth much." It surely is.

Is there one who is not a Christian but you want to be? Have you weighed it over in your mind? Can you say, "That is right"? Then will you do it tonight?

What does it take to be saved? Just in your heart a turning from your own sins and trusting in Jesus Christ. That is repentance and faith. Trust Jesus, not self. Trust Jesus, not feelings. Trust God alone. Trust Jesus who died to save sinners. Will you depend on Him? Come like the beggar and get forgiveness. Tonight you can be saved if you will.

How many can say, "I came like that to Jesus"? How many can say, "I admitted I was a sinner and I trusted Him and He forgave me and I am saved and I know it"? Will you hold your hands just a moment? Oh, yes. Thank you.

I am going to ask a question that I believe everybody here can vote on. How many can say, "Brother Rice, I believe you weighed the thing fair and honest. I believe every argument proves a man is wise to be a Christian and foolish not to be, that it is wise and right and safe to be a Christian and wrong and wicked and foolish not to be. I am convinced everybody ought to be a Christian and ought to be right now. It makes one happier to be a Christian. There is joy in being a Christian and there is an eternal reward in being a Christian. I am convinced of that whether I am a Christian or not"?

How many can say, "Brother Rice, I believe you are right. It pays to be saved and to trust the Lord. It pays in peace and salvation and heavenly mansions in the skies. It pays in your heart and in glory to come. I am sure it pays now and it pays hereafter"?

4—Bitter Words and Wicked Hearts

(Preached Sunday, October 29, 1939, in Fundamentalist Baptist Tabernacle, Dallas. Stenographically reported.)

PRAYER: Our Heavenly Father, wilt Thou open our hearts as we turn to Thy Word. Create in us a clean heart. Let us say like David in the 51st Psalm, "Purge me with hyssop, and I shall be clean." I pray, dear Lord, you will purge me tonight without and within, and, Lord, if tomorrow it needs to be done again, do it again. We pray tonight that Thou wilt have Thy way in our hearts as we come to this place of prayer, where Thou hast blessed many times before. We pray hearts may be blessed and souls may be saved. We pray, dear Lord, speak through this unworthy preacher tonight, that some man, some woman, some young person, may be saved. Tonight may people come out boldly and claim Thee. We pray people may seek and find the blessing in the heart that may express itself outwardly in their words. Tonight speak to our hearts, revive us for Jesus Christ, and let the Gospel bear fruit and God be honored and the Holy Spirit have free course—that people may go home blessed. For Jesus' sake. Amen.

* * *

You will pray for me while I preach, won't you? I feel that you will. Please pray also for these girls, Miss Lola and Miss Viola, who take down this message. They have taken three messages today; one this morning on the radio, one at 11:00, and now this one, and it is a great strain on them.

Turn to Matthew, chapter 12, and there I will read a few verses, beginning with verse 33 and reading through verse 37.

Either make the tree good, and his fruit good; or else make the tree corrupt, and his fruit corrupt: for the tree is known by his fruit.

O generation of vipers, how can ye, being evil, speak good things? for out of the abundance of the heart the mouth speaketh.

A good man out of the good treasure of the heart bringeth forth good things: and an evil man out of the evil treasure bringeth forth evil things.

But I say unto you, That every idle word that men shall speak, they shall give account thereof in the day of judgment.

For by thy words thou shalt be justified, and by thy words thou shalt be condemned.

I. God Is More Concerned About His Fruit Trees Than About Their Fruit

There are four things about this passage I call to your attention.

First, there is a tree and there is fruit, and God is more interested in trees than He is in the fruit.

Second, our hearts are inherently wicked, so much so that by nature we are snakes, poisonous snakes, with the taint of sin and Satan in us, and no man can ever see God without a new heart, without being made a new creature.

Third, the heart expresses itself best and most clearly in our words. Our mouth, out of a good heart, brings forth good words, and out of an evil heart, evil words.

The *fourth* and last point is: Men are justified by their words and by their words they are condemned. God is going to bring every man to judgment for every word, every idle, critical, slanderous, cursing word. I say, God is going to bring men to judgment. So with that in mind, I call your attention to verse 33:

Either make the tree good, and his fruit good; or else make the tree corrupt, and his fruit corrupt: for the tree is known by his fruit.

There is much said in the Bible about fruit. Jesus said, "If ye abide in me, and my words abide in you, ye shall ask what ye will, and it shall be done unto you" (John 15:7). I think seven times in six verses in that passage it tells us how to bear fruit. We are much concerned about bearing fruit. In fact, we mortals are more concerned about living a good life than we are about having a good heart, but God is not.

Dr. Will Houghton, late president of Moody Bible Institute, said a very striking thing: "The main business of Moody Bible Institute is not to turn out good Christian workers but to turn out good Christians, and let God make the workers." If you turn out the right kind of a Christian, he is going to be a good worker. God is more interested in trees than He is in fruit.

All over the country we find men trying to produce good works. One may think if he is going to be saved he must be in church every Sunday morning, take the Lord's Supper, give a tithe of his income, be baptized, and stay straight. It is all do, do, do, do, do! Many times when I ask a man if he is a Christian, he thinks I mean is he living right, so he says, "I am trying the best I can." A colored woman told me yesterday, "I am doing the best I can to be a Christian." She was thinking about the fruit and not about the tree. But God is interested in the tree. The Scripture says, "Either make the tree good, and his fruit good; or else make the tree corrupt, and his fruit corrupt."

All over the country pastors are concerned about the fruit-bearing of their people. And I am concerned about it, too, and I ought to be. If you think I am hard, then remember that the Bible commands, "Obey them that have the rule over you, and submit yourselves: for they watch for your souls, as they that must give account" (Heb. 13:17). I must give an account to God for you. I take this to heart about having the right kind of Christians who win souls and give freely and walk uprightly.

Now then, suppose I say I will try to put the pressure on you to get you to give up picture shows and bridge parties and cigarettes and try to get you to tithe, try to enlist you to go down to the jail services and park services and on Monday night to go to the hospital to win souls. I want you to do all those things. Those fruits are pleasing to God. But most of all, I want you to get dying souls on your heart. With a heart broken for sinners, the outward fruit will come.

I say, what God is really concerned about isn't for people to tithe. What He wants is a heart that will trust Him, a heart that says, "God will do what He said. He will take care of me. God is good to me." So with grateful heart overflowing with praise, you say, "I am just bound to give!"

That is good. You need to work on the heart, Brother Greer! God says in His Word, "Keep thy *heart* with all diligence; for out of it are the issues of life" (Prov. 4:23). God says to watch your heart.

We watch our tongues. You say, "Boy, I have a time keeping my tongue straight!" I know why. It is because your heart isn't straight. You cannot put dirty water in the water mains and by washing the faucets expect good water to come out. You must go back and purify the source of the water. You cannot grow Elberta peaches on an old scrub oak tree. You have to have the right kind of tree to produce Elberta peaches.

And you cannot turn out real soul-winning Christians unless Christians have compassionate hearts, with part of the burden the Lord Jesus has for sinners, knowing that Hell, Heaven, and eternity alone can tell the value of a soul. Until you come to that point, you are not going to be a soul winner. I can argue with you, I can teach you how, I can get study courses for you, and put you to teaching a Sunday school class, but that will not do it.

I remember when I was in a revival meeting with Rev. Harvey Springer in 1937 in Englewood, Colorado. When I got there, everything was all set.

Brother Springer said, "John, I know how you like it. I don't do it that way, but we fixed it up like you like it. At every four seats we have placed a personal worker, ready to go when the invitation is given." He expected to get results.

I said, "God bless you, Harvey. Oh, but first of all we have to get hold of the hearts. You don't make a soul winner out of a man with a cold heart."

I tell you now, what God wants is a tree, then He will get the right kind of fruit. What God wants is the heart that is right, that puts God first. Thank God for these words: "Either make the tree good, and his fruit good; or else make the tree corrupt, and his fruit corrupt: for the tree is known by his fruit." You are not going to have good fruit from a bad tree.

A lot of you people don't tithe because your heart is set on money. The love of money, the love of riches, the cares of this world and the deceitfulness of riches make it so you have trouble tithing. You made up your mind you would, you vowed you would, and you tried it for a time. You thought you could do it. But there is something in your heart that is not right—the love for money, an evil, wicked thing that needs to be taken away. You need God to change it. You need God to make you a liberal Christian *in your heart.*

A man came to Dr. J. B. Gambrell many years ago and said, "I tell you, when I give I just can't help but begrudge it. I give, but it hurts. What ought I do about it?" He thought Dr. Gambrell would say, "I wouldn't give, then," but wise Dr. Gambrell said, "I would quit grudging." God wants you to fix the grudging part instead of the giving part.

That widow who gave two mites gave more than all the others, Jesus said, because she gave all she had to God. What God wants is a heart that is willing to give all. And Jesus stood there at the treasury and rejoiced because she put in all she had, because she trusted Him and had faith and love and surrender.

If we have that kind of giving, it is only incidental whether we have rich folks in our churches. What God wants is the heart, the tree. We are concerned about the fruit, but God wants the tree.

The Pharisees tried to produce the fruit. They tithed, they prayed in public, they went to church. They did all the outside things. They were a fine bunch. Yes, they had fine fruit, but they had wicked trees, and Jesus said to them, "Either make the tree good, and his fruit good; or else make the tree corrupt, and his fruit corrupt: for the tree is known by his fruit."

This Scripture says you can't have one without the other, and

God wants the heart fixed. Oh, watch your hearts!

I hope in this church we will more and more be concerned about being good Christians. I have thought a good deal about this. I don't win as many souls in Dallas as I used to. There are difficulties. We don't have concern about going after them. I win more souls outside of Dallas than in Dallas. I made up my mind I am going to win them where I can. That is what God called me to do and I am going to do it.

Listen! I am not going to preach all the time just to have outward results, with great groups of people coming down the aisles every time I preach. Sure, I want visible results, but I want to first be sure that there are invisible results. We can sin in looking for numbers. We need a revival, but we need it inside to make us good. We need an earthquake inside out hearts so we can get down and have an old-time weeping, old-time praying, and an old-time transforming of lives. Then there will be plenty of people coming down the aisles.

Oh, what God is most concerned about is the heart. He wants the heart kind of religion, the tree made right, regeneration in the soul of a sinner. And God surely wants a refiring, a reinvigorating, a resanctifying of hearts of the saved people. With us we think about the fruit. God wants fruit but God wants a good tree to bring forth fruit.

And right hard on the heels of that truth comes the matter of regeneration. "O generation of vipers, how can ye, being evil, speak good things? for out of the abundance of the heart the mouth speaketh."

My friends, I promised God I will preach again and again that you must be born again. I need to stress to church members to make sure they are saved.

You may say tonight, "Brother Rice, I am as good as the church members. I go to church as much, pray as much. I am good to my neighbors; I don't get drunk; I don't curse; I am a pretty good guy."

That may be true, but if you are not born again you are a poisonous snake.

What does a snake mean spiritually? Sin first showed itself to the human race in the form of a serpent. When Adam and Eve were in the Garden of Eden, Satan came in the form of a snake. The Bible speaks in Revelation 12:9 and Revelation 20:2 of "that old serpent, called the Devil, and Satan."

When Jesus was to be pictured in the Old Testament bearing all our sins, God used a snake. You remember the fiery snakes came in among Israel and much people of Israel died. The people said to Moses, "What are we going to do?" Moses prayed, and God said, "Make a snake out of brass and put it on a pole, and whoever looks at the snake will be healed."

That snake pictures Jesus bearing my sins and yours. "For he hath made him to be sin for us, who knew no sin; that we might be made the righteousness of God in him" (II Cor. 5:21). I say that picture is showing Christ bearing our sins. Sin is pictured by a snake.

II. Our Hearts Are Inherently Wicked

And now the Lord says to the Pharisees in our text, "The trouble with you is that you have the Devil in you. You are a child of the Devil. The trouble with you is that you are a generation of vipers." That is what is wrong with men.

You say what is wrong with men is ignorance. No! No! What is wrong is a rotten heart.

You say they do not have proper organization, or they do not have the right kind of an education. I say that is not what is wrong. What is wrong with war and communism and divorce and modernism and crime and unrest? What is back of it is *sin.* It is wicked *hearts,* the Devil in the *hearts* of people. Jesus said, "You are a generation of vipers." "How can ye, being evil, speak good things? for out of the abundance of the *heart* the mouth speaketh."

The matter of speech is the closest revelation of the heart. Your mouth is like a mirror which shows the heart. One can't see it otherwise. My friends, what is wrong with your speech is that you have a poor, rotten heart inside. May God help you to see it tonight. If you are not born again, if you do not have God's grace in your heart, then you are not saved.

I can never get over the thing, someway the marvel of it, the freshness, the sweetness, the way God makes a real change in a sinner's heart. I think of that Catholic man who came and kneeled at my bedside when I was sick with the flu three years ago this November. He knelt down after I showed him how to be saved, and I put my hands on his head and prayed, and he got up, and sat down on the bed and said, "You know, I feel different. Isn't that strange? I have such peace in my heart! I never had this before. Isn't this wonderful?"

After awhile he said again, "Listen, isn't this wonderful? Isn't this strange?"

I told him, No, it wasn't strange. I have seen so many other people have the same thing when they put their trust in Jesus.

I remember a man named Clyde Barrow (not the Dallas Clyde Barrow but a West Texas man). He was six feet, five inches high, and weighed 235 pounds. He got saved, but before he was saved he drank heavily. He drank up his farm which he had inherited, and finally lost. He had a very beautiful stepdaughter whom he greatly loved. Yet he drank.

One day he let his crony get in on his secret. He had a half-barrel of wine. When he went to the field he always took a jug full. So this crony of his was going along with him, and this Clyde Barrow said to him, "Come on with me and I will give you a drink out of my jug."

So he did and they both drank. This friend did not drink as much as Clyde, so Clyde told him where the half-barrel of wine was that was back at the house. This crony who didn't drink quite as much excused himself, thanked Clyde Barrow, and went on his way. But he went back by the haystack where this wine was and stole nearly all of it.

When Clyde Barrow got home that night, he made his daily rounds. He would always turn out the horses and then go to the haystack. When he went to milk the cows, he would always go down by the haystack. But when he drank this time, he found it was almost all gone! He said, "Somebody has been in my wine and I know who it was. That son-of-a-gun!"

So he got in his car and started out to find this man, and he found him out in the street. Clyde said, "You so-and-so, you got in my wine," and biffed him one, knocking him out in the street. As soon as the fellow could get back on his feet, Clyde would knock him down again, until finally he knocked him out.

Clyde's brain began to clear. He said, "I have played the fool a lot of times, but I was never in a street brawl before. What will Maggie think [his stepdaughter]? What in the world will Maggie think? And what will my wife think? I have played the fool plenty of times. I have wasted a farm on drink, but I never before was in a street fight over being drunk."

All the way home he said the wheels of his car said, "You have played the fool! You have played the fool!" He was ashamed to face his wife. He went down to the haystack and got what was left of that half-barrel of wine and took a cultivator axle and broke in the head of it, and rolled it off down the hill. He went around mourning two or three days.

Finally I met him at a blacksmith shop. He was sick. I tried to get him to my house for dinner, but he wouldn't come. He was afraid of my wife. Finally he went with me out in the field and out there he trusted the Lord and was wonderfully saved. I won't tell you all the details. There were some comical things.

But Clyde Barrow would come to my house between Sunday and Wednesday night. He would wake me up before he went to work about 6:30 and say, "Brother Rice, I have been reading my Bible and I found something I can't understand, so I decided to come and ask my pastor." He couldn't wait for Wednesday night, if he found a verse he couldn't understand, so hungry was he for the Word of God. With great joy he began to win souls to Christ.

One day he brought his own kid brother down the aisle. The Lord just transformed him. One day he said, "Preacher, something has sure happened to me! Do you remember how I used to fight at the drop of a hat? I am big and everybody was afraid of me. I went around looking for trouble. I would get mad at anything. Well, I went downtown and was talking to some guy about the Lord, and this man cursed me to my face. You know, Brother Rice, I just stood there and cried and laughed at him. I said, 'I am not afraid of you. You know I could break you in two with my two hands. You know I would have done it, too, if I hadn't been saved. I don't hate you; I am not mad at you. I am just going to pray for you.' Something sure has happened to me!"

"God bless you," I said, "something *has* happened to you!"

And what you need tonight is for *something to happen to you inside.* God does not want so much tying some fruit on the outside of the tree. God wants a different tree. Then it will bring forth a different fruit.

I tell you tonight, poor lost man, what you need is a new heart. What you need is for God to make your wicked heart right, for God to make you, a snake, into a child of God. John the Baptist said, "God is able of these stones to raise up children unto Abraham." God wants to make your poor, vile heart clean, and He will and can.

I talked to a Jewish girl, a bootlegging woman, in Chicago who was one of seven women rum-runners. There were many men but only seven women known to the federal forces, and she was one of them. She lived a wicked life and was heartbroken. One day I announced that I was going to preach a certain Friday night on "Whiskey-Prescribing Doctors and Druggists, Malt-Selling Grocers, and Bootlegging Skunks." I laid it on. I rubbed people's hair the wrong way. That night when I gave the invitation she held her hand for prayer, but when the invitation came, she got up and left.

I didn't know what was wrong. She was going to Detroit, across 300 miles into Canada, to get another carload of booze. All those 300 miles she kept saying to herself, "Yes, that is right. You are nothing but a bootlegging skunk." She didn't hear that sermon. She just heard me announce that I would preach it on another night. But I gave enough preview that she got that much. She thought, "That is right; you are nothing but a lousy, bootlegging skunk. You have no friends but those you bought or bribed. You have to work to get by the officers of the law. You are a lawbreaker. All you are is a bootlegging skunk" (talking to herself).

She went on across the bridge and came back, and all the way back to Chicago the wheels kept saying, "Bootlegging skunk! Bootlegging skunk!"

She came back on Sunday night to hear me preach. After the service had already dismissed she said, "There is no chance for a woman like me." I did all I could to win her to Christ, but I couldn't. She was cut to the heart with the Scripture, was convicted of her sin, but yet she didn't see any way out of the dirty business and how she could live for God. I was at the end of my rope.

Finally another woman came up to me as I talked to the dear rum-runner nearly an hour. She stood by the high platform in Paul Rader's tabernacle in 1932, and said to the one I was talking to, "You think you can't be a Christian? Let me tell you what I was. I was the madam who ran a house of prostitutes down here on such a corner [and she gave the address]. I was in that awful business for twelve years. I am ashamed of it, but I want to tell you what God can do for sinners." And she stood there and unfolded that story, weeping as she told how God had saved her, a poor, fallen woman who ran a house of ill fame, and made her happy and clean and gave her a good husband and a happy family and made a soul winner and a respected Christian woman of her. And then she said, "If God can do that for me, He can do it for you, too."

Her word did what I couldn't do, and that Jewish girl, that woman rum-runner, trusted Christ and went back and reported to the chief who worked over her that she was through with that business. She said, "I am not going to sell it. I am done with it."

My friends, what God wants is not just to get a man to start living a different life, but He wants to give him a new heart that will sow a different life.

I am afraid about a lot of people who have such trouble trying to come out, trying to get in the church and give their testimony. I am afraid about a lot of people. The trouble is they are working on the fruit end when what they need is a new tree that God can make right and make it so it can bear good fruit.

Jesus said, "O generation of vipers, how can ye, being evil, speak good things?" Oh, unsaved men, you are a bunch of snakes. A man with a wicked heart is a poisonous snake. The poison of Satan is in your veins. You need a new heart. You need God to make you into a new man so that old things will pass away and all things will become new. God will help you to love what you hate, and hate what you now love. God will give you a new heart.

I don't know who is here unsaved, but let me give you this good news. God is in the business of making sad hearts happy. God is in the business of making failures into successes. God is in the business of making harlot women pure! God is in the business of making drunkards sober! God is in the business of making infidels into believers. God is in the business of taking Hell-bound sinners and making them fit for Heaven. God can make a new tree in your heart so you can bear new fruit. What people need is to be born again.

You may be a Pharisee like Nicodemus, but you need to be born again. You may be a moral woman, you may live a good life; but you are as rotten as Hell inside and you need to be born again. Maybe on the other hand you have hopelessly gone in sin and feel no peace. What you need is the grace of God to fix things inside.

III. In Christian Living One Must Have Renewal From God

That is true not only about salvation but on the matter of Christian living. There are people here tonight who can go back and put their finger on the spot when they trusted Jesus Christ and got all their sins forgiven.

> O happy day that fixed my choice
> On Thee, my Saviour and my God!
> Well may this glowing heart rejoice,
> And tell its raptures all abroad.

You can remember that time. I am talking to people who would say you are not Christians, who have forgotten you were purged from your sins, as Peter tells us in the Bible. But if I get you to go back and talk about the time and how sweet it was when you surrendered to Christ and had sweet peace and forgiveness, the assurance will come anew.

Some are here tonight who have lost their joy. At times you have doubted about it. May I tell you what you need? You say, "I am going to start attending church, going to start tithing, going to start giving my testimony, going to get in a Sunday school class, or I will go to teaching." I know, but wait. You need God to clean you up inside.

David prayed in the 51st Psalm, "O God, against thee and thee only have I sinned. Lord, take not thy holy spirit from me and cast me not away from thy presence. Purge me with hyssop, and I shall be clean; wash me, and I shall be whiter than snow. Thou desirest not sacrifice, else would I give it. The sacrifices of God are a broken spirit. A broken and a contrite heart, O God, thou will not despise." And David said, "O God, renew a right spirit within me."

God wants to give you a clean heart. And tonight everyone here needs to say, "O God, make my heart clean." You say, "I wish God would help me live better." Brother Reeves, haven't you often thought, "I wish I could live a better life"? Haven't you? Sure. But what God is after is not so much the outward life. He wants you to get something inside that will shine out.

You say, "I wish I could make that window so the light would come out." But you must have the light to have it shining. You need to get right inside. You have to get the dynamo working inside.

I may drive my car into a filling station and say, "I believe I need more air in these tires." The air does not raise it up. What is wrong? You don't have line trouble; the compression tank is low. Start the engine pumping.

God, give us plenty of compression back in the tank and we will get air in the line! In other words, get compression in the heart, a cleaning up in the heart.

I know why you people don't say "Amen" when I preach. You don't have it in your heart. You don't have enough praise. When you talk to sinners, you have to force it, don't you? You ought to be bubbling over until you can't contain it. You are bound to tell it.

Listen, some of you cold Christians ought to come tonight and say, "O Lord, work me over. Make me the kind of tree that can't help bearing fruit. Make me the kind of tree than *can* bear good fruit." What we need is our hearts made right. May God clean our hearts! God give us fresh hearts. May God make us over in our hearts. We need to be fixed inside.

Now the next point I want you to get it this:

IV. The Heart Expresses Itself by Words

Do you have trouble with your mouth? I do. I wonder how many talk too much. Isn't that strange? You don't look like you would. You talk fine, and you look pretty, and you sing sweetly. You have nice smiles! No one would ever think you would say anything bad about others. No one would think you would ever wrong anybody. No one would think you would speak sharply at home. Isn't it strange that we have trouble with our mouths? Do you know what our real trouble is? It is not with our mouth. We work on our mouth, but that is not what we need work on. *It is your heart that needs fixing!*

Here is somebody who works with a bad crowd. He hurts himself some way, and he curses. He says, "Boy, I must quit that! What if my wife were to hear me curse?" But do you know what needs fixing? You need your heart fixed, for the Scripture says, "Out of the abundance of the heart the mouth speaketh." That is the reason Jesus said here about this matter, "O generation of vipers, how can ye, being evil, speak good things? for out of the abundance of the heart the mouth speaketh. A good man out of the good treasure of the heart bringeth forth good things: and an evil man out of the evil treasure bringeth forth evil things."

Why do you curse? You are a snake in the heart, so you have a snake's language. Oh, my heart is so sick about Christians and the way they talk!

My people—how many need comfort! There is so much bitterness, there is so much temptation, there is so much criticism. How people need comfort and kindness! I need it myself. Couldn't you get off and think up something nice to say about people? We do not love people as we ought.

I am always getting funny letters. Every now and then these girls who work for me take me to task for spending so much time answering silly questions and writing long letters to "Church of Christ" people and others who ask every kind of a question. A woman wrote me the other day and asked, "Brother Rice, what is charity? I read about it in the Bible, but I don't know what it is." I wrote her that it is a love that God puts in the heart for a Christian brother.

You know I would not have to try to get you to say nice things if your heart were filled with nice things. If you have enough gratitude in your heart, you will have some praises. We need our hearts made right. I wish I could get you to go out and win souls, but you have to have a heart to do it. If you had enough compassion in your heart, and if your heart were burning for these people, you would go tomorrow night to Parkland Hospital and give out tracts.

A man at Woodland wants someone to come talk to him. He has T.B. A woman called me yesterday about him. This man is a Seventh-day Adventist. He got some copies of THE SWORD OF THE LORD with an article on law and grace and he is so burdened and upset. He wants to talk to someone about it. He wants to be able to come to church, too.

Listen. There is so much to do. Mrs. McKinney wants somebody to go to the hospital and teach her the Sunday school lesson.

There ought to be something in you that is burning to do something for Christ like Jeremiah when he said, 'I will speak no more in the name of the Lord,' but there was a fire in his bones and he could not contain it. He had to speak. Jeremiah was trying to quit the ministry but he couldn't quit. Jeremiah said, 'Oh that my head were a fountain of water that I might weep over the slain of the daughter of my people.' Our trouble is that we have to squeeze terribly hard to get out one tear for sinners. Jeremiah wept out his soul until he had no more tears. What we need is for God to work on our hearts, then our mouths can be right.

I started to say about comfort—it is so sweet when there are burdens. It is a strange thing, but nobody ever thinks I need any spiritual help. People come to me and say, "Pray with me about this." Or they call me over the phone and say, "Pray about this." They write in letters asking prayers. They meet me on the sidewalk and say, "Pray with me about this," and I do, and I will. But God knows I need prayers, too.

You say, "Brother Rice, I have a heavy burden; I am having a hard pull. Please join with me and ask God to hold me up." I am glad to share your burdens, but I need holding up, too. I am using myself only as an example. This poor, tired, sick, over-burdened world needs people to go around giving comfort, some joy; someone overflowing to make other people happy.

Nobody ever asks me if I am a Christian, though I am always asking other people. No one ever asks me if I am saved. I ask, "Are you letting your light shine? Are you reading your Bible? How are you getting along with the Lord?" No one asks me if God is good to me and if I am getting along all right with the Lord. Do you think I am an angel from Heaven? Do you think I am not made out of the same dirt you are? I need somebody to help me along.

I think of the time when I tried to win a twelve-year-old boy to Christ in a barber shop here in Dallas. I said, "Son, where do you go to church, and do you go to Sunday school?"

He said, "I go to Sunday school."

But his dear mother who was sitting there said, "Friend, let me tell you that just being a member of a church isn't all you need. Just going to church isn't enough."

I said, "No, that's right."

But she didn't give me a chance to say more. "Listen, what people really need is to be born again and have their hearts made right. There is something real about this business. Going to church is not enough." She said, "I know there is something to this business of being a Christian."

I sat there, and my heart was like a desert that just took in the rain. It blossomed as she talked on.

As we came back through the desert from California I was surprised to see how bright green everything was. They said they had had more rain out there in ten days than in the past twenty-eight years. Half a mile of road was washed away in places—in the desert. The desert was blossoming. That is the way my heart was. It just drank it in as that woman talked to me about the Lord.

She said, "Mister, I was sick and about to die. The doctor gave me up. He had a consultation with other doctors. They told me they had done all they could do. 'Then I will call another Doctor.' They said, 'We have already called five of the best.' I told them: 'But the best One you haven't called yet. I am going to call Him. If you can't get me up, God can. I am going to call Him. I want to live for my children. You can go on away. You needn't leave me any medicine.'"

And she said she turned her face to the wall, so weak that she couldn't pray much, but she asked God, "Lord, let me live today! Lord, keep me alive today. I am too sick to pray, but just keep me alive today." And then the next day she prayed, "Lord, you kept me alive yesterday, now keep me alive today."

She told how she didn't feel like agonizing in prayer; she was too sick. But it wasn't long until she began to feel better, then she prayed, "Lord, now get me well." She said to me, "I want you to know God answers prayer. This is real."

Oh, I have thought about that a thousand times. My heart is hungry to hear people talk like that, who have really talked with the Lord and know what it is all about. You don't have praises like that because your heart is not running over with it inside. "Out of the abundance of the heart the mouth speaketh."

Sometimes people here hold their hands for prayer but nobody talks to them. And if you do, you have to force yourself to, because you are not running over inside with the love of God.

I would like to be like the old colored man on the dock at Memphis, Tennessee. Down the Mississippi River there came a steamboat, and as the ship whistled, the old Negro always ran to the dock, and as that big side-wheeler boat passed, he cried out, "Dar he goes! Dar he goes! Look at the captain on the bridge!" When the boat had passed, the old fellow would wipe his eyes and say to somebody, "I jist loves to pint him out!"

The story is that this black man was in a little rowboat in the muddy waters of the Mississippi. One day a larger ship came too close to his rowboat and it turned over, throwing him in the muddy waters, and he didn't know how to swim. The captain of the larger boat jumped off his ship and pulled the old man to shore, saving his life. This old black man couldn't forget him. He said, "I jist loves to pint him out!"

You had better get fixed up inside so the fire is burning and so you will have something to talk about, then you can talk for Jesus. You can point Him out to others. You surely can.

You had better practice up on gratitude in your heart and get the fire burning inside, then you can say "Amen" which you do not do now. You never say "Hallelujah!" do you? You have no hallelujahs in your heart, so you don't have them in your mouth.

Right now you haven't old-time manifestations of the Spirit. Well, you need something to be manifested. You need something inside. You won't have to show it; it will show itself. You ought to pray, "O God, give me the kind of heart that will make me talk for You, the kind that won't listen to criticism."

Are you critical? Do you listen to talk about people? You garbage collectors! God help you! A good woman out in California—the Lord really got hold of her—got up one night and gave a testimony. "I have had a critical spirit. I listened to gossip. The Devil made a garbage pail out of my ears. I had them out listening all the time. I am going to look after my heart."

That is a pretty good idea.

You had better make up your mind to get your heart right, and ask God to give you a distaste for that kind of garbage. If you always listen to gossip and bad talk, ask God to make your heart pure and clean inside, "for out of the abundance of the heart the mouth speaketh."

If you have trouble about cursing, your real trouble is not with the mouth, it is deeper than that. If you have trouble about idle chatter—chatter, chatter, chatter—you have an idle heart. You have no burden, your heart is not filled with the Scriptures, it is not warmed up inside. O God, revive our hearts! Oh, the heart is where we need it!

V. God Is Going to Bring Men to Judgment

Another word. You are going to come to judgment. The Lord will judge you very largely by the way you talk. God is going to bring you up and put you on the witness stand about every idle word you ever said. He just means if it wasn't any good, if it didn't bless anybody. Then you had better be careful about your talk!

The Lord spoke to me not very long ago. About a certain woman in a certain revival, I had a way of saying, "I am satisfied she wasn't as wide as she was tall." It has always been funny about how that fat woman began to shout. And just as I was telling that, I stepped off a chair and lost my balance and everybody laughed at me. I said, "All right, Lord, I will quit making a joke out of that point in the sermon."

I think God wants preachers to be on fire and in earnest. There are times when humor can serve a point and purpose and be used with a lesson. But God will bring you to judgment for words that have no good purpose, especially, words that edify nobody, that win nobody, that comfort nobody. They are wood, hay, and stubble, and will be burned up at the judgment seat of Christ. Oh, my friends, God is going to bring you to judgment for the way you talk! He will judge you by your talk!

"Well, Brother Rice, I pay my debts." I know. This is not what I am talking about. God says you will be justified by your words, or by your words you will be condemned. You say you are out and out for Jesus. Wait a minute! By the way you talk—are you a Christian? Does everybody find out you are a Christian by the way you talk? Do you have the mind of Christ as is pictured in your talk? Oh, the tender voice of Jesus! Do you talk like Jesus? If not, watch your step.

Christians, let's come back tonight and say, "O Lord, purify my heart!" You are always wanting the fruit but you need to get the tree fixed up, then you will bear plenty of fruit.

If you are a lost sinner tonight, I beg you, say, "O Lord, change my heart." He will.

Come and trust Jesus Christ, who knows all about you and He can and will change your heart. Will you give Him a chance to do it tonight? Will you trust Christ to save you and make your heart right?

How many will say, "Tonight, Brother Rice, I want God to revive my heart." You want to live a different life and bear more fruit. But you will have to start deeper than that. Why don't you say, "I want God to revive my heart and put enough gratitude in my heart so that I will just have to praise Him"? Then I would not have to coax a testimony out of you every Wednesday night. Then we would not have to beg you to come to the choir. Nobody would have to beg you to go out and win souls. You would have such compassion that you would have to go and talk to lost people. How many Christians here will pray, "O God, revive my heart"? He will.

PRAYER: Our Heavenly Father, do bless tonight. Revive our hearts. Out of the abundance of our heart may we bring forth good things; may we have a heart that is pleasing to Thee. O Lord, make us soul winners, gentle in our talk because we are gentle in heart. Lord, let us watch our words. Let us remember that a soft answer turns away wrath. Take away bitterness, selfishness, and suspicion and give us tender hearts; gentle, loving hearts. Make us clean in heart. Amen.

(Many came for a rededication of heart and a fresh cleansing.)

5—Three Fathers

(Preached Sunday night, May 8, 1938, at Fundamentalist Baptist Tabernacle. Stenographically reported.)

I am going to speak about three fathers in the Bible. Now today is Mother's Day but I have felt like it wouldn't be right to leave out Father. For one thing, our fathers need preaching to as bad as our mothers do.

How many here have the honor of being a father? God bless you! Many of you boys and young men will one day have a family of your own, and you need the message God has laid on my heart. I will mention three fathers in the Bible, and from these will bring lessons that come very close to my own heart and home, and I believe to yours.

I. Lot Who Moved Into Sodom

In the 13th chapter of Genesis is named the first father I will mention—Lot.

> *Abram dwelled in the land of Canaan, and Lot dwelled in the cities of the plain, and pitched his tent toward Sodom.*
>
> *But the men of Sodom were wicked and sinners before the Lord exceedingly.*

Lot was a saved man. In II Peter 2:8 we read,

> *(For that righteous man dwelling among them, in seeing and hearing, vexed his righteous soul from day to day with their unlawful deeds).*

1. He Moved His Family With Him Into Wicked Sodom

So we know that he was a saved man even though he lived a sorry life and led his family to ruin.

What was the mistake of this father? He "pitched his tent toward Sodom." It is bad enough that Lot himself went to Sodom. It was bad enough when he sold his cattle and got a bottle of wine and brought it home. But he moved the family, the whole house, toward Sodom and then farther toward Sodom and then one day *into* Sodom. Therefore, on an occasion like this, I speak of him not as an individual but as a father who pitched his tent toward Sodom.

But the men of Sodom were wicked and sinners before the Lord exceedingly.

May I say this: every man is accountable for his family whether he would have it so or not so. You can't live one way and expect your wife to live another way. A man who does that is not only a shirker and a slacker and a quitter; he is a fool. If a man says he is the head of his family and doesn't expect his family to pattern after him, he is making a big mistake. I have no boys to follow after me but I have six little girls who are watching my steps. It would be foolish and sinful for me to expect them to live a righteous and clean life if I did not live the same way. I wouldn't drink a bottle of whiskey for that right arm. I am afraid of it. It has the poison of death in it, the deception of Satan in it. I know my sin would one day find me out in my girls.

Lot made a fatal mistake when he moved his family into Sodom.

Men here tonight may curse and you don't want your wife to curse. You are not only a crook and a dishonest hypocrite, but you are a fool. You are wrecking the foundations of your own home.

A man will smoke but he doesn't want his wife to smoke. You may not like to see it but your wife has the same right to smoke as you have. Neither one has any right at all; but God is not the Author of a double standard. He doesn't expect one thing of a man and another thing of a woman.

God wants Christian men to lead the way. You men ought to say, "I will live right and I want my wife to live true after me. I want my children to live true after me."

A man who curses and doesn't want his wife and children to take God's name in vain is a fool. I know men who had certain habits and their boys followed on that way and these men punished the boys for doing the same things they did. I say to you, that is wrong and a sin.

Lot moved his tent into Sodom. When he went into Sodom he took his family with him. And you take your family with you when you move into Sodom and into sin. You think you can perhaps spend time in gambling with a bunch of gamblers, among those with lewd lips, licentious thoughts, lustful appetites and habits, those whose time, energy, and desire are all spent in the things against God—and yet think your family can stay clean! Lot went wrong because he took his tent with him and his family with him. He cursed and doomed his home by moving into Sodom.

Listen to me, you fathers! I promised God and you in the announcement that I would speak plainly and sharply. I am not talking to sissies; I am talking to men. I am not talking to women and children; I am talking to men. Tonight men ought to say, "God helping me, I will toe the line. I will be as clean as I want my family to be. I will keep the same kind of company I want them to keep. I won't drink since I don't want them to drink. I don't want them to curse, so I won't curse."

No man has a right to read what his wife can't read. You ought not go where your wife can't go. You should not have any thoughts you wouldn't want your wife to have.

A man should not go into Sodom unless his family can safely go with him. Lot took his family and pitched his tent toward Sodom. They will go with you, too.

2. Lot Called Wicked Men "Brethren"

Let's see the result in this case. He called these wicked men "brethren."

The sad story is found in the book of Genesis, chapter 19. Down where Lot lived they were so wicked God said, "I am going to destroy it. I will send fire and brimstone and wipe out that town." God did. But God said, "I will tell Abraham about it. He is My good friend." So God went down with two angels and met Abraham and had dinner with him, and He told Abraham what He was going to do about Sodom.

Abraham prayed, "Lord, you don't want to destroy all the righteous and wicked too, do you?"

But God said, "Here are not even ten righteous persons in the city. I will send two angels to get Lot and his family out. I will do it for Abraham's sake." And for Abraham's sake He sent two angels to get Lot and his family out. The wicked men of that city compassed the house around and would have raped the angels of Heaven who came that night, but Lot went out and shut the door and said, "I pray you, *brethren*, do not so wickedly."

Be careful who you call "brethren." Be careful who you compromise with. Be careful who you run with. If you have the wrong kind of friendship, the wrong kind of associates, the wrong kind of companions, then one day it will be the ruin of your whole family. No man can resist bad company, I don't care how strong you are. David didn't when he fell into sin with Bathsheba. Samson didn't when he laid his head in the lap of Delilah. His character was gone, his strength was gone. God forsook him. They cut off his hair and put out his eyes. Samson, grinding at the mill, was in shameful disgrace. Poor, blinded man of God!

No man in this world is strong enough to move into Sodom and live like the Lord's people should live. You won't do it. You will laugh like Sodom and talk like Sodom. You will call that crowd "brethren."

One reason I made up my mind a good while ago not to run with some people who call themselves Fundamentalists but lie, exalt self, are shameful in their private lives is because I couldn't have evil company. I will not trim corners just to please people. I will run with the Lord's people. I will not call the other crowd my brethren.

I wish people everywhere would say, "I will not have association, I will not have dirty conversation with the Devil's crowd and call them brethren."

"Brethren, do not so wickedly." I always thought Lot would have done a good deal better if he had taken a single-tree or an axe handle and waded in on that dirty crowd and driven them from his door. He would have saved his own family. But he lost the respect of his wife and children and all self-respect and the power of God, and he went to the dogs himself and his family was destroyed.

3. Is Your Religion a Mockery to Your Children?

Old Lot got anxious about his family when the angel said:

Hast thou here any besides? son in law, and thy sons, and thy daughters, and whatsoever thou hast in the city, bring them out of this place:

For we will destroy this place, because the cry of them is waxen great before the face of the Lord: and the Lord hath sent us to destroy it.

"Up, get you out of this place: for the Lord will destroy this city." And Lot said, "My, here's my family about to be burned. What will I do?" Poor girls, they married unworthy men. Lot went out to his daughter's house and said, "Sally, get up. The Lord is going to destroy this city." His sons-in-law wouldn't hear him. They wouldn't believe it. They said, "He has gone crazy about religion all of a sudden. People are like that when they get drunk. They feel that way."

The Scripture says this, and I believe it is the saddest thing that can be said about a Christian man, *"But he seemed as one that mocked unto his sons in law."* His religion was a mockery, a joke to his own loved ones.

My friends, I can know just what kind of religion you have, I can tell what kind of life you live by talking to your kinfolk, your married in-laws, your own family, those closest about you.

Somebody here tonight says, "Brother Rice, my boys won't listen to me about the Lord," or, "Brother Rice, my girl won't listen to me about the Lord." If that be true, I tell you what I would do: put on sackcloth and ashes and not eat or drink until I got right with God and until I got the kind of religion my children had confidence in.

I cannot think of any tragedy so horrible to a mother and father as to learn that they have no influence over their boys and girls whom they brought into the world and see those boys and girls go through this world doomed to Hell.

Listen to me! You had better pay a price, whatever it is, to have power with God and influence over your children. You had better quit your wicked, evil companions and turn your heart from covetousness and repent of your sins and start the family altar. Just admit you have failed and then get busy for God and have it settled so your children will have some confidence in your kind of religion.

It is a horrible thing that some of you people who claim to be Christians—there are those in your own home and of your own blood who have no confidence in the way you live and in the way you serve God. Lot was "as one that mocked unto his sons in law."

You fathers had better sit up and take notice. I am looking in the face of some of you men who wear pants and have a job and draw a man's wages, but your own children are going to the dogs. When your boys never go to church, what is wrong? Something is bad wrong at home.

A woman came to me the other day about her poor, troubled boy. God bless her, I wouldn't embarrass her at all, I am anxious to help her. Her boy is now in the penitentiary, and she urged me to pray for him. I am praying for him, but I told her she had better go home and get down on her knees before God in tears and confess to God she had failed, that she put her boy in the pen, didn't rear him right.

"Oh, but I did rear him right," she said.

"No, you didn't," I said. "The Bible says, 'Train up a child in the way he should go: and when he is old, he will not depart from it.' "

"Oh," but she said, "I did train him right."

"You have come to me for help, and I will talk plainly to you. Did you have a family altar?"

"No, I never did."

"You didn't win him to Christ, did you?"

"No. But I have a good boy."

"He is in the pen at any rate. You didn't get him saved."

She needed to confess her failure. And some of you men here tonight ought to confess your failure to God. I would go home with a broken heart and confess, "Lord, I have failed. My family is going to Hell. I have led them into Sodom. I didn't have enough religion that they could have confidence in me."

You remember Lot was as one that mocked unto his own children and sons-in-law. If that is your case, it is time for old-fashioned repentance and confession in sackcloth and ashes.

God knows what is wrong in Dallas. Wicked church members. Churches are full of people in Dallas with no influence over their own children. Your children grow up and are out and gone before you know it. One day you will get concerned about your children and wonder why they are going to shows, drinking, gambling, going to night clubs and keeping bad company. One day you will sweat and cry and pray and wonder why the great calamity has come to you. You will come to me and say, "Brother Rice, I don't know why he curses, and why he won't listen to me." And when you pray, God will not listen. You have pitched your tent toward Sodom.

Your mind is on other things such as making money. You had better repent of your sins, or one day you will wake up like Lot, when he was as one that mocked unto his sons-in-law. That is a horrible case. If that is your case, I tell you, all the weeping and tears and agonizing, all the years of sorrow that you have ahead of you can never make up for the time you have right now before your children are out and gone and you have lost your influence with them and all is gone. God help you not to move into Sodom!

4. Lot Ruined His Life and Daughters With Drink

What else about Lot? He called that wicked crowd *"brethren,"* and lost his influence with his children. He was as one that mocked to his sons-in-law. What else? He ruined his life with drink. Did you know a man can be a drunkard after he is really saved, after he has been born again? I do not mean he can be lost. He is a child of God, bought by the blood of Christ. You cannot save yourself and you cannot keep yourself. "The blood of Jesus Christ his Son cleanseth us from all sin" (I John 1:7). "He that believeth on the Son hath everlasting life: and he that believeth not the Son shall not see life; but the wrath of God abideth on him" (John 3:36).

My friend, I am not talking about losing the soul. Lot didn't lose his soul, but he lost his family and his influence, and he lost his joy. And as he went out of Sodom that day his wife turned and looked back and became a pillar of salt. Others of his daughters burned to a crisp in the fire and brimstone from God out of Heaven that destroyed that city. Only two daughters remained and they went with him into a mountain and there Lot had to have his wine.

Somebody says, "I don't see any harm in wine." If you read the 19th chapter of Genesis, you will find plenty of harm in wine. Those poor, silly, worldly girls, brought up in Sodom, with the customs of Sodom, made their father drink wine and committed incest with him. Read the 19th chapter of Genesis.

Fathers, listen to me. Unless you want to ruin your family, I would not touch it. I wouldn't do it—not a glass of wine, not a glass of beer, not a toddy at Christmas, nor eggnog. If you do, a time will come when you will reap it in your children.

Lot is one example of a father in the Bible. I wouldn't want to pattern after him. I wouldn't want to move into Sodom and lose my influence and call those wicked men brethren and be as one that mocked unto my sons-in-law and have my life ruined by drink. That happened to a church member, a man who had been born again, one who was a child of God.

II. Joshua: A Second Example

I will read you the story of another example in the Bible. He is one of the two oldest men in the entire nation. How do we know they are the two oldest? Because when the nation Israel came into the land of Canaan everyone of the men twenty years old or more, when they came to Kadesh-Barnea forty years before, died in the wilderness.

Even Moses just looked over the river but didn't go in. Every man in the nation who was twenty years old or more died at Kadesh-Barnea, before he went into the Promised Land, except two—Joshua and Caleb, the two spies who brought back a good report. Joshua, one of the oldest men in the nation at this time, was a saintly man of God. God had used him for thirty years to take the land. He is an old man now, and ready to die. This man, one hundred or more years old, called the people of Israel together and said,

> Now therefore fear the Lord, and serve him in sincerity and in truth: and put away the gods which your fathers served on the other side of the flood, [that is, on the other side of the River Jordan] and in Egypt; and serve ye the Lord.
>
> And if it seem evil unto you to serve the Lord, choose you this day whom ye will serve; whether the gods which your fathers served that were on the other side of the flood, or the gods of the Amorites, in whose land ye dwell: BUT AS FOR ME AND MY HOUSE, WE WILL SERVE THE LORD.—Josh. 24:14,15.

Now there is a contrast. Lot was a saved man, and Joshua was a saved man. Lot goes the way of the world. Joshua quits the world. Twelve men were sent over to spy out the Promised Land. The spies came back, and they couldn't take it. "We are no bigger than grasshoppers. There are giants over there. We couldn't do it." Ten of them said that!

But old Joshua, one of the spies, got out before that crowd and said, "We can do it! Our God is with us. We can do it! We ought to do it!"

They brought the grapes of Eschol back from the land of Canaan, and one cluster was so big it had to be carried on a pole between two men. They brought other fruit, too. It was a goodly land, a land flowing with milk and honey, and Joshua said, "Our God will take up for us. We can do it."

I want to find a man who is not afraid to face other men and say, "I will stand up for what is right. I am for God and the Bible and for justice. I am going to do right." Now any time you find a man who doesn't go with the current but bucks it and stands up for God and the Bible, that man will have influence back home. His wife will listen to him. His children will wake up when he calls. That man's children will be the kind who read the Bible at the breakfast table. That man will have influence.

Joshua and Caleb said, "Yes, sir, we can do it!" And God saved and kept them alive in the forty years of wandering while all the other mature men perished in the wilderness.

Joshua led the army of Israel for thirty years. Now he is old. He calls the people together and says, "All right, make up your minds. If you are going to serve idols, go to it. If you want to serve the idols of the Amorites, go to it. If you want to serve the gods of Egypt, go to it. But as for me and my house, we will serve the Lord."

1. Joshua Put God First

There are several things that I admire about old Joshua. One is, he put God first. Any kind of religion that does not put God first is not much good. If you put one other thing ahead of God you won't win out. Joshua put Him first. "We will serve the Lord," he said.

I thank God for a man who says, "The Lord is first at our house. The Lord is first in my time. The Lord is first in my family and first in my business. We are going to put God first, we will serve the Lord."

2. Joshua Took Responsibility for His Family

Another thing I like about Joshua is that he said, "As for me *and my house,* we will serve the Lord." He said, "I am free, white and twenty-one. I am married and I intend to make a living for this woman. If my wife needs clothes, I ought to be able to buy them. Since she carries my name I am accountable for her bills, so I ought to be able to get her to serve God. I brought my children into the world; they are not animals; it was not an accident. I intended to have a family. I intended to be a responsible father. I am no cheapskate, no slacker, no quitter. I am a grown man, I will take the responsibility for my family. So as for me and my house, we will serve the Lord.

"You put it down that I am going to serve the Lord and my wife and my children and my grandchildren and my servants." Joshua will serve the Lord, Joshua's wife will serve the Lord, Joshua's children will serve the Lord and the whole family will serve the Lord.

Joshua said, "I will answer for my children."

Will you men answer for yours? "As for me and my house," Joshua said, "we will serve the Lord." I am talking to men here tonight. I am glad you women are here, but I am talking to men. God wants you men to sit up and take the part of men. God never did intend for you to hide behind the skirts of women.

Some of you say, "I will leave it to my wife as to whether the children mind and as to whether they go to Sunday school. I will leave it to my wife about whether or not the debts are paid." You are a dirty slacker and a quitter and not fit to be a father if you can't say, "I will be the head of my home by the grace of God and set the pattern my children can follow, and I will make my children mind and teach them about God and tell them how to do and show them how to do not only by precept, not only by example, but discipline too."

You ought to say, "I will see that they do it." Joshua said, "That is the kind of man I will be." He said, "As for me and my house, we will serve the Lord."

Oh, we need this tonight. We need a bunch of men who will say, "By the grace of God, I will take the lead in my family."

I talked to a man the other day who said, "My wife is a member of the church, but she is backslidden."

"You are not a Christian? And your wife is backslidden? All right, mark this down. God holds you accountable as a slacker and a quitter because you have kept your wife and family away from God."

A man may say, "My wife may do as she pleases," but she didn't marry you to do as she pleases. She didn't marry you to serve her own god. Any man is accountable for his wife's religion, for the way she lives, for the way she dresses, for the way she talks. God knows that is the biggest thing a man can be accountable for about a woman! If you are head of a family, you should take the place like Joshua who said, "As for me and my house, we will serve the Lord."

This morning we had the women come down to the front. Some came with tears, with sincerity and said, "I want to be a better Christian and a better mother. I want to put God first and set the right example before my children."

But, oh, what we need tonight is for men, heads of families, to come down and say, "By the grace of God, as for me and my house, we will serve the Lord."

I don't believe in women and men going fifty-fifty in the home. That is like the Italian who got a permit to make rabbit sausage. After a while he was arrested for selling adulterated sausage. Somebody accused him of putting dead horse meat with it.

He was called up before the court and the judge asked him, "Is that really rabbit sausage?"

"Yes," he replied.

"But somebody said it had horse meat in it."

"Well," he answered, "it is 'fifty-fifty.' "

"What do you mean, 'fifty-fifty'?" they asked him.

He answered, "Fifty-fifty—one horse and one rabbit!"

Any time you have a home on the basis of "fifty-fifty," you can put it down—one horse and one rabbit, and the man is the rabbit, as sure as the world! God didn't plan it that way.

Listen to me, you men! Some of you go on with your big talk and you smell strong like a man who uses tobacco, but you don't take the responsibility as head of your home. You smell strong and talk big and wear pants, but the plain, simple truth is you are a sissy, a slacker, a cheater, a shirker. You let all the responsibility fall on the shoulders of that woman you promised God to love, cherish and take care of.

You are accountable before God for the children you brought into the world. And when you leave the rearing of them on that wife, you sin against God. We need men to say, "By the grace of God, like Joshua, as for me and my house, we will serve the Lord. The whole gang is going to serve the Lord. And I will see that they do it."

Somebody may have said, "Joshua, you talk big but, old boy, you have something on your hands."

Joshua said, "Yes, I know I have a job, but I have a big God, too."

"What about the wild boys of yours?"

"Oh, I know," Joshua said, "but I am the father of these boys and I know how to make them get up, wash their faces and see that they go to church." And so old Joshua said, "I am going to do it."

"Yes, but you can't."

But old Joshua said, "Praise God, here at my place, as for me and my family, we will serve the Lord."

"But what about the bad influence elsewhere?"

But Joshua said, "We will have more good influence at home than the Devil's influence they get outside. As for me and my house, we will serve the Lord."

Oh, tonight, men, let's follow Joshua and Joshua's God and say, "As for me and my house, we will serve the Lord."

III. The Jailor Who Was Saved and All His House

There are two examples of Bible fathers: Lot and Joshua. There is one more in the New Testament. I turn to the 16th chapter of Acts and find a happy incident of a father. This man was not a Christian. I suppose he must have been a very rough, cruel and wicked man. There are many indications that he was. He had two preachers in jail, put in there without anything to eat. He helped tear their shirts off and beat them. He was a tough nut. That is the reason he was a jailor.

When those preachers were put in jail, they didn't fight back but they began to pray and sing praises to God. The prisoners heard them, but God heard them, too. It is all right to pray when other folks hear you. But something happened when the Lord heard these two. He said, "Gabriel, we will have to do something about that. We can't get any sleep [I don't think they sleep in Heaven]. Gabriel, go down and shake things up a little bit." And some way the old jail began to rock and the doors flew open, and chains fell off, and the prisoners were all loose. But the old jailor—now listen:

> *And at midnight Paul and Silas prayed, and sang praises unto God: and the prisoners heard them.*
>
> *And suddenly there was a great earthquake, so that the foundations of the prison were shaken: and immediately all the doors were opened, and every one's bands were loosed.*
>
> *And the keeper of the prison awaking out of his sleep, and seeing the prison doors open, he drew out his sword, and would have killed himself, supposing that the prisoners had been fled.*
>
> *But Paul cried with a loud voice, saying, Do thyself no harm: for we are all here.*
>
> *Then he called for a light, and sprang in, and came trembling, and fell down before Paul and Silas,*
>
> *And brought them out, and said, Sirs, what must I do to be saved?*—Acts 16:25-30.

1. The Gospel Is Good for Bad Sinners

One thing I like about tough cases. These tough customers are good for the Gospel. The Gospel is good for an old jailor. It has always been a special joy to me to see drunkards saved. It is a joy to go down to the jail and see men, like we did today, weep and come to Christ. A man this afternoon, already condemned to die in the electric chair, heard me preach today and lifted his hand for prayer and said he would take Christ as Saviour. My friends, the Gospel of the Lord Jesus Christ is good for a man like this old tough nut, this jailor.

Perhaps someone is here tonight who is a drunkard, or a gambler, or a woman chaser. Maybe you have made your wife miserable and been untrue to your vows and set a bad example by cursing that would make one's ears burn with shame.

My friends, a man can go until he hits bottom and he can come back to God. This jailor came and asked, "What must I do to be saved?"

If I had played the fool all my life and run with the Devil's crowd; if I were a lost sinner, I would turn to Jesus Christ and be saved. A woman today in jail said, "If I wouldn't take Christ out of the jail, I won't do it here. I won't do it while I am still in jail."

I said, "You didn't need a lawyer while you were out of jail, did you? But you need one now, don't you? And you need a Saviour, too."

My friend, if I had gone into sin and my heart was broken and shame was my portion, I would turn to Christ like that jailor and ask, "What must I do to be saved?"

2. But the Gospel Was for His Family, Too!

Paul and Silas said, "Believe on the Lord Jesus Christ, and thou shalt be saved, and thy house." I am not just talking about men; I am talking about fathers. This man had a family. This man lived for the Devil. His wife and children were lost because he was lost. Because he lived for the Devil, they did, too. Paul and Silas said, "Believe on the Lord Jesus Christ, and thou shalt be saved, and thy house." You can be saved, and your family can be saved the same way. We have a Gospel that is good for Father, Mother and children—the whole family.

Notice this. First, this man asked what to do to be saved. Listen! If you have boys not saved, or girls not saved, you had better take the matter to the Lord. If you have a wife unsaved, she may die tonight and go to Hell. You had better take the matter to the Lord.

I was in a home where a boy died. This mother told me how her boy died, begging Mother to tell him how to be saved. She said, "Brother Rice, I didn't know how to tell him!" That was a sad thing.

I wouldn't go on like this jailor did. Up to this time he let his family go. I honor a man who has got what it takes to say, "I want to get right with God. I am tired of sin. I know I am a sinner. I want to be saved." Paul and Silas answered and said, "Believe on the Lord Jesus Christ, and thou shalt be saved, and thy house."

Let me say just this word. It is a short distance to God. You may have gone a million miles from Him. Your heart may feel so cold. You may feel that God hates you because you have sinned against Him. Every impulse to turn to God, every warning He has given, you have not heeded. You have resisted the Holy Spirit and ignored the Bible and run away from God, but if you will now simply trust Jesus Christ, you can be saved. Just admit to the Lord you are a poor, old sinner who ought to go to Hell, that you need mercy and want forgiveness now. He will hear and save you.

3. How Easy for Any Penitent Sinner to Be Saved! How Wrong to Delay!

If you will trust Him, you can be saved. "Believe on the Lord Jesus Christ, and thou shalt be saved." Isn't that good news for a troubled soul, for a man like this jailor who knows he is a sinner and knows he must do something to be saved? "Believe on the Lord Jesus Christ," He will fix it for you. He will fix your family, too, "Thou shalt be saved, and thy house." God promises the plan of salvation for the rest of the family, too.

As soon as this fellow learned how to be saved, he settled it. This old jailor came trembling and brought them out and fell down before them and said, "Sirs, what must I do to be saved?" But he didn't sit down on a mourner's bench and cry and weep. No, he didn't want to wait until tomorrow; he wanted it settled now.

I was in a revival in East Dallas, at the end of Main, on Carroll. One night I preached and we had a number of conversions. When the service was over we stood around and rejoiced. I answered some questions. After awhile when we were ready to go home a man came running up the sidewalk. "Brother Rice, I have got to settle it! I walked those six blocks home and every step I took something said within me, 'You are making the biggest mistake of your life. You are acting a fool. You had better settle it tonight, you had better get saved tonight.' As I stepped up on the porch of my home, something said, 'Don't go in that door. If you do, you are doomed forever.' And as I put my hand on the doorknob something within me said, 'Don't turn that doorknob. Don't go in that door unsaved. You will never be saved if you are not saved tonight.' And, Brother Rice, I turned and ran all the way back here. I was afraid you would be gone home. I want to be saved."

Praise the Lord, he was saved! This jailor said, "I want to be saved. What must I do to be saved?" He didn't get just something in the head; he got something in his heart. He did not just learn how; he trusted Christ for salvation.

Two years ago when I preached in a revival campaign in Binghamton, New York, a man heard me preach one cold winter night. We had a great crowd. When the invitation was given, Mr. Gregory, an executive for one of the shoe companies, went to talk to him. Mr. Gregory put his arm around his neck and told the man how to be saved.

"Not now," he said, and held on the seat and trembled. Beads of sweat broke out on his forehead, but he wouldn't surrender. He struggled with God. A fight went on in his soul. After awhile he keeled over in a dead faint. Two men got on each side of him and led him out into the cold zero air. There was snow and ice on the ground.

Soon he was revived and he said, "I dare not go home! I had better go back."

"You want to go now and tell it?" Mr. Gregory asked him.

He said, "If I don't do it now, I may never do it. I am afraid I will never be saved if I don't do it tonight."

They brought him back in and he came around through the wings and up on the platform where I was and said, "Brother Rice, I can't go home without settling it. I must get it settled tonight." And he trusted Christ right then.

This jailor said, "I will do it," and he trusted Christ. Paul and Silas told this jailor how to be saved and then he got saved right then. He didn't say, "Let me think about it." That is the reason your family is going to Hell. "Maybe I will do it tomorrow." That jailor didn't say that. He said, "I will do it," and he settled it right then.

But that isn't all. He got his whole family. Listen to the Scripture:

And they spake unto him the word of the Lord, and to all that were in his house.

And he took them the same hour of the night, and washed their stripes; and was baptized, he and all his, straightway.

And when he had brought them into his house, he set meat before them, and rejoiced, believing in God with all his house. — Acts 16:32-34.

You know that old wicked fellow, bless his heart, surely meant business! He got busy. He didn't waste any time. No grass grew under his feet. When he trusted Christ, his whole family got saved. The whole bunch then got baptized, the whole family, and he brought Paul and Silas back and washed their stripes and had a big supper cooked for them at midnight. The whole family sat around the table and rejoiced that they were saved.

Wasn't he thorough-going? I wish I had that man for a deacon in my church! I would have a floor in the basement then, and we would have lights in here. I would sic him on some of you and he would get it done. I wish I had that man for a deacon in my church. I would call on him and he would get the work done up brown, wouldn't he?

Oh, my friends, listen to me! Some of you men say, "God helping me, I am going to take Christ as my Saviour." You ought to make sure about your wife, too. And I would see every child I could tonight. If I had a boy away from home I would call him long distance before I slept and tell him that Dad has trusted Christ and you want him to be saved. I would say, "I wouldn't sleep before I heard you tell me you will take Him, too, Son." Get your whole family in tonight. That is what the jailor did. He got it settled, he and his house. He got them all saved. Isn't that blessed?

4. Not Only Saved But Out and Out; He Was Baptized

Now the next thing. He wasn't a half-way guy! He not only

got them saved but he got them baptized. You folk say, "Next Sunday, if it is not too cold and if the water is warm, I will be baptized." But the old jailor said, "Get out here and baptize me tonight."

They didn't have electric lights, and Paul might have said, "It is midnight."

"Yes, I know," the jailor said, "and the water is pretty cold, but I have been on the Devil's side long enough. Let's do it tonight, Paul."

I really don't think Paul held back very much, but if he did, that guy out-talked him. I like him, don't you?

If I were you and I had lived on the Devil's side as long as you have, I would say, "Good-bye, old Devil! I am going to be saved now." And if I were saved, I would get in the church and be baptized and I would be in prayer meeting next Wednesday night, and next Sunday morning I would be in a Sunday school class. I would say, "Preacher, what can I do? Can I stand back there and shake hands with the folks? Preacher, what can I do next?"

You poor, half-baked, wishy-washy men who never could make up your minds! I am sorry for you. God be praised for a man like the jailor who got his whole family saved, then got them baptized the same hour of the night. Bless his heart! He had been a bad customer up to this time, but when he turned to the Lord, he turned all over.

Did you hear about the little girl who had a little curl in the middle of her forehead? When she was good she was very, very good, and when she was bad, she was horrid. That is what I like about the jailor. He was horrid a long time and he got very, very good. When he got saved, he got saved all over. He got saved and got baptized. He got his family saved, too, and got them baptized! He was out and out! I like that fellow, don't you?

D. L. Moody went to England and had a great revival. One man met him and introduced him to another. When he met this other fellow, he said, "Is Moody O. and O?"

The other fellow said, "Yes, he is O. and O."

Moody said, "What did he mean?"

This man said, "He wanted to know if you are OUT and OUT for Christ."

Moody said, "I am glad you could tell him that I am O. and O."

This old jailor was O. and O. for Jesus Christ. How many here are saved and not in a church? I would apologize to my wife and children and beg God to forgive me and get the whole kit and caboodle in tonight.

Some of you people have moved to town. You did not forget to have your mail transferred. You are not quite sure how long you are going to stay, but you haven't moved your membership. You are a slacker and a quitter. Your heart is not in it. You don't win your children to Christ. Why don't you get into a church and let your light shine? If you are saved, get your family saved and then get them baptized.

Twenty people here tonight ought to join this church. You men are to blame—you men, you heads of families, you fathers. Brother Cherry, I thought about you the other day. Your boy is there beside you, your wife is beside you there. You went a long time. Cherry, I would not waste any more time. You got on the Lord's side, your family is all in and baptized. Let the light shine. I would say, "The Devil's got all the gray hairs he is going to have. From this time on, all is for Jesus, everything for Jesus Christ." I wouldn't waste any more time. No, I wouldn't.

Some folk here tonight are saved but your companion isn't saved. You are saved but your family is not. Your boys are going to Hell. You are saved, but your girls are living for the Devil. I would say, "God helping me, as for me and my house, we will serve the Lord." I would be like the old jailor—get saved, then get my family saved.

Several women came this morning weeping to confess they had failed and wanted to make a new resolution and start again for God. Some of you men ought to come as the women came. There is a man sitting back there who came this morning and trusted Christ. He said, "I am not ashamed of it, Brother Rice." You are not sorry, and you are glad you came to trust Christ this morning right in the middle of the thing, aren't you? Where is Mr. Hall? Bless his heart, he came claiming Christ this morning. We had a blessed time.

Do you want to have a revival? If we ever have a revival, T_____ will have to quit waiting for his wife to do all the leading, quit waiting for his boy. You ought to get in the church with God's people and be baptized, start the family altar and start living for Jesus Christ and start winning souls. If you get that and other men get that then something will happen for Jesus in Dallas, Texas. "As for me and my house, we will serve the Lord."

Don't you want to come tonight and say, "God helping me, I will be out and out for Jesus Christ and lead my family right"? Don't you feel like doing that? Do you feel like saying, "If the Lord will take me, He can have all I have tonight."

I would go home and say, "Wife, the Lord is first in this house from now on." I would call the children and say, "Children, I have failed so many times. The Lord has a right to the best in every one of us." Don't you want to? God is calling tonight. I am glad you men came. I am glad you women came, too. You men, you Christian men, let's have prayer, then step out here boldly.

PRAYER: O God, give grace to do so. Help them to start the family altar, to start winning souls, daily reading of the Bible, to set a pattern for boys and girls, winning them to Jesus Christ. O God, bless these men. Give us grace. Give a triumphant, glorious victory tonight for Thine own sake. Amen.

6—Leaving Nets, Ships, Father

(Sermon preached Sunday morning, October 31, 1937, at Fundamentalist Baptist Tabernacle, Dallas, Texas. Stenographically reported.)

In Matthew the 4th chapter we read, verses 18 through 22:

> *And Jesus, walking by the sea of Galilee, saw two brethren, Simon called Peter, and Andrew his brother, casting a net into the sea: for they were fishers.*
>
> *And he saith unto them, Follow me, and I will make you fishers of men.*
>
> *And they straightway left their nets, and followed him.*
>
> *And going on from thence, he saw other two brethren, James the son of Zebedee, and John his brother, in a ship with Zebedee their father, mending their nets; and he called them.*
>
> *And they immediately left the ship and their father, and followed him.*

Peter and Andrew had left their nets and followed Him, and James and John too left their ship and their father and followed Him.

Now in Luke the 14th chapter, verse 33:

> *So likewise, whosoever he be of you that forsaketh not all that he hath, he cannot be my disciple.*

That is a strange and a hard verse but it is true and we had as well accept it. Once the Jews came and wanted to make Jesus king. They liked it when He fed the five thousand and they didn't have to work for something to eat. They like that. It didn't cost money to eat that way, and they had plenty left over, the twelve baskets of fragments, enough to start on for supper. That was the kind of king they wanted.

They wanted a king without having to repent. They wanted a king who would take all—good and bad alike—one who did not divide, did not split, one who did not demand repentance.

But Jesus did not come that way and would not have that kingdom. Satan had offered Jesus a kingdom without a crucifixion, but it could not be that way. For Jesus, there is no kingdom without a crucifixion, no reigning without first suffering. So Jesus started this doctrine of separation, and He said, "So likewise, whosoever he be of you that forsaketh not all that he hath, he cannot be my disciple."

I wonder, have you left everything behind to serve Christ? If you have not, then I want to lay on your heart this important message. You cannot serve Christ without leaving some things behind, without quitting something. You cannot please Christ without displeasing someone else. You cannot have peace with Christ without war with somebody. If you are going to be a happy, successful Christian, it will mean turning your back on some other things to follow Christ.

They left their nets to follow Jesus, and James and John left their ship and their father and followed Jesus. Throughout the Bible we have accounts of people who followed Jesus by leaving some things. So the first thing you will have to do is to leave something. You cannot follow what you are following now and follow Jesus, too.

I. The Bible Doctrine of Separation

That doctrine is expressed in James 4:4:

> *Ye adulterers and adulteresses, know ye not that the friendship of the world is enmity with God? whosoever therefore will be a friend of the world is the enemy of God.*

Oh, my friends, you cannot have the friendship of God and the friendship of everybody else. Here is a Bible doctrine of separation, of leaving some things. If you follow Christ, you must leave the world. "Whosoever he be of you that forsaketh not all that he hath."

In II Corinthians we have this teaching likewise. In the 6th chapter we read verses 14 through 18:

> *Be ye not unequally yoked together with unbelievers: for what fellowship hath righteousness with unrighteousness? and what communion hath light with darkness?*
>
> *And what concord hath Christ with Belial? or what part hath he that believeth with an infidel?*
>
> *And what agreement hath the temple of God with idols? for ye are the temple of the living God; as God hath said, I will dwell in them, and walk in them; and I will be their God, and they shall be my people.*
>
> *Wherefore come out from among them, and be ye separate, saith the Lord, and touch not the unclean thing; and I will receive you,*
>
> *And will be a Father unto you, and ye shall be my sons and daughters, saith the Lord Almighty.*

If you are going to be with believers, then leave unbelievers. If you are going to be for righteousness, then leave unrighteousness. If you have communion with Light, then do not have communion with darkness. If you are going to have concord with Christ, then do not have concord with Belial. If you are going to have part with believers, then do not have part with unbelievers and infidels. If you are going to have agreement with the church of God and agreement with public worship of God, then do not have agreement with idolators that are against God. How could you take pleasure in a beer joint if you take pleasure Sunday morning in a church house?

No, what agreement hath the temple of God with idols? Your body is the temple of God. If it is for Jesus, then it cannot be for the Devil. Cursing and blessing cannot come out of the same mouth. Out of the same fountain you cannot have both bitter water and sweet (James 3:10, 11). You cannot have coming out of the same mouth a testimony for Jesus and curses against men. The Lord said, "What agreement hath the temple of God with idols? . . .Wherefore come out from among them, and be ye separate, saith the Lord." I am talking about leaving some things, about sacrificing.

Now the Saviour said, "If you want fellowship with Me, you cannot have fellowship with everybody else. If you follow Me, you will have to leave somebody else. If you run with Me, you cannot run with everybody else." God wants you to come out and be separate. He does not want you to have fellowship with the unclean thing, or to have part or concord or agreement with things against God.

Here is a Bible doctrine of separation. You will have to leave some things to please Jesus. "Whosoever he be of you that forsaketh not *all that he hath,* he cannot be my disciple," the Saviour said.

We have the same message in the 13th chapter of Hebrews.

Wherefore Jesus also, that he might sanctify the people with his own blood, suffered without the gate.
Let us go forth therefore unto him without the camp, bearing his reproach. —Vss. 12, 13.

He left the town to go outside the gate to the place of ashes and mourning. He suffered outside the gate. "Let us go forth therefore unto him without the camp, bearing his reproach. For here have we no **continuing** city, but we seek one to come."

According to this verse, Jesus left Jerusalem and was crucified on Mount Calvary. He left the city for the cross. Therefore let us go with Him without the gate, leaving city, leaving friends, leaving homes, and let us suffer with Him without the gate, bearing His reproach, for we have no continuing city but we seek one to come. God wants you to be separate. God wants you to leave some things.

Here this morning are many mothers and fathers. How can you rear your children for Christ? You had better settle it now in your hearts that you cannot possibly rear your children for Christ unless you give up some things.

The question comes up in my own life with my children. I do

not want my children to go to picture shows. Someone says, "But you can't keep them from it." That is what you think.

A preacher told me once, "But my boys want to go, and you just can't keep young people from the movies," so he let his boys go to picture shows. If you follow Jesus, you will have to leave some other things behind. Every person who follows Jesus has to leave some other things. A Christian cannot please Christ unless he turns his back on some other things.

We have a group of Sunday school teachers, the finest we have ever had. Most of you are taking it to heart about your teaching and your classes. You have not all paid the price, but you mean to, and you want to. Twelve or fifteen more of you ought to be teaching. You had better get ready, get filled with the Spirit, nail self to the cross and leave some things behind and separate yourself. Then you can be a good Sunday school teacher.

I spoke last Wednesday night on paying a price. You cannot be a soul winner without paying a price. You cannot be a good Sunday school teacher without paying a price, either. And one cannot be a preacher without giving up some other things. You cannot be a Sunday school teacher unless you give up some things. "My life is so busy," you say, "I do not have time to be a teacher." I know it is busy. I wouldn't want you unless you had something to do. That is not enough qualification, having nothing else to do. I am not looking for somebody to serve the Lord who is not doing anything.

Some preacher feels, "I am a failure at everything else. I do not have anything else to do, so I am going to preach." The best reason for preaching is a definite call. One should say, "I am going to turn my back on some things to do the Lord's work." It is not enough to work for the Lord when you have just run out of something else to do. There are things so important that we should leave some things to do the other. I hope you will say, "God helping me, I will give up some things and turn my back on some things. I am going to leave some things behind." You cannot be disciples of Jesus otherwise.

You may be saved, but you cannot be useful without turning

your back and saying good-bye to this old world. Jesus said here, "So likewise, whosoever he be of you that forsaketh not all that he hath, he cannot be my disciple." That is a Bible doctrine of separation that ought to get into our hearts.

We find many instructions of that kind in the Bible. First, here are these disciples. Jesus came to Peter and his brother Andrew and said, "Follow me." Immediately they left their nets. I believe the way Peter laid that net down was like a fellow who has been digging a ditch and lets his pick fall behind him when the whistle blows, instead of bringing it over his shoulder again. Oh, yes, he did it with his whole heart. Simon Peter said, "Fishing for fish, making money, buying food and eating it and buying clothes and wearing them out—what does one get by all that? I wish I could win souls." Jesus came along and said, "Follow me, Peter, I will help you fish for men." "Good-bye, old nets," Peter said, and he left them.

Peter, Andrew, James, John and their father were all in a company together. They were partners. At least that was so about Peter, James and John. They had good ships and nets and all that. But they did not stop and argue about how to take care of their families. They just said, "Good-bye, old nets," and dropped them there. You know Peter made a lot of mistakes, but he could make up his mind.

I see him again later when he left his nets again. He had already played the fool. He had denied Christ, and had cursed and sworn and brought disgrace on Christianity, and had gone back to fishing.

But one day Jesus came to the shore, as we see in John, chapter 21, and said, "Children, have ye any meat?" They said, "No, we haven't a thing." Peter said, "Who is that out there?" John said, "That is Jesus. Did you see when we let down the net we got 150 fish?" Old Simon Peter said, "Good-bye, nets!" and he left them for good, forever, that time.

If you cannot say good-bye, you are no good as a preacher and no good as a soul winner. If you cannot say good-bye, you will never be any good for Jesus Christ. "Whosoever he be of you that forsaketh not all that he hath, he cannot be my disciple."

Peter and Andrew "straightway left their nets, and followed him."

And then He came to James and John, the sons of Zebedee, in a ship mending their nets. He called them, "and they immediately left the ship and their father, and followed Him."

You are going to have to say good-bye. I don't know what I would have done in the business world, or educational world, but I am glad I left it all behind. It is mighty little to give up for Jesus Christ when He gave up Heaven for me. I was glad to say good-bye to all and leave it all behind.

I know God can use anybody to preach. Charlie Simpson, while sending your trucks out, I hope you will win somebody to Christ. I believe you ought to be a preacher. Brother Walker ought to be a preacher. God wants you to be a preacher in some sense, to give your testimony. If ever you amount to anything for Jesus, you will have to leave some other things alone. I know Paul made tents on the side. There is no disgrace in making tents when you need to. But every preacher ought to have a holy ambition to get his hands off everything else as soon as he can. The trouble with most preachers is that they hold on until God has to whip them loose.

Have you said good-bye to the dearest on earth, to your business, to your job, to your reputation, to your home that you had? Have you said good-bye to your ships and nets? If you want to bid good-bye to your ships and nets, then say, "Lord, call me and I will follow."

You would be surprised how many cases there are in the Bible of people leaving everything for Jesus.

II. Elisha Left Farm, Oxen and Family

Yonder is Elisha. In I Kings, the 19th chapter, the Lord says, "Elijah, you are old. I will have to have another prophet. You are going to Heaven one of these days riding in a chariot of fire. I want you to go out and get another prophet." God led him.

So he departed thence, and found Elisha the son of Shaphat, who was plowing with twelve yoke of oxen before him, and he with the twelfth: and Elijah passed by

> *him, and cast his mantle upon him.*
>
> *And he left the oxen, and ran after Elijah, and said,*
> *Let me, I pray thee, kiss my father and my mother, and*
> *then I will follow thee. And he said unto him, Go   back*
> *again: for what have I done to thee?*
>
> *And he returned back from him, and took a yoke of*
> *oxen, and slew them, and boiled their flesh with the*
> *instruments of the oxen, and gave unto the people, and*
> *they did eat. Then he arose, and went after Elijah, and*
> *ministered unto him.*—Vss. 19-21.

Elisha had eleven servants out there with eleven yoke of oxen,
and he had the twelfth.

> *And Elijah passed by him, and cast his mantle upon*
> *him. And he left the oxen, and ran after Elijah, and said,*
> *Let me, I pray thee, kiss my father and my mother, and*
> *then I will follow thee. And he said unto him, Go back*
> *again: for what have I done to thee?*

When Elijah saw a prosperous farmer with twelve yoke of
oxen plowing, and when God said, "Elijah, lay your mantle on
this man," I wonder if Elijah did not say, "This is God's doing,
not mine, but I wouldn't pick him. He wouldn't give up that big
farm to be a preacher. He has his father and mother and others
to look after. That man wouldn't do to be a preacher." I am
satisfied Elijah may have thought, "God is doing it, and He
must know what He is doing, but I wouldn't choose him."

When Elisha ran after him and said, "Let me, I pray thee,
kiss my father and my mother, and then I will follow thee,"
Elijah said, "Go on back; I didn't call you." I think Elijah was
afraid to say, "Come on."

Many times I have said to a young preacher, "Go slow. You
had better sit down and count the cost. Do you really mean
business about this? Are you sure you mean business? Are you
ready to go with nothing but mush to eat? Sometimes when
your wife doesn't have new clothes and must make over her old
ones or wear clothes given to her and she starts complaining,
will you still mean business for God? Then when you have done

your best and poured out your soul and those for whom you have spent your life trying to help—what about it when they mock you and doubt you? Are you ready for that? You need not try to be a preacher unless you are." "Whosoever he be of you that forsaketh not all that he hath, he cannot be my disciple."

Elisha said good-bye. Listen to what he did.

And he returned back from him, and took a yoke of oxen, and slew them, and boiled their flesh with the instruments of the oxen, and gave unto the people, and they did eat. Then he arose, and went after Elijah, and ministered unto him.—I Kings 19:21.

"I am not going to need these oxen any more," said he. "I have quit plowing. I am now going to preach." But Elisha, you will have to, for a long time, be a servant. When Elijah wants to wash his hands, you will have to bring a pitcher of water and pour it on them. What about that?"

"I know, but I have made up my mind."

So Elisha killed the oxen, had a big dinner and invited all the people to eat all they wanted, then told them, "God is going to make a prophet out of me."

Oh, my friends, it is a blessed thing to say good-bye. You may say, "I have this thing or that to look after, but from now on, it is not mine, but God's." Elisha said good-bye to his oxen, to his plantation, to Mother, to Father. "Whosoever he be of you that forsaketh not all that he hath, he cannot be my disciple."

I have been thinking about other cases. Would it not be fine if today some would just leave everything—leave it all. We have to leave property, or leave business sometimes to serve God. If business is not second to God's will, you will never be a soul winner. You are a sorry kind of a Christian unless you put Jesus first, in the first part of the day, the first part of your time, the first part of your thought, first part of your love. If that is not so about you, then you are not fit to be a disciple of Jesus Christ. Unless you can say good-bye to other things, you are a poor Christian.

III. Samaritan Woman Left Her Waterpot

Then here is the woman at the well. Turn to the 4th chapter of John and read with me about a woman who was not very good. She had had five husbands and was now living with a man to whom she was not married. Jesus said to her, "Give me a drink."

She said, "It is a funny idea, You asking me for a drink of water when You are a Jew and I am a woman of Samaria, for the Jews have no dealings with the Samaritans."

He went on to say, "If you knew who it was that asked you for **a drink, you would have asked of Him and He would have given** you living water, so that you would never thirst again."

"Give it to me," she said.

"Go call your husband, and I will," Jesus told her.

She said, "I have no husband."

"I know you have had five husbands and the man you are now living with is not your husband," Jesus replied.

She said, "I see You are a prophet," and she tried to argue.

Jesus led her little by little until she saw her need of a Saviour and said to Him, "I know that Messias cometh, which is called Christ: when he is come, he will tell us all things."

Jesus said, "I am the Messias! I am He!"

She immediately left her waterpot and ran into the city. How could a woman like that be a soul winner? Everyone must have known about her past. One might have said, "I do not want a harlot talking to me about the Lord." But she left everything that day.

No matter what the past has been, if in your heart you say good-bye to it all and leave everything you have for Jesus, He can use you. He has use for you—even people like you—if you will leave everything for Him.

When she left her waterpot that did not mean she would never need water and would not come back and get her waterpot. At times you will have to leave your dishpan. At times you will have to leave sweeping and making beds and cooking dinner. There are times to leave other things to win souls to Jesus Christ. If you cannot do that, you cannot follow

Jesus. If you put God first you will often leave even necessary things till God's work is done.

That woman left her waterpot.

What if she had said, "First of all I will carry this pot of water up to my house and be sure I have a good drink of water and look after my day's work, then when I get time this afternoon, when I go downtown and if I see any of the men, I will tell them I have found the Messias"? Had she done that, there would not have been a soul saved. Had she sauntered down after awhile and said, "I saw a man I rather believe to be the Messias. So after I got my housework done, I decided I would come by and mention it to you since I happened to see you," not one of the men would have thought there was anything to it. But she left her waterpot and ran into the city and told the men, "Come, see a man, which told me all things that ever I did: is not this the Christ?"

IV. She Helped Win Her Boy at Midnight

I was in Paris, Texas, in a meeting. About midnight a woman came out to Brother Lee's home where I was staying. She had phoned that she was coming. I got dressed. She said, "Will you go down and talk to my boy? He has been bitten by a black widow spider. If he dies, he is lost. I don't want to go through this night without his being saved. The doctor thinks he will be all right, but I can't afford to wait. I wonder if you are willing to go and talk to him?"

When we woke him up in the middle of the night and she said, "Son, I am not willing for you to wait until morning; you had better have God," then he was saved right now. It only took a little bit.

I will tell you why you do not get people saved. You do not leave your waterpot and your fish. If you will follow Jesus, you must leave your nets, leave your father, leave your plane and saw and figures.

Mr. Stark, if you are going to be superintendent of the Intermediate Department, it will mean leaving your waterpot, leaving your nets, leaving your ship, leaving your plane and saw and having less to eat at your house because you did not get enough time to do your carpenter work. You have to leave some things. You cannot serve God and have everything else. You cannot have your cake and eat it, too.

Brother Carpenter, if it is so about the Intermediates, it is so about the Juniors. You cannot have everything else and be superintendent, too. You must leave your waterpot. There are times for us to leave other things to win souls to Jesus Christ.

Brother Fisher, there is a constant drag. The Devil would like to get you interested in other things such as prohibition, etc. Now I am for preachers speaking boldly on the liquor question or on anything else that comes up, but I am not for it drawing one away from the Gospel. We must leave some things undone. We must say, "For the one thing worth doing, I will leave some others. I can say good-bye to some things."

V. Sometimes We Must Neglect Loved Ones, or Leave Them

But there is another thing, and this is the saddest. You would not mind leaving some old nets, would you? You get along all right without that. You can buy another net sometime, can't you? You would not mind leaving a waterpot, would you? You could go back sometime and find it, if you get thirsty, or go down and draw another pitcher of water. I would not mind leaving some oxen, would you? There are more calves growing up all the time. I could buy some more oxen. And I could cut down a tree and hew out a beam for a plow. That would not take very long; so I would not mind leaving my plow. I would not be so bad off to leave oxen and a plow. But when it comes to leaving Father, too—! James and John left their father.

Elisha goes in the house and kisses his mother and says, "Mother, I have been the stay of your old age. The plantation may run down, but I have got to go, Mother. The prophet of God came by and laid his mantle on me, and I have got to go. God wants another prophet, and when Elijah goes on to Heaven, I will get that mantle and be that prophet of Israel."

He kissed his old father and said, "Dad, you have quit farming. You are too old for that. You don't get about very well and I have taken the burden off you. But I am going to leave you." You might not think he ought to go away and leave his old father that burden.

You say, "The only opportunity I have to see my mother is on Sunday." So you take the Lord's time to see your mother, and use the rest of the time for pleasure or business.

"I do not see how I can leave my mother and father," you say. Elisha did not say that. He went in, kissed Mother and Father good-bye. He killed the oxen so everybody would know he meant business.

You have to leave your folks, too, some of them, maybe Mother and Father and brothers and sisters. That ought not be bad. Every girl is supposed to do that when she marries. She is to cleave unto her husband. Every man is supposed to do that when he marries. He is to cleave unto his wife. One is not an honest wife or husband if she or he does not do that. One is to cleave to husband or wife only, in some sense leaving everyone else out.

It is a sad thing, but every mother will learn one of these days that the child she bore in her body and that nursed at her breast and to whom she taught little things, how to walk and talk, and for whom she made the little clothes—that little one of whom she is so proud will grow up. Finally some girl will come along and win his heart away and the mother will find she is on the outside. I have seen it many times. Even when a boy gets grown, his mother may still call him "Mother's Baby." "I want you to meet our baby," she will say, as she calls a nineteen-year-old boy into the room.

Some little silly flapper with a painted face will come along. She can't understand him like Mother does, the mother thinks, and she resents it that that little bit of a flapper gets her boy's heart!

Then he goes to see his wife's kinfolks instead of his own. That may be the first time he ever missed Christmas dinner at home, and his mother cannot understand that. But you have to say good-bye to Mother. You can't marry and not say it.

Oh, my friend, is Jesus less worthy than that? Elisha kissed his father and mother and told them good-bye and went out to pour water on the hands of Elijah and to get ready to be a prophet of God. It costs something to follow Jesus. "Whosoever he be of you that forsaketh not all that he hath, he cannot be my disciple."

VI. Abraham Failed at First to Leave Father

There is the case of Abraham who turned his back on the land of his birth in the 11th chapter of Genesis. If you read in the 12th chapter first, you see that God *had said* to Abram—later called Abraham: "Now the Lord had said unto Abram, Get thee out of thy country, and from thy kindred, and from thy father's house, unto a land that I will shew thee."

The Lord had said, "Get out and leave your kinfolks, Abraham." Notice God told Abraham to leave his kinfolks. But Terah, his father, was getting old.

You say, "But my father and my mother are getting old." Abraham thought that, too. He stayed in Ur of the Chaldees for a time, then after awhile got started. But he took with him his father and his nephew, Lot. "This business of moving around I don't like," Terah, the old man, said, so they settled down in another place. They didn't go on to the land of Canaan. "And they went forth with them from Ur of the Chaldees, to go into the land of Canaan; and they came unto Haran, and dwelt there." They did not get to Canaan. They started, but they did not get there. The Lord had said, "Abraham, go on and leave Lot, and leave Terah, your old father, and your father's house." But Abraham said, "Well, my father is old. I had better listen to him." Terah said, "All right, son, let's go. We will travel on." But they camped at Haran and stayed there.

There is an unwritten story between those lines. Listen very carefully. You may save yourself much heartache. God had said, "Abram, I want you to come on and leave your father and your family." But Abram did not leave his father. He took him with him. God said, "All right, Abraham, then I am going to take your father out of the way." That is not written, but down there in Haran his father died. Then Abraham said, "Let's go on and do what God told us to do."

Grady, (addressing Grady Matthews), your mother is old. She is as good a mother as a fellow ever had. Her husband, your father, is dead. They look to you to look after things. But, Grady, would you rather God would take your mother out of the way, or would you rather say, "No, Mother, I will go on and do what God says. I will always have you at hand until God's good time, but I must put God first."

Abraham lost by staying around there. He went on and did what God said AFTER God took his father out of the way. You had better say good-bye to your father's house and kindred and go on and follow the Lord.

VII. Ruth Left All and Became Immortal

One of the sweetest stories in the Bible is that of Ruth. She was a beautiful character. Her mother-in-law Naomi lived among the Moabites. Naomi had had two sons, but now those two sons had died, and her husband had died and Naomi was left with her two daughters-in-law. She said, "I am old, and my heart is hungry for my kinfolks. My husband has died and my sons have died and I am going back."

Ruth said, "I will go with you."

"No, no," said Naomi, "I have no more sons for you. And you would be a stranger. Don't leave your mother and father."

"But I am going," Ruth said. "Intreat me not to leave thee, or to return from following after thee: for whither thou goest, I will go; and where thou lodgest, I will lodge: thy people shall be my people, and thy God my God."

Orpah kissed Naomi and turned and went back weeping, but Ruth, with bold and smiling face, followed Naomi to the land of promise because it was the land of the true God. She said good-bye to her mother and her father and her kinsfolk and the people of her own land and went with Naomi to a strange land.

There she met a rich man, Boaz, who learned to love her and then married her. They had a child, and that child was Obed, the father of Jesse and the grandfather of King David. She was put in the ancestral line of Jesus Christ because she said good-bye and went into a strange land and said, "Thy people shall be my people, and thy God my God."

The people who get somewhere with God are those who leave something. The children of Israel left Egypt and the leeks and onions and garlic.

Abram must leave Ur of the Chaldees and come to the place of God's promise.

Ruth must come from Moab into the land of promise.

So you, my friend, must say good-bye and leave all if you are going to be His disciple.

One of the disciples came to Jesus one day and said, "Master, we have left all and followed Thee. What shall we have therefore?"

Every man's faith fails sometime. John the Baptist doubted. Elijah doubted. So Peter said, "It isn't going to pay. What are we going to get out of this anyway? We have left everything. This Man is not getting to be King." Jesus said to him, "In this life you shall have an hundredfold and in the world to come, life everlasting."

Oh, the other day when Brother Hughes was here from Illinois and some friends with him, a carload or two, Brother Hughes said, "I pray for you every day." And Brother Stith said, "Yes, Brother Rice, every day we pray for you." Brother Hughes said, "I will never forget that old corner of the tabernacle where I knelt down and got some things settled." He got on fire for God at that time and started preaching. Now he is pastor of two country churches.

My friends, listen, you will have a reaping time. You will have plenty of time to gain after awhile. If you say good-bye, you will get it back some day. Don't you worry when you leave all to follow Jesus.

Jesus left His home in Glory for us and went to the cross. "Who for the joy that was set before him endured the cross, despising the shame [and so you can], and is set down at the right hand of the throne of God."

Say good-bye and follow Jesus. "Whosoever he be of you that forsaketh not all that he hath, he cannot be my disciple."

Suppose we sing, "Where He Leads Me, I Will Follow." Do not sing it unless you mean to give up something and go His way.

You cannot follow Jesus without that. Can you say, "Good-bye to my brother, good-bye to the friends, good-bye to the success that I hoped to have, good-bye to the little nest egg I have saved up. Jesus can have that, too. Good-bye to home, my job. He can have that." Can you say good-bye and mean it?

I have done so little. I have no claim on God, nothing to boast of. In the Pacific Garden Mission in Chicago, I guess I played the fool in human sight—at least everybody thought I did. I had gone to Chicago to do graduate work in the University of Chicago. I had worked hard. When God told me to go preach, I left nets; I did not even take my examinations. I did not get credit on the work I had done. I got up and went to work and earned enough money to come back to Texas. I gave up my job with the college in New Mexico, and let it be known I would sing or preach or do anything I could get a chance to do for the Lord. I planned to enter the seminary that fall.

Let's cut the rope. Have you been trying to please men? You cannot please men and Christ, too. "Whosoever he be that forsaketh not all that he hath, he cannot be my disciple."

There is a man here unsaved this morning. I hope he will say, "God helping me, I am going to turn to Jesus and trust Him and give Him my heart."

Listen. I guess a foreign missionary is a good illustration of this thing. A foreign missionary must leave Mother and Father and go overseas among people he doesn't know. He may not get back alive. Or Mother and Father may die before he gets back. That is not too much to give up for Jesus. He did more than that for you.

If anybody feels called of God to be a missionary or a preacher, wouldn't you like to openly and publicly say, "Today I am saying good-bye"?

Somebody ought to come in the church this morning and get on record for God.

Dear sinner, trust Christ this morning!

7—Christ—First or Second?

(Sermon preached Sunday morning, April 24, 1938, at Fundamentalist Baptist Tabernacle. Stenographically reported.)

Let's start with Matthew 6:33, and we will skip around in the Bible in preaching on it.

You are thinking about something to eat and about clothes. Heathens do that. You are no better than heathens if that is what your mind is on, for "after all these things do the Gentiles seek." Don't you think God knows your need for clothes or food? And now verses 33 and 34:

> *But seek ye first the kingdom of God, and his righteousness; and all these things shall be added unto you.*
>
> *Take therefore no thought for the morrow: for the morrow shall take thought for the things of itself. Sufficient unto the day is the evil thereof.*

Now let's memorize verse 33. Everybody read it together. You had better repeat where it is so you will know where to find it. Matthew 6:33:

> *But seek ye first the kingdom of God, and his righteousness; and all these things shall be added unto you.*

Now that is very important. What is the most important word in that entire sentence? It is *"first."* "Seek ye FIRST the kingdom of God." Everybody does that if you leave out that word *first.* Everybody can say "yes" to that verse, and every Christian does, except that one word, *first.*

Even lost people in some sense seek the kingdom of God if you leave off that word *first.* You ask a lost man if he loves God and his answer will be yes. But he isn't telling the truth. He doesn't love God, he never believed in God, never trusted God. But he is more or less honest in his expectation at least.

Every drunkard wishes he could be sober sometimes. He didn't want to be a drunkard. Every thief wishes he could be honest. He feels, "Well, when I get to where people will give me a fair start, and I get a good job, and have money, I am not going to be a thief." Everybody likes morality and righteousness, and so everybody would be willing to seek the kingdom of God, but they don't want to seek it *first*. The most important word in that verse is *first*.

I. Glory in First Things

There is glory in first things. There is the first baby. Oh, the first baby! I talked to a mother on the telephone last night, and she was telling me about her baby, and of course I had to talk about my baby, too. She told me how much the little one weighed, and how he was getting along. It was her first baby. My wife said that the way to a mother's heart is through her baby. And she asked about our baby. I was interested in hers because she was interested in mine.

There is a freshness about the first baby. Isn't there glory around the first child? You mothers and fathers remember when God gave you that first baby! How precious he was! He was the brightest little thing! Do you remember that?

My brother Bill has a lovely baby. Bill told me, "Now look here, John, my baby—you may think I am joking or partial, but I am not—she has more human expression than any baby I ever saw! She really looks smart!" And I laughed. But Bill said, "Sure enough! I am not joking! My baby *is* the most sensible looking baby I ever saw." Of course his baby looked like anybody else's baby, but to him she was different. "My baby wasn't red like the other babies," he said. But his baby was as red as anyone's. "Most babies don't have any shape to their face," he went on, "but my baby is different."

The first baby—there is a glory about the first baby. There is always a freshness about first things.

There is the glory of young fresh love. I want to say this to you young people, and I say it to the boys as well as to the girls: I would keep myself so that when true love comes, when Prince Charming comes riding on a white horse with a plume in his hat, I would keep myself so that when I gave myself to him, I could know I was giving him my first love.

If you young men expect a good girl to respect you and love you, then keep yourself pure.

There is a sweetness in the first love, isn't there? I didn't mean to tell this, but my wife said she could tell the first time I ever kissed her that I was inexperienced and awkward! I didn't know enough to keep my nose out of the way! I had rather go at this business with the freshness of the first love, hadn't you?

And God wants the first, too. And girls, if that man is going to love and respect you, and if you are to be the mother of his children, he wants you not to be soiled. He doesn't want you to already be handled, slightly reduced in price because you are shopworn. Freshness and sweetness and joy ought to be that of any woman whose marriage is true. You ought to be able to offer the sweetest of the first love. The first things are always sweet!

I can remember when God called me to preach and I marvel that He ever called me. I said, "Lord, I don't know whether I can preach or not." I hesitated and held back and prayed, "Lord, I will try. If anybody is saved, I will know it is right and will praise You."

I preached the first time one Friday night in Pacific Garden Mission in Chicago. And some people were saved! There was a glow in my heart—this was a seal on my ministry!

Then I gave up my work in the University of Chicago and came back to Texas and held my first revival! I have had many revivals since that time, with many more people saved—there were twenty-four saved in that first revival. But what joy I had in that meeting! It was in a little brush arbor about the size of two of these sections, not wider than from here out to there (pointing to posts in auditorium). But, oh, I can remember that first revival! I can remember most of those who were saved.

I remember the songs that were sung and the people who

came. Oh, the freshness and sweetness of that first revival! I thought, "Isn't it glorious to be a preacher!"

Oh, the first things! The first things! God wants the first! I have built a number of tabernacles, but the truth of the matter is, I sometimes go over to Fort Worth and see that old lopsided tabernacle in North Fort Worth, the first one I ever built. It wasn't very carefully put together. The rafters were not notched in on the wall. I didn't know so much about how to do it, but that was my tabernacle, and, oh, the joy of building the first one!

And then the first church. I remember how, with fear and trembling, at Decatur we decided to organize a new Baptist church. It was the first time I had ever organized a church. We started with an independent revival. God blessed and prospered, and many souls were saved. There were some wonderful things about it.

I remember the first time I was pastor of a full-time church. Oh, the sweetness of it, the joy of it! Wasn't I getting to be somebody!

The Lord wants the first. "Seek ye first the kingdom of God, and his righteousness; and all these things shall be added unto you," the Scripture says.

God wants the freshness of the first. He demands it. "Seek ye first the kingdom of God, and his righteousness; and all these things shall be added unto you." God wants the FIRST.

II. The Firstfruits Belong to God

In the Old Testament we find where God demanded the firstfruits. Turn to Exodus 22:29.

> *Thou shalt not delay to offer the first of thy ripe fruits, and of thy liquors: the firstborn of thy sons shalt thou give unto me.*

And verse 30:

> *Likewise shalt thou do with thine oxen, and with thy sheep: seven days it shall be with his dam; on the eighth day thou shalt give it me.*

God says, "Don't make any delay about it. Give me the first of thy ripe fruits."

I can remember when I was first in love. In the spring I would watch for the first ripe peaches. All you have to do these days is go to the store and get fresh fruits. But in those days I can remember—can you?—the first mess of greens you got out of the garden. Oh, wasn't it good? You remember the first time the green onions and radishes, and lettuce (not lettuce like we get today, but the lettuce that spreads out—and you cut it up and put on it a dressing made with cream)—do you remember how good the first ones were? In the springtime the doctors say, "Well, what you need is a good tonic. Just as soon as the garden sass begins to come in, you will be all right."

I remember when I was in love. Love is a strange thing. There is something in the heart of a boy that makes him love a girl. I am talking about real love, with respect, not some foolish, wicked, lustful love.

I remember how when the peaches began to get ripe I would watch them. I wanted my girl to have the first ones. I remember so well the first roses that bloomed. I picked them, and took them to my girl, who is now my wife.

Can you remember the first watermelons that got ripe—how good they were? When the tassels began to turn on the cane, then we knew it was sweet.

God said, "When the fruit begins to get ripe, take the first ripe fruits and do not delay to bring them to me." You may think God would want a man to take the first for his family. But, no, God says, "The first belongs to me—the first of the fruits, the first of the grape juice, the first of all you have, the first of your crops, the first of your cattle, the first of your sheep—give the FIRST." That is what God demands and insists upon. Exodus 23:19 says the same thing:

The first of the firstfruits of thy land thou shalt bring into the house of the Lord thy God.

God says He wants the very first of the firstfruits.

"Wouldn't it be all right to feed my cattle some of this grain first? Wouldn't it be all right for me to pull the first sheaf for myself?" "No," God replies. "Wouldn't it be all right to pull the first melons and cut them for company and kinfolks?" No, the first of the firstfruits belongs to the Lord.

Maybe you haven't yet counted what it costs to be a Christian, what it costs to have victory over sin, what it costs to have power with God and man. You will have to go back and put first things first. "Seek ye first the kingdom of God."

Turn to the 18th chapter of Numbers and we will begin reading with verse 12:

> *All the best of the oil, and all the best of the wine, and of the wheat, the firstfruits of them which they shall offer unto the Lord, them have I given thee.*

[He is talking to the Levites and priests.]

> *And whatsoever is first ripe in the land, which they shall bring unto the Lord, shall be thine; every one that is clean in thine house shall eat of it.*
> *Every thing devoted in Israel shall be thine.*
> *Every thing that openeth the matrix in all flesh, which they bring unto the Lord, whether it be of men or beasts, shall be thine: nevertheless the firstborn of man shalt thou surely redeem, and the firstling of unclean beasts shalt thou redeem.*
> *And those that are to be redeemed from a month old shalt thou redeem, according to thine estimation, for the money of five shekels, after the shekel of the sanctuary, which is twenty gerahs.*
> *But the firstling of a cow, or the firstling of a sheep, or the firstling of a goat, thou shalt not redeem; they are holy: thou shalt sprinkle their blood upon the altar, and shalt burn their fat for an offering made by fire, for a sweet savour unto the Lord.*—Vss. 13-17.

The very first of the ripe fruits, the very first of all grain, and the firstborn are the Lord's.

We read in another place in Leviticus when the grain begins to get ripe in the spring or early summer, you are to bring the wavesheaf into the Temple. When you glean the ears of corn, take the first sheaf and bring them in and wave them before the Lord before the altar. Before you take any for yourself, bring it to the priest and offer it to God. God wants the first.

My people, don't fool yourself and say that is Old Testament law. Don't fool yourself and say that is not for us. God was driving hard to get a lesson on the hearts of the people. Nobody can ever get along with God who doesn't accept His right to the first and best. He has a right to it. He demands that we bring Him the firstfruits. You say that is ceremonial law. But God didn't change when the law changed. He demands the firstfruits.

In Proverbs 3:9, 10, He says:

> *Honour the Lord with thy substance, and with the firstfruits of all thine increase:*
> *So shall thy barns be filled with plenty, and thy presses shall burst out with new wine.*

Now God says, "I will bless you, I will give you your crop and your cattle, but you give me the first part." That theme runs throughout the Bible.

Do you remember how Elijah came to the poor widow? She was picking up sticks to build a little fire. It wouldn't take much, just a little, for she only had a handful of meal and a little oil. She said she was going to make a little cake for herself and for her boy and eat that and die.

But Elijah said to her, "Make me a cake first."

She might have thought, "Well of all things! Talk about selfish preachers! I never saw a preacher quite so selfish as Elijah!" Here was a poor widow making her last cake, and was going to eat it and then expected to die. She just had a little handful of meal left and just enough oil to make one cake. And yet Elijah said, "Make me a cake first."

Was he not hard on that widow? No, he wasn't. For when she made Elijah the cake first, she had plenty left. They had some more then for breakfast and dinner and the barrel never did give out. There was always plenty of oil and always plenty of meal.

"Give Me the firstfruits," God says. "Make that cake and give Me the firstfruits." Many a barrel of meal has gone dry because God's part wasn't taken out first. Many a cruse of oil has gone dry because we didn't take the Lord's part out first. And many a cow was barren and didn't bring the calf because you didn't give God the first calf that came.

You wouldn't put everybody before God, just your wife or your children. But God wants the first, and the best of the first, the first of the firstfruits and the best of the firstfruits. God demands *the best*. You may feel that is exorbitant and unreasonable and you can't do it. All right, but don't argue with God about it. Either say you will put God first or you won't.

The subject this morning is, "God—First or Second?" Everybody feels that nobody would put God last, that everybody loves God to some extent. It is not a question of whether you put God last or not. Nobody wants to put God last. But you have a temptation to put Him *after* your business, or *after* your wife or your children and *after* a few other things. It is not even a question of whether you are going to put Him before the first things, but whether you will put Him before the first of the first things and the best of the best. That is what He demands and He has a right to it, "the first of the firstfruits."

III. God Is Jealous

Back in the Ten Commandments the Lord said,

> *Thou shalt not make unto thee any graven image, or any likeness of any thing that is in heaven above, or that is in the earth beneath, or that is in the water under the earth.*
>
> *Thou shalt not bow down thyself to them, nor serve them: for I the Lord thy God am a jealous God, visiting the iniquity of the fathers upon the children unto the third and fourth generation of them that hate me.*—Exod. 20:4,5.

God is jealous. He is not willing to be second to anybody. He has no right to be second to anybody and ought not to be second to anybody. Your family has no business coming between you and God. God has a right to the first and the best of the best, the first of the firstfruits, as He said. That is what God requires and demands and insists upon.

I read you in Numbers 18, beginning with verse 12. What did He say?

All the best of the oil, and all the best of the wine, and of the wheat, the firstfruits of them which they shall offer unto the Lord, them have I given thee.

And whatsoever is first ripe in the land, which they shall bring unto the Lord, shall be thine; every one that is clean in thine house shall eat of it.

Every thing devoted in Israel shall be thine.

Every thing that openeth the matrix in all flesh, which they bring unto the Lord, whether it be of men or beasts, shall be thine: nevertheless the firstborn of man shalt thou surely redeem, and the firstling of unclean beasts shalt thou redeem.

And those that are to be redeemed from a month old shalt thou redeem, according to thine estimation, for the money of five shekels, after the shekel of the sanctuary, which is twenty gerahs.

But the firstling of a cow, or the firstling of a sheep, or the firstling of a goat, thou shalt not redeem; they are holy: thou shalt sprinkle their blood upon the altar, and shalt burn their fat for an offering made by fire, for a sweet savour unto the Lord.

And the flesh of them shall be thine, as the wave-breast and as the right shoulder are thine.

All the heave-offerings of the holy things, which the children of Israel offer unto the Lord, have I given thee, and thy sons and thy daughters with thee, by a statute for ever: it is a covenant of salt for ever before the Lord unto thee and to thy seed with thee.

And the Lord spake unto Aaron, Thou shalt have no inheritance in their land, neither shalt thou have any part among them: I am thy part and thine inheritance among the children of Israel.

And, behold, I have given the children of Levi all the tenth in Israel for an inheritance, for their service which they serve, even the service of the tabernacle of the congregation. —Vss. 12-21.

You may say, "Well, Brother Rice, now here, I don't believe in bringing in all the firstfruits!"

But the Lord commands, "Honour the Lord with thy substance, and with the firstfruits of all thine increase." Yes, that is the way.

IV. Pay the Tithe First

You say, "I will tithe after I pay my other bills so as to keep my good name, then if I have any left, I will tithe." Or somebody says, "When I get my grocery bill paid, I will tithe." I say, if you are going to please God, He demands the first of your money.

Somebody says, "Brother Rice, we would surely not be required to tithe when we can't pay our bills." But I Corinthians 16:2 says:

Upon the first day of the week let every one of you lay by him in store, as God hath prospered him, that there be no gatherings when I come.

You feel that you owe so much, that you owe so many people, but you don't owe anybody as much as you owe God.

I received one of the saddest letters the other day from Seagraves, Texas. I will not read the name.

Dear Brother Rice:
I read your powerful sermon on "Hidden Sins." I think it the strongest I ever read. . . . It seems like it was all for me.
I am guilty of all the charges you made. I am penniless and friendless on account of hiding the wedge in my tent. Time and again I have promised the Lord a tenth and when He would let me prosper, I kept it all! I have lied and robbed God! At last, He has collected all! I pray the Lord to ever keep you humble and bold to preach the truth. That is what the world needs. A very few preachers now will preach it that way. Pray that I may rededicate my life and all to the cause of our dear Lord. I have been greatly blessed from the good sermons you write. . . .
Find enclosed $1.00. Use it any way you see fit.

"At last, He has collected all!" That is the point I want you to get. He said, "I am guilty of all the charges you made. I am penniless and friendless on account of hiding the wedge in my tent. Time and again I have promised the Lord a tenth, and when He would let me prosper, I kept it all!" And then again, "At last, He has collected all!"

Now, brother, don't think you can get by. God is a jealous God. God doesn't need your money. He doesn't need anything you have. He doesn't need you. But He wants your love, He wants you to put Him first. He has a right to be first. If you don't put Him first, He will not be close to you. He will not bless you and prosper you. He demands to be first.

He has a right to be first in money matters. I only begin on that because God began on that. That isn't the end of it, but the beginning. If you don't put God first in things that come to your hand, if you do not put Him first in money matters, if you do not put Him first in house and first in field and first in fruits, you are going to fall short and miss your blessing.

I want my people to tithe, but that is not the main thing I want. I want you to love God first and put Him first in your heart. That is important for your own sake. If you don't you will be saying like that man who wrote me, "I have lied to God and robbed God. I am friendless and penniless. At last, He has collected all."

Now I tell you, you can't get along with God and make Him a secondary matter and use Him as a tool, just an incident to prosper you and take care of you. You must put God first. He wants the first and the best. He demands it. He has a right to it. He is a jealous God.

V. The Firstborn Are the Lord's

And not only the firstfruits but the firstborn belong to God. There are many Scriptures on that. Turn to Exodus the 13th chapter, verses 1 and 2:

> *And the Lord spake unto Moses, saying,*
> *Sanctify unto me all the firstborn, whatsoever openeth*

the womb among the children of Israel, both of man and of beast: it is mine.

God doesn't say, "You ought to give it to Me." He says, "It is Mine; set it apart. It is already Mine. You just sanctify it. It is holy. You dedicate it. It is Mine."

Moses said unto the people, Remember this day, in which ye came out from Egypt, out of the house of bondage.

(Don't forget, God set this day apart because you are His.)

For by strength of hand the Lord brought you out from this place:

And further down in the same chapter, in verses 10 and following the Lord says:

Thou shalt therefore keep this ordinance in his season from year to year.

And it shall be when the Lord shall bring thee into the land of the Canaanites, as he sware unto thee and to thy fathers, and shall give it thee,

That thou shalt set apart unto the Lord all that openeth the matrix, and every firstling that cometh of a beast which thou hast; the males shall be the Lord's.

And every firstling of an ass thou shalt redeem with a lamb; and if thou wilt not redeem it, then thou shalt break his neck: and all the firstborn of man among thy children shalt thou redeem. —Exod. 13:10-13.

It isn't yours. If you can't pay for it, don't use it. If you can't pay for it, break its neck. It is God's, not yours.

And it shall be when thy son asketh thee in time to come, saying, What is this? that thou shalt say unto him, By strength of hand the Lord brought us out from Egypt, from the house of bondage.

When your boy says, "What is this? What do you mean by bringing in the tithe?" then you shall tell him that the first money that comes in has to be the Lord's.

And it shall be when thy son asketh thee in time to

come, saying, What is this? that thou shalt say unto him,
By strength of hand the Lord brought us out from
Egypt, from the house of bondage:

And it came to pass, when Pharaoh would hardly let us
go, that the Lord slew all the firstborn in the land of
Egypt, both the firstborn of man, and the firstborn of
beast: therefore I sacrifice to the Lord all that openeth
the matrix, being males; but all the firstborn of my
children I redeem.

And it shall be for a token upon thine hand, and for
frontlets between thine eyes: for by strength of hand the
Lord brought us forth out of Egypt.—Exod. 13:14-16.

My friends, it isn't just the money but a token between you and God that you love Him first, that you love Him best and first of all and that all you have is His. God demands the firstfruits and the firstborn.

How dear my children are to me! You heard them sing on the radio this morning. I try not to be foolish about them. People spoil preachers' children anyway. I was so proud of them and I enjoyed so having them with me on the radio and having them sing. I could not then realize what it meant, but when my baby, Grace, was born, the first one, and she was laid in my arms, I knew I held not just a little body but an immortal soul for Heaven or Hell. As I looked down upon her, I begged God to make me fit to be her father. I thanked God that she was well formed and had no disease. We gave her to the Lord that day, my wife and I, and we prayed God to take her and use her.

How glad I was when she was saved! Through the years I have dreamed she would be my helper and play the piano for me and be my secretary. And so about the other children.

But God said, "I want the first baby that is born. The firstborn among the cattle is mine. The first calf from every cow, being male, the first sheep, the first male lamb and the first of every kind of beast, clean and unclean, is mine." If it is the firstling of an ass, you are not to offer it as a sacrifice, but you must pay a lamb for it. Every unclean beast you are to redeem with a lamb. If you don't have a lamb, then break the donkey's neck. It is not yours. You can't have it unless you buy it.

The same way about your children. If some of you are having trouble with your children, and they are a burden to you, if you would really turn them over to the Lord and say they are His, then He will take them and use them for Himself. If you could say they were His altogether, a lot would be settled. God would take them in charge. And God would bless them in it.

I haven't any boys to be preachers. I have thought of it many times. If my six girls were all boys, I think I would want every one of them to be a preacher. I guess I would have been so vain and so proud that maybe God saw I had better not have any. I don't think it is such a curse to have girls though. I am very well satisfied with them! But I would like to have had boys to preach the Gospel. If God wants my girls to be preachers' wives or missionaries' wives and go to Africa or China—if He wants the first, He has a right to it.

The first are the Lord's. He wants the first of animals, He wants the firstborn son, and you ought to give it to Him and I ought to give it to Him. If that seems hard to you, then remember that "God so loved the world, that he gave his only begotten Son." He gave His firstborn. We shouldn't be afraid or shouldn't hold back on giving Him the first.

VI. God Wants to Be First Every Day

God also wants the first day. That is mentioned in I Corinthians 16:2:

> Upon the first day of the week let every one of you lay by him in store, as God hath prospered him, that there be no gatherings when I come.

The Old Testament Sabbath came on the seventh day. The point was this: We will give the Lord the seventh day, a picture of rest, a picture of Heaven when you have earned it. One must work the first day, and the second day, work number three, work number four, work on the fifth day, work on the sixth day, now then you have earned your rest. Now you can have rest.

But that leaves God out. That makes salvation by works. That pictures a type of salvation by your own good deeds. Nobody was ever saved that way. There was nothing wrong with that, but through the wickedness of sinful men it failed. Nobody ever got any real rest or peace in his heart because he worked. Nobody ever got to Heaven because he earned it. But since the law failed to save, God sent His Son in the likeness of sinful flesh, and for sin, condemned sin in the flesh.

Now that Christ has died, what do I do? Praise the Lord, on the very first day of the week Jesus arose from the dead, so I enter into rest! That isn't fair having a rest before you work! But that is right! You rest before you do anything at all! I have peace in my heart. I have ceased from my own works before I ever started any works, and I have trusted in Christ for peace and salvation, and I have Heaven here! I am going to Heaven resting! I am resting my way to Heaven. I have entered into rest, and the first day of the week belongs to God. The Old Testament says about the Jewish Sabbath,

> *And on the seventh day God ended his work which he had made; and he rested on the seventh day from all his work which he had made.*—Gen. 2:2.

That is the Old Testament Sabbath.

But turn to the New Testament and it is the Lord's day. I start out preaching and working on the first day for the Lord. But I already have peace in my heart. I give the Lord the first day. The Lord's Day is on Sunday, the first day.

Would you want to wait until the last day of the week to serve God? No! No! Today is the first day of the week. Today is a new beginning, a new dedication. I take out what money belongs to the Lord on the first day, as the Scripture commands. "Upon the first day of the week let every one of you lay by him in store, as God hath prospered him." Then you pay the rest of your bills on Monday. But take the Lord's part out today. It comes first. It is the first day that God wants. So let us put Jesus first.

Some people say, "I have to go see Mother." Well, go on your own time then. Don't go on the Lord's time. You say, "I want to have a little recreation." Then take it on your day. Don't take it on God's day. Or some one says, "But I am tired and need to catch up on my sleep." All right, but don't take it all out on God because this day is the Lord's day. That is what the Bible called it. God wants the first day of the week. It belongs to Him. All the days belong to Him but this is a type, a token, an evidence that your heart puts Him first.

That is why Christians ought to be faithful to attend services. You ought to be glad to be in Sunday school and to attend prayer meeting, to go to the parks and jails for services and win souls. You ought to be a lot more tired on Monday morning starting your work than you are Sunday morning going to church. You ought to give the Lord the freshest and the best.

I like to have half a day off on Saturday so I can get a little rest and then hit the ball Sunday morning for the Lord. It is the Lord's day, put Him first. The Sabbath, the Old Testament day of rest, came after six days of work, but Sunday, the first day, is a picture that we have already entered into rest. Let us put Him first.

God not only wants the firstfruits and the firstborn and the first day, but He wants the first place in your heart, the first place in your life. He wants the first part in every day.

Did you read in the Sunday school lesson this morning how the Lord Jesus arose "a great while before day . . . and departed into a solitary place, and there prayed"? I set the alarm this morning at 6:30, but a good while before that time I was awake and felt some way the quiet call, and I got up and got my Bible, and in my heart I was saying, "O God, I don't want to preach about the thing and not have it so myself." I want to be like I am telling others to be.

My constant prayer for the last few days as I tried to get ready to preach this sermon was, "O Lord Jesus, be first to me."

And I just wonder how many in this group every day, the first part of the day, put Him first?

When do you read your Bible? Do you read it at night? That is a good time, all right. Do you read it some other time of the day? Or do you read your Bible the first thing in the morning? If Jesus, early in the morning, a great while before day, rose up and went into a solitary place and prayed, don't you think that would be a good thing for us?

Do you want to know the secret of D. L. Moody's life? He made up his mind, "If I am going to be much of a preacher, I must learn the Bible and learn to pray." All his life he got up at 5:00 in the morning (sometimes at 4:00) and spent a couple of hours alone with his Bible and God before others got up.

If we learn to give God the first thoughts, the first plans, the first devotions of the day, some way the day seems better and brighter.

I went through a day not long ago when my burdens got really heavy. Oh, the burdens! You have no idea the burdens, the details, the bills to pay, all this Sunday school to see after. Other preachers have an educational director, other preachers don't have a paper to edit. There are so many things piling up.

And along in the middle of the afternoon these burdens were becoming too heavy. I didn't understand. And something down inside said, "You were so busy today, that is your trouble. You were so busy you didn't take time out to get God's smile on it and your heart cleaned anew before you began." That is the reason I had a hard time today.

Martin Luther said, "My work is so heavy I have to pray at least three hours a day. If I don't, I can't get it all done."

We leave off praying and think that will give us more time, but it doesn't. It never gives you more time to leave off praying. It never gives you more money to leave off tithing. It does not make you any more rested when you take the Lord's time for it. The thing we need to do is to give Him the first and He will make the rest of it go farther. Let's give Him the first part of the day.

I wonder this morning, does God speak to you this way: "Give Me the quiet hour in the first part of the day"? Go alone and there read the Bible and meditate and pray. Lay everything on the altar afresh. Your sins will have to be confessed again. You have a fresher mind in the morning.

I used to work on arithmetic problems but I couldn't work them. Then I would wake up in the morning early. I think they must have been settled in my sleep. I would get up and work them right.

God gives you a fresher mind in the morning. Your heart is clearer and happier in the morning. How sweet that God gives sleep! "He giveth his beloved sleep," the Scripture says. Isn't God good to refresh us! That fresh part, that best part—give it to God. It is His. Put Him first.

You say you can't remember the Bible like you used to. Do you know why? You read it at night when you are tired. You put it last. After you have read other things, you read the Bible. After the dishes are washed and you have put the children to bed, you take your Bible and read a little. You have the place marked and say, "Where did I read last night?" You don't know where you read to. "I can't remember where I read." I know you can't. The reason is this: You are giving God the tail end of everything. Your mind is tired. But as a matter of duty you read it. Sometimes you go to sleep while reading. You read over a whole page and go back and read it again and wonder what you read. "Well, I must have read that," you say. The trouble is, you didn't put God first in the freshest part of the day. He demands the first. "Seek ye *first* the kingdom of God."

VII. God Demands the First Love

God wants the firstfruits, the firstborn and the first day, the first part of the day, and then He wants your first love. In chapter 2 of Revelation, God gave a message to the seven churches of Asia, and to the church of Ephesus He said, "I have somewhat against thee, because thou hast left thy first love."

Now I used to think first love meant to go back to the joy and zeal one had when he was first converted. I think that is true, but I think what God likes about that first love is that God was loved first in it. That is the point.

Many a man here today loves his wife as much as he did back yonder. But this is the difference: Insensibly other things have stolen in between to occupy your mind. You still love her, but your attention has been given to other things. You love her, but you may love something else better. It is not enough to love your wife second to other women.

You say, "God, I will put you right after my business, or right after my wife, or right after the baby." But God doesn't want second place. He wants your first love. And He said, "I have somewhat against thee, because thou hast left thy first love."

I love Him today. God sees my heart and knows I love Him. He knows you love Him, too, but that is not the question. Is He second or first this morning? Does He have your first love, first of all? Can you say with the words of the old song:

> The dearest idol I have known,
> What e'er that idol be;
> Help me to tear it from thy throne
> And worship only thee.

Oh, put Him first this morning! The secret back of tithing is, it is not your money God wants but your love, your first love. He has a right to that. "Seek ye first the kingdom of God, and his righteousness; and all these things shall be added unto you."

Many of you Sunday school teachers are growing in grace. Bless your hearts, forgive me if sometimes I talk sharply. I don't mean to. I do appreciate the work you are doing. Sunday school teachers and officers, you think sometimes your burdens are heavy. You have to go see all your absentees, and sometimes you don't have a car, and you have to have this, that and the other, and you think you can't do it. You think it too much of a burden to come to the teachers meetings, and to give up other things. But you wouldn't think it was too much if you got it settled that He is to have first place.

When Elijah, that man of God, said to the widow when she just had a little meal, "Make me a cake first, and out of what you have left, you may eat. You and the starving boy be second," she might have said, "That is too much to ask. A preacher shouldn't ask that of a widow woman." But when she put the Lord first through His prophet, she had plenty left.

Last Sunday morning a woman trusted Christ in my Sunday school class. I don't know whether she had ever before made a start or not. But she stood to claim Christ as her Saviour. And Mrs. McBeth came to me to tell me about a girl saved in her class. Then someone else told me of a conversion in the Sunday school. There were four saved in Sunday school last Sunday. What little visiting you did, what did it matter? What little time you spent, what did it matter if we had four people saved in the Sunday school last Sunday? That is worth all the visiting. You get things out of proportion. When you put Him first, it pays.

> It pays to serve Jesus,
> It pays every day,
> It pays ev'ry step of the way;
> Tho' the pathway to glory
> May sometimes be drear,
> You'll be happy each step of the way.

Learn to put Him first and give Him the best. I know it may take you away from your family. And your husband doesn't like for you to leave the beds unmade. Two or three women told me, "I feel I can't neglect my home." Another woman said, "My health is bad and my children get out of school in the afternoon. I just can't do the visiting." "I am not very strong and I have to ride the streetcar to see every one of my pupils," another says. If you would just remember that it isn't for the church primarily, it isn't for the preacher, it is for Jesus and you ought to put Him first, it wouldn't seem too much. You ought to say, "Lord Jesus, my day belongs to You. It doesn't belong to my job."

Brother _____, Sears Roebuck didn't die for you. Your job isn't first. Let's put first things first. Consumers Plumbing didn't die for you, Brother _____. They pay you for a little work, but what about your heart and soul? They don't have eternity for you. They didn't prepare Heaven for you. It is right for you to make a good hand, but, Brother _____, Western Auto didn't die for you. Somebody must hold first place.

I would put Jesus Christ first and say, "The Lord Jesus is going to be first in my life." Give Him the first fruit, the firstborn, the first day, the first time of the day and seek first His kingdom.

A song says:

> Early let us seek Thy favor,
> Early let us do Thy will;

Blessed Lord and only Saviour,
With Thy love our bosoms fill;
Blessed Jesus, Blessed Jesus,
Thou hast loved us, love us still.

Oh, if God would put it in our hearts to put Him first, all our problems would be solved. We would have all the Sunday school teachers we need. One of the superintendents said he needed a couple more teachers. There are plenty of folks to teach, but the trouble is that Machinery Sales and Supply is first, or Atleta-Cunningham Cycle Shop is first, or something else is first. I am picking out the folks who are not teaching. I mention these two for illustrations. I am as certain as I am living that God has all the workers we need. The only trouble is that some cheat God and don't give Him first place.

Plenty of folks can teach, and plenty are called to teach, plenty are anointed to teach, and some have taught with great blessing. If we would put God first, we would have all the teachers we need. If people would do this, we would have all the singers, all the personal workers, all the money we need. All God wants is first place, and that means everything. He has a right to it. He will prosper the rest of it, if He is first.

Who are you to leave God out? You can't work for God, you don't know how or you haven't time. But wait, God says, "Seek ye first the kingdom of God, and his righteousness; and all these things shall be added unto you."

VIII. Christ or Self?

But this is what is wrong. Today if it isn't Jesus first, it is self. You say it is your job, or your family, or your health. It isn't that. It is self first—what I like, what I enjoy. Come off that throne, you imposter; you have no right there. That is the throne for Jesus Christ. I say, step down out of that place of authority. It isn't yours. You are bought with a price.

When you were baptized, when you went down into the watery grave, you said, "Jesus died for me, so I die to self. My sins are buried and the old sinner is dead." And when you came out of the water you said to the world, "Jesus rose again. My old sins are nailed to the cross with Him and now I am living for

Jesus. Christ lives in me. All my thoughts and actions are His. He is raised from the dead and lives in me."

Christ in you the hope of glory, the Scripture says, so then "reckon ye also yourselves to be dead unto sin."

Some of you use that strong right hand. You hold the hammer and the saw. Go ahead, but I want you to know that that right hand is bought by the blood of Jesus Christ.

You can talk with that tongue, but you had better beware. That tongue is bought by Jesus Christ.

Be careful about the scenes you look upon with those eyes—they are His, not yours.

Beware what you hear, because those ears belong to Jesus Christ. Some of you listen to that rotten stuff on the radio. Some songs are a shame and disgrace. Your ears belong to God. Take heed what you listen to.

No wonder the Scripture says, "If thine eye offend thee, pluck it out." If that hand doesn't serve God, then you are a cheat. You lied to God when you made a public profession and were baptized and joined the church. You are a cheat and an imposter if you take what is not yours. You are sitting on the throne that belongs to Jesus Christ. Get off today and put Him first. It is Christ or self. A little poem says:

> **When Christ is on the throne,**
> **Self is on the cross,**
> **When self is on the throne,**
> **Christ is on the cross.**

Jesus said,

> *If any man come to me, and hate not his father, and mother, and wife, and children, and brethren, and sisters; yea, and his own life also, he cannot be my disciple.* —Luke 14:26.

We ought to have a purging in this church, a searching of our hearts. We ought to face this thing fair and square and vow, "I will put God first," or you ought to say, "No, I am not going to give up my way. I am not going to give God the first meal out of the barrel. I am not going to give God the tithe. My wife and I do not have enough as it is. I can't give God the first day when it is my only day of recreation and the only day to visit with my family. I won't give God the first of my children, the first of my time, the first of my heart. No, that is too much."

I would like to have a purging here this morning. It would be better if some would say, "I don't like it," and go some place else. We would get somewhere for God if half of the crowd would leave and go some other place, saying, "That is too strict for me. I can't stand that. That is asking too much." And if those left here would pray, "O Lord Jesus, take me, I am bought with a price, I am not my own. I don't belong to myself. My hands are not mine, my money is not mine, my family is not mine, my time is not mine. Take me, Lord Jesus. Take my silver and my gold, not a mite would I withhold. Take my voice, and let me sing, always, only, for my King. Take me, Lord Jesus."

Yes, that would be better. We need a purging. There are those who count the cost and find it too much, and say, "I will not do it." Let us search our hearts this morning.

One man said, "Lord, let me follow You." Jesus said, "The foxes have holes, and the birds of the air have nests; but the Son of man hath not where to lay his head." Another man said, "Lord, I will follow You after I go bury my father." The Lord said, "Let the dead bury their dead." Jesus said, "If anybody follows Me, let him sit down first and count the cost and see whether it is too much."

Brother, let us count the cost today. Is it too much when Christ died for you, when He kept you out of Hell? Is it too much after what He gave you? Is it too much when Christ died for you, when He kept you out of Hell? Is it too much after what He gave you? Is it too much?

Lord, take the first of my time, the best of my talents—whatever it is. Lord, my friendships and my love and my heart's devotion, Lord—take the first love, the first place, take the first day, and the first time of the day. Let me seek first the kingdom of God. Can you say that today? You ought to say it and you had better say it. You can't have victory without it.

It is self or the Lord today. Let's put first things first. He that is first will be last. If you put yourself first, you will come out last.

I read you that sad letter where the man said, "I have hid the wedge in my tent and now I am friendless and penniless. I have robbed God and lied to God and now at last He has taken all." My friends, He loved you so that He gave His first.

When you bring God the firstfruits, God will bless the rest of it. When you bring the first offering, "your barns shall be filled with plenty and your presses shall burst out with new wine." He always pays back more than you give. Seek first His kingdom.

Today put Him first. Maybe somebody here today is not a Christian. If that be so, I am sorry. If you are not a Christian, I know what your trouble is. You don't want to put Him first. You want your own way, your own stubborn, wicked way. "There is a way that seemeth right unto a man, but the end thereof are the ways of death." It may look beautiful but it doesn't turn out that way. No, it doesn't. You had better turn.

A young woman came weeping and asking me, "What shall I do? I don't know what to do. I didn't dream when my mother told me not to go to that country club dance it would turn out this way."

No, and nobody ever dreamed sin would turn out like that. But it does. Adam didn't believe it. Eve didn't believe it when the Lord said, "Thou shalt surely die."

Self means ruin, poverty, heartbreak. I wouldn't go on in my selfish way. I would say, "Today, come in, Lord Jesus, take charge of my life. You can have the first today."

> All my heart's love,
>   All my fond dreams,
> Make them, Lord Jesus,
>   Only for Thee.
> All that I am,
>   All I could be,
> Take me, Lord Jesus,
>   Wholly for Thee.

8—"Present Your Bodies"

(First sermon in new building of Fundamentalist Baptist Church in Dallas, preached Sunday morning, December 10, 1939. Stenographically reported.)

I call your attention to the text in Romans 12:1:

I beseech you therefore, brethren, by the mercies of God, that ye present your bodies a living sacrifice, holy, acceptable unto God, which is your reasonable service.

"I beseech you therefore." Paul's *therefores* always point to something gone before. In this case it is to the manifold mercies of God. Since God has been so good to us, "I beseech you therefore, brethren, by the mercies of God, that ye present your bodies a living sacrifice." Because of God's goodness to us we ought to give ourselves wholly to serving Him, pleasing Him. ". . . Present your bodies a living sacrifice."

I wanted today to talk to you on *Stewardship* of the things God has given you to use for Him. I want to talk to individuals about what God has given you and what God wants you to do about it.

I. God Wants Your Body

First of all, God wants you to give Him your *body*—". . . present your bodies." Today God wants you to bring your body and lay it on the altar. Just as truly as a lamb or a bullock brought to the priest in the Old Testament times was laid on the altar as a burnt sacrifice, just so God wants you and me to bring our bodies.

Now in general the Devil has a way of telling people that it doesn't matter about the body, that what God wants is the heart. People sometimes say to me about a service, "I wasn't there in person, but I was there in heart and in spirit." The truth of the matter is that if you follow what the Bible says you will find that the Lord is not much concerned about your spirit if your body is not given over to God. God is not much interested in your spirit if it is a hypocritical kind of consecration that does not involve the body.

God says about the body, "I beseech you therefore, brethren, by the mercies of God, that ye present your bodies a living sacrifice, holy, acceptable unto God." A holy body, an acceptable body, is a reasonable service for you to give. The same thing is said in I Corinthians 6:19,20:

What? know ye not that your body is the temple of the Holy Ghost which is in you, which ye have of God, and ye are not your own?

For ye are bought with a price: therefore glorify God in your body, and in your spirit, which are God's.

Not just your heart; He is wanting your body. Glorify God in your body first and in your spirit which are His. The body first, then the spirit. There is no sincerity in any Christianity that doesn't include the body. Present your body a living sacrifice.

Now there are several reasons why our bodies ought to serve God. First, because our bodies are in the image of God. If Jesus Christ were here this morning, He would have a body that could wear clothes. And He would have hands and eyes and ears and feet like we have. He could listen, He could talk, He has all the attributes of humanity, the Lord Jesus Christ. He could sit on these benches. Now a horse could not, or a dog could not, or a monkey or an ape could not. But Jesus Christ is a man. He has a human body, born of a woman, nursed at a woman's breast. Jesus Christ has a human body. We are in His image. "In the image of God created he him; male and female created he them," says the Word of God.

Now your body, my body, belongs to God, and it ought to be kept holy. It ought to be given over and consecrated to God because He said that our bodies are in His image.

Your body is made in the image of God. We are, after all,

divine creatures. We are a fallen group, and in us is the taint of sin, and on us the curse sin brings, and all about us there is the enmity of nature to mankind.

The ground is cursed and we must dig and labor to make it bring forth fruit. Animal kind is against man. When a woman brings forth a child, there is suffering that God said was a special mark or curse on the race.

Yes, to be sure, we are fallen under sin, but for all that, there is yet in us the image of God. He made us in His image and your body belongs to God and you ought to give it up to God.

God wants your body this morning. He wants your body because it is in His image.

In the second place, your body ought to be given to Him because it is His temple. God lives in your body. You say, "I came into this house, and I feel the presence of God in the house." But I remind you that God doesn't dwell in temples made with hands.

As God came, Solomon prayed, and the glory of the Lord filled the Temple, and fire from Heaven came and consumed the sacrifice. As God came upon the Temple in Solomon's day, I want the glory of God to fill this house, too. But I want you to know God does not live in houses made with hands, made of brick and steel and wood and plaster and concrete.

This new building is precious to us, and it may be in one sense dear to the heart of God, but it is not as precious as the body of even one Christian, the humblest, lowest, poorest, most ignorant Christian in the world. The body is the living temple of God. God wants your body because it is His home, and it is rightfully His. Your body is His church house. I am talking about the consecration of your body, not only that your heart loves Him, but your body belongs to God. He lives in your body. The Spirit of God talks in your voice and sings in your voice and grips sinners through your handclasp. God wants your body.

Oh, how we worked last night. We carried four pianos, three of them upstairs, and my shoulders are still sore. These good men worked here late last night building this platform. The good women put up these curtains around the platform. We did lots of work last night. That is well and good. We ought to keep this building as clean as it is right now. But much more important it is that every boy and girl who is a Christian ought to wash your face and bathe your body and watch your body and count it as a holy and beautiful thing. Every man, every woman, ought to say, "I haven't revered my body as perhaps I ought, but I will. My body is the temple of the living God. He lives in my body. His Spirit literally has His home in this body."

Some Christians sometimes say, "If you go to certain places, if you go to the picture show, God will not go with you. God won't go with you if you go into a beer parlor."

But, my friends, it is sad but true that if you are a Christian and if you are a child of God and go into a beer parlor or a picture show, the Spirit of God goes in with you because He lives in your body. He is offended and grieved, and it is a horrible sin to take Him where He is not at home and isn't happy, but He lives in your body. "For ye are the temple of the living God; as God hath said, I will dwell in them, and walk in them; and I will be their God, and they shall be my people" (II Cor. 6:16). Your body is the temple of the living God.

This morning we ought to give our bodies to Christ as a temple, as we give this building to God.

I say, third, present your bodies a living sacrifice because it is His purchase. May I remind you that when Jesus died, He didn't just die to save our souls from Hell. The Scripture says about Jesus when He healed the sick, "That it might be fulfilled which was spoken by Esaias the prophet, saying, Himself took our infirmities, and bare our sicknesses" (Matt. 8:17).

The Lord Jesus Christ Himself bore our sicknesses and our sorrows and all the strain and trouble we human beings have. The Lord Jesus Christ had a human body. He was born in a human body, and when He died, He died to save human beings. Those who believe in Him get to Heaven, but they are not ghostly, eery spirits floating around in an intangible way. We will have human bodies that will eat and drink. There will be twelve manner of trees to bring forth twelve manner of fruits, the leaves of which will be for the healing of the nations. And the Scripture tells when that good time comes, when the Salt Sea will be cured and in the Dead Sea will be fishermen who will go out and fish with nets in the millennium age.

When Jesus rose from the dead He called His disciples around Him and said, "Behold my hands and my feet, that it is I myself: handle me, and see; for a spirit hath not flesh and bones, as ye see me have" (Luke 24:39). Then He asked for something to eat, and they brought Him a piece of a broiled fish and an honeycomb, and Jesus plucked the meat from the bones of the fish and ate with a human mouth and swallowed the food into a human stomach after He had risen from the dead. He took the honeycomb and ate it and it was sweet to His tongue as it is to mine and to yours. He ate with an ordinary human body. When He rose from the dead, Jesus came to purchase for us a perfect human body. Your body is the temple of God which was bought on the cross, salvation was paid for and joy is promised to Christians.

I know we do not have all the things He bought for us yet, but one day we will have. God has it for us. We haven't yet attained to the perfection of the body, healing and other things, but we will. The body is purchased. Your body is bought by God and it belongs to God. You ought to say, "Today, God helping me, I will give my body to Him alone." When Jesus died, His human body died. When His human body died, it died for my body. His hands were pierced instead of mine. His blood was poured out instead of mine. His body gave up the ghost instead of mine.

Frankly, I am deeply concerned about soul winning in this church. My heart's desire is to find the will of God and not grieve the Spirit about this church. God has had some dealings with us and He wants us to take it to heart. You may think a building like this is the main thing in your life. Thank God we have a good place to bring in the crowds, but the building should not be our main concern. God wants a place in which He can dwell.

Unless every member of this church, and every member of the committee, and every Sunday school worker has a cleaning up and comes in this building to be a different kind of Christian, with a new kind of living and a new kind of dedication, then we had as well be out in that barn. (The temporary tabernacle used while building the new building.) What difference does it make unless we please God and have His blessing and power?

I am asking you today to lay yourselves on the altar and say, "O God, take my body." "I beseech you therefore, brethren, by the mercies of God, that ye present your bodies a living sacrifice, holy, acceptable unto God, which is your reasonable service. And be not conformed to this world: but be ye transformed by the renewing of your mind, that ye may prove what is that good, and acceptable, and perfect, will of God."

And this holy day, this new day, I ask you to lay your body on the altar and say, "God, you can have my body. And if anything defiles that body which is in the image of Christ, that temple of the Holy Spirit that is bought by the blood of Christ, if anything grieves Him and defiles it, God helping me, I will lay it aside."

You brought in money for this building and for these seats. You brought yourselves. But I tell you what God wants. He wants men to bring your cigarettes up here and lay them down for God. I don't believe any kind of giving will please God if it can't include your cigarettes or a can of Prince Albert, if that is what you use. If it doesn't go deep enough to affect the way you live, your habits, the way you act day by day, it is poor consecration.

You say, "This body I will use for my own. I will eat what I want, drink what I want, listen to what I want to, say what I want to say, look at what I want to . . . I will leave God out." I believe any kind of worship or consecration that doesn't surrender that body to the Lord isn't enough and will not get the blessing God wants you to have today.

Oh, beloved, why not say today, "O God, here is my body. I present my body, the human body. God, You can have this body"?

That is what Paul said to the Romans and that is what I say and what you ought to, today.

II. God Wants Your Members

Next, our members are His. It is a strange thing, but God wants our hands and our feet and our lips and tongues, as He says so many times. The Bible is very definite. Men like to talk about loving God in their hearts and feeling wonderful. And a lot of people had rather go home and say, "Oh, how I love Jesus!" Talk is cheap: but what God wants is for something to happen in the way you live. Your hands and feet and mouth and pocketbook, what you smoke, or drink or what you don't smoke or don't drink—God wants that settled. For instance, our hands. Ecclesiastes says, "Whatsoever thy hand findeth to do, do it with thy might" (Eccles. 9:10). I believe we had some of that last night. Some of the work was paid for last night but some of it was done with hands, and out of love. He wants hands that will work for Him.

These Christians whose hearts are for the Lord and whose hands are for the Devil—something smells about that; there is something rotten and insincere about that. This kind of Christianity that says, "Oh, I am for the Lord; you have no idea how I love Him"—yet you have plenty of time to make a living and no time to work for God! Brother, listen, I tell you, you are a fake, a fraud. There is something insincere about any kind of Christianity which says, "I will give God my heart but not my hands." "Whatsoever thy hand findeth to do, do it with thy might."

We find that Peter in Acts, chapter 3, deals with a lame man. This man had never walked. Peter told him that he didn't have any money—"Silver and gold have I none." Peter told him that he could not give him money; but he said, "Such as I have give I thee: In the name of Jesus Christ of Nazareth rise up and walk." This lame man had never stood up. How was he going to stand up and walk? How was he going to have that much faith?

Peter reached down (that is a picture some way of Christ reaching down) and took him by the *right hand* and lifted him up, and as he lifted him up, immediately his feet and ankle bones received strength. Peter's talking would not have gotten anywhere had his hands not been for Jesus, too.

That is one reason I use my hands when I preach. God wants my hands when I preach as well as my talk. God wants your hands for Him.

Notice that when Jesus healed a blind man, He touched his eyes. And in another case He spit in the dirt and made mud and with His hands anointed the man's eyes.

My friends, it is a wonderful thing to have Jesus' hand to touch you. He touched people with His hands. You remember occasion after occasion where Jesus put His hand upon people. Oh, if God would touch our hands and use them to touch others for Him!

No animal in the world has hands like a man. A monkey has sort of a hand, but a monkey can't play the piano, and can't do the things a human can do. God gave us, as part of our souls, as part of our immortal beings, as part of the image of God, our hands. And He wants these hands for Him.

When we ordain a preacher or deacon, we lay our hands upon him. What does that mean? Paul said to Timothy, "Don't neglect the gift that is in thee which was given you when they laid their hands on you." In many cases in the Bible they laid their hands on people. Why? God wants to use hands, and the Spirit of God Himself can bless hands.

I know there have been times when the power of God was on me and when I laid my hand on the shoulder or arm of a poor sinner, immediately he would tremble and break down and weep with conviction. The Lord can use your hands. If He wants my hands, He can have my hands. I give them to the Lord Jesus this day.

"Take my hands and let them be Consecrated, Lord, to Thee."

Give Him your hands this morning to work for Him. We need people who will say, "My hands belong to Jesus Christ." Lots of people say that about one dime out of one dollar. But why not give your body and all its members?

Not only hands, but your eyes. Job said in the midst of sorrow and trouble, "I made a covenant with mine eyes; why then should I think upon a maid?" (Job 31:1). I do not know all of the hidden, unwritten context. It may be that Job, as a man with authority like a king, with many slaves around about him over whom he had power of life and death—it may be that Job was tempted in a particular way about a maid. But Job said, "I made a covenant with mine eyes; why then should I think upon a maid?" I think perhaps Job means by this the temptation men have to face in their minds about a lovely woman, to imagine a woman's body and beauty. "But I made a covenant. I won't look at things that tempt me to do wrong," and so he said, "I made a covenant with mine eyes." In a time of great distress and temptation Job remembered God and made a covenant with Him about what he would look on.

Some people say that they do not see any harm in going to picture shows, but the first thing about that statement is that it is not sincere, not frank. No intelligent being who considers this honestly will say that there is no harm in picture shows. If you have ever been to many shows and still say that there is no harm in them, you are not very smart. If you have two good eyes you can see plenty wrong.

Oh, this holy day, this new day, this day of dedication, this day of consecration—oh, why don't you on this day make a covenant with God about your eyes, that you will only look at things that will honor Jesus Christ? Why don't you covenant with God that you will not look at a magazine, a picture, people, books, shows, etc.—things that dishonor God? Why don't you say, "My eyes belong to Him. I give them to Him today"? If you will do that, you will not have any trouble about shows. You will sure settle that business.

I have made up my mind to a new dedication not only for myself but for this entire church. Ordinarily churches grow more worldly as they become prosperous, as they get into a nicer building. It is nearly always true that such churches grow a little more worldly minded. What once they would not put up with, now they will cut the corners. They need more income, they have more bills to pay, etc. But I have made up my mind. Now I believe under God we ought to draw straighter lines than we ever have. Our Sunday school teachers cannot teach and attend movies. And if that is too great a temptation to you, I would get out now. If the lives of precious boys and girls are not more important to you than the dirty picture show, you are not fit to be a Sunday school teacher in our Sunday school.

We ought to not only say no *teacher* can smoke or attend picture shows or play bridge, but I long for the time to come when this church, like the great Moody Church in Chicago and some other fundamental churches around the world, will ask EVERYBODY who joins this church to make up their minds whether they will be for God or the Devil on the matter of the theater. Why not ask people if they will be out and out or not? Why have just another church? Dallas is full of churches. There are a lot of churches where you would never be embarrassed about attending picture shows, where you would not be embarrassed to step inside the church and take a last puff at your cigarette and throw the butt outside on the church steps. The preacher would say nothing about it. You can belong to a lot of churches and still be active in lodge work. You can dance and they think there is no special harm. You can have bridge parties and never be especially criticized for it.

If you want that kind of church, get in that kind! Dallas has plenty of that kind of churches. I think our church should set a higher standard. Let us pray and teach it. Let us have a church of people whose bodies are surrendered to Jesus Christ, who look at the things a Christian ought to look at, who live the way Christians should live. We have people who believe the Bible. Why don't you say like Job, "I will make a covenant with mine eyes: I will look at the things that will honor God, that a Christian has a right to look at, and nothing else"?

You ought to give God your eyes this morning. Would you be willing to meet in judgment everything you read? You say, "I don't see any harm in the books I read." But is it idle reading? Is it profitless? If so, I would make a covenant that what I read will be for good, and for God. Why not say to God that you will only use your eyes to glorify Him?

Yield your members, your hands, your eyes, and surely your tongue. David prayed, "Set a watch, O Lord, before my mouth;

keep the door of my lips" (Ps. 141:3). David said, "Lord, send a corporal's guard of angels to watch my tongue. Set a watch." David said that he needed a bunch of angels like guards in time of war. "You will have to send angels to watch my tongue and mouth," David said.

In James the 3rd chapter, we are told that out of the same fountain, a Christian's mouth, sometimes comes both sweet water and bitter. And we are told, "Brethren, these things ought not so to be." The same kind of plant brings forth briars and thistles. Why should not Christians have a tongue that is given over to the Lord?

Now why don't you vow that today you will give your mouth to God? I am ashamed today that before our visitors, twice or three times we had to announce and beg for you to come to the choir. If I were you, I would give my voice to the Lord. God gave you a tongue, a voice; use it for Him. Those who can sing should say, "I present my body a living sacrifice." Then we would not have to corkscrew it out of you to get you to sing. Instead of that, people ought to say, "I will give myself to God. I want my tongue to glorify Him, my voice to please Him. I will give myself to witness for Him. I will please God."

There are a lot of church organizations, most of them to try to enlist people in getting out the Gospel. It ought to be so a Christian would settle that thing back in his own heart with God. He ought to say, "I belong to Him—my mouth, my tongue."

I say, God can use your hands, but of all the instruments of the human body, the Holy Spirit uses the voice more than anything else. In the New Testament anybody filled with the Holy Spirit spoke for God. Acts 1:8 says, "But ye shall receive power, after that the Holy Ghost is come upon you: And *ye shall be witnesses unto me* both in Jerusalem, and in all Judaea, and in Samaria, and unto the uttermost part of the earth."

Oh, the power of the Holy Spirit loves to anoint a human voice, a mouth and tongue and throat and lips that speak for God. How beautiful in God's sight!

**"Take my voice and let me sing,
Always, only for my king."**

Don't you want to say today, "I will give my voice for God. I will ever   try to say things that would please Him. I will try to daily use my voice for Jesus. I present my body a living sacrifice"?

And now your feet. Did you know it is hard to get people to do the kind of work that uses the feet for Jesus Christ? Soul winning is largely a matter of the feet. Psalm 126:6 says, "He that *goeth forth* and weepeth, bearing precious seed, shall doubtless come again with rejoicing, bringing his sheaves with him."

And Romans 10:15 says, "How beautiful are the feet of them that preach the gospel of peace, and bring glad tidings of good things!"

And Ephesians 6:15 says, "And your feet shod with the preparation of the gospel of peace."

Wouldn't you like for the Lord to have your feet? Wouldn't you like to go where He wants you to go? After all, that is the answer of every call of God, "I will go."

"Here am I: send me." I will *go* is the idea. Jesus said, "Go ye into all the world, and preach the gospel." So God wants your feet.

III. God Wants Your Talents

I have said that God wants your body, your members; and third, God wants your talents. This is a holy day. I hope the Lord will take this building and see fit to use it. I hope He will keep it as a holy place, and that no men will spit on the floors and no child will mark on the walls. I want it to be a holy place where God deigns to dwell and bless.

Wouldn't you like to give Him not only the building but your talents?

I think God has touched me in some ways. I know I am ordinary, weaker than anybody knows. I remember when God called me to preach, I mourned and mourned about it. I heard Dr. Truett, and I said, "I am not fit to be a preacher. It takes a marvelous voice which I don't have." I felt the grace and majesty of preaching with dramatic power, as Dr. Truett does so grandly. I said, "I can't Lord. There are lots of things I don't have."

My friends, I would tell God today to use what I do have.

God wants Sam Ray. God has given him unusual opportunities and abilities, and that business of an object lesson or art talk, drawing before you while you speak, is a gift of God. And that isn't the only gift he has. God has laid His hand on young people. I want to say to young people, you will sin against God if you don't say to Him, "What I have, you can have it; I lay it on the altar."

I never will forget the time when I, a twenty-year-old lad, went out past the woodpile and out through the pea patch and through a wire fence and under a chapparel bush in West Texas and got down on my face and said, "Lord, I don't have any money to go to school. I only have nine dollars and some cents and I can't sell my horse and can't borrow the money and Dad doesn't have any money to loan me. But I am giving to You everything I have. I want You to use me. I will tithe every penny that comes to me (and I have). Lord, if You will let me preach, I will preach. If You want me to be a singer, I will do that. What You want me to do, I give myself to You to use." I prayed and had a holy covenant with God.

I packed my trunk and saddled my horse and rode off for Decatur College. I told my dad I would send word where to send my trunk, when I had arrived.

I would say, "Lord, You can have my talents and what I have. It will take money, it will take training and hard work and long hours. It will cost money and time and giving up pleasures, but if You want me to sing, I give You my voice, I give You my talents today."

This business of a teacher teaching with no training and teaching preparation—God forgive us! It is a shabby way to do the God who loves you and the Saviour who died for you. Your talents belong to God. Give your talents to God to develop, use—turn it over to Him. Give it to God today.

IV. God Wants Your Heart

Another word and I close. The time is gone. God wants your heart. I prayed that today some soul would be saved. Unless we have the fire of God, people will not be saved. I wonder who will today give God what you have?

My friends, first of all He wants your heart. Someone today who is not a Christian ought to give God what you have.

Is there someone here today who is not a Christian? Why don't you give God what you have? Give Him your heart. Don't you want to do that?

We hired a couple of colored boys to help carry benches and pianos last night. When they were through, I gave them a check and asked each, "Are you a Christian?" One said, "No." The other said, "I'se been a member of the church for eight years, and I sure is saved."

To the non-Christian I said, "And you are not a Christian? Is your mother a Christian?"

"My mother is dead."

"Is your father a Christian?"

"My father is dead, too."

"Don't you want to be a Christian? You would have to mean business with God and give Him your heart and trust Him," I said. "Suppose we go out to a quiet place and get down on our knees and have prayer."

We went out that door and around to that little closet there and got down on our knees last night about ten o'clock, and that colored boy bowed his head; the other boy prayed and I prayed and this boy prayed, "I want the Lord to forgive me and save me right now." And he took my hand on it and went away. I trust he was saved—I know he was if he trusted Christ.

If you haven't said to Jesus Christ, "Take my heart's love and devotion, all I am and hope to be, and make me what You want me to be," then you are an ungodly sinner.

Don't you want today to give the Lord your life and trust Him as your Saviour? Don't you want to say, "Yes, today I will let God take my heart's devotion, my love, and all I am, and make me His today"? And this morning you can go home happy, and there will be a dedication, not only of a church house but of a heart and mind and soul for God.

Let us bow our heads for a moment.

Our Father, we thank Thee for this good day, for the attendance and for Thy presence and for Thy Word. We rejoice and praise Thy name. We pray we may wholeheartedly give Thee our hearts and lives today. For Jesus' sake. Amen.

(Invitation followed. Scores came forward for rededication: some confessing and forsaking picture show attendance, two or three volunteering to teach in Sunday school, a young preacher came to confess his backsliding. Five came for membership. One other came to openly confess Christ as Saviour.)

9—Seven Fundamentals of Christian Faith

(Preached June 12, 1938, in Dallas, Texas. Stenographically reported.)

If ye believe not that I am he, ye shall die in your sins. —John 8:24.

If there come any unto you, and bring not this doctrine, receive him not into your house, neither bid him God speed; For he that biddeth him God speed is partaker of his evil deeds. —II John 10,11.

But though we, or an angel from heaven, preach any other gospel unto you than that which we have preached unto you, let him be accursed. —Gal. 1:8.

I thought nothing would be more fitting in this first Sunday night service of the Bible School than my laying out the great fundamentals of the Christian faith. What does it mean to be a fundamentalist? Is it a new denomination? Is that a new idea somebody started? As I rode to Fort Worth the other day with a Dallas businessman from whom we bought the material for the ceiling of our auditorium, I told him what I would preach about, what it meant to be a fundamentalist.

He said, "That is nothing new. That is what I was taught by my mother when I was but a child."

I am not bringing anything new. The things I am talking about are the bedrock principles of the Christian faith. There are some things on which men cannot differ and stay with Christianity. There is a dividing line. On one side are believers; on the other side are infidels, pagans and heathens. Some facts, some doctrines, some teachings are so essential that without them a man cannot be a Christian.

I come to speak on this because the Bible so clearly teaches that I ought to, because some men, even in pulpits, deny the very fundamentals of the faith, because the Scripture foretold there would come people denying even the Lord that bought them. There are certain doctrines that cannot be trifled with.

There are some things I may see one way and you may see another way, but I can still be your brother. There are some matters about which people can differ and yet be Christians and have the finest Christian fellowship. Other matters are so important that I will not shake a man's hand as a Christian if he does not agree to them. They are so important that I will not invite a man to eat dinner with me, I will not say, "God speed you," if he does not agree on some things. The Bible plainly forbids it. Some doctrines are so important that I will not call a man brother, I will not call a man a Christian unless he agrees to them.

What are those differences? Somebody says, "All the doctrines of the Bible are important." I grant that everything the Bible says is important, but not all things are as important as some others. The Bible makes a clear distinction that a gnat is not as important as a camel. Some people gag at a gnat and swallow a camel. So then, according to the Bible, a camel is bigger than a gnat.

The Jewish Pharisees, the Saviour said, tithe mint, anise and cummin but have omitted the weightier matters of the law.—judgment, mercy and faith. According to Christ, therefore, tithing mint, anise and cummin is not as weighty a matter as judgment, mercy and faith. Isn't that so? There is a difference in the relative importance of some doctrines.

And certain fundamentals must be counted essential. I want you to see what it is to be a fundamentalist. Some people have the idea that to be a fundamentalist means to be a follower of one man, and he has so led some men to believe that. But one man is an incident. The truth of the matter is, many, many people who themselves are fundamentally sound would not follow a man they could not trust, in whose life they could find no harmony with Christ, and whose word could not be believed.

Let me make it clear once and for all that to be a fundamentalist is not to be a member of any denomination, nor a part of any man-made movement. It is not to be a member of a new denomination nor of an old denomination. One may be in a denomination and be a fundamentalist, or one may be out of a denomination and be a fundamentalist. Or one may be in a denomination and not be a fundamentalist, or one may be one of these gun-toting, law-suiting, slandering, Hell-raising, self-exalting fundamentalists by name and not be a fundamentalist in his heart at all. It is not a question of having your name on a certain kind of church book or having the approval of a certain organization to be a fundamentalist.

What I wish to say is that being true to the Bible does not mean following one man any more than being saved means following a man. Being true to the Bible as a fundamentalist does not mean to be a member of a certain church or to meet their requirements any more than being saved means being a member of a certain church.

There are certain fundamentals of the faith which people must hold to if they are to be true Christians. I will bring them to mind tonight.

Don't misunderstand me. For instance, about baptism. I believe baptism is important. I was baptized, and I teach others to be baptized. I do it by the command of Jesus Christ. But baptism is not as important as getting saved. Water is not as important as blood. Local congregations are not as important as the whole body of the saved, the bride of Christ.

I say there is a difference in importance. I can call a man brother who has been sprinkled, but I cannot call a man brother who does not believe in the deity of Christ, the virgin birth, the blood atonement, the inspiration of the Scriptures, direct creation, and Heaven and Hell. There are some essentials that a man must believe in if he is to be a fundamentalist, or if he is to be a true Christian.

Some twenty-odd years ago, a group of great men who were against modernism and against evolution and against worldliness in churches, got together and organized what has become known as the World's Christian Fundamentals Association. The leading spirit was Dr. W. B. Riley. Others were Dr. R. A. Torrey, Dr. William Pettingill, Dr. P. W. Philpott, I believe, and Dr. J. Frank Norris was not one of them. They organized the World's Christian Fundamentals Association. Dr. Riley was a Baptist. His church was in the Northern Baptist Convention. Dr. Torrey was an independent, though known as a Congregationalist. Others of these men were Presbyterians and Plymouth Brethren, I believe. Dr. W. B. Riley started a magazine called *The Christian Fundamentalist.* Later on the name was taken by others and used, and Dr. Riley finally discontinued publishing it. William Jennings Bryan was an active leader in the World's Christian Fundamentals Association. *The Sunday School Times,* which was one of the greatest Christian magazines in America, with a circulation of over 100,000 weekly, sponsored the movement. The *Moody Monthly, King's Business,* and a great group of Christian magazines and papers sponsored the Christian Fundamentals movement. They are fundamental in the same sense that I call myself a fundamentalist. They believe exactly what I believe about the blood of Christ, the atonement of Christ, the deity of Christ, about the new birth, about sin, about Heaven and Hell, and about the second coming of Christ.

The Moody Bible Institute was behind that movement. The Los Angeles Bible Institute was behind it. The National Bible Institute in New York City, the Philadelphia School of the Bible and other great seminaries, colleges and Bible institutes were behind it. The World's Christian Fundamentals Association was made up of people in various denominations. Some were Methodists, like Dr. B. H. Shadduck of Ohio. Some were Baptists, some were Presbyterians, as was Dr. Gresham Machen, for instance. Some were Congregationalists. Dr. James M. Gray was nominally an Episcopalian.

SOME ABSOLUTE ESSENTIALS NAMED

There are certain fundamentals without which one cannot be a Christian. One must believe there is a God. He must believe the Bible is the infallible Word of God. He must believe in the fact of sin. He must believe that man is fallen and a sinner, and must be born again. He must believe that salvation is by the blood of Christ. He must believe in the bodily resurrection of Jesus from the dead. He must believe in the virgin birth of Christ, the miracles of Christ. He must believe in a Hell for Christ-rejecting sinners.

Great groups of people in the churches and out of the churches, in all denominations and in no denominations, hold those fundamentals.

To be a fundamentalist does not mean to follow one man. It does not mean to be in one denomination. It means to believe certain things about the Bible, about God, about Christ, about man, about sin, about Heaven and Hell and salvation by the blood.

I am anxious that all minds be clear on that matter since it is essential and fundamental, because it is so important.

The Scripture I am going to read to you is II John, verses 7 to 11:

> *For many deceivers are entered into the world, who confess not that Jesus Christ is come in the flesh. This is a deceiver and an antichrist. Look to yourselves, that we lose not those things which we have wrought, but that we receive a full reward. . . .*

Now somebody says it doesn't matter what you believe, it is the way you live. That isn't so. Satan never told a bigger lie. You can live the best you know how, but if you do not believe Jesus Christ is the Son of God, you will die in your sins. If you do not trust Him to be your Saviour, you will go to Hell, no matter how you live. People are not saved by the way they live. They are saved by a certain attitude toward Jesus Christ, and—

> *Whosoever transgresseth, and abideth not in the doctrine of Christ, hath not God. He that abideth in the doctrine of Christ, he hath both the Father and the Son. If there come any unto you, and bring not this doctrine, receive him not into your house, neither bid him God*

speed: For he that biddeth him God speed is partaker of his evil deeds.

Now that Scripture says that there is a certain doctrine so important that if a man does not have the proper attitude toward that doctrine, if he does not abide in that doctrine about Christ, he does not have God, and you are not to take him home to eat at your table and you are not to have him sleep in your bed. You are not even to say, "God speed you." If you do, you are a partaker of his evil deeds.

That means there are some men whom I must not, I will not, invite to preach in this pulpit. I will invite men who do not call themselves by the same name as I do. I will invite men who do not have the same attitude on some minor matter—important matters but not the most important. But I will not invite anybody to come to this pulpit who doesn't believe certain doctrines, that Jesus is the very Son of God, that He was born of a virgin, that He died for our sins, that He arose again the third day, that He ascended to Heaven and is coming again, that sinners must meet Him in peace under the blood or in wrath and judgment if they reject Him.

I will have nobody in my pulpit, I will have nobody as a guest in my home, I will approve of no work of schools and hospitals if anybody in them denies those fundamentals of the faith. I want you to know what I mean by being a fundamentalist.

Let's read another Scripture. This is so important that Paul said in I Corinthians, the 15th chapter:

Moreover, brethren, I declare unto you the gospel which I preached unto you, which also ye have received, and wherein ye stand; By which also ye are saved. . . .

And this is it:

. . . how that Christ died for our sins according to the scriptures; And that he was buried, and that he rose again the third day according to the scriptures.

Now notice. You were saved by a certain Gospel. Some people believe a man may be saved any way. One cannot be saved *any* way. There is only *one* way. The Gospel is the power of God unto salvation. Nothing else is the power of God unto salvation.

Masonry never won a soul no matter how moral. Masonry might get people to quit drinking whiskey and be true to their marriage vows and be kind to their neighbors, but Masonry has nothing that will save a soul. It takes the Gospel of Jesus Christ to save a sinner.

Some people say it doesn't matter what you believe. Oh, yes it does matter. If you don't believe the Gospel you are going to Hell. If you do not teach people the Gospel, you will never get anybody saved. God's way is still the Gospel, how Christ died for our sins according to the Scriptures, that He was buried, that He arose again the third day according to the Scriptures. The Gospel as laid out in the Scripture must be believed or you cannot be a Christian. There is no such thing as being a Christian without accepting certain Gospel doctrines as facts.

A lot of people do not like doctrine. But if you do not hold to certain doctrines, you will never be saved. Some doctrines are essential. Some are not. But the doctrines about Christ's death, His resurrection, His atonement, are essential doctrines without which men cannot be Christians.

Any preacher who stands in anybody's pulpit anywhere who does not believe it all, does not believe that Christ was born of a virgin, who says it does not matter, and perhaps he does not believe in the miracles of the Bible, doesn't believe Christ lived a sinless life, doesn't believe that He died in my place and for my sins and paid my debt and redeemed me to God—if a man does not believe He died as my Substitute and for me, that man is not a Christian. If he stands in a pulpit to preach, he is a lying hypocrite who ought to be scorned and thrown from the pulpit as what he is, an infidel. And you ought never hear a man who claims to preach if he does not believe those essential, fundamental doctrines about the death of Christ for sinners, His deity and His blood atonement.

Paul said in Galatians 1:8,9:

> *But though we, or an angel from heaven, preach any other gospel unto you than that which we have preached unto you, let him be accursed. As we said before, so say I*

now again, If any man preach any other gospel unto you than that ye have received, let him be accursed.

There is one Gospel, one doctrine by which men can be saved, and it is based on a certain attitude toward Jesus Christ. You do not have to know all about these Bible doctrines and have a theological training in them, nor do you have to understand all the Bible; but unless you accept Jesus not as a man but as God-man, not as a good prophet, but as the very Son of God, our Substitute, not just one who will show us how to live but One who died in my place—if you do not accept Christ like that, you are doomed and damned, eternally lost!

A Christian must believe certain fundamentals of the Gospel. I want you to get them. I want you to know what I mean when I say I am a fundamentalist. I want you to know what God says a man must believe to be saved.

To believe certain facts is not enough. To say I believe the doctrine is not enough. Jesus said to the Pharisees, "If ye believe not that I am he, ye shall die in your sins." But even those who believed Jesus was the Son of God were not saved without personal surrender and dependence on Christ.

But there is no use to talk about trusting Christ as your Saviour unless you trust Him as the virgin-born, sinless-living, bodily-resurrected Saviour. Don't trust any man as saviour who is just a man!

So you see there are some fundamentals which are so important that you are not to receive anybody into your house or bid him God speed unless he accepts these fundamental doctrines of Jesus Christ. There are some so essential that we ought to be narrow, as narrow as the Gospel of Jesus Christ. On the matter of the blood, on the matter of the inspiration of the Bible, we must be narrow.

We ought not be easy-going and "broad-minded" about whether the Bible is so or not. We ought not be "tolerant" about whether there is a Hell or not. If there is no Hell, then there is no such thing as salvation, there is nothing to be saved from, Christ didn't save anybody, and the Bible is a lie, and there is nothing to Christianity—if there is not a Hell.

There are some things on which I could disagree with a man and still call him my brother. But I cannot call any man brother who does not believe certain fundamentals. He is not my brother, he is not a Christian and cannot be classed as a Christian by thinking people who believe the Bible.

I. A Personal, Prayer-Answering God

What are these essentials? Let me name some things that are so essential that there can be no room for disagreement. When talking about God, there may be some things you think about God that I do not agree to. But if you are a Christian, you must believe that there is a God. Hebrews 11:6 says:

> *He that cometh to God must believe that he is, and that he is a rewarder of them that diligently seek him.*

In that verse is the Bible doctrine of God. One must believe there is a God if he is ever to be saved. If you come to God, you must believe that He is.

Note the teaching of this verse. First, you must believe that there is a God, a personal God. Second, you must believe that He may be reached by prayer. The third thing is that God reaches down to man in answer to prayer. Isn't that right? There is a God. "He that cometh to God must believe that he is, and that he is a rewarder of them that diligently seek him." People can reach Him by prayer, and God answers prayer.

That doctrine of God—what do you mean? I mean this: If you believe there is a God, then in heart you believe in miracles. Dr. Charles Blanchard, one-time president of Wheaton College, said, "If there is a God, He would have to act like a God." To say that God cannot work miracles is the same as saying there is no God. If there is a God, He can work miracles.

Man says, "Yes, I believe there is a God; but I believe nature has inherent forces, that by inherent forces in nature evolution takes place, and life came into being. Some one-celled animal grew on up until after awhile it got to be a many-celled animal, then it got to be a little floating piece of protoplasm. Then it got an eye-spot, then finally got to have legs and a tail, maybe. Then it was a fish and then a turtle, and on it developed—into a land animal and after awhile into a monkey and then a jackass and then an evolution-teaching professor!"

That is the silly theory of those who do not believe in a personal, prayer-hearing, prayer-answering God, the God of miracles revealed in the Bible. If evolution is a fact, then there is no God, that is, no God like the Bible talks about.

There is a God, there is a Person who answers prayer, and that isn't nature. Evolution does not answer prayer. Nature does not answer prayer. "He that cometh to God must believe that he is." He is in the sense that He lives as a person—not that He just exists as an influence. He lives. There is a God who made us, a God who loves us and hears us and answers us; there is that kind of a God, and one cannot be a Christian without believing that.

II. A Divinely Inspired, Infallible Bible

The next essential doctrine is: There is a Bible. That Bible is the revelation from God. It does not just contain the Word of God, it *is* the Word of God. What do I mean? I mean what the Scripture says: "All scripture is given by inspiration of God." That is what the Scripture claims about itself. Holy men of God wrote down what God told them, 'not in the words which man's wisdom teacheth, but which the Holy Ghost teacheth" (I Cor. 2:13). The Scripture tells us God said to Isaiah, "I have put my words in thy mouth" (Isa. 51:16), and practically the same words were said about Jeremiah. God told Moses to write all the words of the Lord in a book. "And Moses wrote all the words of the Lord" (Exod. 24:4). The same thing happened with Jeremiah. God gave the very words. The thoughts were God's thoughts, but the words were God's words, too, a revelation from God as literally as I dictate letters to a stenographer. I see that it is what I meant and what I said when I dictate. God is more particular than I am, and I am pretty particular.

God gave the very words of the Bible in the original manuscripts. The Bible is a revelation from God. This Word of God is true about science, it is true about history, it is infallible, with no mistakes. There are mistakes sometimes in men's translations of the Bible, and mistakes sometimes as men copy the Bible, but as God gave the Scriptures, this infallible revelation from God is perfect, the Word of God, and it will live forever.

The 19th Psalm tells about nature:

The heavens declare the glory of God; and the firmament sheweth his handywork. Day unto day uttereth speech, and night unto night sheweth knowledge. There is no speech nor language, where their voice is not heard. . . .

But that Scripture continues in verse 7:

The law of the Lord is perfect, converting the soul.

That is something nature never did do. Many a man with a poetic soul has stood sometimes by the seashore with a sense of awe as he sees the grandeur of the mountainous waves. Every man with any sense has sometimes, I suppose, looked out at the stars at night and been overwhelmed with the sense of God.

One evening when I was a boy growing into my teens, I went out into the stack lot and climbed up on a great stack of feed, and far into the night I lay out there and looked up into the stars. My soul was thrilled: I knew there was a God. I know it now. There must be! Nature claims there is a God. But notice this: Nature never saved anybody. Looking at the stars never saved anybody.

I preached the funeral sermon of a man not long ago who had just gone to Heaven. I had been with him before he died, and he told how he was converted. He told how when he was a young man one night a group of children were playing around the door. He heard one little girl say, "Oh, if the wrong side of Heaven is so pretty, don't you know the right side must be beautiful!" And that little girl's words about Heaven went like an arrow to his heart. When he came to himself he was away down in a lane by himself looking up at God's Heaven. But he was not converted until he later heard the Gospel of the crucified Saviour and the blood shed for sinners, and then he was saved!

The law of the Lord is perfect, converting the soul!

Nature tells about God, but nature has never saved a soul. Nature is under a curse. There is nothing perfect in nature. It brings forth thorns and cockleburs and mosquitoes. But the Word of God is perfect, converting the soul. The Word of God, the unchanging, eternal, infallible Word of God, with no mistakes, no errors, is true.

It is true about science. Up and down the country I have laid down the challenge. I am not afraid to face any college professor to show one place where this Bible is scientifically wrong. It is not. Nobody can point it out. I dare any history professor to show where the Bible is incorrect historically. You may put it down that the Bible is true in every detail. It is the very Word of God. Without requiring a knowledge of all the Bible doctrine of inspiration, one must believe the Bible is the Word of God to be saved.

If a man does not believe the Bible, he will not believe what the Bible says about God, about Christ, about Heaven, about Hell, and about salvation.

That is one of the essentials, then, an attitude of faith toward the Bible.

III. Man, a Fallen Creature, a Sinner

Another essential is the Bible doctrine about man. There are two, and only two, principal theories about man. One theory is that man is pretty good. That theory is that man may make mistakes, but that essentially men are good. That kind of doctrine talks about the Fatherhood of God and the brotherhood of man. It says, "That is all right. You are a child of God, and those little slips don't matter so much. You are still a pretty good fellow." That doctrine pats man on the back and says, "You are all right. All you need is to join the church. You are all right because you are a member of a lodge and live a good life."

That is the Devil's doctrine about man. The Devil said to Eve, "When you eat of that fruit you will be wise. You will be like God to know good from evil!" On that doctrine of the Devil about man's goodness we honor ourselves, brag on our goodness, make excuses for our wickedness, and do not repent.

The other doctrine is the Bible doctrine about man. It doesn't flatter man, to be sure. The Bible tells of our ancestry, but it doesn't say man came from apes and monkeys. Instead, the Bible says God made man of the dust of the ground and breathed into his nostrils the breath of life and man became a living soul. The Bible says, "So God created man in his own image, in the image of God created he him; male and female created he them." The Bible says man was made in the image of God.

Man is not a beast. He is not an animal. He didn't come from monkeys or other animals. Man walks upright to be nearer Heaven. His conscience came from God. Man has an immortal soul that will spend an eternity in Heaven or Hell. Man was made in the image of God, the Bible says.

Another thing is that man is a fallen creature. Did I say in the image of God? But man is so marred! Did I say you were made in the image of God? Yes, but how far we have fallen!

Sometimes we get dolls for our children, and it isn't long until the doll doesn't look the same. You don't know what an expert I have become. I know how to put arms and legs back on dolls. The children think Daddy can fix anything. I want to postpone just as long as possible the time when they learn I can't fix everything brought to me. But I get a strong rubber band and fish with a hairpin and hook on the legs and arms. It isn't very long until the little girls push the doll's teeth out; and if they have moveable eyes that go to sleep, after awhile the eyes come out; and if they have hair, the little girls all like to wash the baby's hair, and the top of the head comes off! I know, I am an expert on dolls! If you had reared as many girls as I am rearing, you would understand about that! It isn't long until the doll is such a poor, abused thing, not the lovely baby it once was!

And I look in your faces tonight and I see the marks of sin. We have fallen so far, so far! These men and women who were made in the image of God, why do we have weak eyes, and why do our teeth come out, and why do we get baldheaded? Why do we lose our temper? Why all the marks of sin in our face? And why the disease in our body?

Man is a fallen creature. And I read in the Bible here an explanation of it. "For all have sinned, and come short of the glory of God." He said, "All," "*All! All! All!*" God help us!

And we who are saved, too. All have sinned and come short of the glory of God. And the Bible says sin demands the wages of sin which is death. It says, "the way of transgressors is hard," and what a man sows he is going to reap, and "the soul that sins shall die." Before we get through the Bible we have the race cursed, under sin, lost, away from God, aliens and strangers!

After Adam sinned in the Garden of Eden, he hid himself from God. When God called, "Adam, Adam, where art thou?" Adam said, "I hid myself because I had sinned."

My friends, man is a fallen creature, a doomed creature, a sinning creature. You needn't talk to me about people being essentially good. Maybe they are in Houston, but they are not in Dallas. Maybe they are in your family, but they are not in mine. Men are not good! Men are essentially sinners! In the heart of all of us is sin. We are sinners, sinners! sinners! That isn't flattering, but that is what the Bible says about us. We are sinners!

And now another thing. Because men are made in the image of God, therefore men have souls, immortal souls. Men, I say, have sinned, and men are lost, and men are condemned! The Bible talks about the goodness of God and the sin of man. I wish I could go through the Bible with you on this question. The longer I went, the more we would hear about sin, and sin and sin and the sinner—until down in a horrible bottomless pit is man! Man's sins have made him a million miles away from a just and holy God and there is a gulf between God and man and sinful man cannot face God.

Yet man must meet God. He is afraid and doomed and righteously damned because of his sin. And I say the God of the Bible and the race of men the Bible tells about are an ocean apart. Unless someone is revealed in the Bible that can bring a just and holy God and sinning man together, man is forever lost!

IV. Jesus the Virgin-Born, Miracle-Working, Bodily-Resurrected Son of God in Flesh

And now we come to another doctrine. That is the Bible doctrine of Christ. That is an essential doctrine, a fundamental doctrine. Without this Bible doctrine one cannot be a Christian. Unless one takes the Bible attitude toward the fact of God, the Bible, the deity of Christ, the fact of sin, the blood atonement, regeneration, and Heaven and Hell—those seven things—one is not a Christian; he is a heathen or a pagan. One is not a believer; he is an infidel.

I can't go into all of the Bible doctrine of Christ. What about Jesus? This same Jesus was in the beginning with God. This Baby brought from the womb of a virgin was the Creator of Heaven and earth. Turn back to Isaiah and let the prophet of God answer:

> *For unto us a child is born, unto us a son is given: and the government shall be upon his shoulder: and his name shall be called Wonderful, Counsellor, The mighty God. . . .*

Who is this little Child born?

> *. . . The mighty God, The everlasting Father, The Prince of Peace.*—Isa. 9:6.

He is not just a man but God in human flesh who nursed at a woman's breast, a defenseless Baby. God emptied Himself of His glory and came in the likeness of sinful flesh. Jesus Christ was no ordinary man. No wonder those who heard Him speak said, "Never man spake like this man" (John 7:46). No wonder doubting Thomas said, when asked to put his hand in the pierced side and to put his finger in the nailprints, "My Lord and my God!"—not just Rabbi nor good Master nor Teacher, but, "My Lord and my God!"

Jesus Christ is God in the flesh. Jesus Christ is God by whom the Scripture says the Father made the world and without Him was not anything made that was made. Jesus is God! That involves certain things. If Jesus is God, He is different from any other man. If Jesus is God, as we are not God, there is something between us and Jesus Christ, something altogether different. Jesus Christ was born in this world, but the Scripture said He is the only begotten of the Father. Nobody else was ever born like Jesus. He must have been born differently, and He was. How did it happen?

The angel came to Mary and said: "Fear not, Mary: for thou hast found favour with God. And, behold, thou shalt conceive in thy womb, and bring forth a son, and shalt call his name JESUS. He shall be great, and shall be called the Son of the Highest: and the Lord God shall give unto him the throne of his father David: And he shall reign over the house of Jacob for ever; and of his kingdom there shall be no end."

And Mary said—I say it reverently—"How can I, a virgin girl, have a baby?"

And the angel answered back: "The Holy Ghost shall come upon thee, and the power of the Highest shall overshadow thee: therefore also that holy thing which shall be born of thee shall be called the Son of God."

Oh, Jesus was born with no human father. Jesus was born when conceived by the Spirit of God in the womb of a virgin girl that had never known man after the flesh.

Someone has said, "Well, what does it matter whether Jesus is the Son of God or not?"

He isn't the Saviour if He isn't very God. He isn't God if He wasn't born as He was, if He didn't work miracles, and I can't believe on Him, I can't risk my soul with Him. How could you believe He made the world and then not believe Christ is more than a man? Unless you accept the miracles of the Bible you are not a Christian. The virgin birth is essential to the deity of Christ.

Some may argue, "I believe the body of Jesus rotted away. In some spiritual sense I think He was resurrected." No, if His body didn't come out of Joseph's tomb, then He is not the Son of God. He said, 'There shall no sign be given you but the sign of the Prophet Jonah. As Jonah was three days and three nights in the belly of the whale, so the Son of man will be three days and three nights in the heart of the earth' (Matt. 12:40; 16:4).

Jesus came bodily from the grave or He was not the Son of God. He could not be our Saviour and the Bible is not true and there is no God of the Bible, no hereafter, no Heaven and no Hell, and nothing to Christianity but superstition unless Christ arose bodily from the grave like He said He would. And five hundred witnesses saw Him and handled Him and heard Him and felt of Him after the resurrection (I Cor. 15:6). No, He arose from the dead, thank God! I know it is true! Jesus Christ is the very Son of God!

V. Christ's Blood Atoned for Man

We come to another doctrine that is connected with this. That is the doctrine of the atonement. Righteous Abel set up an altar and brought the firstling of his flocks. God says, "By faith Abel offered unto God a more excellent sacrifice than Cain, by which he obtained witness that he was righteous" (Heb. 11:4).

God told Abraham to take Isaac to the top of Mount Moriah and offer him there for a sacrifice. And then as he was about to offer Isaac, the Lord called to him, "Abraham, Abraham . . . Lay not thine hand upon the lad. . . ." And Abraham turned and saw a ram caught in the thicket and Abraham put the ram on the altar instead of his son.

In the pouring, spouting blood, I see God's picture of atonement for sin. I see the high priest when he takes the mourning dove which pictures the Man of sorrows, the tender, brokenhearted Saviour who would come, and as the blood drips I see God's picture of atoning blood. I see the priest bring two goats before the high priest and I see them lay their hands on the head of one of the goats and confess their sins and the goat is led away out in the mountains bearing away the shame and disgrace of sin. I see them take the other goat and kill it, cut the throat of that animal, and as they dress the body, then blood is poured out at the altar and I see God's picture of atonement for sin.

The Bible has chapter after chapter about blood and sacrifice and altars. Then the Bible says, "Without shedding of blood is no remission" (Heb. 9:22). The Bible says, "The life of the flesh is in the blood" (Lev. 17:11). Oh, my friends, there is no life outside the blood and there is no salvation outside the blood. Men are not saved by being good or by church membership or by baptism.

You say, "Brother Rice, you have to live it." If you could live it, you could have done it without a Saviour. Man isn't saved by man living. Man is saved by Christ dying! Oh, my friends, understand it is *salvation by the blood*, "Not by works of righteousness which we have done, but according to his mercy he saved us, by the washing of regeneration, and renewing of the Holy Ghost" (Titus 3:5).

It is not by man; it is by God. It is not by works lest any man should boast. It is by grace. "For by grace are ye saved through faith; and that not of yourselves: it is the gift of God: Not of works, lest any man should boast" (Eph. 2:8,9). And again the Scripture says in the first text I ever preached on in the Pacific Garden Mission in Chicago, "For the wages of sin is death; but the gift [not the pay, not the reward, not the salary, but the gift] of God is eternal life through Jesus Christ our Lord." That gift is in the Son of God. That gift is in the shed blood. That gift is in Calvary. Hallelujah for the cross!

What can wash away my sin?
Nothing but the blood of Jesus.
What can make me whole again?
Nothing but the blood of Jesus!

Oh, my people, when you talk about your fundamentalism, do you mean some tom-foolery of method, some incidental? Do you mean following some man? Or do you mean your belief in these fundamental doctrines of God's Word? Let's learn the fundamental of all the fundamentals—the blood of Jesus Christ shed for sinners on the cross. That is God's answer to sin. That is God's picture of love. That is God's atonement for sin. The blood of Jesus Christ paid for my sins and "Christ died for our sins according to the scriptures."

Let me change it. He died for *my* sins.

My sins nailed Him to the cross. *My* sins are all paid for. *I* am redeemed under the blood. *My* sins are blotted out. *My* sins are buried in the depth of the sea. *My* sins are carried as far as the east is from the west. *My* sins are paid for, thank God! Oh, what a Saviour!

> **Saved by the blood of the crucified One!**
> **Now ransomed from sin and a new work begun,**
> **Sing praise to the Father and praise to the Son,**
> **Saved by the blood of the crucified One!**

The only way you can be saved is by the blood of Christ who died for our sins. Let no one talk about the good example of Jesus saving sinners. Let no one talk about Jesus being a good man, a good teacher. He is the Son of God who paid for my sins and for the sins of every man, on the cross. "He is the propitiation for our sins: and not for our's only, but also for the sins of the whole world" (I John 2:2). Jesus died and atoned for sin on the cross.

That means this then, and I come to the sixth.

VI. Personal Regeneration: the New Birth by Faith

The sixth one of the great fundamentals is this: To be saved, men must be born again. Jesus said to Nicodemus, "Except a man be born again, he cannot see the kingdom of God."

Nicodemus said, "I am too old. How could I go back into my mother's womb and be born?"

Jesus said, "That new cleansing, that new life I am talking about, unless you have that, you will never get into the kingdom of God."

Nicodemus said, "That sounds fishy to me!"

That is one of God's musts. There are some things you might be able to get by without, but when Jesus said, *"You must,"* that settles it. *"Ye must be born again."*

You must be born again or forever be lost eternally in Hell. You must be born again, you must have a new heart, a changed nature, you must become a child of God or you will go to an eternal torment with your old heart and your old thoughts. Every man needs a new heart, must have a new heart.

God and man and sin and the atonement all go to prove that man needs God and can have Him when he trusts Jesus Christ.

That means salvation by faith. That means trusting Jesus, that is all. That means depending on the shed blood, risking Jesus Christ the Great Physician, the great Lawyer, the Advocate. Risk Jesus Christ the Substitute. Risk Jesus Christ the Intercessor, the best Friend man ever had. Jesus Christ is my Saviour. Jesus Christ died for my sins. He is my Lamb by which God made peace. He is my High Priest, my way to Heaven. Risk Jesus Christ, my God, Jesus Christ, God's revelation of His love. Be saved by the blood!

I ask some man if he has been born again, and he says, "I am a good man." But I ask him, "Are you a Christian?" and he says, "I don't know; I am living the best I know how." "But are you a Christian?" "I am afraid I am not living right."

But that is not the question. Have you been born again? Are you under the blood? Have you been transformed inside? Have you turned to God, and has He made you a new creature? If so, tonight you are a child of God. If you are not sure, you had better find out.

I remember one morning I preached at Fort Worth. We had a great revival in the young people's choir. We didn't get away until about one o'clock. As others came, a young woman came at the invitation and said, "I have had my name on the church book, but I am afraid I have never had it on the Lamb's Book of Life!"

If you haven't been born again, you are lost forever. A woman came one night and looked solemnly and sadly into my face and said, "I have been baptized; now I want to be born again." You had better make sure.

When I was at Decatur, Texas, I remember a scoutmaster got all his boys to come to the revival. One by one they had been saved. I felt strangely impressed one day to ask him if he were a Christian. He was very religious and moral. I looked into the face of this church man and said, "Are you a Christian? Have you ever been born again?" He said, "No, Brother Rice, I never have." He looked like a Christian, he acted like a Christian, but he was not. He then and there trusted Jesus Christ. If you have not been born again, you can be and you ought to be. The way is to trust in the blood of Jesus Christ.

VII.   Eternal Happiness or Punishment;
Heaven and Hell

There are two other things: There is eternal joy or eternal torment. Which will it be—Heaven or Hell? You are going one way. You are not an animal, not a beast. You didn't climb up from apes, you were made in the image of God. You are a fallen creature, sinful, a million miles away from God unless you have been born again. Now it will be Heaven or Hell somewhere. Five minutes after you die where will you be? Five minutes after your property has passed to somebody else—you won't need it—five minutes after your life is gone—life is like a bundle of dry grass, burned up and gone—what will it be then?

Will it be Heaven and the joys of Heaven, greeting the saints of God, looking in the face of Jesus, being introduced to the Heavenly Father? Or will it be crying out, "I am tormented in this flame! Send somebody to cool my tongue with a drop of water!" Which will it be? Heaven or Hell somewhere!

These essentials one must agree on. Oh, not in all details must we agree, but on the facts as taught in the Bible.

My friend, what will you do tonight about it? I have talked long. I have been faithful, I trust. I wonder tonight, where do you stand? Do you believe God is a loving God, a personal God who hears man and answers prayer? Do you believe the Bible is the Word of God? I believe it all, do you? I believe it like my mother believed it.

> I believe that the Bible is true,
>> Though the critics have torn it apart.
> All the warnings and miracles, too,
>> I do wholly accept with my heart.

I do, thank God! I do believe that it is the Word of God. I believe man was made in the image of God. But man sinned and is lost and tainted, doomed without Christ. Do you believe that? Do you believe that man must be born again or be forever lost? Do you believe that Jesus was born of a virgin and lived as no man ever lived, and died for our sins, and arose again and ascended back to Heaven and is coming back some day? Do you believe that? Do you believe that Jesus died for us and that His blood paid for sin? Have you been born again, and are you ready for Heaven? Or are you lost, condemned and headed for Hell?

II. SOUL WINNING

10—"A Sower Went Forth to Sow"

(Sermon preached Sunday morning, October 29, 1939, at Galilean Baptist Tabernacle, Dallas, Texas. Stenographically reported.)

In Matthew, chapter 13, we will read the first nine verses:

> *The same day went Jesus out of the house, and sat by the sea side.*
>
> *And great multitudes were gathered together unto him, so that he went into a ship, and sat; and the whole multitude stood on the shore.*
>
> *And he spake many things unto them in parables, saying, Behold, a sower went forth to sow;*
>
> *And when he sowed, some seeds fell by the way side, and the fowls came and devoured them up:*
>
> *Some fell upon stony places, where they had not much earth: and forthwith they sprung up, because they had no deepness of earth:*
>
> *And when the sun was up, they were scorched; and because they had no root, they withered away.*
>
> *And some fell among thorns; and the thorns sprung up, and choked them:*
>
> *But other fell into good ground, and brought forth fruit, some an hundredfold, some sixtyfold, some thirtyfold.*
>
> *Who hath ears to hear, let him hear.*

May God bless His Word to our hearts.

I. Why Jesus Spoke in Parables

Why did Jesus talk in parables? Evidently there is a reason

why Jesus used parables. There are some people who do not like
fiction. I had a letter the other day from a woman wanting us to
stop THE SWORD because she did not believe in novels, and we
advertised some novels in our paper, Christian stories God had
used to bless hearts. But Jesus used the parable or story
method.

The reason why He did is described here at some length. It is
possible for people to have form without substance.

When you had Mother by your side, you could have told her
you loved her, you could have made her happy then. But when
she has gone to Heaven and left only that cold form of the face
and the poor, thin, blue-veined hands, then you come and weep
over that form when she herself is gone.

We think more of form many times than of the substance. We
do for the form what we would not do for the real thing.

People weep and call on God because they so long to speak in
tongues. Then if they talk in tongues, they say, "I have the
baptism," but these never win souls. Now the baptism of the
Holy Spirit at Pentecost meant that three thousand souls were
saved. I say, our custom is to be satisfied with some outward
appearance but with no substance.

So many people get the letter of the Scripture but never really
understand the Word of God. Jesus said He spoke to the people
in parables, because some harden their hearts, some close their
eyes so they cannot see, and stop their ears so they cannot hear
lest they should understand and be converted and He should
heal them. For that reason Jesus said He spoke the Word in
parables.

It is strange that the Gospel cooperates with your heart. If
your heart is wicked and does not want to know the truth, it is
amazing how much truth can be poured out and not a bit of it
soak in. I am amazed that some people read Scripture after
Scripture and it never gets into their hearts. One man on the
radio this morning quoted part of John 3:16 where it tells of
God's love, but he never got the idea that one may be saved by
grace through faith.

Why is it that people pray to the Virgin Mary to intercede

with Jesus to save them? They have the form but no meaning. They have hardened their hearts lest they be converted and healed. Their ears are stopped lest they really hear, and their eyes are blinded lest they really see. Jesus said that was why He spoke in parables.

In this parable you would expect people to get the beautiful story, but they get only the bare facts and no spiritual blessing. They are drawn no nearer to God and get no real blessing from the Scriptures. So He said, "I speak in parables."

You can get a form, the outer story, in your heart, and those who are spiritually-minded can get the spiritual lesson, too. May God open your heart this morning. May you see how important it is to get the spirit of the Scriptures as well as the letter.

Notice the parable of the sower. There are four different kinds of people who hear the Gospel; and these are illustrated by the four different places that the seed fell when the sower went out to sow.

II. "Some Seed Fell by the Wayside"

"A sower went forth to sow. . . ." That is like a preacher preaching the Gospel, or a missionary teaching the heathen, or a Sunday school teacher Sunday after Sunday teaching a class. That is like a mother drilling into the hearts of her children the Word of God.

"A sower went forth to sow."

My children have better forgetters than rememberers. And I would have to say that their father has a better forgetter than a rememberer, too. Children forget. And the truth is, when I preach to grown people, they forget, too. This is what Jesus said in Matthew 13:3-9:

Behold, a sower went forth to sow;

And when he sowed, some seeds fell by the way side, and the fowls came and devoured them up:

Some fell upon stony places, where they had not much earth: and forthwith they sprung up, because they had no deepness of earth:

And when the sun was up, they were scorched; and

because they had no root, they withered away.

And some fell among thorns; and the thorns sprung up, and choked them:

But other fell into good ground, and brought forth fruit, some an hundredfold, some sixtyfold, some thirtyfold.

Who hath ears to hear, let him hear.

What did that mean? Jesus explained it this way, in verses 18 through 23:

Hear ye therefore the parable of the sower.

When any one heareth the word of the kingdom,. and understandeth it not, then cometh the wicked one, and catcheth away that which was sown in his heart. That is he which received seed by the way side.

But he that received the seed into stony places, the same is he that heareth the word, and anon with joy receiveth it;

Yet hath he not root in himself, but dureth for a while: for when tribulation or persecution ariseth because of the word, by and by he is offended.

He also that received seed among the thorns is he that heareth the word; and the care of this world, and the deceitfulness of riches, choke the word, and he becometh unfruitful.

But he that received seed into the good ground is he that heareth the word, and understandeth it; which also beareth fruit, and bringeth forth, some an hundredfold, some sixty, some thirty.

Every time you go out to sow, you are going to see some seed wasted. Many people are not going to hear the Gospel. But you ought to sow it, and keep on visiting even if you don't get the pupils in your Sunday school class.

We are concerned because we feel that some of our money we put in the offering for the Lord does not amount to much. In this building we will have some seats on many Sundays that are not filled, just as there are seats here not filled now. I will preach to many men who are never converted. We will waste some seed; yet we must sow beside all waters.

Now here is what happens. The Devil sits down alongside every sinner who comes in here to hear the Gospel. He says, "Move over." And the sinner says, "Sure, Buddy. I'm glad to have you." I put the Gospel message or a verse of Scripture in his heart. Or it may be a plaintive melody of an invitation hymn sung by the choir. But the Devil is right there and he gets the sinner to look out of the window, or makes him think, "What about this business deal tomorrow?" Sinner, the Devil will take your mind away, or he will take the Word out of your heart—just like a bird comes and catches away the seed when a farmer sows it.

That is what often happens to seed sown by the wayside. The ground is not broken up and the seed doesn't get down into the dirt. A sower goes out and sows broadcast. When he does, some will fall by the wayside and the birds will come and get the seed.

Some Gospel that is preached never gets any further than that. It is forgotten before men leave the church house. Or warnings of a godly mother are forgotten just as soon as they leave her lips.

One young man, when I was in a revival meeting at Roosevelt, Oklahoma, heard his mother at the dinner table urge him, with prayer and tears, to turn to Christ and be saved. He only laughed about it and in an hour's time was dead—killed by a freight train. Oh, people do not always listen. Some seed is taken away.

Here today there are some unsaved people. Whoever you are, if you are not a Christian, if you are not born again, if you are not a child of God, you must beware to fix your attention on the message, for the Devil is here to see that you do not hear.

Lots of Christians are spoiled by my preaching. I go to great pains to get young people not to talk in the services. You think I am hard-boiled. I am trying to plant the seed so the Devil will not take it away. You think I am a fanatic when I run down the aisles and try to make you hear. I want you to hear! You don't voluntarily hear. I do not often get voluntary attention or intentional attention. It is hard to make up your mind to hard work. People don't have it in their hearts to get everything the preacher says. They do not put the outline down on paper nor put down the verses and look up every Scripture. That takes hard work. Attention is hard to get. Most people don't give it. Preachers must fight to make people give attention. The Devil doesn't want you to hear and be convicted and saved; so people must deal against that.

That is why I do plain, sharp preaching against sin. If I didn't make somebody mad, the Devil would get the seed. If I didn't stick it in so deep, you would soon forget it. But I put a fish-hook on to make it catch. I put cockleburs in to make it stick.

Many, many times I have said things almost insulting in order to plant the seed so deep the Devil will never get it. If need be, I try to plant it where it will fester and make a sore so you will never get away from it. God said a lot of seed would be wasted. The Devil is there beside you to take it away, to take it out of your heart; so beware.

Oh, then how much attention you ought to give to understand it! You ought to be careful to understand and to pay attention. I try to make the sense plain by giving you line upon line, precept upon precept, here a little, there a little, as the Bible says. I ought to come and preach again on the plan of salvation. Nearly everybody here has heard me preach on the dance, but I ought to come again and preach on it. It slipped the other time. Some of you weren't here. Others were here but have forgotten or didn't pay attention. And now something comes up and you find you didn't get the answer to it.

Again and again with children you go over the same lessons, repeatedly. The teacher in the Sunday school class ought to do it again and again, for the Devil is there to steal the seed out of their hearts. Do your best now, for one day you won't have a chance. Be sure they understand. The Devil will keep people from understanding the truth. Some people go to church forty years and still believe they are saved by good works. The Devil is there to see that they don't believe the Bible and don't understand it.

Understanding the Bible is a simple thing for a spiritual

heart. It is simply written. Nothing could be plainer than it is.

Take John 3:16, for instance: "For God so loved the world, that he gave his only begotten Son, that whosoever believeth in him should not perish, but have everlasting life." What could be plainer than that?

Or turn to Acts 16 and there you find: "Believe on the Lord Jesus Christ, and thou shalt be saved." What could be plainer than that? But people don't get it and we must pray for them. The preacher must pray for the hearers to understand the Word that the Devil is trying to keep them from understanding.

Notice another thing. The Devil is right there to distract the mind of those who hear. I felt led to pray a little while ago about the radio program we had early this morning. Many times people hear and are convicted and we must pray that the power of God will continue on the Word that was preached, that the Word may become fruitful.

There are certain details of my preaching in the North that please me greatly. The Northerners are plenty slow, but when they do something, they mean business. If a fellow in some areas says, "Yes, I will come to Christ," that means he will quit his business if it is the wrong kind; it means never smoking another cigarette. If he is going to be a Christian, that means he must act like a Christian. They are slow, but many give direct attention to my preaching that brings real results later.

Again and again I have gotten letters from Mr. Frank Sheriff, Executive Secretary of the Christian Business Men's Committee of Chicago, saying So-and-So has written that he has been saved that night after he went home or meditated on it two weeks later and was saved. A good father showed me a letter. His boy heard me on the radio last February when I preached on Hell. He went home convicted in his heart but didn't surrender to Christ. But in April he was saved. But he didn't settle it when he heard me in February.

So, when you hear the Gospel preached, pray that the Holy Spirit will keep the Devil from stealing away the seed.

We ought to be in prayer warfare, in a battle, begging the Holy Spirit to drive away the birds of inattention and lack of interest that steal the seed of the Gospel and hold on to God in prayer as we sow. If you sowed seed and didn't put out scarecrows, the crows may get your seed. If God doesn't rain upon it, you will have no crops. Pray that God will give the things necessary that the seed may bring forth fruit later.

If you are not saved, then you had better beware. Except you give the more earnest heed, you will let the things I am saying slip and will go away unsaved, because the Devil sits beside you this morning to take every word out of your heart.

III. The Seed in Stony Hearts

Then some seed fell in stony places, the Scripture says, where they had not much earth.

Now here again is some wasted seed. But Christians, let's sow beside all waters. I can't see anyone's heart, so I must preach to all, that God loves all. If I had one thousand men before me and I knew that none of them would be saved, and knew that all of them would go to Hell, I would preach to them the Gospel anyway, because God will have it as a witness against them that He loves them and did His best. I will have it as I come before them, that God loved them and that I wanted them to love Jesus Christ and be saved.

"Blessed are ye that sow beside all waters" (Isa. 32:20). Preach the Gospel in season and out of season (II Tim. 4:2). You will find some hard and stony hearts, those who have gone long in sin and who are enamoured with the pleasures of this world, occupied with money-making, absorbed in other things, and have no heart for the Gospel.

When Jesus was crucified, the soldiers kneeled down and cast lots for His garments. They did not care for the groans of Christ our Saviour, nor the dripping of blood. How strange that man hardens his heart after hearing that God loves him and that Jesus died for him!

Here we find that they sowed some seed in stony ground. This is a surprising thing. Some people who are not saved will accept the proposition quicker than those who really accept Christ and are saved. Here the Scripture says, "And forthwith they sprung up, because they had no deepness of earth." This soil was too shallow, the seed was right on top of the ground. Jesus explained that by saying, "But he that received the seed into stony places, the same is he that heareth the word, and anon with joy receiveth it." They are glad to hear it.

"I like that preacher," somebody says.

But dureth for a while: for when tribulation or persecution ariseth because of the word, by and by he is offended.—Matt. 13:21.

Here is a man whose heart is as hard as a stone and he doesn't have much deepness of earth. He hasn't yet developed, his conscience hasn't been stirred and broken. He has no searching of heart, no longing for God. He hears the Gospel in one service and says, "That is fine." He takes it, does it quickly, but that does not mean he is saved.

Anyone who does Christian work and deals with people had as well face some things. Not everybody is saved who says he is saved. Not everybody is saved who takes your hand and says, "Yes, I will trust Christ as my Saviour." Not everybody is saved who joins a church.

This Scripture certainly means there are multitudes who quickly, without any real root in themselves, say yes when they don't mean yes. Later on they fall away because they have never been anywhere. This Scripture certainly means some people are not saved.

That is the same thing Jesus taught in Matthew, chapter 7, when Jesus said some would say, "Lord, Lord, open to us," and Jesus will have to say to them, "Depart from me, ye that work iniquity; I never knew you." There are people who do religious work that God never knew. There are people who have been baptized that Jesus never knew. There are people who say, "Lord, Lord," there are people who have worked in His name, people who did church work and did Sunday school work and gave money and did wonderful things and did it in Jesus' name, yet were never saved. They had a change outside but no change inside. They had reform, but were not reborn. Here Jesus gave ample warning about that business.

Oh, my people, hear me today! You had better be more serious about soul winning. I think I have been guilty in some degree. Sometimes we say something like this: "You know Jesus died for you. Will you trust Him as your Saviour?" And people will say "Yes." "Well, shake hands with me, then." Maybe in those simple words people have been saved. Many, many times I know they have been. If their hearts were not stony, they have been. It is that simple. If the heart really turns to Christ and is changed, if they meant what they said, it was genuine, and they have been saved, but there are many cases when it wasn't genuine.

Many times a man has said to me, "Yes, I will do it." But when I began to lay on hard that this means to come out openly and follow Christ in baptism and let His light shine, then that one said, "I am not ready yet."

Many personal workers have had that experience. They took your hand and said they would accept Christ as Saviour, and when you began to press the matter of coming out openly and confessing Christ and being baptized and joining the church and witnessing for Christ and living a new life, then they said, "I am not ready yet." I have had that happen many times. I do not mean, of course, that baptism and church membership are essential to salvation. But many, seeing duty hard, see they did not really repent, did not mean to wholly give themselves to Jesus.

What Jesus is saying is that lots of people with joy receive the Word but don't receive Christ in the heart. It springs up like seed on top of the ground. It sprouts, but it has no root in itself. So it represents a man who has never really been saved.

I tell you right now, I am becoming more and more concerned that in the church people know nothing about a real change of heart and really being born again. I ask you again, in Jesus' name, whether you have root in yourself. Are you one who loses out when something goes wrong, and turns your back on God because you got mad at the preacher?

Listen, I am convinced a lot of people who are really saved are only baby Christians. On Sundays when I am gone you stay away from church because the pastor is away. And I come back the next Sunday and you are at church. It may be that kind are not saved.

Then this Scripture says,

> . . .*for when tribulation or persecution ariseth because of the word, by and by he is offended.*—Matt. 13:21.

You know, some people look like good Christians until they have a sick spell?

Did you ever know anybody who came to church until they had a sick spell, then when they got well, did not come back? I have known some. Or if somebody mistreated them (it doesn't have to be the preacher, nor even a church member)—they were mistreated, then they quit God. Do you know cases like that? It may be they are not saved. The Scripture says that some seed falls on stony ground and has no root in itself. They haven't any change, they never have been a new creature in Christ. They get along fine until something happens, then they are off the track and are gone.

IV. Christians, Too, Need to Beware of Deep Roots, Steadfast Character

My friend, if you are saved, you had better learn to be a steadfast Christian, the kind that will go on for God. If I were you, even if I were disappointed in every preacher on topside of God's green earth, I would say, "Jesus Christ saved me, the preacher didn't. And next Sunday morning I will be in church for Jesus Christ and give liberally for Jesus Christ, and have family altar for Jesus Christ, and I will be winning souls for Jesus Christ, preacher or no preacher." If you are the kind of Christian who, when the church house burns down, says, "I will look for an easy way out," or if somebody in the church does something you don't like, then you quit, you had better beware. Scripture indicates you may not be saved. And if you are saved, you are just a weak child with the carnal nature on top. You haven't won the victory over the carnal nature. You had better come to Christ all over again and receive Him as your Saviour and Lord.

Listen, we ought to be more than just a crowd who comes here to hear me preach. We ought to be one body, members one of another. If I am not here, what does that matter? God is here. Enough Christians ought to be here every time to pray down the power of God whether you have any preacher or not. We are young, we are babies, and we haven't developed the kind of spirit that people say, "I am going to church and give liberally and sit on my seat and fill my place, preacher or no preacher. The church—Jesus died for the church and bought it with His own blood, and if you have any kind of a preacher or no preacher, there ought to be certain groups of people praying just the same, no matter who is here, and you ought to expect to meet God at church. Then anybody you have who is an open-minded, good Christian will give a real message of God, and you will not need somebody to prime you up and pour it on and make you have a good time whether you intended to or not, and warm you up enough so you will say, "Amen."

What the church needs is not more preachers but people in the pew who have the power of God, people who have roots in themselves and can bring God to church and not come to church to see if the preacher can bring God. God comes with you. The Scripture said, "This people have no root in themselves."

I wonder today, are you one of these Christians with a stony heart? Do you have much trouble with your heart? I will tell you why people are away from God. You need not tell me that it is because a man is so moral that he has a hard heart. No, it is because he has a heart that is against God and loves sin! It is a stony heart that turns down Jesus! That is the reason John the Baptist said, "God is able of these stones to raise up children unto Abraham." May God give us tender hearts, hearts of flesh instead of hearts of stone.

We do not forgive because we have stony hearts. Oh, the melting heart of God toward sinners! Oh, the gentle heart of Jesus and His longsuffering and His mercy! If I have wronged you and I come to you and you don't forgive me, your trouble is a stony heart. And if you come to me and I don't forgive you, my trouble is a stony heart. And if you don't come to me, and I hold it against you, it is still the same thing—a stony heart.

So a stony heart is the reason people are not saved. Christian, if you win souls, you know what I have been talking about. People come forward and I try to make it clear that salvation is only by faith in Christ alone, and what they have to do is to trust Him and they are saved. If there is a man who will say, "Sure, I will do that," a good many times I say, "Don't you want to kneel down here and tell Him so?" You can be saved anywhere, and you don't have to kneel down and cry to be saved, but it pays to count the cost and find out if you really mean business.

You folks who go out in personal soul winning—I am glad you do, that is wonderful. But if you mean business you will try to get them in the baptistry and expect they will be in church next Sunday morning. There is something bad wrong with any kind of Christianity that doesn't have anything happen to the one who claims to trust in Christ. The trouble is that a lot of the people in the church have never been anywhere. They have no root in themselves. You had better beware and make sure that you are not like that.

How are you going to know you are saved if you don't live different? How will you know you are saved? With joy you received the Word. I know you are saved when you trust Jesus Christ alone, but real, genuine faith puts a root inside and makes a difference in your life.

V. Christians Who Bring No Fruit to Perfection

Next, some of the seed fell among the thorns. That is sad. When I was a boy I lived on a farm with a hundred-acre field. There was a big eleven-hundred-acre pasture for outside stock, but there was only one hundred acres of field in that dry West Texas country. And it was all ordinary ground except one place. Down across the corner of that field, deep in the valley, we planted some cane, and it grew ten and eleven feet high. There was no way to cut it but by hand. My, my! I used to sit down in the cane patch and chew that cane and the juice would run out of the corners of my mouth! My, it was good! That soil was soggy. It would make the best crop of any portion in the field—that is, except the weeds would take it in spite of all we could do. That part of the field stayed wet longer than the other did. We would have to dig it and dig it or the weeds would get it every year. If we didn't cut them out, the thorns would take nearly anything we planted.

This is a strange thing, but you find a man who has a pleasing personality and you say, "Wouldn't he be wonderful for Jesus! If we could get that man saved, wouldn't he be wonderful?" But when, possibly, you get him saved, he is still so crazy about making money, or so crazy about some kind of a hobby, or he is so wrapped up in lodges until he isn't worth a dime for God. He is saved, but the thorns choke the Word and he becomes unfruitful. That is what the Scripture said, and Jesus explained it this way:

> *He also that received seed among the thorns is he that heareth the word: and the care of this world, and the deceitfulness of riches, choke the word, and he becometh unfruitful.*—Matt. 13:22.

Now here is a sad thing. Did you know that the best ground will grow the biggest thorns? Here is a banker. You get him saved, and you thought he would have a big influence to win souls, but he is so wrapped up in his business that he never amounts to anything for God. Jesus, in talking about that, said, "How can a rich man be saved? It is harder for a rich man to enter the kingdom of Heaven than for a camel to go through the eye of a needle."

You say a camel can't go through the eye of a needle. No, he can't—unless God works a miracle. The love of money is slavery, it is a wicked thing, it is of the Devil. The love of money is the root of all evil, and you had better beware of it. And the man who has the richest soil will grow the biggest thorns instead of a crop if he doesn't beware.

All over the country people who are truly saved and can put

their finger on the time when they really trusted Jesus and received Him and were saved by grace, never win a soul. Some of them are the most important speakers in the Chamber of Commerce luncheons, with influence and personality and training, with executive gifts. Some are used in big corporations. But they never have time to win one soul to Jesus Christ. If there ever was a tragedy it is a Christian who has many gifts but those gifts are not given over to Jesus Christ.

I have a heavy burden on my heart for the young people in this church: Sam, Madelaine, Noah, Ray Taylor. I have been talking to each of them, pleading with them. I have offered to help them borrow money so they can go to school and get their talents in for God while they are young. Oh, I don't want their lives to be grown up in weeds! It is a sin to have talent and not use it for God.

If you love to sing, I would say, "God helping me, I will give my voice to God while I can." I sing poorly I know, but under a chaparral tree in West Texas in January of 1913 I knelt down and said, "O God, if I can sing, You can have my singing. You can have my voice. If You want me to preach, I will be a preacher. You can have what I have." I am a poor, ordinary writer, but I said, "If God will give me a talent to write, I am going to write. If God calls me for revivals, I am going to hold revivals. If I can sing, I am going to sing."

I don't want God to let thorns grow up in my life and choke out the fruit. They do in the lives of many Christians, though they have been really saved, so that they never amount to anything for God. They can tell foolish jokes, but they can't stand up and give a warm testimony for Jesus Christ. They can sell a cemetery lot or a big saw table or a $10,000 life insurance policy, but they can't sell one sinner on Jesus Christ, and He is free! Eternal life and salvation are free! God have mercy on us! How many of us are so full of thorns that we never get anybody saved! God help us! Oh, the cares of this world!

After all, there is a lot of care, God knows it. I feel more tender than I used to about backslidden Christians. I skin them alive, but I love them. Oh, the care of this world! Everyone has to take care of his family. You have to be at work tomorrow morning at 7:30 or 8:00 o'clock. You must be there on the dot, rain or shine. You have to do it in order to pay your bills. Oh, the cares of this world. But if you don't beware, those very things that are necessary, that you never get away from, will choke the Word and you will never win a soul, and you will have no fruit. Oh, the cares of this world!

There are a lot of burdens in this world. There is sickness and disease and death. I have found that just as soon as someone goes to work for Jesus, the Devil begins his business. A lot of Christians start out, then something happens. If you are not going to work for God even if something is happening, you are never going to work. If you can't work for God when it is not convenient, you will never work for God when it is. The Devil will see that it is not convenient. You will have trouble at home, or sickness, or you will lose money, or you will have to work on Sunday, or work at night, or somebody will steal your machinery, or something will happen to you. If you don't serve God with the Devil after you, you will never serve God.

I go to a football game once in a while. Do you know what makes it interesting? It is not the running so fast, but running with somebody after you, and pushing somebody in the face, and getting out of the way, and going on this way, and dodging that guy, and keeping on going with them after you. The beauty is in getting somewhere in spite of opposition.

And being a Christian is not just getting along when everything goes fine, but you should say, "I don't care if I do live in the world and work for a living. I have to be doubly cautious every day and not let them get the mastery. I know I will meet temptations and heartbreak, but all the time I have God living in me, and I am saved, and God said for me not to let the thorns choke out the Gospel! I am going to live for Jesus Christ, and I am going to let my light shine, trouble or no trouble."

If you can't do that, you won't be any good as a Christian, anyway. You young folk might say if somebody would give you a thousand dollars to go to school, so you could get all fixed with nice clothes, a nice, pretty shirt with figures in it and socks with clocks in them—you would fix up and go to school. But you wouldn't be worth shooting when you got there! If you attend much to the cares of this world, you are not going to do much for God.

Cares or no cares, I would say, "I am going to serve God and win souls." If in your life you have had thorns and temptations and sin, if you have made mistakes, had heartbreaks—God knows about it all, but get busy, and God will help you. Break up your fallow ground.

There is a judgment coming for everybody. There will be one judgment for sinners and another judgment for Christians. There will be a judgment of the people of God. God is going to bring you to judgment. As an illustration, will somebody volunteer to come to judgment? All right, Grady is coming to judgment (Grady Harding, a young preacher).

Grady, you are already saved; you are going to Heaven. Right? Yes, you are saved by the blood. You ought to go to Hell, but you are going to Heaven. All right, he gets up there and sits down at the wedding table, and God says, "I want somebody to reign for Me. I want somebody to reign over ten cities, and someone over five cities."

When Grady gets up there and the Lord looks up his record and sees that Grady worked so many months in the newspaper business, the Lord says, "Burn that up, that is no good! That time was wasted, that time wasn't any good!"

But that isn't all: Grady covers the ground he stands on. He is not going to take any sass or anything. That is right, isn't it, Grady? At least that used to be so. (Grady: "It still is.") But the Lord says, "That is nothing but trash and stubble: burn it up!"

Don't misunderstand me. Some people ought to work at these jobs, but that is only for a day. I think it is all right to eat dinner when you go home today, but remember God says, "Meats for the belly, and the belly for meats: but God shall destroy both it and them."

There is going to be a judgment time, and we will find out one of these days that much we spend our time on is going to be burned up. God says about some of us, "The cares of this world choke the word and he becometh unfruitful."

O Christian, say, "God helping me, I will not let my life be choked off. I am going to win souls."

VI. Some Good Ground Brings Forth Abundantly

Then there is another kind. Let's see what God says here.

But he that received seed into the good ground is he that heareth the word, and understandeth it; which also beareth fruit, and bringeth forth, some an hundredfold, some sixty, some thirty.—Matt. 13:23.

Here is a man who has received the seed into good ground, and he hears the Word and understands it. That man is saved. And not only did he receive the Word in the sense that he understood it, but he took it to heart and had a good heart, ground that was ready and willing to hear the truth, and willing to do what God said. In that good ground the seed sprouted and grew and had root.

Not only was that man saved, but he "also beareth fruit, and bringeth forth, some an hundredfold, some sixty, some thirty."

Oh, it is fine to be saved, but it is fine to have that "also" after you are saved. It didn't say one hundred per cent, but a hundredfold. If you gained a hundred per cent when you make a business deal, that would mean that you would sell a lot for twice as much as you had invested in it. That would be a real gain. You made one hundred per cent on a deal.

But one hundredfold—that is ten thousand per cent. I can go out here and preach hard and sometimes it seems like a waste of time, but now and then the seed falls on good ground and someone is saved and that one goes and gets somebody else. And for that one seed planted, maybe one hundred will be saved.

I preached in Chicago the first of the year on a big radio there, and we had a little handful saved. I preached one day on Hell. Out yonder a fellow driving a milk wagon heard the Gospel and was so convicted that he drove into a garage, knelt down and asked God to save him, and God did. Then he won his sister to Christ. Then he won his boss's wife and daughter. Now he is working on his boss. Before a year is gone, I may get one hundredfold on that.

In Maywood, California, a good doctor brought a woman to the service one night, and asked me to pray for her. He said, "She had tried to kill herself and I was called to save her life and I brought her to church tonight." That night she was saved. She went back and told her sister and she came one night and was saved. This same doctor had also gotten in touch with the sister when she was hit over the head and got cut up with a beer bottle. Then these sisters went back home and got the mother, and the mother came and was wonderfully saved.

And then on Sunday morning Miss Viola stopped a man at the back and talked with him and helped to win him to Christ. He was the estranged husband of the second woman who was saved. He said to Miss Viola, "I can't do it now. I have some stripes to wash first." (I had preached that morning on "Washing Stripes," and used as my text Acts the sixteenth chapter.) She explained to him that in Bible times they washed the stripes AFTER they were saved; so he was saved.

When I think of those four, I think of that good doctor who was saved already but got on fire for the Lord and was bringing forth fruit as the Lord had promised, some a hundredfold, some sixty, and some thirty.

Then I will go ahead and sow the Gospel. Some of it will bring forth good fruit, and some of it won't.

There are two or three conclusions for lost people, too. Don't let the Devil get the seed away, but hide it in your heart. The Bible says take heed how you hear. Take time to understand the meaning of it, get the root of it, get the real change of heart.

And for Christians—oh, don't let the fruit be choked in your life by worldliness or cares of this world! The necessary things—don't let them keep you from being a soul winner and take your heart's affection and keep you from being what God wants you to be!

Now for preachers and teachers and people who want to win souls, let me tell you this: You will have a lot of waste. How prodigal God is with His mercy! Isn't it wonderful how merciful

PREACHING THAT BUILT A GREAT CHURCH

God is with sinners? Give the Gospel and give it and give it! How many here heard it a hundred times before you were saved? I expect some heard it a thousand times. How many times God called! Your mother talked to you, or somebody else. Someone wasted a lot of seed. You can afford to. The Scripture said, "He that observeth the wind shall not sow, and he that regardeth the clouds shall not reap." So don't wait for the clouds and the wind to be right, go ahead and preach the Word.

You think this fellow wouldn't believe; you think he wouldn't listen. But maybe he will when you don't think he would. You will find somebody else whose heart will be broken, and you can reach him. Someone will be gone forever, right away. You thought you could wait, but couldn't. Go ahead and sow the seed and you will win someone and find he will come after a while and bring in a hundredfold. Keep on sowing the seed. The Devil will get much of it, but finally it will find good ground where it will not be covered too much with thorns and it will bring forth good fruit, some thirty, some sixty and some a hundredfold. Praise the Lord!

Sinner, the Gospel seed has been sown in your heart. Don't let the Devil snatch it away. Trust Christ now for salvation and claim Him as your Saviour today. If you will receive Him, the Scripture said, "As many as received him, to them gave he power to become the sons of God," I hope you will copy out the following, sign it and mail to me. I will rejoice with you.

Dr. John R. Rice
Box 1099
Murfreesboro, Tennessee 37130
Dear Brother Rice:

I am glad the Gospel seed has been sown in my heart, and I don't want the Devil to snatch it away. I here and now receive Christ as my Saviour and gladly mail this to let you know.

(Signed)_____

Address_____

_____

11—The Lonely Christ

(Sermon preached Sunday morning, August 9, 1936. Stenographically reported.)

Psalm 69:

> *I am become a stranger unto my brethren, and an alien unto my mother's children.*
>
> *For the zeal of thine house hath eaten me up; and the reproaches of them that reproached thee are fallen upon me.*
>
> *Reproach hath broken my heart; and I am full of heaviness: and I looked for some to take pity, but there was none; and for comforters, but I found none.*
>
> *Pour out thine indignation upon them, and let thy wrathful anger take hold of them.*—Vss. 8,9,20,24.

The Christian who walks with God walks alone. Jesus was lonely. Jesus went further than anybody else, so far beyond any human that He was the loneliest man that ever walked this earth. The 69th Psalm tells of the loneliness of Christ.

Look again at verses 8 and 9:

> *I am become a stranger unto my brethren, and an alien unto my mother's children.*
>
> *For the zeal of thine house hath eaten me up; and the reproaches of them that reproached thee are fallen upon me.*

This Psalm is a prophecy of how the Lord Jesus would feel when on the cross. There is so much about Jesus that we ought to know. If we knew how He felt, we would know the way we ought to feel. If we know how Jesus suffered, we should be willing to suffer, to serve like He did. We should have the mind of Christ. The Bible says we should follow in His steps. "For even hereunto were ye called: because Christ also suffered for us, leaving us an example, that ye should follow his steps" (I Pet. 2:21).

With that in mind, I call on you to follow Jesus in the pattern laid out in the 69th Psalm.

We know this Psalm is about Jesus by three verses. One is verse 9, "For the zeal of thine house hath eaten me up." In John 2:17 when Jesus had just driven out the traders from the Temple, we are told, "And his disciples remembered that it was written, The zeal of thine house hath eaten me up." This verse is about Jesus when He went in and cleansed the Temple; so this Psalm is about Jesus.

Then turn in the same Psalm to verses 20 and 21, and there we read: "Reproach hath broken my heart; and I am full of heaviness: [that is Jesus] and I looked for some to take pity, but there was none; and for comforters, but I found none. They gave me also gall for my meat; and in my thirst they gave me vinegar to drink." Jesus on the cross was given vinegar and gall and there were no comforters. It is clear that this passage is about Jesus.

Notice verse 8: "I am become a stranger unto my brethren, and an alien unto my mother's children." Jesus had brethren, half-brothers. His mother Mary had other children after Jesus was born. Our Catholic friends don't like for us to say that Mary had any other children. They say she was "a perpetual virgin." But the Bible contradicts that. She was a virgin when Jesus was conceived and a virgin when He was born. But Joseph was really her husband, after the birth of Jesus, and she and Joseph had other children. Many Scriptures mention the "brethren of Jesus." Matthew 13:55 gives us their names. Our Catholic friends say they were His cousins. But the verse I have just read proves that Jesus had brothers, children by His own mother: "I am become a stranger unto my brethren, and an alien unto my mother's children." The verse following says it was about Jesus. Jesus had brothers, His mother's children. To those He was an alien and a stranger.

Do you realize how lonely Jesus must have been? One of the

first things to assail Jesus when He was born must have been loneliness. Did He remember Heaven and the angels? He must have suffered. It was a lonely, sad day for Jesus when He left Heaven to be born as a baby; not able to talk and not able to walk. He emptied Himself of His glory and wisdom and might and power and so gave Himself up to become a man.

He must have been lonely down here when He was born in a manger, and when He grew up among poor, wicked, sinful men. His mother was human, and Joseph, His foster father, was just a poor, sinful man, an ordinary man. The children Jesus played with were sinners, and when He got grown, the men about Him were sinners. The people He preached to were sinners. Nobody perfectly understood Jesus. None had perfect fellowship with Him.

Jesus was lonely. He said, "I am become a stranger unto my brethren, and an alien unto my mother's children." That was true on the cross, and in some sense about all His life down here. Oh, the loneliness of the Lord Jesus! How He must have felt it many times!

In the Garden of Gethsemane, He went a little farther. Peter and James and John went into the garden with Him, but they didn't go as far as He went. When He went to pray, they went to sleep. He was lonely. O Jesus! His love and compassion! Jesus had a very tender love for His people. He loved His own disciples. Many things show His tender affection for them.

I. The Affectionate Jesus

I sometimes marvel that John the beloved disciple laid his head on the breast of Jesus. It wasn't dignified; that seems too intimate for John, a poor sinful man, to do. Wasn't that presumptuous for him to lay his head on the breast of Jesus? Do you wonder that Jesus didn't rebuke him?

But Jesus didn't rebuke him. He enjoyed it! He wanted someone to love Him. He wanted this show of affection. He was lonely, a stranger, unknown and misunderstood, in an alien world! The agony of His breaking heart must have been partly because nobody understood, nobody much cared for Jesus.

At that Last Supper when John leaned his head on the breast of Jesus, there must have been a heartache for Jesus to see in the heart of John his desertion on tomorrow. Jesus may have said to Himself, "I know you love Me; you want to lean your head on My breast, but before tomorrow morning when Judas comes out against Me, you will run away with the rest of them."

Jesus had to bear this loneliness. Nobody else could go with Him into the awful loneliness when He was nailed to the cross. He was even a stranger to His brothers. Everybody left Him. Mary Magdalene was near and His mother was near—but they could not feel the agony of His heart. His own brothers up to this time were not even saved. They did not even believe Jesus was the Saviour, didn't believe He was the Son of God. They were later converted, perhaps at the resurrection. Jesus Himself on the cross said, "I am become a stranger unto my brethren, and an alien unto my mother's children."

Were you ever in a hospital when loved ones couldn't often come and when it seemed so long between visits? Even when the nurse came to bring a meal, it was an event, or if a visitor came. The hours are so long. They drag out more when you suffer and there is no one to share it with, no fellowship nor understanding.

You should see then the loneliness of Jesus. He went alone to the cross to pay for all our sins. Nobody else could go where He went, care like He cared, know what He knew, or suffer like He suffered. He was alone and the cry of His heart was, "I am become a stranger, an alien, to my brethren."

II. The Lonely Abraham

Consider the preachers and great men of the Bible. How lonely Abraham was when he gave up his home and was called to leave kinfolks, leave Ur of the Chaldees, leave his neighbors, leave even "his father's house." Abraham tried to compromise. "I will take my father, Terah, with me." But Terah was an old man and perhaps didn't want to go all the way.

They started to Canaan but stopped at Haran and camped awhile. After awhile the old man died, and Abraham went on into the land of Palestine, facing his lonely calling. He let God lead him. He went out not knowing whither he went.

It is a sad business to say good-bye to everybody. Abraham said to them, "I am going out into a far country. I don't know where, but God told me to leave." So he went out by himself, with nephew Lot. If you read the story of Abraham rightly, you will see the loneliness of his heart out there. And even Lot left him.

One day God and two angels came by going down to Sodom. Notice how Abraham ran out to meet them. "Let me get a meal for you." He himself ran to the flock and got a calf and killed it. Abraham was a rich man and could have had any one of hundreds of servants do it, but he was lonely and was pleased to have company. His wife made cakes on the hearth. They were so glad to have company. It was lonely out there in a tent by themselves, away from everybody but their own servants, and with Lot gone. They were lonely. *When you walk with God, you walk alone!*

Another case in the life of Abraham that will help you to see what we are talking about is Genesis 15:2. I think Abraham wept and said, "O God, You promised that my seed would be as the sand of the seashore, and all I have to be my heir is this slave man born in my house, this Eliezer, since I have no child. If I die, I will have to leave my property to him! I gave up family and kinspeople, I left the place where I was born and came to this strange land. I don't have a child of my own!"

Later on when God had said, "I will give you a son," Abraham hardly believed it. He married the Egyptian girl Hagar. To her was born Ishmael, and Abraham said, "Oh that Ishmael might live in Thy sight."

Hunger, loneliness, away from home, loved ones and friends, just he and his wife—a stranger in a strange land, a sojourner, no city about except those like Sodom and Gomorrah, too wicked for godly people.

Abraham was lonely, but in his loneliness he looked far into the future and sought a city whose builder and maker is God. God will comfort the heart of Abraham and give him the city, the New Jerusalem, which will come down out of Heaven from God.

Christians ought to expect to be lonely if they are to live in communion with God and please Him, as Abraham did.

When you condemn Lot, first consider his terrible loneliness. It is a lonely way when you hew to the line and live a separated life. When you walk with God, you walk alone and you leave a lot of people behind!

God said to Abraham, "Abraham, take thy son, thine only son Isaac and bring him over here three days' journey to Mount Moriah and then take him and kill him on the altar of sacrifice." Oh, it was not as if he had been in the midst of a crowd, or kinfolks were all about him, with loved ones on every hand, understanding his sorrow. No, no, no! He set out alone with his boy. God had promised to give him seed as the stars for multitude. He was to be the head of a great nation through that boy! As they walked that lonely road those three days' journey up to Mount Moriah, Abraham knew what it meant, what it cost to walk with God!

That three days' journey! There would have to be two nights on the road. Can you picture Abraham as he lay down on his pallet and looked up at the stars, the multitude of stars that God had used to picture the seed of Isaac? Do you suppose Abraham slept much on that journey? I don't think so. The boy, healthy, husky, tired, lay down and slept.

I can see Abraham in the night hold out his arms toward Heaven and say, "O God, these arms that have been empty for a hundred years—must I go home without my boy? The lonely years—then You gave me a boy, my delight and my joy. I don't have anyone else! Lot has turned back on me for money. I left my other folks behind. My wife is getting old. This boy has been the light of my life. We named him Isaac, 'laughter.'" I can imagine that Abraham, as he lay there and held out his hands, would say, "O God, am I going back with these arms empty, with nobody to lean on, nobody to look to?" But he trusted that God would raise Isaac from the dead, and so gave him up.

Loneliness! Let me tell you, it is going to cost some loneliness if you walk with God.

Can you see the heart of Jesus as He hung on the cross? He said, "I am become a stranger to my brethren, and an alien unto my mother's children." Jesus was lonely. He was homesick for Heaven, away from the angels. Even His Father turned His back on the cross, and He cried out, "My God, my God, why hast thou forsaken me?"

Few others cared. He may have thought, "Judas has betrayed Me, and Peter has denied Me, this crowd mocks Me, and now My Father has turned His back on Me." It was awfully lonely on the cross. That is what Jesus went through for us. You and I need not be surprised if we suffer some of the loneliness that Christians in Bible times had.

I lay awake last night and thought, "O God, people are coming with hurts, with sorrows, with weaknesses and temptations. Lord, You know they need help, and I must provide it!"

Someway, God broke my heart in loneliness last night, I thought of friends I had said good-bye to. I thought of many fine Convention preachers, true to the Word of God, soul-winning, honorable men whom I greatly loved but whose friendship I have lost because of my stand against modernism.

I thought of another man I had loved and with whom I had labored unselfishly long years, writing for his paper, with never a penny's pay, filling his pulpit dozens of times without remuneration, getting hundreds of subscriptions for his paper without commission, trusting him, believing in him; and then in his pride and spite he attacked me, slandered me, and tried to ruin my ministry. Though God has wonderfully worked it out to His glory and to my good, yet betrayal and disillusionment by those you love leave loneliness.

I thought of another friend who has often preached in this pulpit and how, when the pressure came, his courage failed and he signed a statement reflecting on me. I loved him then and love him now and want his fellowship. If you stand true to God, you will sometimes, like Abraham and Moses and Paul and Christ, walk alone.

I thought of Brother Banta whom we so dearly love. God has led him out in revivals and he cannot be here regularly when I am at home. We have had such sweet fellowship in prayer and service. Our hearts are knit together, yet we must go on separate paths some of the time. We cannot always be with those we love best.

I thought of so many others that I have loved and who are out and gone. So many friends I thought of as I lay there last night. It is a lonely business when you walk with God.

That will be one of the blessed things about Heaven. We will see all our friends and loved ones then and will get to be together then. There is loneliness down here for Christians. This world is no home for us anyway. This world is "a wilderness of woe." As Jesus was a stranger and an alien in this world, even to His own loved ones, His own family, so we ought to be strangers. We ought not think it strange concerning the fiery trials that come on us. Our loneliness is not forever. We will not always be misunderstood, neglected, brokenhearted.

III. Lonely Paul

I thought of Abraham; then I thought of Paul. There is something strange about Paul. He was a member of the Sanhedrin, a Pharisee at Jerusalem. He was born at Tarsus but was trained in all the learning of the Jews and grew up to be a rabbi, at the feet of Gamaliel. He was proud, well born, intellectual, educated, a Roman citizen, of the tribe of Benjamin, a Pharisee of the Pharisees; concerning zeal, he persecuted the church. He was popular. Paul was "somebody come."

They sent him to stamp out this "new religion." They sent him down to Damascus with warrants to arrest people, to take men and women and put them in prison and speak against them when tried. How intensely he loved his Jewish brethren!

One day when he was on the road to Damascus there came a light from Heaven above any light he had ever seen, and Paul heard a voice, "Saul, Saul, why persecutest thou me?" And he said, "Who art thou, Lord?"

And the Lord said, "I am Jesus whom thou persecutest: it is hard for thee to kick against the pricks."

And he, trembling and astonished, said, "Lord, what wilt thou have me to do?"

God told him, "I will send you far hence to the Gentiles."

The Lord Jesus was honest with Paul. The Jews would never hear him. God said, "Paul, go to the Gentiles," but Paul always wanted to go back to the Jews. God tried to persuade him not to go. Everywhere Paul went, the Jews hated him. Everywhere he went, they tried to kill him. He went to Lystra and they stoned him and left him for dead. Everywhere Paul went, he tried to preach to the Jews first. You read in the book of Romans how he loved the Jews. "I have great heaviness and continual sorrow in my heart. For I could wish that myself were accursed from Christ for my brethren, my kinsmen according to the flesh. Brethren, my heart's desire and prayer to God for Israel is, that they might be saved."

That is how he loved them. But they hated him like poison! Paul had gone to Gentiles but was always trying to come back to his brethren, the Jews. He went among Gentiles and raised good collections for the poor saints in Jerusalem. He thought, "Maybe they will hear me now."

Agabus the prophet said, "Loan me your belt, Paul." He took it and bound himself and said, "This is what will happen to the man who owns this belt." But Paul said, "What mean ye to weep and to break my heart? I am willing not only to be bound, but also to die at Jerusalem for the name of the Lord Jesus."

God didn't want him to go, and told him, "The Jews won't hear you." But the loneliness of his breaking heart made Paul feel he must see the Jewish people!

If you were in a strange land where nobody talked the English language, and you never had anyone you could talk with, those who knew how you were reared, liked what you like, it would be a sad business. Lonely day by day. Loneliness is the part of a separated child of God.

Paul went back, but they put him in chains and tried to kill him. Then he was shipped to Rome. Paul, after awhile, wrote back from Rome. In his letters, one of the most pathetic things and yet most precious is the picture of Paul in jail. He calls himself "a prisoner of Jesus Christ."

Can you see the shackles on the hands of the aged Paul? To Philemon he said, "I am Paul the aged one." To Timothy he wrote, "I am a bond slave of Jesus Christ." At one place he writes, "Demas hath forsaken me." "Everybody is gone but Luke," he says.

IV. Preachers Must Be Lonely Men, Must Walk Alone With God

It is strange that preachers must be lonely men. Some people may be satisfied with a wife and little family around them. You are content if you have your people and a handful of friends and loved ones. But it is different with a preacher. He says good-bye to kinfolks even. A preacher is almost divorced from his wife.

In some sense, in a preacher's life there is a holy of holies that even his wife cannot enter into. Every preacher's wife feels this and many resent it, but it is a thing that he cannot help. There is a holy of holies in a preacher's life where his wife can't come in, where his children can't come in. His friends who love him can't do it. He must go alone with God, must run ahead, he must go a little farther than others. Others can't quite get there. They must go out as strangers and pilgrims. Shepherds have burdens that sheep never know about.

A preacher, a separated, anointed preacher, is a branded man, a separated man like the Nazarites who couldn't cut their hair nor eat what other people ate.

I want to lay on your heart a little of the loneliness that belongs to Christ, belongs to the preacher, and belongs to anyone who goes the second mile, who goes a little farther than anyone else. Jesus said, "I am become a stranger unto my brethren, and an alien unto my mother's children."

Do you see that loneliness is necessary to the Christian who longs to be like Christ? God is not saying, "Come on and have more friends," but, "Come on, step a little further out in the way of faith and loneliness."

We should go alone the extra mile. Oh, my people, I would that ye reigned and that we should reign with you, but I want you to see how Jesus, the lonely One, the separated One, came and took our place.

I thank God that Jesus on the cross could look up and say, "I am poor, a prisoner. They gave Me vinegar when I wanted water, and gall. . . . Father, all have forsaken Me, but I look forward to the time when I shall receive My reward."

I remind you there is coming a time when everybody will confess Him, when every knee shall bow before Him. They despised Him, pulled out His beard, crowned Him with thorns and beat Him with a Roman cat-o'-nine-tails. But He who suffers will one day reign, will one day be the center of the universe of God. Thank God! "The humble shall hear thereof and be glad." Then I will thank God, Brother Arrant, when you and I see our converts coming in.

I realize what Brother Arrant meant when he said, "I am not old but broken." People don't see what there is about preaching to break a man down. They don't see what there is about praying that would break a man down. People don't see what there is about agonizing for a revival that would break a man down. People don't understand the lonely burdens of a preacher.

But I thank God that one day "when the saints go marching in" and they shall come from the East and from the West and sit down with Abraham and Isaac and Jacob in the kingdom of God, all the humble shall hear thereof and be glad, said the Lord Jesus in this Psalm.

One good day there will be no loneliness of heart for the child of God. I am talking to everybody here. All have sorrows. It may be your own fault, yet you have them. But there is coming a good day when all tears will be wiped away, when our loneliness will be no more, and when we will rejoice forever in the fullness of understanding, in the fullness of blessing, in the fullness of fellowship—one good day! Praise the Lord!

Now I want to say a word to sinners. You who are lonely, flee to the lonely Jesus. Last night in the night I held up my arms and said, "O God, maybe that is part of it. Maybe I must be lonely in order to be driven to Jesus." I think that is why Moses spent forty years in the wilderness, why Paul had to be a prisoner.

Loneliness! Why? I think I know why. Moses learned to have fellowship with another world. Sorrow comes, but, thank God, after awhile comes fellowship with the lonely Christ. We see One wearing a crown of thorns. If I have a crown of thorns, I can understand His better. He was lonely, broken, despised, shamed. When some shame comes, I can understand it better. Loneliness ought to come. Then let it come!

> Let the world despise and leave me,
> They have left my Saviour, too;
> Human hearts and looks deceive me;
> Thou art not, like man, untrue;
> And, while Thou shalt smile upon me,
> God of wisdom, love, and might,
> Foes may hate, and friends may shun me;
> Show Thy face, and all is bright.

Are you lonely? Let it drive you to Jesus. Run to Him. Open your arms wide and let Him fill them with Himself! With loved ones, you can't always be. Sometimes fellowship, understanding with men, you can't have. God can satisfy the hungry heart. He can fill you with Himself. He will, if you will open yourself to Him!

Every lonely heart—look to Jesus. Troubled heart—look to Jesus! If there is a sinner here, Jesus knows about the shame of sin—Jesus bore it. He felt like a sinner feels, was counted guilty like a sinner, was troubled like a sinner, ashamed like a sinner. Though He was no sinner, all sins were piled on Him. He suffered for you. Troubled, lonely sinner, look to Jesus, the Sin-bearer.

Today if you have sin, run to Jesus who came from Heaven to be a lonely alien and stranger and died just to save sinners. God be praised, He loves you! If you want Him, you can have Him!

Lonely heart, no man or woman need stay away from God. The prodigal boy was lonely. It is bad to be lonely unless you can have Jesus. Come back to the Father's house. The elder brother may not like it, but the Father will put His arms around you.

Come on back home. Lonely-hearted sinners, you wish you had forgiveness, you wish you knew you were saved. Then come on while we stand and sing. Will you come to Jesus today? Trust Him as your Saviour. He died for you, was lonely for you. He loves you. He wants you. Come today and give Him your heart and life while we sing. Will you come?

12—The Power of Pentecost

The New Testament Pattern of a Normal Church Revealed in Acts 2

(Sermon preached Sunday morning, January 2, 1938, at Fundamentalist Baptist Tabernacle, Dallas, Texas. Stenographically reported.)

I made a New Year's resolution to seek God more, to ask God more, and to expect more from God. I made other resolutions. I hope you promised God to make room for Jesus.

On this first Sunday morning in 1938 I feel we should study Acts, chapter 2, where the first church, the one at Jerusalem, had an anointing of power from God. If we had the blessing of the Holy Spirit like they had, we would have all we needed to begin this year aright.

So open your Bibles to the 2nd chapter of Acts, and we will read together.

> *And when the day of Pentecost was fully come, they were all with one accord in one place.*
>
> *And suddenly there came a sound from heaven as of a rushing mighty wind, and it filled all the house where they were sitting.*

What a profound impression it made! There was a sound like a cyclone in the house, and not only in the house but in the whole town.

> *And there appeared unto them cloven tongues like as of fire, and it sat upon each of them.*
>
> *And they were all filled with the Holy Ghost. . . .*—Vss. 1-4.

Forked tongues of fire sat on them. One could look around and see people with fire leaping up from their bodies.

> *. . . and began to speak with other tongues*
> [languages], *as the Spirit gave them utterance.*

The word used here for tongues always means languages in the Bible. It is the Greek word *glossa,* translated *tongues* or *languages.*

Here was a group of Christians, fishermen and common folks, who began to talk and preach in various and different languages. Believe me, that town woke up!

> *And there were dwelling at Jerusalem Jews, devout men, out of every nation under heaven.*

The town was crowded. These were right in the middle of town somewhere.

> *Now when this was noised abroad, the multitude came together, and were confounded, because that every man heard them speak in his own language.*
>
> *And they were all amazed and marvelled, saying one to another, Behold, are not all these which speak Galileans?*
>
> *And how hear we every man in our own tongue, wherein we were born?*
>
> *Parthians, and Medes, and Elamites, and the dwellers in Mesopotamia, and in Judaea, and Cappadocia, in Pontus, and Asia,*
>
> *Phrygia, and Pamphylia, in Egypt, and in the parts of Libya about Cyrene, and strangers of Rome, Jews and proselytes,*
>
> *Cretes and Arabians, we do hear them speak in our tongues the wonderful works of God.*
>
> *And they were all amazed, and were in doubt, saying one to another, What meaneth this?*—Vss. 5-12.

"What in the world has happened here?" they said!

> *Others mocking said, These men are full of new wine.*
>
> *But Peter, standing up with the eleven, lifted up his voice, and said unto them, Ye men of Judaea, and all ye that dwell at Jerusalem, be this known unto you, and hearken to my words:*

For these are not drunken, as ye suppose, seeing it is but the third hour of the day.

But this is that which was spoken by the prophet Joel.

Now let's see. Peter is explaining. He told them to turn back to Joel and read in the 2nd chapter where the Prophet Joel said,

And it shall come to pass in the last days, saith God, I will pour out of my Spirit upon all flesh: and your sons and your daughters shall prophesy, and your young men shall see visions, and your old men shall dream dreams:

And on my servants and on my handmaidens I will pour out in those days of my Spirit; and they shall prophesy:

And I will shew wonders in heaven above, and signs in the earth beneath; blood, and fire, and vapour of smoke:

The sun shall be turned into darkness, and the moon into blood, before that great and notable day of the Lord come:

And it shall come to pass, that whosoever shall call on the name of the Lord shall be saved. —Vss. 13-21.

Now Peter did not say, "This is the end of it." Peter said this is what God and the Prophet Joel are talking about—the pouring out of the Spirit. This is that.

Ye men of Israel, hear these words; Jesus of Nazareth, a man approved of God among you by miracles and wonders and signs, which God did by him in the midst of you, as ye yourselves also know:

Him, being delivered by the determinate counsel and foreknowledge of God, ye have taken, and by wicked hands have crucified and slain.

This Jesus hath God raised up, whereof we all are witnesses.

Therefore being by the right hand of God exalted, and having received of the Father the promise of the Holy Ghost, he hath shed forth this, which ye now see and hear.

Now when they heard this, they were pricked in their

*heart, and said unto Peter and to the rest of the apostles,
Men   and   brethren,   what   shall   we   do?—Vss.
22,23,32,33,37.*

They did not say, "What shall we do TO BE SAVED?" though
they wanted to be saved. They wanted not only to be saved but
they wanted what he was talking about. So they said in effect,
"What shall we do to have salvation and the Spirit poured upon
us?" And what Peter tells them is in answer to their question,
"What shall we do not only to be saved but to be filled with the
Spirit or anointed or the Spirit poured out upon us?"

> *Then Peter said unto them, Repent, and be baptized
> every one of you in the name of Jesus Christ for the
> remission of sins. . . .*

The remission of sins that you got when you repented.

> *. . . and ye shall receive the gift of the Holy Ghost.
> For the promise is unto you, and to your children, and
> to all that are afar off, even as many as the Lord our God
> shall call.*—Vss. 38,39.

Here he calls it "the promise," and he says "the gift of the
Holy Ghost" in the 2nd chapter. It was called "filled with the
Holy Ghost" in the same chapter. He says "the promise of the
Holy Ghost." In another place it was called "anointed with the
Holy Ghost." Again he said in Luke 24:49, "endued with power
from on high." All terms are talking about the same thing.
After you are saved by faith, then he said, "Be baptized every
one of you in the name of Jesus Christ for the remission of sins,
and ye shall receive the gift of the Holy Ghost." This is a very
important verse,

"For the promise is unto you, and to your children, and to all
that are afar off, even as many as the Lord our God shall call."
Praise the Lord, the same promise is to us!

And verse 47 says:

> *. . . and the Lord added to the church daily such as
> should be saved.*

I believe that on the matter of New Testament churches and

their needs and their methods, that chapter is the most important in the Bible. I believe in many respects it is the most important chapter in the Bible for one already saved. It does not say as much about the plan of salvation as the 3rd chapter of John, but it certainly gives more of the secret of usefulness and happiness than many other chapters.

This first Sunday in the year is a day of new beginning for churches as yesterday, the first day of the year, was a day of new beginnings for individual Christians. Let's make this day memorable for learning what God's secret is for a happy and prosperous church year.

I will begin at the first of the chapter and see if I can preach through it. You know I can't get it all in.

I. Pentecost, the Climax After Waiting on God

"When the day of Pentecost was fully come. . . ." They had been waiting for Pentecost. They did not know the Holy Ghost would fill them on that day, but they had been waiting for Him, for the power from on high. If you will look back at Luke 24:49, you will see that Jesus had said, "And, behold, I send the promise of my Father upon you: but tarry ye in the city of Jerusalem, until ye be endued with power from on high."

The last words of Jesus were, "Wait, tarry in Jerusalem until ye be endued with power." "I send the promise of my Father upon you." He said, "'Don't leave without it, this promise of the Father from on high."

We come then to the 1st chapter of Acts and verses 4 and 5 say:

And, being assembled together with them, commanded them that they should not depart from Jerusalem, but wait for the promise of the Father, which, saith he, ye have heard of me.

For John truly baptized with water; but ye shall be baptized with the Holy Ghost not many days hence.

A great promise that was. It is *the* promise, the one mentioned in the 14th chapter of John, mentioned repeatedly as *the promise* of the Holy Spirit. "Don't leave until you get it, for," He said, "John indeed baptized with water, but ye shall be baptized with the Holy Ghost not many days hence." And He said, "You wait for that."

They said to Jesus, "What do You mean? Are You going to restore the kingdom to Israel now?" He said, "That is not what I mean." Now verses 8 and 9:

> But ye shall receive power, after that the Holy Ghost is come upon you: and ye shall be witnesses unto me both in Jerusalem, and in all Judaea, and in Samaria, and unto the uttermost part of the earth.
>
> And when he had spoken these things, while they beheld, he was taken up; and a cloud received him out of their sight.

Then look at verse 14. The preceding verse names the apostles with Mary the mother of Jesus and His brethren:

> These all continued with one accord in prayer and supplication, with the women, and Mary the mother of Jesus, and with his brethren.

Now they waited. If it was fifty days from the time that Jesus arose from the dead to Pentecost, and He had gone about among them forty days (Acts 1:3), then that left ten days that they waited before Pentecost. Jesus had not told them to wait ten days . . . He did not say, "It will take ten days to get the power of God." He simply said, "You wait until it comes. Tarry until ye be endued with power from on high." They didn't know how long they must wait. It might be two months. Jesus had said, "Not many days hence." And they set out to wait until that time was come.

So, "When the day of Pentecost was fully come. . . ." This was not the beginning, this was the climax. The beginning was when they were back there on their faces, searching their hearts, waiting on God! Gathered there were James and John and Peter, Thomas, Bartholomew, Andrew, and Philip—all the apostles were up there waiting, waiting, waiting and praying. Mary, the mother of Jesus, was there and some other women. The half-brothers of Jesus were up there, four of them. They were converted about the time Jesus was crucified. Waiting! Waiting! These continued steadfastly in prayer *and supplication.* After awhile they got to begging God; supplication, not just praying and waiting.

The first verse in the second chapter is not the beginning; it is the climax. "And when the day of Pentecost was fully come. . . ." If you want the blessings of the second chapter of Acts, start where they started with waiting. They set their goal. What this church needs to do is not today to look for Pentecost. That is not where the apostles started. Where they started was up yonder in an Upper Room waiting before God.

I like what Daniel did. He "purposed in his heart." Nobody will be baptized with the Spirit until he makes up his mind, "God helping me, I want this power, I want the Holy Spirit to have His way," until he purposes in his heart about it.

Peter might have said, "You know how my mother-in-law talks if I don't supply the needs of the family." But no, sir! They said, "This one thing we are going to do." They set their hearts to this.

Setting out stakes, putting up a standard, making resolves to be filled with the Holy Spirit. You cannot always just say, "Lord, fill me today. Amen. Good-bye." I know sometimes the Spirit of God does come on us in power the first time we see our need. In this case, it was not so. Usually it is not so that the great things of God come at the wave of a hand or a snap of the finger. Set a standard, aim your gun for it, wait for it, pay a price for it! They did back at Jerusalem before Pentecost. So must we do if we are to have that kind of a blessing.

Oh, if we could have that kind of praying in this church! But we must do as they did—set a standard for that, and make high resolves about it. They got what they asked for, and prayed for, and worked for.

So I may have the power of the Holy Spirit upon me. The first verse in the second chapter is not the beginning but the climax after the beginning in the other chapter. And that great revival was not the beginning.

A lot of people get the cart before the horse. We think it is more blessed to receive than to give. We are glad to take a job at the top and work down. We are glad to begin at Pentecost and go backward. But the way to begin is the way they began—waiting on God and paying a price.

II. Physical Miracles at Pentecost

Notice this. When the day of Pentecost was fully come, there were several definite, outward miracles. Talk about publicity and getting a crowd! I have trouble getting a crowd. Any preacher does. When the Cotton Bowl has football games, the newspapers will boost that free, but preachers have to work and pay for publicity.

But the apostles got publicity when a sound of a cyclone swept through the town. "What in the world is that?" people asked.

The answer was, "That bunch of preachers have been praying ten days and the power of God is on them."

And when the crowd got over there, they saw tongues like as of fire sitting on the people; forked tongues of fire running off people. Then people asked, "What has happened here?"

They got further over here and found this bunch of Galilean fishermen talking in sixteen different languages and everyone heard them speaking in their own tongue wherein they were born. "What is that going on?" they asked. "What in the world does this mean?"

Notice these three different, outstanding miracles.

First, there was the sound of a cyclone, a rushing mighty wind, which filled all the house where they were sitting.

Second, there were cloven tongues like as of fire, and it sat upon each of them.

Third, they spake in other languages of people present who heard and understood the Gospel in their own language.

Those are outward miracles. The religion of Jesus Christ is a religion of miracles. Christ Himself was a miracle. It was a miracle the way He was born. It was a miracle the way He taught. The way He lived a supernatural, clean life, with never a sin, was a miracle. It was a miracle the way He died. He did not die like others. The greatest miracle was the way He arose from the dead. It is a miracle when He saves a soul, when He calls a preacher. That is a miracle when He puts His power on the preaching so that somebody is saved. The religion of the Bible is a miraculous religion, a supernatural religion.

But mark you this: you are not to dictate to God about what kind of a miracle you get, and the same kind do not always recur. That is the same thing when someone claims, "If you do not get down on your knees when you are saved, you are not saved," or, "If you do not shout when you are saved, you are not saved," or, "If you do not have a period of mourning, you did not really repent and you are not saved."

There are always people to measure your corn in their half-bushel. God did not put it here as an axiom that we are always to have these miracles, these outward miracles, in the inward miracle of conversion. The power of the Holy Spirit is available for everybody, praise the Lord! But God does not let us choose this outward show, or that, or the other.

This is the reason why. So wicked we are by nature, so is the human mind, so carnal is our nature that we would choose the physical miracle and leave off the inward power. God does not leave it for us to choose about outward miracles, but He does promise supernatural power to every person who is called. Man would like to choose the form instead of the substance. We want things for our belly and not for our heart, for our body and not for our soul. We want things for our own glory and not for the glory of God. God does not leave this to us about miracles.

III. Speaking With Tongues Not Commanded, Not Promised

Someone argues, "If you are baptized with the Holy Ghost, you will talk in other tongues." But the Bible never says so, not once, anywhere! The Bible never says talking in tongues is the Bible evidence of the Holy Ghost. The evidence is in Acts 1:8:

But ye shall receive power, after that the Holy Ghost is come upon you: and ye shall be witnesses unto me both in

PREACHING THAT BUILT A GREAT CHURCH

*Jerusalem, and in all Judaea, and in Samaria, and unto
the uttermost part of the earth.*

Here is another reason it is not tongues. Here were three
miracles, and any one of the three was just as important as the
other. Just as important was the sound of a rushing, mighty
wind. Just as important was the tongue of fire, which sat upon
each of them. You cannot produce the evidence of Pentecost by
jabbering in a tongue.

Besides, they understood here. All heard the Gospel in their
own language in which they were born. It was not this modern
imitation no one understands. If you are going to pick out a
miracle, why don't you pick out a cyclone like they had? Your
answer might be, "No, I can't work the cyclone, but I can work
the jabber."

Some people say, "I was baptized with the Holy Ghost
according to Acts 2:4." Yes, if you are going to pick out an
evidence, why not pick out forked tongues of fire going up from
you? Did you have that when you say you were filled with the
Holy Ghost or baptized with the Holy Ghost? Or did you have a
cyclone of wind heard all over the city like they had? The truth
is, each one of those things was just as much an evidence of the
baptism of the Holy Ghost as tongues, far more of an evidence
than an unnatural jabber no one could understand. God can
work physical miracles, but God does not do it at your whim and
to please you. God does not work miracles to pander to your
carnal pride and make you think you are better than others, or
have more power.

What was the blessing they had? It was not the physical
miracles. They were incidental. People were there who needed
the Gospel, so God said, "I will help you preach to them." The
physical miracles were not the important thing. If a language is
all it takes, people all around you speak the English
language—talk to them. But it takes more than a language. It
takes the power of the Spirit. The language is not what got
people saved. It was the power behind it. The language was an
incident, relatively unimportant. God only gave that because
people were there of sixteen nationalities to hear the Gospel.

What must bring the result? You need just as much miracle if you are talking to a man in English. It must be the power of God to convict and to save. And that is what they had.

Do not be misled. The importance of Pentecost is not the jabber of tongues, not the sound of the wind, not in the tongues of fire. It was not what they heard and felt with the wind on their cheek, or saw of the fire on people's heads, but **the power of the Spirit of God on their testimony.** That was the miracle of Pentecost. That is what made the New Testament church successful.

How foolish we are! Sometimes a preacher feels if he can tell a story and get people to tears, that is all that is necessary. I am for the moving power of sentiment in preaching if used by the Spirit. I am for the right moving of the heart and the will in preaching. But I do not believe that just for me to tell a dog story and bring you to tears does any good unless the Spirit of God works on your heart and conscience. It takes more than emotion. It takes supernatural power, not just a trick of oratory. It takes the power of God, not just a trick of speech, not just a fancy story.

God give us grace to believe it is the power of God, the Holy Spirit working on the hearts of the people. And thank God that is what they had!

IV. "Filled With the Holy Ghost"

Notice verse 4: "And they were all filled with the Holy Ghost, and began to speak with other tongues, as the Spirit gave them utterance." "Filled with the Holy Ghost" is a strange term. What does He mean?

Well, I am a vessel. If a vessel, then fill me full, Lord. And the Holy Ghost came in, and they were *filled* with the Holy Spirit. That is a blessed word, isn't it? Oh, to be *filled*!

> "I would be nothing, nothing, nothing.
> Thou shalt be all in all."

We are filled with so many things, filled with so many desires. There are so many things we want. We want this and that and the other. We are filled with sins, too, aren't we? Oh, how many failures and heartaches, how many things left undone, how many pages left blank because we did not do what we had planned to do!

Few days come that I get done what I thought I would do and had planned to do. Some pages are smeared with things we never dreamed would be on that page. We have sinned against God in the way we spoke, or thought, or when we did not pray, did not have power. So many pages are smeared with sin in the past. We are filled with ambition, filled with selfishness, filled with love of money. We are filled with human conceit and pride and haughtiness. How many things we are filled with!

But we need to be filled with the Spirit of God. Paul put it in Ephesians, "That ye might be filled with all the fulness of God."

You know, for a church to be powerful and to be like it ought to be, it needs to be filled not with human plans, contentions and divisions, not with our own way, but filled with the Spirit of God. And so that is what they had at Pentecost. They were filled with the Spirit.

V. Many Terms for the Same Blessing

I want you to notice the different terms used. My friends, get this lesson. God cannot show poor, ordinary human beings in one term all that He means.

For instance, God is going to give His Son, so He will name Him by a name that you will know. He names Him *"Messiah,"* but you have a poor conception. He calls Him *"Immanuel,"* or "God with us." He calls Him *Christ,* the anointed One. I will call Him, *The Prince of Peace.* Do you see?

I will call Him *The Son of David.* So that involves that He is going to reign. I will call Him *Son of Abraham.* That means He is a Jew. I will call Him the *bright and morning Star.* That means He is a light in this dark world. I will call Him the *Sun of Righteousness.* That means to the Jews He will come to bring in His eternal reign of righteousness. I will call Him *King of kings and Lord of lords.* That means He will reign over the whole world. How many names come to mind! No one name can tell it all.

So when God deals with us poor human beings, He uses several terms about the plan of salvation.

How can a man be saved? He can be saved by coming to Christ. Another place says, "He that *believeth* is not condemned." It is coming, and it is believing. And in another place, He said, "As many as *received* him, to them gave he power to become the sons of God." So it is receiving Him, coming to Him, believing in Him. It is also *repenting*. Jesus said, "Except ye repent, ye shall all likewise perish." It is coming, or repenting, or believing, or accepting. Do you see it? But all mean the same thing. It is the same Saviour, one conversion, one regeneration.

Now in speaking about the filling or baptism of the Spirit, God used the same principle. "And they were all *filled* with the Holy Ghost," as verse 4 says. But go on a little further and Peter said, "This is that which was spoken by the prophet Joel." Let's see what Joel said. "And it shall come to pass in the last days, saith God, I will pour out of my Spirit upon all flesh: and your sons and your daughters shall prophesy, and your young men shall see visions, and your old men shall dream dreams: And on my servants and on my handmaidens I will pour out in those days of my Spirit; and they shall prophesy" (Acts 2:17,18).

All right, now, they were all filled: and the way they were filled was that the Lord poured out the Spirit. See the picture if you can.

The apostles are all waiting in the Upper Room, waiting, praying, making new resolutions, begging God for blessings, submitting themselves, surrendering their wills. After they had waited and tarried and prayed and begged, the Holy Spirit from Heaven was poured out. Every man held his cup up until it was filled, "filled with the Spirit." They got the filling.

In the same chapter, look in Acts 2:38,39. Peter was preaching to others. "Then Peter said unto them, Repent, and be baptized every one of you in the name of Jesus Christ for the remission of sins, and ye shall receive *the gift of the Holy Ghost*. For the promise is unto you, and to your children, and to all that are afar off, even as many as the Lord our God shall call."

What they got at Pentecost was a *filling* with the Spirit. It was a *gift poured* out on them until they were filled with the Holy Ghost.

But that isn't all. Back in the first chapter Jesus had said, "Ye shall be *baptized with the Holy Ghost* not many days hence" (vs. 5). Here are Christians who were filled with the Holy Ghost. But they were also baptized with the Holy Ghost. The baptizing and the filling happened at the same time.

Someone might ask, "But how were they filled and baptized at the same time?" "Why, Brother Rice," someone says, "baptizing isn't pouring. Baptism is an immersion. Here he spoke of a 'pouring out' of the Spirit, and then you say that is the "baptism" of the Spirit."

Is pouring baptism? Is it, or not? Is pouring baptism? Yes, if you pour enough! If you have somebody in the baptistry and pour water on him until he is covered. Yes, if he is covered! Just a little water on the head wouldn't do. But if he is buried, then it is a baptism, isn't it?

Can you see how a filling and a baptism are the same thing? If you put a wooden bucket in a well on a chain, let it down until it hits bottom, it floats, but you bob it up and down, shake it, turn it over, and after awhile it goes over and fills up—then you pull it up. This one goes down while you pull the other up. When you let down the bucket, it is *filled* and it is *baptized*.

You put a cup in the dishpan and turn on the water. You fill the cup up and fill the dishpan up, and the cup is *filled* and *baptized* both, isn't it?

That is what they got at Pentecost—the gift of the Spirit, or the pouring out of the Spirit. They were all filled, all baptized, according to the wording of the Scripture.

I am not talking now about every Christian being buried into the body of Christ by the Holy Spirit. That is another matter. But in this case they were all filled with the Spirit, all baptized with the Spirit. "Behold, I send the promise of my Father upon you:" (What is that promise of Luke 24:49?) "but tarry ye in the city of Jerusalem, until ye be *endued with power from on high.*" There it is called endued with power. It is called a *baptizing*, a *filling,* a *gift,* of the Spirit. It is called the *pouring out* of the Spirit. In other places in the Epistles of John it is called an *anointing* of the Spirit. Don't you see it is the same?

What does it mean? It is not technical. It is not hard to understand. God just poured out the Spirit until He ran over and covered them and filled them and just took possession of them.

God had to use more terms than one. Why? It was so free and so full. It was a filling. But that wouldn't be enough. It covered them, too. It was a baptizing, but that wouldn't be enough, because they want Him inside, too! Some inside as well as outside! They are filled, and they were covered, anointed, endued, they had the gift.

At Pentecost the Holy Spirit was poured out upon them until they were filled, covered, supplied, and anointed. They had what God wanted them to have. The promise was fulfilled. God gave them what He promised.

All this foolish talk and arguing about terms doesn't do any good. We need to open our hearts and clean up our lives and wait on God for what He gave them. God wants us to have what they had. The promise was to them, but the promise is to us, too.

Let us leave off all this frill about outward miracles, cyclones, earthquakes, tongues of fire, other languages, and not mistake what God commanded and promised us. "The promise is unto you, and to your children, and to all that are afar off, even as many as the Lord our God shall call."

VI. God's Purpose in Filling or Baptizing With Holy Spirit

What does the filling or the baptism involve? You tarry in Jerusalem until I send you the power. I tell you, you are to go into all the world and preach the Gospel, but don't go until you get this blessing. It was power for their testimony.

Look again at Acts 1:8: "But ye shall receive power, after that the Holy Ghost is come upon you: and ye shall be witnesses unto me. . . ." What was it for? For witnessing. ". . . both in Jerusalem, and in all Judaea, and in Samaria, and unto the uttermost part of the earth." Do not go until you get this blessing.

The Holy Spirit came that day and everybody, in various languages, told the wonderful works of God and people heard them and were converted.

What is the Holy Spirit given for? Not just to make people happy. A woman may enjoy cooking, but she ought not cook just because she enjoys it. She wants to feed hungry people. A woman may enjoy making beds, but she shouldn't make beds just for beauty and tear them up and make them over again. You make beds so they will be nice and fresh for somebody to sleep in the next night.

Being filled with the Holy Spirit is not just for enjoyment, not just to go around and brag about. We need not pray, "Give me the Holy Spirit so I can brag to everybody about *the baptism*," as some people do, because they say, "I am talking in tongues." The gift of the Holy Spirit is to make you witnesses for Jesus. It is a holy enduement of power to get people saved.

And that is what this church needs. God give us grace! That is what happened at Pentecost, and three thousand were converted.

VII. What Is Lacking in Present-Day Preaching?

Have you ever thought that in modern days and in most modern preaching something is lacking? Isn't it strange that things do not happen now like they did in Bible times? You stop and think. I preach like Bible preachers did. Many preachers are sound in the things they preach but have few great revivals. Isn't it rather strange that things don't happen like they did in Bible times?

In our revival preaching, what is lacking? You know what Peter preached? He preached on the Holy Spirit.

Some people say, "If you have the Holy Spirit, you won't say anything about it." Peter did! That is about all he did do. Isn't it strange that sinners don't hear us preach with the power of the Spirit of God on us and hear us exalt the power of the Spirit of God in a Christian's life? We should make much of what the sinner should be converted to.

Peter spent nearly all the time in a sermon explaining the pouring out of the Spirit of God, the anointing of the Spirit, being filled with the Spirit. He said Jesus was raised up, and this was the promise of the Father. Look if you will at verse 33:

Therefore being by the right hand of God exalted, and having received of the Father the promise of the Holy Ghost, he hath shed forth this, which ye now see and hear.

About all they heard was that Jesus was raised from the dead and the pouring out of the Spirit was the evidence.

In my Sunday school class, I laid on your hearts the importance of the resurrection. The resurrection of Jesus Christ is the overwhelming proof of His deity. Jesus said to scoffers, "I will give you no sign, but the sign of the prophet Jonas: For as Jonas was three days and three nights in the whale's belly; so shall the Son of man be three days and three nights in the heart of the earth" (Matt. 12:39,40).

Jesus said, "I will be three days and three nights in the grave, and I will come out alive. My resurrection is the only sign I will give you scoffers, the sign of the prophet Jonas." He said that to the Pharisees twice in the last three chapters we have studied in Matthew. That is the sign—the resurrection of Jesus Christ.

Listen to me! Isn't it strange since He has risen from the dead, since it is overwhelmingly proven that He has risen from the dead, that sinners do not follow Him when they hear about it? *The proof of the resurrection lies with the Holy Spirit!* The proof that He has risen from the dead is this: He has gone back to Heaven, and has received the promise of the Father, and having received this promise, has poured out this that you now see and hear. The Holy Spirit of God on the church to fill preachers, and workers, is the proof that there is a living Christ who is raised from the dead!

If we do not have that, why tell anybody that Jesus is risen from the dead? Why should a Sunday school teacher go before his or her class and say Jesus is risen from the dead, except that teacher have the evidence of the Spirit's presence there with him?

If you have the Holy Spirit upon you, you can talk about the resurrection, about Jesus gone back to Heaven, because the Spirit is poured out; "this you see and hear," Peter says. Holy Spirit power on Christians should be obvious proof of the reality of Christ's atonement, His deity, His second coming.

There is an element that has been lacking in our preaching, and that is this: *there is a risen Saviour, a resurrected Saviour who pours out His Spirit on His people!* That is a witness of the resurrection. I am to give witness to the resurrection, and the Spirit of God is to give witness to the resurrection. That is the reason Peter said—get this—in Acts 5:32:

> *And we are his witnesses of these things; and so is also the Holy Ghost, whom God hath given to them that obey him.*

The Holy Spirit is a witness of the resurrection. The resurrection proves that Jesus is the Saviour, but any proof has to be presented and augmented by the presence of the Spirit on the Christian. While Peter preached about the Holy Spirit, that this is the proof Jesus is the Saviour, proof He can save you, proof that the Saviour is raised from the dead and has given what He said He would give, the Holy Spirit convicted and saved sinners. "We begged Him for this power and He did give it. Now then, He being at the right hand of the Father poured out this that you now see and hear."

VIII.　The Power of Pentecost, the Best Answer to Modernism

You talk about fighting modernism and exposing modernism and denominational overlordship—those things are not a proof of a living Saviour. No, that is proven by the Spirit of God on His people! Manifestations of the Spirit, the movings of the Spirit, make a difference in the way they live, talk and feel. That puts power on their testimony.

Listen, my friends! It looks as if I need no defense against any modernist in the world. That fool who doubts the Bible! It seems anybody in the world could prove it true to him. But I can't—unless I have something more.

Here is one thing that thrilled me in the life of D. L. Moody. In England he did the most audacious, the most bold and courageous thing I ever heard of a preacher doing this side of Bible times. There was a great infidel club there. Moody announced a service at midnight for infidels only, and sent out word and challenged and dared and begged them to come.

Infidels came to hear Moody preach, and they filled up that hall, a thousand or more of them, scoffers, infidels, those who said the Bible was a pack of lies.

Moody got up to preach. I could understand if that had been some college man, a great scientist who knew enough to prove the Bible historically, scientifically true, but Moody was not that. He had only been to about the fifth or sixth grade. But Moody preached Jesus that night, and the power of the Holy Spirit of God was behind it and in it.

He said to them, "All right, we will sing your favorite song." And everybody laughed. For sad it is, infidels do not have a song. There is no song, no joy in song when you doubt God and turn your back on the Bible. What is there to sing about? Not any talk of seeing mother again, about the Holy Spirit, the crucifixion, nothing to sing about for infidels. No! No! They laughed at that.

After awhile when Mr. Moody got up to preach the Spirit of God moved and filled him. Then he asked them, "Who is going to take Christ as Saviour? Just say, 'I will.' "

A man in the audience spoke out, "I can't."

Moody replied, "You have spoken the truth. But before we are through you will be able to say 'I can.' "

Then he explained the word *believe* and made a second appeal. One big fellow, a leading club man shouted, "I won't!"

Mr. Moody was broken. Tearfully he said, "It is 'I will' or 'I won't' for every man in this hall tonight."

Then Moody suddenly turned the whole attention to the story of the Prodigal Son, saying, "The battle is in the will, and only there. When the young man said, 'I will arise,' the battle was won, for he had yielded his will; and on that point all hangs tonight.

"Men, you have your champion there in the middle of the hall—the man who said, 'I won't.' I want every man here who believes that man is right to follow him and to rise and say, 'I won't.' "

After perfect silence, and no one speaking, Moody burst out, "Thank God no man says, 'I won't.' Now who'll say, 'I will'?"

And the Spirit of God got on that crowd. From all over some five hundred men sprang to their feet shouting tearfully, "I will! I will!" Remember, these were atheists, free-thinkers, skeptics!

The kind of fundamentalism that we have to have is the power of the Spirit of God on us! That is what this church needs. Your pastor needs it. These Sunday school teachers need it. We need the credential of the power of God, a supernatural Presence so manifest everybody will know it. I want it to be so, my friends.

It takes the moving of the Spirit of God to convince the gainsayers and alarm sinners and convert them. May God's Spirit work in our hearts. That is the ideal for this New Year.

I suppose we will finish some on this building, but that is relatively unimportant. I hope before hot summer comes to have the ceiling in here, but there wouldn't be anybody here much any way unless there is a blessing here.

What we need this year is not so much Sunday school organization. We want to have better trained workers, but that is not especially important. The thing that is important, and the only thing that matters is if we can this year have *breathed upon* us from Heaven, *poured out* from Heaven, a *filling* and *anointing*, a *baptizing*, or *covering*, a *gift* of the Spirit of God like they had in the church at Jerusalem. That is what we need in the hearts of individuals here. If we have that, we can have everything else!

I was so rejoiced when Mr. Middleton phoned yesterday and said, "Here is the first soul I won this year!" He said, "I am going to do more this year." But that must spring from the power of the Spirit of God.

IX. The Promise of Pentecost Is to You!

I am going to have to close soon, but here is another word. They were pricked in their hearts when they heard that the Spirit of God had come. That brought conviction to sinners. That saved souls. They said, "What will we do?" Peter said, "Repent, [and you are saved when you repent] and be baptized." He told them to be baptized. Why? My friends, listen to me. You can't trifle or flirt with God on baptism. Do not do wrong about that. If you do, you will get in trouble.

My heart is greatly concerned about somebody who is fighting God on this. You cannot get away with it when you fight God. Baptism is not to save you, but he said, "If you do this, ye shall receive the gift of the Holy Ghost."

And then he said another blessed thing. Look at verse 39:

For the promise is unto [what promise? The promise of the gift of the Holy Ghost], *you, and to your children, and to all that are afar off, even as many as the Lord our God shall call.*

My people, the promise is to us, praise God!

I have heard people divide it up and say, "There is the baptism of the Spirit. That is not for us. That is already over. But the filling is for us." That is sort of the way people explain that. "Nothing to it now, just at Pentecost and no more," or, "Just what you got at conversion and nothing else. There is no other special enduement of the Spirit."

That is like one little boy who said, "That is just like the Devil or Santa Claus; it is just a story. It is your father!" People think it is only a fable, nothing to it of special interest. They think it means growing in grace, or that's what they got when they were converted! No, there is no use explaining it away. It is too important for that.

We can have the same power, the same joy! I mean the same possession by the Spirit, of your body. That is for us today. The promise is to us! I would memorize that verse 39: "For the promise is unto you, and to your children, and to all that are afar off, even as many as the Lord our God shall call."

"Well, God's plan has changed now about the Spirit," you say.

That Scripture does not say it would change. It was that same kind of a promise when Jesus said about the Gospel, "go into all the world." He said, "baptizing them . . . teaching them to observe all things whatsoever I have commanded you: and, lo, I am with you alway, even unto the end of the world."

That does not talk like changing, and this promise about the Holy Spirit power is not changing, either. This is for *you*, and it is for *your children*, too; and to *them that are afar off!* It is to "you, and your children, and to all that are afar off, even as many as the Lord our God shall call."

As long as it is true that Christ died for sinners, just that long it is true that He can pour out His Spirit upon you to baptize and fill you for service.

X. The Filling at Pentecost; the Filling Commanded Now

Look at Acts 2:4: "And they were all *filled* with the Holy Ghost." Now look at Acts 4:31: ". . . and they were all *filled* with the Holy Ghost." And Ephesians 5:18: "And be not drunk with wine, wherein is excess; but be *filled* with the Spirit."

Now they were all filled with the Holy Ghost. That is what they had at Pentecost, and He said to us, "You be filled with the Spirit." We can have the same filling, the same blessing.

I am not talking about the indwelling of the Spirit. All saved people have His indwelling now. I am not talking about being born of the Spirit, which all are who are saved. But I am talking about this *baptism* or *filling* or *gift* or *anointing* for power.

A lot of us do not have that, and that is the reason we are not getting results like they had. You can have that. It is for you!

And of these Spirit-filled people, verse 47 says:

Praising God, and having favour with all the people. And the Lord added to the church daily such as should be saved.

Now that is the kind of a church we can have if the power of the Holy Spirit of God is upon us.

Will you join me in a dedication today that God will make this church that kind of a church more than it ever was, more than we ever dreamed? Do you pledge that this year, waiting on God

for the power of the Spirit, you yourselves will seek that for
yourselves and others and seek it for the whole church? Will you
do that?

Let us pray.

Our Father, we thank Thee for Thy mercies, so many. Let the
words of Thy Book sink into our hearts and let us hunger and
thirst until we are filled with the Spirit of God for soul-winning
power. We ask this in the Saviour's name. Amen.

13—God's Part, Our Part, and the Sinner's Part in Salvation

(Stenographically reported sermon as preached in Galilean Baptist Church, Dallas, Texas, Sunday morning, September 3, 1939.)

Turn to Romans the 10th chapter and begin reading with verse 9. I am going to speak this morning on "God's Part, Our Part, and the Sinner's Part in Salvation." We will read through verse 15. Suppose you read aloud with me.

> *That if thou shalt confess with thy mouth the Lord Jesus, and shalt believe in thine heart that God hath raised him from the dead, thou shalt be saved.*
>
> *For with the heart man believeth unto righteousness; and with the mouth confession is made unto salvation.*
>
> *For the scripture saith, Whosoever believeth on him shall not be ashamed.*
>
> *For there is no difference between the Jew and the Greek: for the same Lord over all is rich unto all that call upon him.*
>
> *For whosoever shall call upon the name of the Lord shall be saved.*
>
> *How then shall they call on him in whom they have not believed? and how shall they believe in him of whom they have not heard? and how shall they hear without a preacher?*
>
> *And how shall they preach, except they be sent? as it is written, How beautiful are the feet of them that preach the gospel of peace and bring glad tidings of good things!*

PRAYER: Lord, open our hearts. We pray that we may learn Thy Word and that Thou wilt impress, teach, and bless here. For Jesus' sake. Amen.

I. God's Part in Saving Sinners

What does God do to save sinners? God has to make some provision before any man can do anything about salvation.

Well, first of all God has to punish sin. He can't save a sinner and ignore sin. He is not a Christian Scientist. He can't say that there is no such thing as sin. If I am going to have a God to look to, I must be able to trust Him to do right. If He does not care whether we do right or wrong, I can't love Him, I can't trust Him and I can't serve Him. God must punish sin.

That means·God must have it clearly understood that there must be a Hell for sinners. There is no such thing as God dealing with the sin question without punishing sin. There has to be a Hell for sinners. There is a law, "The soul that sinneth, it shall die." When God says, "Thou shalt not," man cannot ignore it and the Lord cannot ignore His own law's violation.

There is a certain thing we have to be saved from. He must punish sin to be a just God and a good God, an honest God, a God people can trust, and therefore God must arrange to punish sin.

Now beyond that, if God is going to save people, He must make some righteous way to get around the sin question. There are none to be saved except sinners. "There is none righteous, no, not one" (Rom. 3:10). Our conscience condemns us, the Bible condemns us, our neighbors see that we are condemned. Our own hearts tell us we are sinners, and we can't get away from the fact of sin.

Now if God is going to save sinners, He must arrange some honest way, some righteous way to get around the sin question. Sin must be punished. Sin has to be paid for. You can't get by with sin. You can't sin and God not pay any attention to it. So He has prepared a plan by which He could honestly punish sin and yet righteously save sinners.

God said, "I hate sin." He says, "I will punish sin," and He says, "I will let My own Son take all the sin in the world, and when He takes that sin upon Himself, I will let Him die like a sinner and suffer like any sinner, and taste death for every man." God must provide a way of salvation, and that He did.

The first part of this 10th chapter of Romans teaches about the righteousness of God. He says, "I know the Jews are zealous. They have a zeal of God, but the trouble is they go about to establish *their own righteousness* and have not submitted themselves to God's righteousness." God has a way for man to be made righteous, but here He said they try to establish, prove, their own righteousness.

Most men feel the same way. They say, "Sure, I would like to get to Heaven by doing right." Some of you say the same thing. Your trouble would be that you would have to do right in every detail to be saved and no one ever did that except Jesus. It has to be God's righteousness and not yours. Your righteousness is so insincere, so superficial in God's sight that it is as filthy rags. Your righteousness, so-called, cannot save, so God had to provide righteousness free for sinners!

You have to be righteous to have Heaven, but you are only a sinner, and to cover that over does not change a fact. Just to say, "Well, I am not a sinner," or, "I am sorry I sin," or to sin as little as you can, is not enough. If God is going to be honest, He must punish sin, He must make some way for sin to be punished and yet save the sinner. So God let Jesus die in the sinner's place. He let Him bear all our torments and take all the punishment sin could lay on Him. God the Father turned His face away from the cross, and Jesus cried out, "My God, my God, why hast thou forsaken me?" Jesus died in my place and now I can be a forgiven sinner since my sins are all paid for!

I said before and say again, God has to be a good God, has to be against sin, an honest God against sin, a just God punishing sin, if I can trust Him and love Him. I can't trust a groceryman who is not honest, and I can't trust God if He is not honest. If a parent does not deal rightly with a child and punish sin and keep his promises, love right and hate wrong, the child cannot trust that parent. If I cannot trust a parent who is not honest, then how can I trust God if He isn't honest? God must make a way for sin to be paid for if a sinner can look to God for salvation. So God being just, let Christ die for sinners, and sinners can be saved because sin is all paid for!

If God is honest, He must see that sin is paid for. But if God is honest, it wouldn't be right to pay twice. If a groceryman is honest, he will not require me to pay twice for some beans. And if God is honest, He doesn't require payment twice for sin. God is honest in having Jesus pay for sin and God is likewise honest in not requiring payment from me after He has already collected from Christ. The righteousness of God has paid for sin. Sin has been punished. Sin is condemned. Sin has been dealt with honestly, and then a just God can offer mercy to the sinner. God has made a way of salvation.

Then the third step. First, God is honest in punishing sin. Second, God offered His Son to pay for sin, and third, God had to give the Gospel in a divine revelation to save men. God had to write a Book to save men. The Bible is part of God's plan of salvation in this sense.

Doesn't the Bible say in Romans 1:16, "For I am not ashamed of the gospel of Christ: for it is the power of God unto salvation to every one that believeth; to the Jew first, and also to the Greek"? What is that? The Gospel. And if we are to have the Gospel, then it has to be revealed from Heaven. It has to be a divine revelation whether it is written in a book or angels tell the shepherds on the hillside. God had to give divine revelation of His plan.

He had to give the way of salvation to men. Men get outside the Bible plenty of evidence that there is a God, but nature does not tell how man may be saved. "The heavens declare the glory of God," but "the law of the Lord is perfect, converting the soul" (Ps. 19:1,7).

People who don't believe the Bible are not willing to take the Bible. They always seek some way for man to get the credit. He wants to do the work and earn salvation himself. That kind always fails. But divine revelation had to be made to show us how honest God was to punish sin, how good God was to furnish the Man to suffer for us and to forgive us when we don't deserve it. Only divine revelation tells us that. Man's reason couldn't make such a plan. That Gospel was God-given! The Bible tells how Jesus died to save sinners.

Christ is the theme of the whole Bible, Christ in the Old Testament and in the New Testament. Acts 10:43 says:

> *To him give all the prophets witness, that through his name whosoever believeth in him shall receive remission of sins.*

That is the theme of the Old Testament and the New Testament likewise. It is the same thing—*believe, believe, believe!*—all the way through. It is the same Gospel; "that Christ died for our sins according to the scriptures." The theme of the Old Testament and of the New Testament is the same.

Then fourth, God sends the Holy Spirit to convict a sinner. I don't care if Christ has died for sinners. I don't care if God has given the Bible, and I don't care how many preachers have preached it—if God doesn't do this other one thing, nobody will be saved. Preachers ought to remember this. Sunday school teachers, here is where you fail. If God's Holy Spirit doesn't take the invitation to people's hearts, *you* can invite people and call people, but people are not going to be saved.

People are not running after God to be saved. Did you ever hear of somebody's running after God? If anybody ever runs you down and says, "What must I do to be saved?" you can know that the Spirit of God has already run them down first. Nobody is going to seek God until God seeks them.

Jesus said, "No man can come to me, except the Father which hath sent me draw him" (John 6:44). And again He said, "And I, if I be lifted up from the earth, will draw all men unto me" (John 12:32). God's part of salvation includes sending the Spirit of God to call sinners, convict sinners. That is a wonderful thing to have people saved.

Some poor, ignorant worker may say, "Well, I haven't much. I do not have an education or any training nor a pleasing personality. I am too ignorant to do God's work."

But the Holy Spirit of God is actually the miracle-worker who gets people saved. God sends the Spirit to get people convicted and gets them saved. God calls men by His Spirit. That is *God's* part in salvation, not primarily yours. Depend on the Holy Spirit to do His work!

The fifth thing God must do about saving sinners is this: He must change the heart. Mark this. A sinner never lived who could change his own heart. He can change his mind. That is a part of repentance. But the heart and nature itself, only God can change. This matter of being born again is not your business but the business of the Holy Spirit of God.

Somebody says, "I believe you have to transform your life and learn to love what you once hated and hate what you once loved. You have got to turn over your own life and make a new start."

No. Only God gives that change, and that change is the miracle of God. Man can't make it. Your part is to trust Christ. Your part is to let the Holy Spirit of God do what you can't do. No sinner ever could make himself good. No sinner that is a child of wrath could make himself a child of God. "But as many as received him, to them gave he power to become the sons of God, even to them that believe on his name" (John 1:12). God has to give the power to become a child of God. That is a miracle.

After all, who is responsible for a birth, the child or the parent? It is the parent. All right, who is responsible for a change in a sinner's heart? God is. Though a sinner has to trust for it, God does all the hard work.

II. The Christian's Part in Saving Sinners

Now what is our part? That is my second main point. What is our part? Getting sinners saved ought to be proof that Christ is real. Jesus commands us,"Let your light so shine before men, that they may see your good works, and glorify your Father which is in heaven" (Matt. 5:16). The Scripture says, "Ye are the salt of the earth: but if the salt have lost his savour, wherewith shall it be salted? it is thenceforth good for nothing, but to be cast out, and to be trodden under foot of men" (Matt. 5:13).

A Christian ought to live a life that will prove Christianity is real.

A Christian can prove there is a reality to Christianity.

First of all, you can prove it by the life you live, by living a life that will indicate to lost sinners that something has happened, that you have what he doesn't have. Prove it secondly by your happiness in your heart. A Christian who isn't happy tells a lie on God. Your unhappiness says what you have is no good, that the Saviour you have does not fill your need, that what you have you can't recommend.   A Christian ought to be happy.

I think it was Dr. Truett who said one time that a baby was dying and the unsaved father came to him and said, "Oh, what will I do? My wife is so weak and frail and sickly. The shock will kill her. She worships this baby. Dr. Truett, come and be ready to comfort her."

So when the child died, Dr. Truett was there. But he said that mother came and stood by that bedside and smiled through her tears and said, "It is all right. The Lord gave and the Lord has taken away. Blessed be the name of the Lord. I am not afraid. I can see my baby again."

The father went off with a broken heart and wept and wept. He couldn't get peace. He said to the preacher, "I don't see why it is. I thought my wife would die. I thought it would kill her. Now she stands it better than I."

And Dr. Truett said, "The reason is, she has Christ and you don't have Him. She has Somebody to help her bear her burden, and you don't have."

And a Christian ought to have joy and victory and peace to prove the reality of Christianity, the reality of Christ. That is the duty of a Christian. He ought to have his prayers answered, ought to have a happy face, ought to be able to stand in temptation, thus proving to every sinner round about that it pays to be a Christian.

What else? Every Christian ought to carry the Gospel. "Follow me, and I will make you fishers of men," Jesus said (Matt. 4:19). God wants you to win somebody yourself.

I remember a sweet thing. Every Christian can win somebody. Every preacher is the biggest preacher in the world to somebody. To me it was an amazing thing the first time I had a man come to me and say, "I had as soon hear you preach as to hear Dr. George W. Truett. You are a real preacher. I like to hear you preach."

The first time I ever heard that, it went to my head. I thought, "Wow! I must get a bigger hat after this!" But every preacher has somebody tell him that. Every preacher is the biggest preacher somebody knows.

Every Christian is the best Christian somebody knows! There is someone you can win, and do it easier than anyone else.

How many, many times I preach to the boys in jail—and you know I love the boys in jail. Each boy had a mother, perhaps, who didn't have family prayer. The mother didn't win him to Christ, she didn't read the Bible as she should, she neglected the vital discipline, and so let her boy become a criminal. Yet many such a boy has talked to me about his mother and said, "I have the best mother any boy ever had!"

You are the best Christian somebody knows, and if you don't get that one saved, he is likely not to be saved. In His kindness, God has made it so that if you don't win him, that sinner has lost his best chance to be saved.

Somebody will listen to you who won't listen to me nor to anybody else. You had better be wise. God wants every Christian to win somebody. "Let your light so shine before men, that they may see your good works, and glorify your Father which is in heaven." Then, "Follow me, and I will make you fishers of men." Go ahead and fish; you can win somebody! You can't win everybody, and I can't, but you can win somebody that I can't!

Then, next, the Christian's part is to pray. I wonder if you know how duty bound you are to pray for me? Paul said in that wonderful 6th chapter of Ephesians, 'Put on the whole armour of God, the helmet of salvation, the breastplate of righteousness, the shield of faith, and your feet shod with the preparation of the gospel of peace,' and then use the sword of the Spirit, he said, which is the Word of God, to fight with, and then he said, "Praying always with all prayer and supplication in the Spirit. . .for all the saints," then he pleaded, "And for me, that utterance may be given unto me, that I may open my mouth boldly, to make known the mystery of the gospel."

"And for me!" I wish I could preach to you this morning like an angel from Heaven. I wish I could speak with tongues of men and of angels so that your heart would be stirred and broken and blessed, then when I preached—salvation! PRAY FOR ME! "And for me!" It is the cry of every preacher. It is a Christian's business to pray down the power of God. I want power.

I went out to hear Brother Crimm. One thing that impressed me so much was that when the invitation was given, the people stayed and stood reverently. Some didn't have songbooks to sing by, but they didn't get up and leave, nor talk. I wish my crowd could see that bunch and take a lesson from them. Four churches worked together in that campaign. A woman went out and found a couple of backsliders and brought them in, so happy. Everybody was reverent and prayerful.

I tell you, it is the part of a Christian to pray down the power of God on sinners. Nobody will be saved unless the Holy Spirit draws him, without conviction. Nobody will ever be saved unless the Spirit of God speaks to him. That is your high privilege. "Brethren, pray, and holy manna will be showered all around."

What else? It is a Christian's duty to send others. I read you where the Scripture said,

> *How then shall they call on him in whom they have not believed? and how shall they believe in him of whom they have not heard? and how shall they hear without a preacher?*

We have one missionary now in Brazil. I bless God for that. Brother De Assis, a Baptist pastor, was willing to leave his good church and take $25.00 a month and live on that. He doesn't have money to run his car, so he will get a horse and buggy. A good man in this church gave $40.00 to get him the horse and buggy. Now he is living on $25.00 a month, preaching the Gospel. They started services in his own little house but they are planning to build a church house in the interior of the heathen part of Brazil, and preach. I am glad this church sent him. I think we ought to have a missionary in every continent—somebody in China, India, Africa, somebody in Mexico. Those who are saved themselves ought to tell others and ought to send others to preach.

Paul said in Philippians the 4th chapter, 'I remember you folk at Philippi, how from the very first you sent to my necessities time and again,' and then Paul said, "My God shall supply all your need according to his riches in glory by Christ Jesus," since you have cared for His preacher.

Win others. Win sombody. Do you remember when you played "Button, button, who's got the button"? You put the button on the string and passed it on. You were not supposed to hold the button in your hand, but keep it going. So when you get the Gospel you are not to keep it yourself but you are to pass it on. Send it to others. Pay a missionary, just as you pay your own pastor.

> **Have you had a kindness shown you?**
> **Pass it on!**
> **'Twas not meant for thee alone.**
> **Pass it on!**
> **Let it travel down the years,**
> **Let it dry some other's tears,**
> **Until in Heaven the deed appears,**
> **Pass it on!**

Pass it on to somebody else. That is a good privilege He has given to us.

I prayed the other day as I went to Kansas. I didn't tell you, but I had a blessed trip up there. I got there Tuesday night. Tuesday night we had five saved and one backslider restored. We had about the same number the next night, and there were a number saved on Thursday night; there were over twenty altogether, I suppose.

On the train up to Kansas City, a man got on at Oklahoma City with a five-year-old boy. God through that boy opened the heart of the old daddy. I played with the boy. I petted him and talked to him. And it wasn't long before I said, "Do you have any more children?"

"Yes," and he told me how many.

"Are you a Christian?"

"No."

"You surely need to be, don't you, with this family?"

It wasn't long until he was saved.

I remember that I said, "Lord, help me to win somebody today." I came back from lunch and sat down. (A good man took me to the dining car and paid for my lunch.) I heard behind me a woman crying. The nurse came along and asked, "Is there anything I can do?"

"No, no. Never mind, there is nothing anybody can do. I have just lost my husband."

The nurse talked awhile and tried in every way to divert her mind. She brought by a baby and chatted about the country.

After awhile when the nurse had gone, I said, "Would you mind if I sat down? I am a preacher and I just wanted to talk to you. I couldn't help but hear of your trouble."

"Yes," she said, "my husband died. We were married just last January. I left home and went down to Piedmont, Oklahoma. Now I have just buried him and I am going home to my folk a widow!" She said she hadn't slept for three nights.

"Let me get you something to eat," I said.

"No, no. I haven't eaten in three days."

"Let me get you a cold drink."

"I couldn't swallow it," she said.

I sat down and told her about Jesus Christ. "Do you know there is one Friend that sticketh closer than a brother?"

She knew who I meant, and she said, "Yes."

"Do you know there is One who said, 'Casting all your care upon him; for he careth for you'?"

She said, "Yes." And then she said this, "I don't know why I am not a Christian. I ought to be. I have been going to a Baptist revival some, where I lived."

I thought, "Praise the Lord, He sent me to the right place at the right time!" So I said, "Well, the Lord Jesus loves you."

She said, weeping, "Yes, I know I am a sinner. I am a Lutheran. I was confirmed, I don't know why I never was converted. I want you to pray for me tonight. Will you?"

"I surely will," I told her.

I gave her my booklet, *"What Must I Do to Be Saved?"* She

told me she would trust Christ, and I believe she did, and I went on my way.

Out of a happy heart I tell that experience to encourage you, my people, to get out the Gospel. It is our business to take the Gospel to people. We ought to reach those we can around about us, and those we can't reach, let's send the Gospel, brother, let's send it!

My brother, Joe B. Rice, is going to Moody, but how shall he go except he be sent? That is partly my business. Isn't it yours? Don't you think so? Grady is planning to go to Moody. Grady, God bless you. God help others to send you! There ought to be some of you to care, too. Hillus is at the World's Fair in New York City giving out tracts—don't you think that is your business, too?

"How then shall they call on him in whom they have not believed? and how shall they believe in him of whom they have not heard? and *how shall they hear without a preacher?*"

We can't wash our hands and say, "Well, I am not called to go."

You may say, "I don't believe in this denominational program." But that doesn't release you. You believe in sending preachers to heathen people, don't you? We ought to do it. We ought to train Sunday school teachers, singers and preachers, and send them out.

Jesus said,

> *The harvest truly is plenteous, but the labourers are few; Pray ye therefore the Lord of the harvest, that he will send forth labourers into his harvest.*—Matt. 9:37,38.

God wants you to send some of those He sends. If we pray we must help send. We ought to go ourselves and then send others. That is the reason this church ought to have a big missionary budget, a separate budget, with a half-dozen missionaries, and every day the Gospel being preached all around the world every day the sun shines. Wouldn't it be fine if we had missionaries like that, supported altogether by this church, preaching the Gospel? Will you pray about it? God help us to send out soul winners.

III. The Sinner's Part in Getting Saved

The last thing is this: God's part is all done. It is our part to take the Gospel. And now what is the sinner's part?

First of all, to admit you are a sinner. That is easy. I have a tract, *"What Must I Do to Be Saved?"* and I have a decision slip and on that the first thing I ask the sinner to agree to is, "Realizing that I am a sinner. . . ." All right, that is not hard. You ought to admit that. You will never be saved without it. If you are here today and are not a Christian, why don't you say in your heart, "Lord, I admit that I am a sinner"?

"Realizing that I am a sinner. . .," that is the first thing. And the next thing, "And believing that Christ died for my sins. . . ." That is the second thing you have to do to be saved. Admit you are a sinner, and then believe that Christ died for you.

But this passage in Romans tells us about "the word of faith." What is "the word of faith"?

> *That if thou shalt confess with thy mouth the Lord Jesus, and shalt believe in thine heart that God hath raised him from the dead, thou shalt be saved.*
>
> *For with the heart man believeth unto righteousness; and with the mouth confession is made unto salvation.*—Rom. 10:9,10.

Do you believe that God raised Jesus from the dead? Yes, perhaps you have believed that all your life. That doesn't save you, but it makes it so you can be saved. You can't be saved until you do believe that. If Jesus was an ordinary man, He couldn't save sinners. But if He is God's Son, if He was born of a virgin, if God raised Him from the dead, if He is coming again, then He can save people. Do you believe Jesus died for sinners? God opened the way. God loves you. Christ died for you. The blood has been shed, sin has been paid for. All right, the second thing is, you can be saved, since you know Christ died.

What is the third thing? The third thing is to repent of your sin. Turn your heart from your sins. Nobody will be saved who loves his sins and holds on to his sins, and yet says, "I am going to be saved." No, sir. I don't mean being saved is simply quitting your sin outwardly, but being saved requires turning your *heart* away from sin. Saved people still sin, but saved people have turned their hearts to admit sin and regret their sin, turned their hearts from it and said, "Lord, I am sorry for my sin."

But faith goes with repentance. I don't believe repentance and faith are two different things. I think they are two sides of the same thing.

> *If thou shalt confess with thy mouth the Lord Jesus, and shalt believe in thine heart that God hath raised him from the dead, thou shalt be saved.*

Will you trust Him to be yours? Confession is not a *part* of salvation. Confession is *proof* of salvation.

> *With the heart man believeth unto righteousness; and with the mouth confession is made unto salvation.*

With the mouth people confess or admit or claim the righteousness of Christ which they received in the heart when they trusted. So then if you want to be saved, admit you are a sinner, believe that Christ died for you and turn from your sin and trust Him to save you. That is not hard.

If you want to be saved today, you can. Sinner, can't you say today, "God helping me, I will turn to Jesus Christ and trust Him to forgive me and I will claim Him as mine today"? You will be saved today if you will say that in your heart, sincerely.

I am through. I have preached twenty-nine minutes including the reading of the Scripture. That is a real record for me! Let us all stand. Will you say, "I am going to turn to Jesus Christ and be saved"? Who will say, "I admit I am a sinner, I confess I am a sinner and I believe Jesus died for me and I here and now turn from my sins and trust Christ to forgive me and save me"? If you will trust Him, He will forgive you and save you. He loves you. The debt is all paid. God wants you to come. You can today if you will.

> *For whosoever shall call upon the name of the Lord shall be saved.*

III. SERMONS OF COMFORT

14—Heaven

(Sermon preached Sunday night, March 7, 1937, at Fundamentalist Baptist Tabernacle. Mechanically recorded.)

1. **Tradition, Instinct and the Cry of the Human Heart Are Backed Up by the Word of God**
2. **Heaven a Real Place, a City With Walls, Foundations, Streets, Mansions, a River, Trees, Fruit, Leaves, Physical Bodies**
3. **Heaven Where Jesus Is. Tears Wiped Away. No Sorrow or Dying. Old Things Passed Away**

I am going to speak tonight on Heaven. I will read in Revelation the 21st and 22nd chapters several verses. I hope you have your Bibles and will look on. We will read verses 1 through 8:

> *And I saw a new heaven and a new earth: for the first heaven and the first earth were passed away; and there was no more sea.*
>
> *And I John saw the holy city, new Jerusalem, coming down from God out of heaven, prepared as a bride adorned for her husband.*
>
> *And I heard a great voice out of heaven saying, Behold, the tabernacle of God is with men, and he will dwell with them, and they shall be his people, and God himself shall be with them, and be their God.*

And God shall wipe away all tears from their eyes; and there shall be no more death, neither sorrow, nor crying, neither shall there be any more pain: for the former things are passed away.

And he that sat upon the throne said, Behold, I make all things new. And he said unto me, Write: for these words are true and faithful.

And he said unto me, It is done. I am Alpha and Omega, the beginning and the end. I will give unto him that is athirst of the fountain of the water of life freely.

He that overcometh shall inherit all things; and I will be his God, and he shall be my son.

But the fearful, and unbelieving, and the abominable, and murderers, and whoremongers, and sorcerers, and idolaters, and all liars, shall have their part in the lake which burneth with fire and brimstone: which is the second death.

I will skip a little bit. Then in the 22nd chapter I read verses 1 through 7:

And he shewed me a pure river of water of life, clear as crystal, proceeding out of the throne of God and of the Lamb.

In the midst of the street of it, and on either side of the river, was there the tree of life, which bare twelve manner of fruits, and yielded her fruit every month: and the leaves of the tree were for the healing of the nations.

And there shall be no more curse: but the throne of God and of the Lamb shall be in it; and his servants shall serve him:

(All of our work will not be done. We will work some more.)

And they shall see his face; and his name shall be in their foreheads.

And there shall be no night there; and they need no candle, neither light of the sun; for the Lord God giveth them light: and they shall reign for ever and ever.

And he said unto me, These sayings are faithful and

true: and the Lord God of the holy prophets sent his angel to shew unto his servants the things which must shortly be done.

Behold, I come quickly: blessed is he that keepeth the sayings of the prophecy of this book.

And now skip to the 17th verse:

And the Spirit and the bride say, Come. And let him that heareth say, Come. And let him that is athirst come. And whosoever will, let him take the water of life freely.

Heaven is a wonderful thought, a wonderful place. There is a Heaven! Many arguments prove there is a Heaven. For one thing, every heathen religion in the world foretells a place of blessedness in the hereafter. The Indians on the American Continent believed that when men die here they go to a "Happy Hunting Ground," at least if they were worthy. The Hindus believe in Nirvana, a place of endless peace hereafter.

Heathen rites, ceremonies, point toward and look toward a place of peace, rest and reward for the good in the next world. All heathen religions believe in a hereafter—a Heaven for those who are righteous as well as a place of punishment for those who are not.

Then the instinct of man is the same about the fact that there is a Heaven. There is something in every man that says there must be a hereafter. There is something in a man that says he knows he will not be dead forever.

I am not like a dog nor a horse. I cannot be content to believe I will go into a sleep that will mean oblivion. I cannot believe this body is all there is to me. I know I have an undying soul. Instinctively I cannot believe there is no hereafter, no Heaven, no Hell. Neither can you. There is something that cries out for the eternal.

You say, "But that is no argument for a hereafter, no argument for immortality."

The fundamental and essential needs that God forms in man, He supplies. Someone attends to God's business if there is no God! When God made Adam, He said, "It is not good for man to be alone," so God made a woman. God made something to complement the sex instinct, the mating instinct. The man is for the woman and the woman for the man. God gave the need and He supplied the need.

There is something about the natural body that cries for food. Where God gave hunger, God provided food—vegetable and meat.

The body cries out for water, thirsts after water, needs water, so God provides water. The lungs must have air. We are conscious of a need for breath, and God provided breath. What the fundamental needs and instincts cry out for, God has supplied.

So there must be a Heaven, an immortal place beyond the grave.

I. The Heart Cries for Heaven

That isn't all. Not only the teachings of men, not only heathen superstitions, not only our instincts, but also our hearts cry out that there is a Heaven. I, at six years of age, came one day to stand by the grave of my mother. My heart asked, Would I ever see my mother again? Then after I was a grown man and a preacher, I stood by the grave of my father. I have many times said good-bye to those I love. They were dear to me. Their lives had been a part of my life. In some way we were tied together, bound together.

Is it true that I will never see them again? I cannot believe that! My heart cries out that there must be another place where there will be no more death. There must be a place where I will see my loved ones again, see my friends, see my hopes and dreams fulfilled. My heart cries out that there must be a Heaven.

But, thank God, we have better evidence than any of these! There is as much outward evidence, as much human evidence, as much scientific evidence for Heaven as any other great fact. You could not refute it. There is too much evidence about the immortality of the soul for intelligent people not to believe in it. There is more evidence even outside the Bible than for most other matters people take for granted. There is too much proof to deny it. There has to be a Heaven.

But, thank God, we have a more sure word of prophecy that tells us about it. I say, conscience may tell us, and our instinct and heart cry out for a place where we will fulfill our destiny, where longings will be satisfied, where we will meet our loved ones again.

But, best of all, the Lord Jesus Himself said, "I go to prepare a place for you. And if I go and prepare a place for you, I will come again, and receive you unto myself; that where I am, there ye may be also" (John 14:2,3). Yes, Jesus said, "In my Father's house are many mansions, and I am preparing a place for you and will come and get you. And where I am, there you may be also." We have the pure word of the Saviour Himself, the Son of God, and the abundant testimony of the Bible that there is a place called Heaven. Oh, thank God for that testimony!

I ask you to please consider with me the Bible teaching on Heaven.

Is there a Heaven? Yes there is. I want first to consider just the bare outline of Bible teaching.

II. The Promised City of God

The first clear reference that I recall to Heaven as a place, a literal place, as a city, is in the 46th Psalm. (I am thinking now of Heaven as a city. There are many Scriptures before this that make clear there is an eternal blessedness for the saved.)

There is a river, the streams whereof shall make glad THE CITY of God.

Isn't that sweet poetry! "There is a river, the streams whereof shall make glad the city of God." There is a *city* of God. Heaven is a real place.

The New Testament has many references to Heaven. In the 14th chapter of John the Saviour said,

Let not your heart be troubled: ye believe in God, believe also in me.

In my Father's house are many mansions: if it were

not so, I would have told you. I go to prepare a place for
you.

"I go to prepare a place for you"—a literal place. Heaven is a
real place. There is the same teaching in the book of Hebrews.
In the 11th chapter, we are told that Abraham looked for
Heaven. He was looking for a real, literal, physical city. Verses
8 to 10 say:

> *By faith Abraham, when he was called to go out into a*
> *place which he should after receive for an inheritance,*
> *obeyed; and he went out, not knowing whither he went.*
>
> *By faith he sojourned in the land of promise, as in a*
> *strange country, dwelling in tabernacles with Isaac and*
> *Jacob, the heirs with him of the same promise:*
>
> *For he looked for a city which hath foundations, whose*
> *builder and maker is God.*

Abraham was homesick for Heaven. He dreamed and
planned and meditated on the glories of that city. And though
he was a rich man, he could be content to live in a tent because
he knew one day he would live in a real city, a city of God, a
place called Heaven!

Again in Hebrews the 12th chapter is a very clear reference to
Heaven. Verses 22 and 23 say:

> *But ye are come unto mount Sion, and unto the city of*
> *the living God, the heavenly Jerusalem, and to an*
> *innumerable company of angels,*
>
> *To the general assembly and church of the firstborn,*
> *which are written in heaven, and to God the Judge of all,*
> *and to the spirits of just men made perfect.*

All right, there is a new city, a lovely city of the living God,
the heavenly Jerusalem where the general assembly of the
firstborn will be gathered, all the saints, the church of God.
That will be a wonderful time when we meet together in that
blessed land. There is clear teaching on Heaven.

Then we come to the book of Revelation. The first three
chapters are about this church age. Then from chapter 4
through chapter 18 is the story of the tribulation time on earth.

Then the 19th chapter is a picture of Christ coming back to reign. He will take away the saints in the 4th chapter, then in the 19th chapter we see Him coming on a white horse with an army following Him. The Battle of Armageddon takes place. The 20th chapter tells about the millennial reign, when Christ reigns here on earth. Then at the end of that time, after the great white throne judgment, we enter into the glories of Heaven that I have read you here in chapters 21 and 22.

Heaven a Literal, Physical Place

I want you to notice here that there is a real place called Heaven. Did I say a place? Yes, a place as physical as this ground, as literal as this platform. Houses, literal houses, made out of material, matter that we can feel and walk on, as literal as this house we are now in.

Let's consider some of the terms used in the Bible about Heaven. Jesus said, "I go to prepare a PLACE for you." People have had an idea about Heaven that saints float around up there, ghostly spirits out in space wandering around. That is not Heaven. Heaven is a place. Jesus said, "I go to prepare a place for you"—a real place, a prepared place. Now places need preparing. Out in space emptiness needs no preparation.

If when a young man gets married he just takes his wife to a flivver and lives out on the highway, he does not need to prepare a place. If when Jesus comes for His bride—and we are His bride—He just takes us up to float around, to sing and to wander around in space, all spiritual anyway, all a part of a general whole, if the person in a sense ceases to be, passes out of existence, with no individual personality, there wouldn't be a need for a place.

But the Lord Jesus said, "I am going to get a *place* ready for you." When a young man marries a bride, he first selects the house and the furniture. He gets everything fixed up just right, then he brings his bride to that place. Just that literal is Heaven, a place, a real place that Jesus is making. It is as literal as the creative work when He made this first world, the Garden of Eden. I remind you He said a PLACE.

III. A Literal City With Mansions or Houses, Streets, Foundations, Gates, a River, Trees, Leaves, Fruit

And it is not only a place, but notice these other terms used: "In my Father's house." The Bible says it is a house.

Then, "In my Father's house are many mansions." By mansion we mean a fine, beautiful building. The term indicates riches, luxury. It indicates loving preparation. It indicates expenditure, invested money, plans, a skillfully prepared place. And that is what Heaven is—a literal place with mansions.

We use a lot of terms we don't actually know about but just guess at, such as "the general judgment" and "the general resurrection." Now let's see, in what part of the Bible is that mentioned? I couldn't find it, so I looked in my concordance. Not one time were those terms mentioned. There is nothing in the Bible about a "general" resurrection. As a young preacher, I know I have heard the term somewhere, but where? I found out when I sent to the next Masonic funeral and heard them talk about a general resurrection, something not mentioned in the Bible.

As the farmer said when he first saw the giraffe, "There ain't no such an animal." There is no general resurrection. There are two resurrections—the saved rise first, and a thousand years later the lost; the one to one destiny, the other to another destiny, but altogether different.

It is called a city. If the souls of people who have died are never to go to Heaven, if bodies are never to rise, if your souls do not go to a real, literal place but float around in the air, that would not be called a city.

What is the difference between a city and the country? A city has houses and paved streets. A city has gas lines, water lines, organization, traffic lights. A city has buildings. A city is a prepared place. The open country is not a prepared place. Heaven is a city.

So I thought, Is Heaven a reality? Now we had better find out. We have been talking about "the City Foursquare," that wonderful city, "The Holy City." I began to look for Scriptures that call Heaven a city. Oh, yes, Abraham "looked for a city that hath foundations," a city that needs to be builded. *A city.* I looked in Psalm 46:4 which says, "There is a river, the streams whereof shall make glad the city of God." The city, the city of God. I looked in Revelation and saw "the holy city, new Jerusalem, coming down from God out of heaven, prepared as a bride adorned for her husband." A city!

Heaven is a place. Heaven is a prepared place. Heaven is a physical place, as literal, prepared and builded as any city, but this by the hands of the Lord Jesus Himself. "I go to prepare you a place."

Not only is it a real place, not only is it a city, not only does it contain mansions, but it is a place that has foundations. Now notice this. If you just floated around in the air, you wouldn't need a foundation under you. Do you know why I have such good foundations? (Holds out foot.) Because I weigh enough that I have to have something solid to stand on.

If we were put in Heaven without any weight, without any bodies, without any houses, put in a Heaven without any walls, put in a Heaven with no trees, put in a Heaven without any material substances, we wouldn't need foundations. But if you build a house that weighs anything, you must have a foundation. And if you make it out of brick, you had better have a good one. A masonry house needs a good foundation.

So Heaven has to have such a good foundation because it is a real, physical place, with weight and substance and mass and matter. Heaven is a place, so it takes foundations. "He looked for a city which hath foundations, whose builder and maker is God."

We have a way of explaining away the Bible. It says a city, but we don't believe it. It says foundations, but we don't believe that. We think we will just float around. Get away from that idea and think of Heaven as a place as literal as the Garden of Eden, as literal as this church here, but without any sin, without disappointments, without its partings, its death. Heaven is a place, a prepared place with houses, mansions, a place with foundations.

What else about Heaven? It has streets. Now if we were just floating around in the air we wouldn't need streets. What if we saw a street up in the air with no automobiles on it, nobody walking on it? We have to have foundations for this place.

Now gold is one of the heaviest metals in the world. Streets paved with gold would sure take enough foundations to hold us and the houses, the mansions. They will be like transparent pure glass for purity. The city has foundations. It has streets! It has gates. It has a wall! It has a river! It has trees!

Yes, praise be to God, that is a real place. Jesus said, "I go to prepare a place." He is building a place. Isn't it wonderful to know that Heaven is a real place!

I wonder if you have ever thought about the trees there. And the trees have leaves and bear fruit. And the walls and foundations and streets and mansions show it is a place, a real Heaven.

IV. Physical Bodies in Heaven

I want you to notice this other thing. There are physical bodies in Heaven.

Thank God, one of these days the saints of God, with human bodies, with eyes and ears and teeth and bones and flesh and hands and feet and hair, with literal bodies, human bodies, physical bodies, glorified but still human, spiritual but still material bodies, are going to be in Heaven. Right now if you were in Heaven you could run around and see people. You could shake hands with people.

I don't know if we would stop at shaking hands. If I saw Enoch, I think I would hug him. I think I would do more than shake hands with old Elijah. Praise be to God, were I to go to Heaven today I would see him with a physical body. He didn't die. He went to Heaven in a whirlwind and chariot of fire in his physical body. His body was changed on the way up. God got it all ready for the angel's food, all ready for the music of Heaven, all ready for the company of the Lord! There are some physical bodies in Heaven now. Elijah has one, and Enoch has one.

And not only that, but the Lord Jesus Christ has a physical body. The old Devil is keen. He tries to keep us from realizing that Jesus really died, and then he tries to keep us from believing that Jesus really rose from the dead. When Jesus came out of the grave, nobody was there. But Jesus came out. His body came out, the hands and feet and head and flesh and bones. Jesus' body didn't stay in that grave. It came out. The physical body of Jesus came out. Nothing was left in Joseph's new tomb. It was empty. The resurrection of Jesus was a physical resurrection.

You say it was a spiritual body. Yes, I know it was a spiritual body, but it was the same body, made out of the same material. "It is sown a natural body; it is raised a spiritual body." Both "its" in that verse refer to the same body. The same one that is sown is the same one that is raised. The same body that dies is the same one that lives. The one is made over into a new body, a glorified body.

God will do the same thing for this earth. This old earth is cursed by sin. This earth now has brambles and thorns and thistles and pests. But one day God will purge this earth by fire, and with these ashes, these melted elements, God will form a new earth, but the same earth. He will make it over anew. It will be a new earth.

So one day when Jesus comes He will take this body to meet Him, to be changed in a moment, in the twinkling of an eye. If I die before He comes, this body may crumble back to dust, but God will raise it up. That grave will fall back down empty. There will be a hole in the ground where I come out. I mean there will be a physical resurrection of literal, physical bodies.

When Jesus rose from the dead, the people didn't believe it. Thomas said, "I don't believe it."

"But," they said, "He was right here. We saw Him and talked with Him."

"You were just fooled," Thomas said. "That was a ghost or a hallucination. I don't believe it. Until I put my hands in those places where they drove the nails, and put my hand in the side where the spear went, I will not believe it! Not until I have proof for myself."

A week later Jesus came and said, "Thomas, put your finger

in these scars and see. Put your hand in My side and feel where the spear went in. See for yourself." Jesus said, "A spirit does not have flesh and bones as you see Me have."

And old Thomas fell down on his face and said, "My Lord, and my God!" He was convinced! It was the physical body, the literal body, with bones and flesh and hands and feet and eyes and ears and hair and the lovely features of the Saviour.

I say, Jesus rose from the grave with a physical body. He said to the still wondering disciples, "Have you anything here to eat?" They said they had some broiled fish and some honeycomb. "That is fine. Bring it out," Jesus said. So they sat around and watched the Lord Jesus Christ who came out of Joseph's new tomb, that same body. They saw the nail-scarred hands take a bit of fish. They saw Him take a piece of fish and pick the bones out and eat it. They saw Him put it in that physical mouth and chew it with those physical teeth and swallow it to go to a physical stomach. He ate that broiled fish and honeycomb before them. And that physical body of Jesus is now in Heaven.

Many preachers believe our bodies will have flesh and bones but no blood. But these bodies will have fluid. Jesus ate honey—that is liquid. Jesus said about grapejuice, "I will not drink it until I drink it new with you in the kingdom of my Father." Jesus will drink grapejuice, and so will the rest of us.

My friends, this body will have the normal functions of a physical body—to eat and digest, to see and hear, a literal, physical body in Heaven. Jesus is there now with that kind of a body. Heaven is a real place, thank God!

I am glad God told us about it. You say, "It looks to me awfully dreamy." It is not dreamy to me. It is as real to me as any other place. There are a lot of places I never saw but thank God, I know about Heaven! It is a real place. A literal, physical place is Heaven. Praise the Lord for a *place* where my Saviour is!

Here at the Fundamentalist Baptist Tabernacle we plan to put in a floor and ceiling and partitions when we get a little money for it. So it is in Heaven. The Lord Jesus Christ created it. With a word He could bring it into existence. But He is preparing it now. He is having the finest time. He is like a bridegroom fitting out his house for his sweetheart, who will soon marry him. The Lord Jesus is fitting out mansions in Heaven for us who are His saints and His bride. He is preparing a place for those who love Him, and it is an actual, physical, literal, real place.

V. The Joys of Heaven: We Will See God

What kind of a place is Heaven anyway? I am glad the Lord tells us about the nature of it, not only that it is a place but the spiritual nature of it and what goes on there.

> *And I heard a great voice out of heaven saying, Behold, the tabernacle of God is with men, and he will dwell with them, and they shall be his people, and God himself shall be with them, and be their God.*
>
> *And God shall wipe away all tears from their eyes; and there shall be no more death, neither sorrow, nor crying, neither shall there be any more pain: for the former things are passed away.* —Rev. 21:3,4.

What kind of a place? It will be, first, a place where God is. I am going to see the Lord God! The Bible says that man cannot now see God and live. None of us are fit to see God now. We are carnal, evil. The people couldn't even look on the face of Moses when he came down off the mountain where he had been so close to God for forty days and nights. He had to put a veil over his face, when he had been so near to God. These blinded eyes couldn't look on the face of God and live.

But the Bible says, "Blessed are the pure in heart: for they shall see God." Oh, one good day my heart will be made pure, and made fit to see Him, and I will see Him! I do not wonder that Job, in the midst of his trials and sorrows, said:

> *I know that my redeemer liveth, and that he shall stand at the latter day upon the earth: And though after my skin worms destroy this body, yet in my flesh shall I see God: Whom I shall see for myself, and mine eyes*

shall behold, and not another; though my reins be consumed within me.

Oh, my friends, one day I shall see God! You shall see Jesus! The pure in heart shall see God and they that hunger and thirst after righteousness shall be filled. They that mourn shall be comforted in that good day.

Thank God, I am going where God is! The Lord God will be their God and His tabernacles shall be with men. Won't it be great? One day all the longings of my heart to be fulfilled in Him, the Lord God, the Creator of Heaven and earth.

That isn't all. Jesus will be there, too. Our black people sing:

> I'm goin' to meet my blessed Saviour,
> I'm goin' to meet my blessed Saviour one of these days,
>   Hallelujah!
> I'm goin' to meet my blessed Saviour,
> I'm goin' to meet my blessed Saviour,
>   One of these days.

Amen! And so am I, Brother. I can rejoice and shout just as much as they when I get there. I am going to see Jesus. Praise the Lord, I will be there!

VI. Heaven Is Where Jesus Is

The thief on the cross didn't have much background to merit his getting to Heaven, having lived a terrible wicked life. Now he was dying on the cross for his sins. Yet Jesus turned to him and said, "To day shalt thou be with me in paradise." I am glad He said, *"with me."* It wouldn't have been paradise without Him. I think that thief dying, gasping for breath and begging Jesus to remember him, would have been afraid to die had Jesus said only, "You are going to paradise." That wouldn't be enough. But Jesus said, "You are going to be *with Me* in paradise."

One day I will be with Jesus. My mother saw Jesus when she died. She said so. We will be where He is. I have thought many times of how glad I would be if some way I could only walk up to Him and tell Him, "I am so sorry, so sorry I have sinned," and tell Him how I love Him and hear Him say that He loves me. I want to see Him and speak in His physical ears and hold onto His physical hands and kiss His feet. I want to see Jesus, don't you?

Oh, my friends, the very first thing I want to do is to see Jesus, and I will, thank God! Jesus said, "I have gone to prepare a place for you. And if I go and prepare a place for you, I will come again, and receive you unto myself; that where I am, there ye may be also."

Then when talking about the second coming, Paul says, 'Now, brethren, I don't want you to be sorrowing like the people who have no hope. This is what to tell them: For the Lord Himself shall descend from Heaven with a shout and with the voice of the archangel, and the trumpet shall sound and the dead in Christ shall be raised and we shall be changed and caught up together with them to meet the Lord in the air, *and so shall we ever be with the Lord!*' (I Thess. 4:16,17).

Oh, praise to His name! I don't care where He goes—it will be Heaven where Jesus is. Yes, I will have Heaven when I have Him—His smile, His wisdom, His holiness, His goodness, His love and mercy and righteousness! That will be Heaven. I will see Jesus, and that will be Heaven!

VII. No Sorrow in God's Tomorrow

What other blessings in Heaven? Well, the Scripture says, "And God shall wipe away all tears from their eyes." I thank God that one day all sorrow and sighing will be over.

I had a letter this week that touched my heart. The writer said, "Brother Rice, I long to see you. Thank God, one of these days we will be where there are no partings!"

Won't it be fine when God Himself takes plenty of time to wipe away all tears! I will get in line. I could almost cry some more tears for the fun of having them wiped away by the Lord God Himself! I will then rejoice that I have had burdens. I will then rejoice that I have even been sometimes tempted, if the Lord Himself will take time to wipe away all my tears. That is the kind of place Heaven is going to be. I want you to go there. When God Himself shall wipe away all tears, that is going to be a wonderful time, isn't it?

VIII. There Will Be No More Death

And He said there will be no more death. This past week I

held a funeral here. I said all the words of comfort I could to the family. Then at last the loved ones came by. The daughter said, weeping, "O Daddy, are you going to leave me? And I thought you would get well!" They led her away and took the body of Brother Warren to Waxahachie for burial.

But thank God, there will be no more death in Heaven! One day there will be no more death! Won't that be fine? That is the kind of place Heaven is going to be.

The next verse says:

> *And God shall wipe away all tears from their eyes; and there shall be no more death, neither sorrow, nor crying, neither shall there be any more pain: for the former things are passed away.*

I said at that funeral, "We will be getting good news in Heaven. Now we hear news of death." A woman called the other day to say old Mother Berry had fallen and broken her hip and is now at Parkland Hospital. That is sad news. One day nobody will bring a sad word of accident or a word of death.

A young man brought word that his neighbor was hit by a car and killed over on Jefferson Street. Won't it be fine when there is no more sorrow and no more crying?

You know, I am about ready to say good-bye to this old world. You can have this old world with its poverty, with its sickness. This old world can go. There are too many hospitals for me, too many graveyards for me. This old world has too many strikes, too many wars, too many sorrows, too many broken friendships, too many divorced homes, too many failing eyes. There are too many out of work, too many who can't pay their bills.

One day we will say good-bye to this old world. We are going to a place where all will be made new. Each will have a new sheet of paper to start out anew. We have failed here. But our purity, holiness, righteousness, will not fail then. People won't have homes disrupted by sorrow, broken by sin, when we get to the place where old things are passed away. It won't be the same in Heaven as it is here.

Now listen as I sing this well-known song:

> There's no disappointment in Heaven,
>   No weariness, sorrow, nor pain:
> No hearts that are bleeding and broken,
>   No song with a minor refrain:
> The clouds of our earthly horizon
>   Will never appear in the sky,
> For all will be sunshine and gladness,
>   With never a sob nor a sigh.

Won't that be good in those days? Old things will be passed away and all things are made new!

> We'll never pay rent for our mansion,
>   The taxes will never come due,
> Our garments will never grow threadbare,
>   But always be fadeless and new.
> We'll never be hungry nor thirsty,
>   Nor languish in poverty there,
> For all the rich bounties of heaven
>   His sanctified children will share.

Chorus: (Brother Stroh joins in)

> I'm bound for that beautiful city
>   My Lord has prepared for His own;
> Where all the redeemed of all ages
>   Sing 'Glory' around the white throne;
> Sometimes I grow homesick for heaven,
>   And the glories I there shall behold;
> What a joy that will be when my Saviour I see,
>   In that beautiful city of gold!

Have you lost a loved one? Did death come in at the door? Was sorrow and parting yours? Listen then:

> There'll never be crepe on the doorknob,
>   No funeral train in the sky;
> No graves on the hillsides of glory,
>   For there we shall never more die.
> The old will be young there forever,
>   Transformed in a moment of time;
> Immortal we'll stand in His likeness
>   The stars and the sun to outshine.

Brother, I am going! Thank God, I am going to be there when the old things will be passed away and sorrow and sighing shall be no more and there is no more pain, no more dying, and when God Himself will make all things new! That is the kind of a place Heaven is, and I am going there!

IX. Will We Know Each Other in Heaven?

The question arises, Will we know our loved ones when we meet them in Heaven? The answer is without a shadow of a doubt, we certainly will! Perfect, immortal, glorified, resurrection bodies will look very, very much like the mortal, corrupt, earthly bodies from which they will be made. All of us then in the next world, both in Heaven and Hell, will have perfect memories and we will recognize each other.

Elisha knew Elijah even after he was translated and caught up to the Lord in a whirlwind and a chariot of fire. Jesus, after His resurrection, was recognized by His disciples. He had the same scars in His hands, the same wound in His side. Even doubting Thomas was convinced against his will that it was the Saviour.

Lazarus and Abraham knew the rich man in Hell and he recognized them—Lazarus whom he had known and Abraham whom he had never seen. All three, saved and lost alike, remembered the things that had transpired on earth and knew about the five lost brothers who were yet alive.

Certainly, in Heaven, with perfect knowledge and perfect memory and with physical, recognizable bodies, we shall know each other.

Elijah and Moses certainly knew each other and knew Jesus when they met on the Mount of Transfiguration. And they all knew and there discussed the future atoning death of Jesus on the cross, "His decease which he should accomplish at Jerusalem."

People in Heaven, then, know what is transpiring on earth, though they do not communicate with us. Hebrews 12:1 says, "Wherefore seeing we also are compassed about with so great a cloud of witnesses," which indicates that the Christian dead look down upon us and are concerned about the race we run here.

In Revelation 6:9-11 we are given a glimpse of "the souls of them that were slain for the word of God, and for the testimony which they held," and we are told, "They cried with a loud voice, saying, How long, O Lord, holy and true, dost thou not judge and avenge our blood on them that dwell on the earth?" **These** martyred saints in Heaven are interested in what is going on on earth and have it explained to them why we should wait with patience for justice to be done on earth!

Certainly, then, people in Heaven know each other, know how things are going on the earth, and in fact, know far more than we do here on the earth.

First Corinthians 13:9-12 says:

For we know in part, and we prophesy in part.

But when that which is perfect is come, then that which is in part shall be done away.

When I was a child, I spake as a child, I understood as a child, I thought as a child: but when I became a man, I put away childish things.

For now we see through a glass, darkly; but then face to face: now I know in part; but then shall I know even as also I am known.

In this world we know only in part. Now we only see through a glass darkly. Now we only partially understand. But, thank God, one day we will see each other face to face, will know each other's hearts. Yes, then we shall know even as we are known. In other words, we will know each other as God knows us, in that good time!

On her dying bed, my mother looked up into Heaven and said, "I can see Jesus and my baby now!" Do you suppose that was merely hallucination? No, no! She saw and recognized her baby who just a few months before had gone on to be with the Lord. After my mother bade us good-bye, she closed her eyes and went to be with Jesus. I am sure she still could recognize her baby and all her loved ones gone on before.

I have heard the flimsy argument that in Heaven we could not be happy if we knew that some loved one was not there. The answer is this: We will love all people then, not merely and selfishly our own. And if some reject Christ and miss Heaven, we will feel just as our Saviour does about it, that we are sorry they are lost but we know that God did right about it. Brother, if you get to Heaven, you will be mighty well satisfied with everything the Lord has done. Certainly we will know our loved ones in Heaven.

X. The Future Heaven Will Come Down to Earth

There is another important word about Heaven that I want to bring before I close. My friends, notice this. One day Heaven is going to come down and be on earth. I read many times this Scripture before I noticed this: "And I saw a new heaven and a new earth: for the first heaven and the first earth were passed away; and there was no more sea. And I John saw the holy city, new Jerusalem, COMING DOWN FROM GOD OUT OF HEAVEN, prepared as a bride adorned for her husband" (Rev. 21:1,2).

Then in the same chapter, verse 10, "And he carried me away in the spirit to a great and high mountain, and shewed me that great city, the holy Jerusalem, DESCENDING OUT OF HEAVEN FROM GOD."

Yes, it is coming down. It is coming down to the earth. Why is it called new Jerusalem? It has got to come down here and land at Jerusalem and be the center for the new earth, a new Heaven on a new earth. Yes, that holy city will only be the capital city. Abraham "looked for a city." He gazed out all over that country—the land of Canaan—and wondered just where the Temple would be. The mansion I will have will come down. Yes, Abraham looked for a city.

As Abraham followed the will of God and camped on the prairies and valleys of Palestine, God said to him, "Lift up now thine eyes, and look from the place where thou art northward, and southward, and eastward, and westward: For all the land which thou seest, to thee will I give it, and to thy seed for ever" (Gen. 13:14,15).

The same promise was repeated to Abraham, Isaac and Jacob, and to David and Israel, that God in the future would give the land of Palestine as an eternal home of blessedness, Heaven on earth, for Abraham and his seed (Gen. 17:8; Gen. 26:3,4; Gen. 28:13; II Sam. 7:10; Ezek. 36:24-28). All of these promises teach that the believing seed of Abraham will eventually have an everlasting possession in Palestine, which would mean an eternal Heaven on earth.

Abraham, Isaac and Jacob all died in faith not having received the promises. We are told of Abraham, "By faith he sojourned in the land of promise, as in a strange country, dwelling in tabernacles with Isaac and Jacob, the heirs with him of the same promise: For he looked for a city which hath foundations, whose builder and maker is God" (Heb. 11:9,10).

Then in verse 13 we are told, "These all died in faith, not having received the promises, but having seen them afar off, and were persuaded of them, and embraced them, and confessed that they were strangers and pilgrims on the earth."

They obtained possession of not even so much of that land as to put foot upon (Acts 7:5). But they knew that God would one day keep His promises, and so they looked forward to that wonderful city of God!

So here in Revelation we are told of how this holy city that Abraham looked forward to, the new Jerusalem, will come down from God out of Heaven to be the capital city of Heaven on earth, to be literally a new Jerusalem, not Palestine.

XI. God Selected Jerusalem As the Site of the Temple Hundreds of Years Ahead of Time

The Lord said to Abraham one day, "Take now thy son, thine only son Isaac, whom thou lovest, and get thee into the land of Moriah; and offer him there for a burnt-offering upon one of the mountains which I will tell thee of."

He made that journey of three days. What heartbreak! Finally he took the fire and laid the wood upon the altar, bound his son and took a knife to slay him, but God said, "Stop, Abraham! I know you believe in Me." Abraham thought God would raise his boy from the dead. He then saw a ram caught in the thicket and he killed it for a sacrifice. God had picked out that place eternally as the site of Jerusalem and the Temple.

The next time we find Mount Moriah mentioned, a plague was on the nation Israel and they were about to be consumed for their sin. God led David to go out to the outskirts of the city and

buy the threshing floor of Ornan the Jebusite as a place to build
an altar and offer sacrifices. He did that and the plague was
stayed. That was at the same place, on or by Mount Moriah.

The next time we hear about this place is in II Chronicles the
3rd chapter, verse 1, which says, "Then Solomon began to build
the house of the Lord at Jerusalem in Mount Moriah, where the
Lord appeared unto David his father, in the place that David
had prepared in the threshingfloor of Ornan the Jebusite."

And so this holy spot where God has placed His name
perpetually will be the site where the new Jerusalem will come
down from God out of Heaven to the earth.

There will be a new Garden of Eden on the earth, sin will be
done away, and the tabernacle of God will be with men, and God
Himself shall be their God for an eternity of Heaven on a new
earth. Brother, I am going to be here!

XII. Unregenerate Men Not Fit for Heaven

Another word. Don't you know that men are not fit for
Heaven? What would you do if when you got to Heaven you had
a poor, frail mortal body and everybody else had perfect bodies?
If you had poor eyesight, ears not perfect, your body stooped
with age, disease germs, decay—that would not be Heaven! Oh,
you are not fit to go to Heaven this way: where there is no
sorrow, no crying, no pain, no death. . . . You can't get to
Heaven unless something happens to you. You must have
something mortal man does not have, by nature, in both body
and mind and soul. God alone can make you fit for Heaven.

Do you know what the difference in Heaven and earth is?
This is it—sin! There are folks like you on earth, folks like me.
That is what is wrong with this earth! We are not fit for
Heaven. No wonder the Saviour said, "Ye must be born again."
And, "Except a man be born again, he cannot see the kingdom
of God." You must be born again. Why should anybody have to
argue that a sinner needs to be born again? Don't you know you
are not fit for Heaven, not fit for the company of angels? You
are not fit to walk those streets and eat of the tree of life and
drink of those celestial waters, clear as crystal that proceed out

from under the throne of God, not fit to see the holy face of God. You couldn't see His face and live.

Sinners, don't you see we must be born again? This vile nature must be changed. You need a new heart and a new nature. You must be a partaker of the divine nature. You need to be made into a child of God before you are fit for God's home and God's tabernacle. You must be born again! You need a change of heart!

This other thing becomes obvious. Can you just get ready and go up? Every plane has a "ceiling." With extra care you could get a little higher, put on more wings, a bigger motor and get a little higher. You can seal up the cabin of the plane, take an oxygen tank and supercharger and get a little higher. You can get in a stratosphere balloon and you may get as high as twelve or thirteen miles, but you can't go any higher. You would never get to Heaven. You miss Heaven a million miles that way. *The Lord* has to take man to Heaven.

Here is the whole secret. Jesus said, "*I* am the way." He said, "*I* am the door: by *me* if any man enter in, he shall be saved." Jesus said, "Let not your heart be troubled: ye believe in God, believe also in me." He said, "*I* go to prepare a place for you. And if *I* go and prepare a place for you, *I* will come again, and receive you unto *myself*; that where *I* am, there ye may be also. And whither *I* go ye know, and the way ye know."

Thomas—good old Thomas cleared up lots of things for me. If he hadn't been there to ask questions I might be in doubt and troubled. But for his lack of faith for the Lord to explain away, what would we have done? Thomas said, "Lord, You say we know the way. I don't know the way. How are we going to get there?" Jesus said, "Thomas, I am the way, the truth, and the life, and no man cometh unto the Father but by Me. I am the way." Oh, if you have Jesus—

> **Jesus, Jesus, Jesus,**
> **Sweetest name I know.**
> **Fills my every longing,**
> **Keeps me singing as I go.**

If you have Jesus, you are safe for Heaven. If you have one to change your heart, to give you a name there, you can go. I have

One who writes my record clear there, have One to intercede for me, have One who will someday call me up and I will go, not because I climb up or fly up but because He calls me and carries me. He who made me lifts me. That is the only way. Just get taken to Heaven.

If you don't get a free pass, you will never get there. "The wages of sin is death; but the gift of God is eternal life through Jesus Christ our Lord." Everybody who goes to Hell works his way, but the man who gets to Heaven was given a free ride for nothing!

The blood of the Saviour paid for sinners, my friend, when you trust in Jesus for salvation. You will get to Heaven no other way. "This is the record, that God hath given to us eternal life, and this life is in his Son. He that hath the Son hath life; and he that hath not the Son of God hath not life."

My dear friend, if you have Jesus, you have a home in Heaven.

You remember the story of the king who made a marriage for his son and bade many. He sent his servant to say, "All things are ready, mine oxen and my fatlings are killed. Come to the marriage." They made their excuses, but later some came. One man came not having on the wedding garment. A poor man couldn't dress fit for a wedding of the king's son. The king provided the wedding garment. He said, "Friend, how camest thou in hither not having on the wedding garment?" And he was speechless. The king said, "Bind him hand and foot and cast him into the outer darkness. There shall be weeping and gnashing of teeth."

Outer darkness! Outside in the darkness are sorcerers, whoremongers, the fearful and the unbelieving and the abominable and whosoever loveth and maketh a lie! On the outside! Oh, don't be on the outside!

XIII. Are You Ready for Heaven?

My friends, you surely know I wouldn't come tonight just to do some Bible teaching alone, however sweet this truth is. It would make me happier in Heaven to meet you there. You surely know I couldn't come just to give a lecture. If I could get you to be saved who are unsaved, get your minds more set on Heaven, the rest of you, that is what I want. I want you to be ready for Heaven. And the only way is to take Jesus and be saved, have your sins forgiven, be born again while you can.

Don't you want Christ? He is the only hope for sinners. Don't you want forgiveness and salvation tonight?

This 22nd chapter of Revelation closes with that marvelous invitation, "The Spirit and the bride say, Come. And let him that heareth say, Come. And let him that is athirst come. And whosoever will, let him take the water of life freely."

My friends, if you want it, you can have it. Heaven says, "Come." The Holy Spirit, the saints all say, "Come to Heaven." Even I say, "Come. I want you." The Spirit says, "Come." The bride says, "Come." Everybody who hears ought to say, "Come."

Come on to Heaven! Whosoever will can come to Heaven.

Your sins may be as scarlet, but they can be white as snow in a moment. You may be a harlot, but you can be made pure. If your hands are dripping red with human blood, Jesus can cleanse them. He died for you. The way is all paid. He said, "Come to Heaven." The Spirit says, "Come on; be ready for Heaven." Let every Christian say it, and tell people, "Come on and go to Heaven with me."

Years ago a president's mother was dying back in Ohio, Cincinnati—I think it was President McKinley's mother. The duties of state were very heavy upon him. He sent word, "Mother, I am awfully busy. The burdens are heavy, but when you tell me, I will come."

One day his mother said, "You had better wire William." So they sent the wire. "If you want to see Mother alive, you must come." He wired back, "Tell Mother I'll Be There."

He drove to the station. They had a special train on the track steamed up and ready. Everything was put on the sidetrack for this train as it rushed through.

When the train got to Cincinnati, carriage and team were waiting. The Chief of Police had cleared the traffic. In a gallop they drove to the cottage where his mother lived. He got out and went in. He got there in time to tell his mother good-bye. She said, "I knew you would get here." He saw his old mother and kissed her good-bye and she went on Home.

That telegram, "Tell Mother I'll Be There" was put in the newspapers that day, and a certain man saw that telegram the president had sent to his mother. He thought of so many, many mothers in Heaven longing to see their children, so he sat down and wrote the words of this song Brother Stroh is going to sing, "Tell Mother I'll Be There."

As he sings it, my friends, I hope everyone here—preachers, other men, women—will make a new resolve. Oh, let's make sure it is settled! Let the angels sing it in Heaven, "He'll be there. He trusted Jesus. He has been born again. He'll be there!" Let the mothers in Heaven hear it. "God, I will meet my mother and my Saviour and my loved ones in Heaven. I'll be there." As he sings you pray, and may God open your heart to heed its message.

> When I was but a little child
>   How well I recollect
> How I would grieve my mother
>   With my folly and neglect;
> And now that she has gone to Heav'n
>   I miss her tender care:
> O Saviour, tell my mother, I'll be there.
>
> *Chorus*
> Tell Mother I'll be there
> In answer to her prayer—
> This message, blessed Saviour, to her bear!
> Tell Mother I'll be there,
> Heaven's joys with her to share,
> Yes, tell my darling mother I'll be there.

Let's bow our heads before Brother Stroh sings this next verse. I think it is not wrong for me to remember my mother in Heaven, not wrong for me to have a holy ambition, to make a holy resolve that by the grace of God I will meet her.

I wonder how many now have mothers and fathers or wives or babies or someone very dear to you in Heaven? Let me see your hands. Thank you. God bless you.

How many of you can say, "Brother Rice, I thank God that my Saviour can give them the word that I am saved and I am ready and will be there because I trusted Jesus"? How many can say, "By the grace of God, I will"? How many can say, "I am saved and I expect to be there. I have been born again"? Can you?

Oh, my friends, if you are not saved, don't you want to be? Listen to another verse of it as Brother Stroh sings. Everybody pray. (With bowed heads people listen while Brother Stroh sings.)

> When I became a prodigal,
>   And left the old roof-tree,
> She almost broke her loving heart
>   In mourning after me;
> And day and night she prayed to God
>   To keep me in His care:
> O Saviour, tell my mother, I'll be there!

15—Are You Thirsty?

*(Stenographically reported sermon preached Sunday
night, June 4, 1939, Dallas, Texas)*

*For I will pour water upon him that is thirsty, and
floods upon the dry ground: I will pour my spirit upon
thy seed, and my blessing upon thine offspring.*—Isa.
44:3.

This verse is a clear promise of the Holy Spirit. How happy I
was in reading a book by D. L. Moody to find these words: "God
said, 'I will pour water on him that is thirsty.'" I must have
read that verse many times, but I never did get it until D. L.
Moody called attention to it. God said, "I will pour water upon
him that is thirsty, and floods upon the dry ground: I will pour
my spirit upon thy seed, and my blessing upon thine offspring."

I. The World Cannot Quench Thirst

Water for the thirsty! Water for the thirsty! This world is
thirsty. On the cross the Lord Jesus said, "I thirst! I thirst!"

There are two reasons why Jesus was thirsty. He was thirsty
physically. The blood was pouring from the wounds in His body,
and with the sweat pouring from His body, His tongue
thickening in His mouth, the sun shining down in the hot
climate—Jesus was thirsty, physically. But let me remind you,
Jesus was taking the part of sinners, and He was suffering as a
sinner suffers. When Jesus said, "I thirst," He meant with the
thirst of Hell.

The world is thirsty. Every man you meet is thirsty. If you
could see in people's hearts the trouble and heartbreak, you
would find that the whole world has unrest, unease and
dissatisfaction. People are longing for what they do not have.

This world is thirsty. Sometimes people do not have sense enough to know what they seek and what their hearts long for, but they are thirsty.

Last week an ocean liner was anchored at Havana, Cuba, with more than nine hundred Jewish refugees who wanted to land there. They sent representatives to government officers, but were told they could not land. Finally the authorities said if the Jews did not move their ship away from the Havana harbor, it would be escorted out into the sea. They said, "We will not have these Jews land here." And the paper this morning said that the ship started steaming slowly back toward Hamburg, Germany, for the Jews to be put off again on the soil of those who hate and despise them. They were radioing and trying to get arrangements with the Dominican government to get off there and start life again in that strange land.

I will tell you what is wrong with our Jewish friends. There is a hunger in their hearts that will never be satisfied until they turn back to God.

Do you know what obsessed Hitler with that wringing fire in his bones and heart that made him crazy for land and created such a hatred against the people of God? After all, people are thirsty. Hitler thought he would be satisfied if he had power. And people all around us think if they had money they would be satisfied. This world has a famine; it is dry ground. This world needs a rain from God. God says, "I will pour water upon him that is thirsty."

The Bible says many things about those that thirst. In John the 7th chapter, Jesus stood and cried that last great day of the feast and said, "If any man thirst, let him come unto me, and drink. He that believeth on me, as the scripture hath said, out of his belly shall flow rivers of living water" (vss. 37,38).

In the 4th chapter of John, Jesus came to the woman at the well of Sychar who was thirsty and had come for water. She had brought her pitcher, but Jesus gave her water that was not in the well. Jesus said to her, "If thou knewest the gift of God, and who it is that saith to thee, Give me to drink; thou wouldest have asked of him, and he would have given thee living water."

And little by little He brought out her deep dissatisfaction and uncovered the thirst of her heart, and showed her her need of what He had, and turned her away from her hatred of the Jews and of Himself. Finally she said, "I know that Messias cometh, which is called Christ: when he is come, he will tell us all things."

And Jesus said, "I that speak unto thee am He. I am the Messias."

When she knew that He was the Messias, she dropped her waterpot and forgot all about the water she had come out to get, and ran into the city to tell the men. She had living water "springing up into everlasting life."

This matter is all through the Bible. In Isaiah 55:1, the Lord says, "Ho, every one that thirsteth, come ye to the waters, and he that hath no money; come ye, buy, and eat; yea, come, buy wine and milk without money and without price."

In the last chapter of the Bible, Revelation 22:17, the Lord Jesus says again, "And the Spirit and the bride say, Come. And let him that heareth say, Come. And let him that is athirst come. And whosoever will, let him take the water of life freely."

If anybody is thirsty, let him come. The Bible is full of invitations to the thirsty. There is water for the thirsty.

I have found this: anything that is a legitimate desire, God has the answer for. My father said something one time that touched me as a boy: "Love begets love." If you love somebody, and if you pour out your soul in love, there is something about love that must have an answer. God never put a hunger in the heart unless He had something to satisfy that heart.

Oh, if we could just realize today that for all the things we need, God has the answer. If you are thirsty, God has water for you. You may think you want this or that or the other, but really you do not.

It is not money you want. Maybe you think if you had money you would educate your children. But it is not money you want. It is the end of the thing you want. If you had money, you might ruin your children. It is not money, but something else you want. I use that only as an illustration.

We have a thirst for something only God can give. God has water for every thirsty heart, and He says, "I will *pour* water on him that is thirsty." We Christians ought to expect more, ask more and want more than we do.

Sometimes people say to me, "You expect too much of a Christian life. You cannot expect God to give you everything you want." They have the "disappointed" attitude and they discourage young Christians from asking a lot.

Many people say to young Christians, "Be careful. You are asking so much. God will not change all nature in order to have it when you want it to rain, or quit raining when you want it to stop." Older Christians sometime say to young Christians, "You cannot be on the mountaintop all the time; you have got to come down to drudgery," thus discouraging young Christians from wanting to be happy and filled with the Spirit.

I know a good preacher, pastor of a good church in Texas, preacher with a keen mind, a good knowledge, a good delivery, a good personality, but on this thing he fails. He never has a great pouring out of the Spirit of God on him. One time when I was just a young preacher, I said to him, "I must go. I am bound to get out in revivals. I am dying to preach."

He said to me, "John, I had that unrest lots of times, but you cannot always be on the mountaintop and in the midst of revivals. You must learn to be content without it."

Well, I have not learned to be content without it, and I ought not to. He sinned when he put the lid on that hunger of his own heart and did not ask for what he wanted and did not have God fill the hunger in his heart. He should have gotten the power and let God pour water on him.

God says, "I will pour water on him that is thirsty." If you are thirsty, God has the answer. If you have a hunger in your heart, God has the answer. If there is a need in your soul, God wants to fill it. He said, "I will pour water on him that is thirsty."

II. Not Just a Glass Full but Floods!

Are you thirsty? Do you want God to give you a glass of water? God says, "I will do more than that; I will turn the hose on you." God says, "I will POUR water on him that is thirsty."

Is it just a sip of water you ask for? Is it like the rich man in Hell who asked for Lazarus to dip the tip of his finger in water and cool his tongue? A lot of Christians are like that rich man. They just want a drop of water. They just want to get by. They do not expect to be happy in this life.

I asked a preacher how he was getting along, and he answered, "I am as near happy as I can expect to be in this world." A preacher of the Gospel talking like that! My friends, God has an abundance! If you are thirsty, He will just turn the hose on you. He will *pour* water on you who are thirsty, *and floods* of water on the dry ground.

Some people have an idea that a man can drink a little of the water of God, and wipe his lips and nobody can tell he has had a drink. But God wants you to get water all over you. "I will POUR water upon him that is thirsty."

Some people cannot understand how one can be *filled* with the Spirit, and *baptized* with the Spirit, too. He is filled inside and baptized outside. God turns the hose on you, and you get plenty outside and plenty inside, too.

I will tell you what is wrong with many of us. What we need is a fresh pouring out of the Spirit of God upon us, a thirst for God until God will pour out afresh His Spirit upon us. God is ready now, and willing. He has plenty and you and I should not be satisfied with just a little that does not show.

Is my preaching old to you? It would not be were you really on fire for God, and if I were really filled with the Holy Spirit of God. God is not old to you. The Spirit is not old to you. If we were filled with Him, He would burn in your heart while I preach, and there would be a joy you could not control, and you would be praising God all the time. That is what you need in your life and what I need on my ministry.

Too many Christians are like the young man who was working with ungodly people, and when his pastor asked him how he was getting along, answered, "I am getting along fine. Nobody there knows I am a Christian yet." Nobody had found out he was a child of God! Nobody had embarrassed him, because he had not told anybody that he was a Christian!

That is the kind of water that just gets inside and does not get on the outside. You have not had a flood poured out on you. But God wants to turn the hose on you. He said, "I will *pour* water upon him that is thirsty, and floods upon the dry ground."

I want you to get this clear. The Lord is not talking about just having the Holy Spirit to dwell in a Christian. Every child of God does have the Spirit of God dwelling in him. If you are saved, the Spirit of God lives in your body. But the Bible does not talk nearly as much about the Spirit of God living in your body as it does about the fact that you can have the Holy Spirit upon you.

The Holy Spirit *in* you is one thing; that is being saved. But the Holy Spirit *upon* you is another thing. You can drink, and that is salvation. But then, "He that believeth on me, as the scripture hath said, out of his belly shall flow rivers of living water"—that is salvation for somebody else. God is not just talking about your getting saved. He says, "I will water your parched soul and pour floods on the cracked ground."

III. The Freshness of a Spirit-Filled Life

Sometimes there is a drouth in West Texas and the sky is like brass, the earth is like iron, and the ground is cracked in great fissures. I have gone all over the land with an auger. Down, down we would go, trying to find water. Then we would tie a rope in a ring, and let it down twenty or thirty feet. Everything had gone dry in the whole county, and we were hauling water for ninety head of stock. The grass was burned and the fields were bare. Even the cane was curling and brown. A drouth in West Texas is a terrible thing.

But a drouth on your soul is worse. Do you have a drouth today? Don't you want the flood of rain to make your life green again with a richness of the Spirit you used to have? Do you want the rejoicing you had as a young Christian? Do you want power and freshness of the Spirit of God?

Some Christians have no greenness in their lives. The Bible says about a righteous man, "He shall be like a tree planted by the rivers of water, that bringeth forth his fruit in his season;

his leaf also shall not wither; and whatsoever he doeth shall prosper."

But a lot of Christians not only do not have any fruit; they do not have any leaves on the tree! Jesus came to a fig tree and cursed it because it had nothing but leaves. But a lot of Christians do not have even the leaves of rejoicing. There is no sweetness, no summertime in your heart.

The song says, "There is springtime in my soul today," and there ought to be springtime, the song of the birds, the blooming of blossoms, and the growing of green things in the hearts of Christians.

If your life is drouth-stricken, with the fields barren and the pastures dried up and eaten by grasshoppers and the streams all gone and dry, then come to God today and say, "Lord, I want You to pour out upon me the Spirit of God and give me a freshness and a greenness, and the joy and fruitfulness again."

Out in West Texas it gets so hot the cotton droops and it looks like it is going to die. And a lot of you droop down in your seats like these cotton leaves. Your joy is about gone. After awhile a good shower comes and the cotton freshens up and straightens up and grows out again.

If the Lord would pour upon us His Spirit, our lives would be green with blessing.

God says, "I will pour water upon him that is thirsty and floods of water upon the dry ground." God has plenty. Do not think that God has a limited blessing for us. Everywhere I go I find defeated Christians who try to excuse themselves for not having joy and power. They are just living on the husks in the hogpen, as the prodigal son did.

It is not right for the sons and daughters of God to go hungry and thirsty when their Father has plenty. We can have the floods of water, and we should have them.

IV. Are You Satisfied With What You Have?

You are saved, and you should praise the Lord for that; but do you have all you want? The Lord says, "I will pour water on him that is thirsty."

One of the greatest sins of Christians is that they are not thirsty. They are dried up, yet are not thirsty.

A man told me the other day that because his wife did not drink enough water, she was always ailing. One day a friend said to him, "If you will cooperate with me, I will get your wife well."

This man then saw his friend's wife and said to her, "I have invented what is known as an electro-bar."

"What is it?" she asked.

"It has in it certain radium and chemical properties. If it is put in water and left to stand, then when you drink that water off the electro-bar, it will revitalize you inside and make over your whole body entirely. It will make old folks young again."

"Is that so?" she asked.

"Yes, I sell them for ten dollars each, but if you will use it, I will give you one. You have been going to a doctor and taking medicine, but this will cure you. Will you follow the directions if I give you one of them?"

"Yes, I will," she said.

He went down to the brickyard and got a brick—just an ordinary brick—took it to a steel lathe and had it ground off smooth. After he had it ground to the size and shape he wanted, he then took it to the lady and said, "Now you put this in a certain size vessel, and leave it so many hours, and then drink all the water in that vessel."

She did that every day religiously, and she drank all the water, as instructed. She drank and drank and drank. Then she would fill the vessel up again—of course with the bar in it—and drink the water.

It wasn't long until everything wrong with her got all right. She began to think she was all right. She drank that water until the disease was conquered and everything was all right.

It is one of the saddest things in the world to find Christians who are not even thirsty enough to drink. God has for you an abundance, all of Heaven's floodtides of blessing, but you do not drink. If you are thirsty, He will pour water on you. The trouble is that you are not thirsty. We can have the blessing of God, and springtime in our hearts, and a song in our life all the time. When there is a praise service, you would jump at a chance to testify. A word for sinners would be burning on your lips. You would feel that you must speak for God. You would wake up in the morning with joy because it was a new day in which to serve the Lord. You would have a joyful floodtide, an irrigated life, with your roots down in the abundance of water.

Oh, poor, drouth-stricken Christian, with your leaves all withered and your fruit knotty or no fruit at all, God wants to give you plenty and make you a blessing! "I will pour water upon him that is thirsty, and floods upon the dry ground."

God is still in the flood business. Everywhere I go preachers are teaching that the Holy Spirit came at Pentecost and then there was a flood of power, wonderful power, and three thousand were saved in a day. But they teach we cannot have that any more. They teach He came like a flood once and that was enough.

But it is a strange thing. It is true that Simon Peter had to preach to the crowd that crucified the Lord Jesus Christ. But I go to Hastings, Minnesota, tonight, and I will have to preach to people just as wicked, just as Hell-bound, just as Hell-bent as they were. And I need the same power Peter had, the same joy, the same answers to prayer, the same wisdom.

As I sit down to write for my paper, I need wisdom. I must have wisdom from God. I cannot write so as to bless hearts and feed Christians and inspire preachers unless I have what they had in Bible times. I have a right to the floods if I preach as I ought to.

Some people are dry-weather plants. They get accustomed to living in a desert. You will find certain kinds of plants out in Arizona that grow only in the desert. Most of them are cactus. They are accustomed to the desert air and the desert climate. It takes very little water for them.

That is the way it is with some Christians. They are perfectly content to barely get by. If they get a prayer answered once a year, just as long as there is "no visible mark of Thy displeasure on us," as they say in their prayers, that is good enough for them. They are not concerned as long as they are getting by without God whipping the socks off them. They are desert Christians.

They ought to be like the place I saw out in that same desert country. Away back up in the mountains the wonderful Coolidge Dam is across the Gila River, and the water from the mountain sides forms a lake out there close to Phoenix. That water is used for irrigating. And my, my! the dates and figs and tomatoes and grapes and all kinds of things! They are the richest and finest in the country for flavor and size. In that irrigated part they can raise anything. They have the sunshine and the soil; all they needed was the water.

Some of you Christian people never win a soul. It would be wonderful if God really turned the hose on you! You might turn out to be a fine soul winner. We ought not to be content to be ordinary, dry-land Christians. God wants to pour floods upon the dry ground. He said, "I will pour water upon him that is thirsty and floods upon the dry ground." Floods of water! You know the sin everywhere is that people are content without Holy Spirit power. People do not have the power, but they do not worry about it.

Brother Robert Hughes said to me one time, "Brother Rice, pray with me." He had not won a soul, but he was told that was all right, he would later on, that he had to grow in grace. But he did not feel that was right; Robert felt he should win souls now.

I said, "Robert, you go to a private place and pray now and ask God to take all hindrances out of your life and pour out His Holy Spirit on you so that you can win somebody to Christ today."

After praying, Robert went up to the courthouse and met some fellows sitting on the courthouse lawn. Robert was in despair and was distressed. He got it on his heart to talk to some of the men. He talked to one of them, but he did not win him to Christ. Robert came back disappointed to tell me. I said, "Well, we will pray and keep on praying." We had prayer again.

Robert saw the man the next day and stopped to talk to him again. Lo and behold, he found the man had already been saved!

I said, "Robert, the reason people are not soul winners is because they do not make up their minds that they can be and ought to be. They have no business waiting about this matter and hoping later to grow into it."

Some people think they are not called to win souls and are not supposed to have blessings like others.

One preacher not long ago said, "I want to have all the power Moody had." And somebody said, "God does not want many people to be Moodys." Maybe He does not want everybody to be a Moody, but He wants us to have as much power and love as Moody had, as much of the Holy Spirit working in us as Moody had.

It is a sin that we do not expect great blessings. We are content with a dribble from the faucet. Some of us are like a bird that sees a drop of water on the faucet, and he will sit down there and get that drop of water in his bill. That is the way you dribble along—just a drop, just a bare existence of a Christian life—when God wants to pour out upon you floods of water on the dry ground.

V. What Is Our Duty, Then?

If we can have the power of the Holy Spirit, what are we going to do then? In the first place, each of us should say, "God helping me, I am going to get thirsty."

How does one get thirsty? For one thing, good, hard work will make you thirsty. You get a pitchfork and take a bundle wagon and wade in. Begin in the morning about 4:30 and work until sundown with a pitchfork loading a string of wagons, and you will get thirsty. It will not be long until your overalls will be soaked through. They will dry and then you will sweat some more and dry again. Your clothes will begin to look salty. You will be bound to drink some water. Good, hard work is one way to get thirsty.

And another thing. Salt will make you thirsty. The Bible is like salt. Brother, if you take the Word of God and read the Bible like you ought to, you will get thirsty.

I never will forget when as a boy about fifteen or sixteen I read in the 2nd chapter of Acts how at Pentecost the power and joy came and three thousand were saved in a day. I thought that was wonderful. I thought so then and I think so now. That is one of the most fascinating chapters in the Bible. How wonderful that God Himself would just come and get in men until they speak with power and three thousand are saved in a day. That is a marvelous, glorious thing.

I read it and read it. Brother, if you read the Bible, you will get thirsty.

It is a sin that we do not ask much when we pray. Everywhere I go, people say, "Do not go meddling with God's affairs. Do not ask so much. Do not expect so much." Or they say, "Maybe it is not God's time." I tell you, God wants us to come with hungry hearts and ask. Is that not what He said in Luke 11:13: "If ye then, being evil, know how to give good gifts unto your children: how much more shall your heavenly Father give the Holy Spirit to them that ask him?"

He will give the Holy Spirit to whom? To them that ask Him. Then ask Him. If you want Him, then why do you not ask and have? We can have power, we can have blessing, we can have refreshing and joy, we can have the greenness of living, we can have the fruit of the Spirit. But if we want, we must ask.

Do you want Holy Spirit power? Somebody says that is out of date. What a funny idea! Or you say you do not believe in praying for the Holy Spirit. Do you believe in praying for revival? What is that but praying for the Holy Spirit? Did you ever pray for a sinner to be convicted? Who does that? You are praying for the Holy Spirit to work then, aren't you? Did you ever pray for the Holy Spirit to bless a preacher as he preaches? You ought to. If you pray for that, what do you pray for? Really, you are praying for the Holy Spirit of God to be on the preacher to anoint him and help him preach.

Well, did you ever pray for God to help you pray right? How does He do that? The Holy Spirit of God prays for us and with us with groanings that cannot be uttered (Rom. 8:26). That is praying for the Holy Spirit to take charge of you and move in and fill you.

It is silly to say that you do not believe in praying for the Holy

Spirit. You do not know what you say. If you are a Christian, you ought to pray for the Holy Spirit. Jesus told us to pray for the Holy Spirit. "If ye then, being evil, know how to give good gifts unto your children: how much more shall your heavenly Father give the Holy Spirit to them that ask him?"

I am not talking about the Holy Spirit coming in to live in your body. I am saying that the Holy Spirit will be poured out upon you and cover you until you will be a wet-weather Christian, an irrigated Christian, a green Christian; until you will be a fruit-bearing Christian, a happy, contented Christian.

May God pour out water upon us! He said, "I will pour water upon him that is thirsty." Are you thirsty? God has plenty for you.

VI. Poor Thirsty Sinner, Let Jesus Fill Your Empty Soul With the Water of Life

Here is another word to unsaved people. God has a promise for you. You ought to be saved. Brother Joe was telling me about a woman who would not be saved because she said she could not yet give up her pleasures. And yet she and her husband cannot meet their bills with what money they have, and they have a good salary. She said she was afraid to read the Bible because it condemned her sin. She had no peace and was constantly afraid. And yet she was saying she could not give up her pleasures! Is that not a strange thing?

The Devil catches us as monkeys are caught. The way to catch monkeys is to put some nuts in a jug with a hole just large enough for the monkey to get his hand in. So Mr. Monkey comes along and he wants that nut, so in goes his hand and he grabs the nut. He gets his hand in there and cannot pull it out. But he will not turn loose of the nut. He works and works trying to get his hand out. Still he will not turn the nut loose. Finally they come back and put a sack over his head and carry him off. He does not have any pleasure, but he will not give up the nut.

And this girl said, "No, I will not give up my pleasure."

I talked to two young men. Both of them were out of work. Both were poor. One of them was out trying to get a little work in the harvest fields. One of them had been out working, and was heading back toward Post, Texas, where they lived. I tried to get them to be saved. No, they said, they were not ready to give up their pleasures. They did not have any pleasures to give up!

What do you have to give up for Jesus Christ? Some people say, "I feel sorry for a preacher's wife." I do not want anybody feeling sorry for my wife. She is happy. In the first place, she has more friends than she otherwise would have had, and does more good, and has more blessings and joys and treasures in Heaven. Nobody has any business feeling sorry for a preacher's wife. It is a glorious thing for God to put His hand on a man to preach, and God gives the wife blessings that she would not otherwise have.

You are not giving up something for God, you are just letting God pour water on you when you are thirsty. We need to wake up to the fact that God has what we need. Other things do not satisfy.

After God had sent a thousand dollars and we had paid up the printing bill about which we had been praying for more than a year, then I was praying again for the same thing. The Lord had answered prayer, but I had to pray again, because we had another week's printing bill and had to have money again for THE SWORD OF THE LORD.

I found that what He gave back there was not enough; I must keep on praying. God has the money, but He may want me to sacrifice. Money will not satisfy. I need the freshness of God Himself. I need His riches, His blessing, His power. I need communion with Him, fellowship with Him. I need that, and I can have that, and I am not going to be happy or satisfied with anything less.

Are there some here today who are not saved? It may be you are thirsty, or it may be you are not. If you are not, there is nothing I can do for you.

I told you about two men I picked up, two young fellows. I had one read the 3rd chapter of John. When he read, "Ye must be born again," I had him stop and I would talk a bit, then he would read more. "The wind bloweth where it listeth, and thou hearest the sound thereof, but canst not tell whence it cometh, and whither it goeth: so is every one that is born of the Spirit." When he read that, I would explain the mystery of the new birth. Then he would read, "As Moses lifted up the serpent in the wilderness, even so must the Son of man be lifted up." I told the story and illustrated what it meant. Then he read, "For God so loved the world, that he gave his only begotten Son, that whosoever believeth in him should not perish, but have everlasting life." He read all the chapter. Finally they had to go, but they did not accept Jesus Christ. They turned Him down. I was sad. I tell you, some are hungry, and some are not.

I stopped in a little filling station at Whitesboro, Texas, and had a bottle of orange-ade. I asked the attendant where he went to church. He said he was a Methodist, was once a member of the Methodist Church. I asked him if he was saved.

"I don't know."

"Have you ever been born again?"

"No, I guess not. I don't know."

I talked to him awhile. He told me he had lost his wife, or that she had lost her mind. He had two children, but both had gotten married. He did not have anybody left, so he moved into town and it was so lonely. He was living in the filling station. We talked about the Lord. I asked him if he would mind if I prayed before I left.

"No, I would be glad for you to."

So in that filling station we prayed, and when I got through and looked up he was weeping. He said, "I am so glad you came by."

I said, "I want to meet you in Heaven."

"I want to meet you, too."

I asked him if he was willing to trust Jesus Christ and depend upon Him now. "Are you willing to do that?"

"Yes," he said.

I said, "Here and now will you shake hands with me and put your trust in Jesus Christ and depend on Him to take you to Heaven and satisfy your heart and give you comfort for your sorrows?"

He said, "Yes, I will."

He stood there and wept as I went away.

If you are thirsty, God has water for you. That poor woman at the well of Sychar in Samaria had a deep thirst in her heart, though she hated the Jews and hated Jesus. But when He began to pry, and she saw her sins, she said, "Oh, when the Messias cometh, He will tell us these things."

Jesus said, "I am the Messias."

She had walked all the way from town down to this well to get this pitcher full of water, but she forgot all about it and left her pot and ran back to town to tell the men she had found the Messias. God had poured out on her thirsty soul the water of life. And you can drink, too, if you are thirsty.

Don't you want Jesus? Some are thirsty, and some are not. If you are not thirsty, there is nothing I can do for you. I am sorry if you do not have a hunger for God. I am just sorry you are going on to Hell.

There is nothing I can do for you if you are satisfied. But now you have your family about you. One day you will not have. You do not have time to come to church now, but you will have time to go to a funeral one of these days!

You are not thirsty? Well, one day you will lose your job. You have good health now, maybe. One of these days you may be flat on your back—in a week's time, maybe. You will get thirsty then. I cannot help you if you do not have a thirst for God.

But if there is a dissatisfaction, a thirst, then God says, "I will pour water upon him that is thirsty, and floods upon the dry ground: I will pour my spirit upon thy seed, and my blessing upon thine offspring." And He said, "The Spirit and bride say, Come. And let him that heareth say, Come. And let him that is athirst come. And whosoever will, let him take the water of life freely" (Rev. 22:17).

Are you thirsty? Then God has water for you, and you can have it and be saved and go away happy.

16—Flowers, Birds and Oxen

Does God Take Note of Our Needs and Troubles? Will He Care for Us When We Trust Him? Will God Pay Us When We Work for Him?

(Stenographically reported sermon preached Sunday morning, July 30, 1939.)

Are not five sparrows sold for two farthings, and not one of them is forgotten before God?

But even the very hairs of your head are all numbered. Fear not therefore: ye are of more value than many sparrows.

Consider the ravens: for they neither sow nor reap; which neither have storehouse nor barn; and God feedeth them: how much more are ye better than the fowls?

Consider the lilies how they grow: they toil not, they spin not; and yet I say unto you, that Solomon in all his glory was not arrayed like one of these.

If then God so clothe the grass, which is to day in the field, and to morrow is cast into the oven; how much more will he clothe you, O ye of little faith?

And seek not ye what ye shall eat, or what ye shall drink, neither be ye of doubtful mind.

For all these things do the nations of the world seek after: and your Father knoweth that ye have need of these things.

But rather seek ye the kingdom of God; and all these things shall be added unto you.—Luke 12:6, 7, 24, 27-31.

For it is written in the law of Moses, Thou shalt not muzzle the mouth of the ox that treadeth out the corn. Doth God take care for oxen?

Or saith he it altogether for our sakes? For our sakes, no doubt, this is written: that he that ploweth should plow in hope; and that he that thresheth in hope should be partaker of his hope.—I Cor. 9:9, 10.

There are three things I want to lay on your hearts: *lilies, sparrows* and *oxen.*

I. Does God Care About Sparrows?

Consider, first, the sparrows. The Scripture says, "Are not five sparrows sold for two farthings, and not one of them is forgotten before God?" Brother preacher, when we first begin to preach, we often use the same illustrations. Jesus used illustrations. He said, "When you sell a sparrow, you get one farthing for two sparrows." Another time He said, "When you sell more than that, you give five sparrows for two farthings." In one case there was one illustration and in another there was a similar illustration. Sparrows are very cheap, aren't they?

Few people thought that one of the least bits of money, the smallest piece, would buy two sparrows. In our case the least money we have is a penny, but if we had a mill like the tax money, we could buy two sparrows. And if you had two of them, you could buy five sparrows.

The Jews set their nets around the eaves of the houses, and the sparrows could be caught easily in the nets or traps. One could buy two sparrows for a farthing. But Jesus said, "Do you know that not one sparrow ever gets caught but that God knows it? And not one sparrow ever falls to the ground but that He knows it?"

We come down the sidewalk and see a dead sparrow. We do not know what parasite or tick or disease killed it. But God knows. You don't care, but God cares! God takes note of sparrows. Sparrows were so unimportant that if a Jew sold two, and then if the fellow wants two more, the Jew would say, "All right, I will give you another one free." He just throws in one free. But God cares about that extra sparrow.

And then Jesus said, "If God cares for sparrows, you are worth more than fowls; He will care for you."

The question, then, for Christians: Does God care about you? Let's put it this way, making it more definite: Does God take note of you and your sorrows and your troubles? We have a feeling that some things are too little to pray about, but they are not too little to worry about! There are some things that you do not pray about, but you fret about them. You know, the Lord says, "In nothing be anxious; but in every thing, by prayer and supplication with thanksgiving, let your requests be made known to God" (A. S. V.). You are not to pray only when your home is about to be sold, not pray only when your wife and children are sick and about to die, but *"in every thing."* God is a God of details and He knows and cares.

He cares so much that He says the very hairs of your head are all numbered. Not one hair falls when you comb your hair without His knowing about it.

Take this little girl. Honey, when you combed your hair this morning before you started to Sunday school, maybe one little blond hair came out of your head with the comb. God knows about that. He said, "Gabriel, change your record. This little girl has only so many hairs now." God says that He keeps up with our hairs and knows how many we have.

You say, "Does God care that much?" Yes, God cares about sparrows and God counts the very hairs of your head. There isn't anything too small for God.

Nearly all our fret is over little things. Nearly all of it is over little things. Listen. Brother Harris, if you had six little girls and if just one of your girls should chew half a stick of gum and leave it in the seat of your chair, and you sit down on it, that would be enough to fret you more than if you lost some money. Isn't it strange? Most of our troubles are little ones. Aren't most troubles small troubles? But they can run you crazy.

When nervous people have a nervous breakdown, it is nearly always over little frets and little worries which we do not take to God. Oh, God cares about our little troubles. Why don't we take every one to God who cares and counts our hairs? You haven't anything so small, anything that worries or bothers you, but that God cares about it. If it worries you or bothers you, God cares about it.

I printed in my paper this week a part of a sermon I preached in January a year ago, and I call to mind this. One day when Mrs. Rice was out of town Mary Lloys called the office and said, "Daddy, may I fry some potatoes for supper?" (At our house fried potatoes are a great luxury. It takes a lot of them.)

"All right, go ahead," I told her.

After a while she phoned back and said, "Daddy, I am in trouble. I got two or three potatoes peeled and sliced and put them on to fry and started to peel some more, and we haven't any more."

"Go across to NuDeal Grocery and get some potatoes, and get a can of spinach, and I will come by and pay for them," I told her.

But I felt in my pockets, and I didn't have any money. The afternoon mail was brought to me, and somebody had sent in a subscription, and sent fifty cents extra, and said, "This is for Brother Rice to use as he wants to." When I got down to the NuDeal Grocery on the way home and paid that forty-four cents I owed, I had six cents left.

You know, I have prayed a lot of times and gotten money; I have prayed and gotten fifty dollars, or a hundred dollars; I prayed last week and God's mercy made it so we could pay a bill we didn't think we could pay—the printing bill on THE SWORD OF THE LORD. I have prayed and God has given an average of thirty dollars a day for five months. But I had rather have that fifty cents that day to cover that little bill. That meant that God was saying, "Don't worry, old boy, I am looking after your little needs."

God cares for sparrows—the hairs of your head are all numbered. Take to God your burdens and sorrows. He knows every sharp word someone speaks to you. You do not have to talk back. Don't you worry, leave that to God. Don't you worry, every need you have—whether big or little—God remembers it.

You know the Lord thinks a lot of me. He has all my hairs counted. He knows everything about me. God has our hairs counted, and not one sparrow falls to the ground without the Father's knowing about it. Blessed be God who cares about little things and makes note about little things.

Nothing is too big and nothing is too little for God.

Does Jesus care when my heart is pained
  Too deeply for mirth and song;
And the burdens press, and the cares distress,
  And the way grows weary and long?

O yes, He cares; I know He cares,
  His heart is touched with my grief;
When the days are weary, the long nights dreary,
  I know my Saviour cares.

He cares about little things.

II. If He Cares for Sparrows, Then We Ought to Trust Him

Jesus made an application here in this Scripture and I ought to make it, too. He said, "Whosoever therefore shall confess me before men, him will I confess also before my Father which is in heaven" (Matt. 10:32).

You know, when you come to a man and say, "Listen, you need Jesus," and he says, "I would like to be a Christian but I do not see how I can. I do not see how I can get by if I live as strict as a Christian should. I have got to make a living," then you can tell him, "But listen. He notes the sparrow's fall, and He has your hairs all numbered. He cares about you, and you can afford to trust Him."

God is a God of detail. He is the God of the oceans. He holds the sun in its place. He keeps the planets in their orbits. You can take a telescope and look out to the magnitudes and immensities of God and prove there is a God. But you can take a little microscope and look into one drop of water and see the animal life—too small for man to see with his natural eye—and prove there is a God, too. God is a wonderful God who knows details, and He cares.

You could tell him, "And if God loved you enough for Christ

to die for you and save you, don't you know He loves you enough
to take care of the details of every day?"

Oh, why fret? Why care? God cares, and He takes note about
it. Don't you worry. If you really believed that, you would never
try to get even with anybody. You would leave it all to God. He
said, "Vengeance is mine; I will repay, saith the Lord." If you
believed that, you would never fret about tomorrow. God cares.
Why fret over tomorrow? Let God worry about that. It is His
worry, not mine. There is plenty of money in His treasury.

God cares for sparrows. If that is the kind of Saviour He is, I
can trust Him. I wouldn't be ashamed to claim that kind of a
Saviour. If that is the kind of Saviour He is and if He loves me
and watches and even one baby sparrow cannot fall out of the
nest without His notice and care, then I can trust Him as my
Saviour.

You say, "I wish they were all dead. They stop up the gutters
of my house and cover the place with fleas." But if one falls out
of the nest they made up there in the gutter of your house, God
knows and cares, even if you don't. God cares. And I am glad He
is that kind of a Saviour. Don't you think you could trust your
soul to Him? If He cares for sparrows, then He cares for
bricklayers, Mr. Hoover. Yes, He cares, and He knows. He is the
God of the sparrow.

God loves the raven, too. The raven doesn't have barns to lay
by food in. What will birds do in the winter, then? The Bible did
not use the squirrel as an illustration because he cooperates and
lays by nuts and everything he can get, but the Lord uses
something that doesn't have barns and doesn't hide anything in
a hollow tree. He takes the bird that lives from day to day,
never laying anything by.

God cares for birds, but He cares more for Harris than for
any crow or than any pretty field bird that He ever made. God
cares, and He looks after details. You ought to be able to trust a
Saviour like that with your soul.

III. God Cares for Flowers, Too

The next thing is, God cares for the lilies. That is a little
different. Does God take note about me and does He know my

troubles and sorrows? Yes, He knows. If I trust Him, will He care for me? I want you to know that it is a matter of faith. You say, "Faith is easy. I have lots of faith in God." Listen, faith is not a feeling; faith is risking something. Faith is something you cannot see but something you must trust.

I am reminded of a good preacher brother who wrote me the other day. He reads the paper, and was especially blessed by the article in THE SWORD OF THE LORD last week on "Five Reasons for Tithing." He told of bills that he needed to pay, but he said, "I have made up my mind that you are right; I ought not to rob God in order to pay my bills. I am going to put God first and I believe He will help me pay my debts. You convinced me I ought to tithe and I am going to do it," he said.

Listen, will God take care of me if I trust Him? That is real faith. You can't say you trust in God if you do not trust Him enough to tithe. To just say you have a warm feeling in your heart toward God is not faith. If you trust, you try God out. Really trusting God gets some things settled. If you live the same way, and if your mind is on laying by for the future or on making a living, and you say, "I am trusting God," then I frankly say you are not. For the Lord says, "Lay not up for yourselves treasures upon earth, where moth and rust doth corrupt, and where thieves break through and steal." The Bible even says, "Take. . .no thought for the morrow." Don't worry about what is coming tomorrow. Don't try to save up, and save up, and save up. *Real* faith says, "God is going to take care of me tomorrow."

Someone says, "That business of staggering off into the dark and not seeing tomorrow: I don't know if I will be well enough to work or not. I don't know if I will have a job. I may have a doctor bill to pay. Who knows? I had better save up for tomorrow." And God says, "Can't you trust Me?" God says, "You must believe, you must trust Me." It isn't faith if you do not live a different life. You are not really trusting God about your daily life.

"Consider the Lilies," Jesus Said

"If I risk Him, will He really look after me?" you say. God

says, "Look at the lilies. See these lilies growing here, these wild flowers? Aren't they lovely things?"

From my childhood I have been fascinated with flowers, wild flowers particularly. I think they are lovely. God has never made anything prettier than a flower. Did you ever open up a flower and look down at the dainty colors, the pastel shades, the pistils that come up with their dainty pollen, how they are made and the sweet odor? Only God could make the flower. God loves flowers. God is the only one to smell most of them and look down in their hearts and see their beauty. God must love flowers. That is the reason the poet said in Gray's "Elegy Written in a Country Churchyard":

> Full many a gem of purest ray serene
>   The dark, unfathomed caves of ocean bear:
> Full many a flower is born to blush unseen,
>   And waste its sweetness on the desert air.

God loves flowers. He says, "Consider the flowers. Even Solomon in all his glory, as a king with robes of purple and scarlet, a crown of gold and a sceptre—even Solomon in all his glory wasn't dressed up as pretty as one of these flowers." You worry about something to wear. "O ye of little faith," Jesus said. If God so clothed the grass of the field which tomorrow is withered and some one comes along and gathers it up and uses it to heat their oven, and it is burned up and gone, if God cares that much about the grass in the field, so lovely today and tomorrow gone—don't you know He cares for you? "O ye of little faith."

Flowers do not get out and spin and toil and work. There is some virtue in working. There is some virtue in not being lazy. God is pleased with a fellow who is willing to work, but when work comes to be translated into covetousness, a lack of faith, and unbelief, then work becomes a sin.

When I was in the Seminary at Fort Worth, I was then a college graduate. I would get out there on the campus and cut weeds for thirty cents an hour and make enough to get us a little hamburger meat for the next day. We had a soup bone one day and then in about a week we had hamburger meat. It was always good when we would have soup bone, for we would have soup one day and hash the next! My wife would say, "Why do you work just enough to pay for what we have to have right now? Why don't you go ahead while you have a little time and work?"

"No sir! God called me to preach. I will work what I have to work and the rest of the time I will put in studying my Bible and winning souls. I will not lay by any money. I am just hoeing to pay expenses."

A Christian ought to learn this. God says He takes care of flowers when they do not spin, and do not sow. They can't shop, and they do not have a bank account. And the flowers, look how pretty they are dressed! Then won't God clothe you, too? "O ye of little faith!" God says, "Take no thought what you will wear."

You say, "I think a man who is a preacher ought to dress well," or "I think a preacher's wife, or a Sunday school teacher, ought to dress well," or you say, "I think I ought to dress nice and not have people thinking I am trampy." Don't you think God knows about that as much as you do? Let God worry about that. The God who cares for birds and flowers will care for you, too. That is His worry. "Seek ye first the kingdom of God, and his righteousness; and all these things shall be added unto you."

I am not saying that you should go without decent clothes. I am saying, Let God do the worrying about decent clothes. You attend to God's business and leave it to Him about food and clothes. Don't worry about it. God in His mercy is going to take care of flowers. And if He cares for flowers, He will care for anybody else who will look up to Him and drink the dew of God's Heaven and breathe the perfume of a consecrated life into God's air. God is going to breathe His blessing on the flower or on the Christian like that.

IV. "Doth God Take Care for Oxen?"

He cares for flowers. He cares for the ravens. Does God care for oxen? He cares for donkeys. One time one donkey was mistreated, and God gave that donkey a mouth to talk back to the fellow, Balaam, who was beating her. God said that a merciful man will be merciful to his beast. God cares for oxen, but He was not writing that for oxen.

God said when you are getting ready to thrash out the grain, you cut it with a hand scythe and tie it with a bunch of straws. And then you lay it around in a circle, and yoke some oxen up together, tie a string to a ring in the nose of one of the oxen and to a stake in the middle, and you let the oxen tread around and around on the grain. Now they are treading out the grain. When they get that all out, you have to pitch it up and the wind will blow the threshed chaff away, and pitch it up again and the wind will blow some more away. After awhile you have it all winnowed, and you have the grain thrashed.

I know how you feel about those oxen. You say, I have gone out and cut that grain with a hand scythe to make wheat and bread out of it, and I want to put a muzzle on these oxen. I can't let them eat up this wheat while they are tramping it out. But God says, "Don't do it." Well, but they eat so much. "Let them go ahead and eat," God says, "and you do what I tell you to do."

So for fifteen hundred years every Jew who followed the Bible did not put a muzzle on his ox. Jews may have said, "My, these oxen will eat a whole bushel of wheat!" But they went on this way for fifteen hundred years. Then Paul said, "I will tell you what God is talking about. He wanted every burdened preacher to know that God cares about him and his family. God looks after him, and He says, "Don't muzzle the preacher that works for you."

Don't you know you ought to let a preacher go unmuzzled if he treads out the corn of the Gospel for you? God is not caring for oxen so much as He is caring for preachers.

Now, I come to answer the next question: Does God take thought of my sorrows and burdens? "Yes, I do," God says. "I note every sparrow that falls."

The second question I ask is: "If I trust Him, will He care for me with food and clothes?" Yes, He clothes the lilies of the field, so He will clothe you, "O ye of little faith."

But if I cut loose of everything else to work for Him, will He pay me? That is a question that comes many times in the Bible. Back yonder people drifted away in the Old Testament in the book of Malachi. They said, "It is vain to serve God." They said that it doesn't pay to serve Him.

One preacher came to me who was about out of the ministry. He said, "I do not have any education and they will not pay me without an education." He was saying, "It is vain to serve God."

Old Peter said the same thing. "Lord, listen, I sure had a good fishing business. If I do say so myself, I had a humdinger of a fishing business. My brother and I caught lots of fish and we made a good living. Jesus, You know I left my family and my fishing business; in fact, I left everything; now what will I get for this?" Peter said, "You don't mind my asking, what are we going to get for this? We have left all to follow You."

And Jesus said, "You twelve are going to sit on twelve thrones judging the twelve tribes of Israel. And everyone that hath forsaken houses, or brethren, or sisters, or father, or mother, or wife, or children, or lands, for my name's sake, shall receive an hundredfold, and shall inherit everlasting life" (Matt. 19:29).

My wife went down on Zangs Street the other day to look at a house. She said that someway God keeps putting it on her heart, and she just wondered. . . .We gave up a home in Fort Worth and moved to Dallas, a six-or-seven-room brick veneer. We loved it so because we planned it ourselves. We claimed the promise then, "If we leave houses or lands for His sake we will receive an hundredfold," and my wife said, "I wonder if God meant this house to be part of the hundredfold?" I don't know, dear heart, whether that is what God meant, but don't worry, God means every bit of it.

If I work for God, will He pay me? If I leave all for Him, will He pay me back? I answer back—God said, "Watch the oxen when they are treading out the corn. They do not have a muzzle on them." I tell you, if you want to work for God, get to treading out the corn, and you will get some of the corn. You surely will.

I get a certain letter regularly from Oklahoma, from a woman to whom I preached the Gospel back yonder. She heard me over radio WBAP, and was saved. And every now and then when we are in a tight, God puts it in that dear woman's heart to send some money. Usually it is an uneven amount, because it is her tithe.

If God didn't want a muzzle on the oxen, if you work for God, He is going to see that you get paid. Praise His name!

Does God care for oxen? Yes, but He primarily cares about preachers. He cares about His workers. If you get out here and spend your time away from home and your business, working for God, how will you come out? I will tell you how. "Seek ye first the kingdom of God, and his righteousness; and all these things shall be added unto you." That is God's plan from the Word of God. Wouldn't it be wonderful if we believed it?

Does God care for oxen? He said, "Don't muzzle the ox." The fellow who sows has a right to reap. If he sows spiritual things, he has a right to reap some carnal things. And I tell you, Nichols, it is a wonderful plan of God. If I had that kind of God, I would cut loose and go to preaching. I would head straight for a Bible school, and the God who cares for sparrows, the God who has all your hairs numbered—that same God knows about the lilies of the field, and He has plenty for you. He is the God who clothes the lilies, and He will do the same for you. He feeds the birds and He will feed you.

God does care for oxen. Yes, He wants them to have something to eat when they tread out the corn. If you had that kind of a Saviour, you could say, "All right, I will go on and serve God and trust Him and live and work for that kind of a Saviour." Oh, God cares for birds and flowers and oxen, and God cares for His children. God cares for preachers. Bless His name! Why doesn't somebody shout Hallelujah? That is a wonderful Saviour!

Does God take note of my sorrows and my burdens? Yes, He does. He cares about birds, and He cares for you.

Will God supply my need if I start out in the dark on His Word and risk Him? Yes, all these things shall be added unto you, the Scripture says.

Will God pay me if I work for Him? Yes, a hundredfold in houses and lands and brothers and sisters and mothers in this world and in the world to come a wonderful life. God will pay me because He cares for oxen and He will not allow anybody to muzzle the ox.

You will find a lot of folks who try to muzzle a preacher. But God doesn't want preachers muzzled—either about what they say, or about what they eat. If we have a God like that who cares for them, I could preach for that kind of a God. Yes, sir! I believe I could serve that kind of a God and risk Him to take care of the future.

What a wonderful Saviour! God cares for us. God cares for sparrows, and so God cares for Christians.

Somebody says, "I am only a poor widow." But if God cares for sparrows, He cares for widows. Or someone may say, "I am but an orphan and I do not have anyone to take my part." God takes care of birds and He takes care of orphans. You are very poor, you say, and if you do not work awfully hard, you will not make it. Don't depend on your working. Depend on God. I believe you ought to work, "But seek ye first the kingdom of God, and his righteousness; and all these things shall be added unto you."

Somebody says, "Well, but is it really worth what it costs to be a preacher?" Yes, the God who will not allow a muzzle to be put on the ox will take care of you.

I have repeated it a good many times, but I want you to get it. It pays to serve God. You ought to say, "If that kind of a Saviour loves me like that, I will love Him and trust Him with all my heart, and claim Him as my Saviour."

17—Abounding Grace

(Sermon preached Sunday morning, August 30, 1936.
Stenographically reported.)

Turn in your Bibles to the 5th chapter of Romans, please. I am going to speak to you this morning on "Abounding Grace."

But not as the offence, so also is the free gift. For if through the offence of one many be dead, much more the grace of God, and the gift by grace, which is by one man, Jesus Christ, hath abounded unto many.

And not as it was by one that sinned, so is the gift: for the judgment was by one to condemnation, but the free gift is of many offences unto justification.

For if by one man's offence death reigned by one; [That is, when Adam sinned everybody died.] *much more they which receive abundance of grace and of the gift of righteousness shall reign in life by one, Jesus Christ.*

Therefore as by the offence of one judgment came upon all men to condemnation; even so by the righteousness of one the free gift came upon all men unto justification of life.

For as by one man's disobedience many were made sinners, so by the obedience of one shall many be made righteous.

Moreover the law entered, that the offence might abound. **But where sin abounded, grace did much more abound:**

That as sin hath reigned unto death, even so might grace reign through righteousness unto eternal life by Jesus Christ our Lord. —Rom. 5:15-21.

Abounding grace and reigning grace! Now we are not the

authors of grace; we are the subjects of grace. We are not the ones who make grace; we are the ones who receive it. Grace is the unmerited favor of God. That means God loves us, God has mercy upon us, looks with favor upon us.

One of the most startling things in the Bible is that it says God loves us. God looks with favor upon us. He is pleased with us. God delights in us. He wants us. God wants us! He paid for us. He bought us. When nobody else would have us, God thought us worth buying with the blood of His Son, and redeemed us to Himself! Oh, the abounding grace of God!

We are the subjects of such marvelous blessings. I want you to think about it this morning with me. "Where sin abounded, grace did much more abound." Then we are taught that Christ died for sinners that grace might reign, that grace might *reign*, that grace might REIGN!

When a man was a lost sinner, sin reigned. Now when one is saved, grace reigns. Grace is the sovereign, the only thing greater than sin. All the Bible speaks of abounding grace, reigning grace.

I. Sin Abounds

You know sin reigns in the human heart. Sin is a most terrible fact, a most potent fact. Sin is a most obvious fact about sinners everywhere, about any man in the world—this preacher, the man on the street, a saved man, a lost man. The most obvious fact about any human being is the fact of sin. Jeremiah 17:9 says, "The heart is deceitful above all things, and desperately wicked: who can know it?" That is the reason in I John 1:8 we are told, "If we say that we have no sin, we deceive ourselves, and the truth is not in us."

When Solomon prayed at the dedication of the Temple as told in II Chronicles and in I Kings, in both cases we are told, "For there is no man that sinneth not." There is not a man on the earth who does not *sin*. The most obvious fact about man is sin. Sin reigns in the natural man. Sin reigns in the unsaved man. Sin reigns in the carnal nature. Sin is abounding.

The most abounding thing in the world of carnal men is sin. There is more sin than money. There is more sin than food.

There is more sin than air or water. The freest and biggest thing in this world is sin. There is more sin among men than anything else. Sin is more abounding than all. There are millions of human beings and there is not one but who has been tainted with sin, mastered with sin.

Sin reigns in the heart of every newborn babe. That baby grows and the carnal nature remains and he is a slave to sin. The Scripture says, "He that commits sin is a servant to sin." Sin reigns in the carnal nature in the natural man, in the heart of all mankind born in sin.

Sin has pervaded every nation, every country, every city. Never a little village somewhere hid in the mountain pass, cut off from the rest of the world, but that sin reigned there. Never a home so happy, with true love founded, where a man loved a girl and took her to himself but that trouble and heartache came in, for sin was there! Sin reigns!

Take every home in Dallas, every home in the nation, and one thing reigns there—sin. Sin reigns wherever man goes. In the natural man sin reigns. Sin is above all in the carnal man, reigns over everything in the natural man.

Now then, as sin reigned and abounded, so God said, "Where sin abounded, grace did much more abound." Where sin reigned, now then by the death of Christ, grace reigns.

> **"Marvelous, infinite, matchless grace**
> **Freely bestowed on all who believe."**

II. Moody and "Grace"

Dwight L. Moody said once that he got his concordance and turned to His Bible, reading everything he could find about grace. He had just started preaching in Chicago. He said there never was a man who did such big business on such small capital. He would get what the Bible said about the blood and get a bunch of people together and give them a Bible reading on the blood. Then he would be set on fire from Heaven as he studied another subject. He would get all the Bible said about that. He didn't have a wonderful knowledge of the Bible or a college education, but he would take what the Lord said.

One day while studying about *"grace,"* he got so enthused and so exalted with the marvelous grace of God that he threw his book down, rushed into the street and the first man he met he asked, "Say, do you know grace?"

The man said, "Grace who?"

"The grace of God that bringeth salvation!"

The grace of God! The marvelous grace of God that reigns and abounds. Where sin did abound, grace did much more abound.

Let us look to the cross of Jesus Christ and think about the grace of God, the loving favor of God toward sinful men who didn't deserve the love of God.

I want you to remember that men are sinners. The best Christian here today may hold a big revival, or go down to the service this afternoon at the jail and get people saved, or have a fine revival service at the lot and a lot of people get saved, but you must kneel down and humbly say, "O God, I am such a poor, sorry, unprofitable servant. I haven't even paid the interest on the investment when You bought me for Yourself. I am an unprofitable servant."

The results are from the abounding grace of God, the reigning grace of God. The abounding must be of grace. The reigning must be of grace. Not our righteousness but the righteousness of Jesus; not our deserts but the mercies of God give us what we don't deserve and couldn't buy. Not good works, but grace.

"For by grace are ye saved through faith; and that not of yourselves: it is the gift of God: Not of works, lest any man should boast." Grace is the gift of God. Grace is the mercy of God. Grace is the favor of God. Grace is the abounding, loving mercy of God. God loves us. Not that we love Him but that He loved us and gave Himself for us.

III. Salvation Is Free

The first thing we need to consider about grace is the matter of salvation. Salvation is by grace. "For by grace are ye saved through faith." Turn to Ephesians, chapter 2. There we are told that we are saved not by works of righteousness; not by good deeds, but by the grace of God.

For by grace are ye saved through faith; and that not

of yourselves: it is the gift of God:
Not of works, lest any man should boast.

Look, begin at verse 4:

But God, who is rich in mercy, for his great love
wherewith he loved us,
Even when we were dead in sins, hath quickened us
together with Christ, (by grace ye are saved;)
And hath raised us up together, and made us sit
together in heavenly places in Christ Jesus:

(Now what for? What is the object of grace? Why does God love us?)

That in the ages to come he might shew the exceeding
riches of his grace in his kindness toward us through
Christ Jesus.
For by grace are ye saved through faith; and that not
of yourselves: it is the gift of God:
Not of works, lest any man should boast. —Vss. 4-9.

No man in the world has any right to boast, "I am doing all the saving myself because I am good." No, not because man is good but because God is good.

Get that on your heart this morning. It will help you never to have doubts about salvation. Salvation is wholly of grace, altogether of grace. Not if I carry my end, God will carry His end. We don't have any end. All we can do about salvation is to take it.

Somebody asked a good Scotchman, "How did you get saved?"

He answered, "Me and the Lord together got it fixed."

"How did you have anything to do with it?"

"I did everything I could to go to Hell, and the Lord did all He could to save me."

Nobody here ever did anything to merit salvation. Nobody here ever did anything to make it so God would want to save you. You didn't beg God into the notion of saving you. You didn't deserve saving. You weren't fit to save. God in His mercy loved you when you didn't love Him. He sought you when you went astray. He saved you when you were not fit to be saved. It is the grace of God by which people are saved. Get that straight.

People ask me why we don't have a mourner's bench. A mourner's bench is all right, but it is not to get God in the notion of saving people. The God I serve is already in that notion; so why have a mourner's bench? The God I serve and preach about is ready to save sinners. It is all right for a man to mourn over his sins. But that comes just as well after a man is saved as before.

Maybe we ought each to have private places of mourning. We should lament over our sins and be sorry for them. But I want everybody here to remember that nobody deserves salvation. Nobody pays for it. You take it free or you don't get it. Grace is offered you free. God pours out His abundant mercy. Nobody would seek God unless God called him. Jesus said, "And I, if I be lifted up from the earth, will draw all men unto me."

It wasn't because you ran after God that you got God to save you. God put things in your heart. He pulled you, and drew you, until you couldn't get away.

That prodigal boy who went home—do you know why he went? The father was praying for him, and that father had some way through the years put such bonds on that boy's heart that he couldn't forget about Father's love. He knew his father loved him. He couldn't forget how good he had been, and it pulled him home. It wasn't of his own goodness.

When you and I were saved, it was because God in His mercy ran after us and sought us.

When Adam sinned, he ought to have gone immediately and begged God for forgiveness. But he didn't do that. He did what every one of us does—he hid himself from God, and God had to call, "Adam, where art thou?" He called Adam. After awhile when God finally ran him down, Adam let God forgive him.

Nobody here was saved until God ran you down to get you saved. The first time God called, you should have been instantly willing, glad to be saved, but you were not. God finally put it in your heart to be convicted and put it in your heart to seek God. That is the reason you are saved. The mercy of God, the grace of God, the abounding love of God overcame your sins.

Your sins just abounded, and abounded, and abounded. You were a fountain of wickedness—just turned out wickedness and grew wickedness and spread wickedness everywhere. But the grace of God abounded more than our sins and caught up with us and ran over us and one day got us saved when we didn't deserve it.

Oh, my friends, the abounding grace of God is the only explanation why any poor sinning man could ever get to Heaven. Where sin abounded, grace did much more abound. Where sin reigned, so must grace reign. My friends, it is the grace of God, the infinite grace of God by which people are saved. If you get that settled, then you are fit to talk to sinners and tell them God loves them.

IV. Sinners Cannot Make Peace With God—It Is Already Made

"Have you made peace with God?" one asks a stranger. You can't make peace. Jesus made it. "Make your peace with God," we exhort. I want you to know Jesus has already made peace. All you need do is accept it. It is already made. You don't have to come and say, "Now Lord, look here! I am trying to make peace with You." God has already made peace; given His Son, the blood is poured out. The record is all ready to be changed in Heaven. You should only take what God offers you free and pushes on you and pours out on you—the abounding grace of God.

If any sinner here wants to be saved, all you have to do is to want to.

God never expected you to do anything that would change your own heart. He does not expect you to do anything to earn credit in Heaven. You can't earn it. The only thing that you can do is to admit that sin abounds, and God answers back, "My grace abounds more than sin does." Your sins may be piled as high as a mountain, but He is willing to wash them away in the fountain filled with blood. The grace of God abounds more than all your sins. God's love goes on after you and after you and after you (pointing to individuals).

The thing for us to do is to take what is so freely offered. If there is a boy or a girl, a man or a woman, one who is unsaved, not a Christian, put this down: The Lord Jesus died for you.

Why do people have trouble getting saved? They are looking in their own heart and are afraid they can't make it. They don't feel right . . . looking at their own feelings . . . looking at the life they think they have got to live here later on. They say, "I don't believe I can live it." "I am afraid I can't last long . . . sin so abounds!" I know it, but what you ought to remember is that where sin abounds, grace did much more abound. People are saved, not because they make up their minds, "I will live without sin and I will live a perfect life." Not because one says, "All right, I will do the thing . . . I will do my part and the Lord will do His, and we will struggle along together." No! People are saved because God's wonderful grace is so free and so great.

One is saved when he says, "I can't make it! I am undone! I will let Jesus do it. He loves me! His grace is my only hope!" If you want to be saved, just look to the crucified Saviour. Remember that God loves you. His abounding grace is all that can keep man out of Hell.

Someone says, "Brother Rice, are you certain you are going to Heaven?" Absolutely certain, as certain as I am standing here. Jesus died for me. His blood paid for my sins. Grace abounds! Grace reigns!

V. Not Perseverance but Preservation

The next thing is, people are kept by the abounding grace of God. That is the way they are saved. People are saved by grace and they are kept by grace.

There is an old Baptist Confession of Faith, and part of it I don't like. It says in effect, "We believe in the perseverance of the saints" and that "if they are truly saved they will persevere unto the end." That sounds like the Lord is saying, "All right, I am going to set you on the track. If you persevere, you will go to Heaven. Root hog or die!"

That is not true! I wasn't saved by perseverance to start with. I believe in the *preservation* of the saints, not the perseverance. The fact of the business is, I couldn't risk any thirty seconds of my life to get me to Heaven. I wouldn't persevere that long.

When I would do good, evil is present with me. I can't save myself, nor keep myself saved.

How are we kept then? This is a wonderful story. The way we are kept is "grace did much abound!"

Do you believe Christians sin? I know they do. I not only know about me, but I know about Mr. Renz even. I know something on Mr. Renz. I have some secret information about his sins. I found it in the Bible. "There is none righteous, no, not one." "If we say that we have no sin, we deceive ourselves, and the truth is not in us." I have secret information, positive, authentic information about anybody who says you don't have sin.

There is only one way in the world to get to Heaven, and that is on the train of grace! "For by grace are ye saved through faith; and that not of yourselves: it is the gift of God: Not of works, lest any man should boast."

VI. We Need a "Done" Religion!

You say, "Well, but Brother Rice, if a Christian gets drunk, and then gets in a fight while he is drunk and somebody shoots him and he dies in that state, don't you believe he is a goner?"

No, I believe he *deserves* to be a goner. You say, "Will he be saved?" Not *will* he be saved; he is already saved if he trusted in the blood. It is not whether he *will* be saved. You had better not risk anything about what is going to be; you had better get it done. Too many have a *do, do, do* religion. . . . What you need is a *done* religion. I can look back and say, "On the cross Jesus said, 'It is finished.' Thank God, it is done! Mine is already done! Praise the Lord, it is done!"

A famous prizefighter was converted in a meeting held by J. Wilbur Chapman in Atlanta, Georgia. Mr. Alexander, the singer, urged the preachers to come shake hands with the new converts. One preacher, a very staid, quiet, formal preacher, came to shake hands with the converted prizefighter, and he said, "Well, Brother, I hope the Lord will bless you." This prizefighter jubilantly answered, "He has done done it, Brother!" Already done!

The Lord has already done it for me, too. I am saved. I have a *done* religion. It was finished on the cross of Christ. The unceasing, abounding grace of God saves and then keeps. Brother, if He saves, He does the keeping. After God saves, He does the keeping. Oh, the abounding grace of God!

Now here is a man who abounds in sin. Do you think if a man is really saved, he will then get drunk? Some have. "I don't think he was really saved," you say. It doesn't matter what you think. That didn't keep Noah and Lot from getting drunk, and the Bible plainly says Lot was saved. It says he had a 'righteous soul,' yet he got drunk.

A man who has been active for years in Christian work, after he was converted, went on drinking and trying to quit. Finally he was expelled from college because of drunkenness. He was called then to a special work for God. He is well known and we sing some of his songs.

You don't know what a fellow will do. *Sin abounds!* There are two things you can't talk too much about and can't make too big. One is the sinfulness of man; the other is the grace of God. Where sin abounded, grace did much more abound. The biggest thing about mankind is sin, and the most wonderful thing about God is grace. Where sin abounded, grace did much more abound.

Someone might say that I am encouraging sin. No, I preach against sin and warn against sin. But get it settled this morning that if you are saved, you are going to stay saved. You are going to get to Heaven and enjoy endless bliss through the countless ages of eternity. Nothing we can do can undo it. It is in the hands of God and His marvelous grace.

The next chapter says, "Shall we continue in sin, that grace may abound?" No, we should not do that. God forbid. I must reckon myself dead to sin. But sin does abound and has abounded, and I can only rely on the abounding grace of God.

Some people believe that if you feel so and so, you are saved. If you feel so and so, God will forgive you. It is not settled on feeling! It is settled altogether on the wonderful love of Jesus that He doesn't withdraw!

Read in the 8th chapter of Romans these words:

For I am persuaded, that neither death, nor life, nor angels, nor principalities, nor powers, nor things present, nor things to come,

Nor height, nor depth, nor any other creature, shall be able to separate us from the love of God, which is in Christ Jesus our Lord.—Vss. 38,39.

And love here is another synonym for grace, the grace of God, the love of God that will not let thee go, will not let you be lost, will not let the one He has bought and paid for go to destruction. God's grace will take us Home. That is the way people are saved. That is the way they are kept saved.

VII. Abounding Grace Cleanses From Sin

We are not only saved by grace, but we are kept by grace and cleansed by grace.

We can't deny the sin question, and ought not deny it. The sin question is still there. Grace does still abound. Brother Renz, it is bad to be under the control of sin before you are saved, but it is a horrible thing that we still have to fight sin after we are saved. The sin question is a terrible thing. With my mind I serve the law of God, but with my flesh I still serve the law of sin.

What can I do about it? There is one thing that can attend to sin, can whip sin, and that is the abounding grace of God. But that is available to all—God's marvelous grace.

Do you know what we need to do to get cleansing from sin? First John 1:9 tells us: "If we confess our sins, he is faithful and just to forgive us our sins, and to cleanse us from all unrighteousness." If you want forgiveness and cleansing for sin, you can look up and say, "O God, I have sinned. Please forgive me."

A young man came to me in Fort Worth and said, "Brother Rice, I am in terrible trouble. I want to talk to you." I told him to wait until after the preaching service, then the radio service running until 1:00 p.m., then wait till after baptizing, then I would talk to him. He followed me through the services that day, and about 1:30 or 2:00 we sat down on that winter day in the sun against the side of the tabernacle.

He said, "I was converted. I know it. I lived a good life for a time. Before I was saved I drank and went with wicked women. After I was saved I got in the wrong crowd and slipped. I fell. Then after a time I prayed and promised God that if He would help me, I would never do this any more. After awhile I got a sense of forgiveness and peace.

"But after about two weeks I slipped again and was as bad as ever. I can't control myself. I tried again and promised God this time, sure enough, I would not do it any more.

"I straightened out, but in a little while I got into some bad company, and again the first thing I knew I was drunk and then out with the wild crowd."

He was in such terrible distress. He said, "I can't enjoy sin. Something happened to my heart that causes me to be miserable. I can't enjoy sin like I used to, yet I don't have strength to resist it. But this is the main trouble. I can't go back to God any more. I have lied to God. I do not believe God will believe me if I tell Him I won't do it any more, and I can't come and pray about it. Now what in the world can I do?"

I said to him, "Your mistake was in telling God you weren't going to do wrong. What you ought to make up your mind to do is this: If I sin a million times—I hope you won't—you see it brings trouble and heartache; you see it is wrong and does not pay—if I sin a million times, I still belong to God. He is mine and I am His. I am bought with a price and I don't belong to myself. I have no right to go my own way. If I do wrong, I will come back and confess it to God. Don't make any promises that you will do better, but tell Him you are His, that He bought you, and He will have to take care of you. Confess your wrong."

He said, "But I promised. . . ."

"I know you promised, but sin is so abounding, you failed. But God said, 'If we confess our sins, he is faithful and just to forgive us our sins, and to cleanse us from all unrighteousness.'"

Why should God be faithful? It looks as if it would be our part to be faithful. But grace indicates that the righteousness is all on God's side. If you find favor with God, get along with God, it is not your faithfulness but it is taking the faithfulness of God, calling on the faithfulness of God, counting on the faithfulness of God. It is taking what He so freely gives. Grace is ours! It is in the bargain when we are saved. It is part of the plan of God.

I have sins, but God's grace abounds where sin abounds, and He answers back, "But My grace is sufficient." "Grace does much more abound!" And so if you sin and sin until you say, "I can't quit, I can't cleanse myself, I can't trust myself, I have nothing at all to promise," then listen! Don't look beyond this minute. This minute say, "I am a sinner. I want mercy. God loves me and His grace is sufficient. If I have gone far in sin, He has gone farther to save me." Our sins are not so dark but what the blood of Christ can settle it all. Grace will abound where sin abounded and He will cleanse us! He is faithful and just to cleanse us. That young man got the victory that day, and what I told him helped my own heart.

I never will forget when I backslid the first time and lost all my joy, and how I came back as they sang

Pass me not, O gentle Saviour,
Hear my humble cry,
While on others Thou art calling,
Do not pass me by.

I remember how I came back that night and promised God faithfully that I would not drift any more. But I did. My way of peace with God was not in saying, "I will not do wrong," nor in living a sinless life. But my peace lay in His grace! And when sin again overtook me, I confessed it and claimed that grace that abounds more than sin. Though I know I can't live a sinless life, I can every day get all the cleansing I need, get the peace in my heart. If you have sins that need cleansing, the grace of God is sufficient.

VIII. Grace Can Give Daily Victory

And not only cleansing but victory. Victory is on the basis of the grace of God. Paul said one day, "Now Lord, I have a thorn in my flesh." I don't know what it was, whether some weakness or a habit, but it was in his flesh, either in the literal body or in the fleshly nature. It was a messenger from Satan to buffet him. He said, "Here it is in my flesh, Lord. Remove it." And he besought the Lord thrice, but the Lord didn't do it. He then said, "My grace is sufficient for thee: for my strength is made perfect in weakness." Paul said, "All right, then, Lord, I will glory in my infirmities." God's Word says that God chooses for us to be weak.

God is not responsible when we sin, and we must not make it so or claim it so. We must not ever believe God is to blame when we sin. Now listen! If anybody gets any praise out of getting you to Heaven, it must be God. He says, "If you get to Heaven, I get the glory. I would rather you would be weak and know it." He would rather you would come and from Him have help and victory.

Somebody may say, "I am a strong Christian. Liquor doesn't bother me. I can live a good life." If you say that, then you are a Pharisee claiming false credit for yourself. God doesn't want that. God said, "In your weakness, my strength is made perfect. Paul, you go on hollering for help all the time. My grace is enough." Paul said, "Lord, if you will give grace every day to overcome this thorn in the flesh, I will go on with the thorn and stay humble and call for help every day." And the Lord said, "I will give you grace. My grace is sufficient." Paul said, "Yes, it is. We will make that trade, and I will glory in my infirmities that the power of Christ may rest upon me."

My friend, listen to me! If you want all God has, then get down low. Look at all the meanness of your heart and see that you don't deserve a thing. Then say, "O God, have mercy." He said, "I will. My business is to have mercy."

When we get to Heaven, what will we brag on the Lord about? "That in the ages to come he might shew the exceeding riches of his grace in his kindness toward us through Christ Jesus." Oh, the mercy of God! Victory? Yes, victory.

I think sometimes of how I used to be. I thought, "I will try to keep myself out of bad company. I will try to study the Bible and do this and that and the other." But I have learned the Devil is too strong for me. I don't care how big you get; the Devil is bigger. I can't depend on John Rice. I have made up my mind to risk Him. I will pray the prayer of David, "He leadeth me in the paths of righteousness for his name's sake."

When I get to Heaven, the Lord will say, "John, remember when you thought you were a pretty good guy because you didn't get drunk? when you thought you were pretty smart because you didn't do this or that or the other? when you thought you were a pretty good Christian? Well, it wasn't you. Come here, angels. John, I put the angels down there to guide you in the path for My own name's sake. After all, it was the mercy of God that hemmed you in." God put a hedge about me that would not let me stray. We are supposed to pray every day, "Lead us not into temptation, but deliver us from evil." When you do something good, it is the mercy of God. Oh, may I abandon myself to the mercy of God! Oh, marvelous grace! I will risk it! I will depend on it.

I have had so many times of sorrow over my own sins. I am gaining though, thank God, and this day I have sweet comfort to my heart in this. God says, "The steps of a good man are ordered by the Lord: and he delighteth in his way. Though he fall, he shall not be utterly cast down: for the Lord upholdeth him with his hand." It is the mercy of God that He places around us and covers us and surrounds us when we sin. Where sin abounded, grace did much more abound!

Victory through the Lord Jesus Christ!

IX. God Answers Prayer Through His Amazing Grace

Now what else? I have learned something about prayer. I believe in the prayer of faith. God's best reason for answering prayer is His own grace. I believe in prayer according to the will of God expressed in the Bible. We should be willing to do what God's Word says, have God's Word abiding in us. We should ask in Jesus' name. I believe in being persistent in prayer. When you pray, be humble in prayer. All those things are good, *but answer to prayer is after all a matter of grace!*

What is the main reason we ought to pray? "If ye then, being evil, know how to give good gifts unto your children, how much more—how much more, *how much more*—shall your Father which is in heaven give good things to them that ask him?" He did not say, "If ye then, being evil, know how to give gifts unto your *good* children, or now you pay them back when they behave themselves"—No! You give to your children freely, good or bad, whether they are right or not. If that is in your heart, how much more is it in the heart of God to give. He did not say pay; He said *give*—to give good things to them that ask him. Grace is the main reason a fellow ought to pray.

I talked to a businessman last year. He was heavily burdened. Business deals were tight and he had a great investment, heavy loans at the bank and was nearly up against the wall. He said to me, "Brother Rice, when I pray, I am so poor and sorry and I haven't anything much to pray about. I can only pray to the Lord every night, 'Lord, remember these twenty-five families who are supported by my wages. Lord, help me hold this thing together so I won't have to fire these men. Take care of these families.' That is the only way I know how to pray."

I told him, "You are surely passing up the best way of praying."

"How is that?"

"Why, you act as though you have to put up a big argument so God will see where He can get some returns on His investment. That is not the way to pray."

"What should I do then?"

"You go right straight up there, knock on His door and say, 'O God, you are my own Father. I am Your child. You love me and Your grace is enough. I need this, just because I need it.' Whether you are good or bad, you are God's child. He loves you. And He said, 'If ye then, being evil, know how to give good gifts unto your children, how much more shall your Father which is in heaven give good things to them that ask him?' Ask Him." I said, "You have a right to come to your Heavenly Father and say, "Father, I don't deserve a thing, but You are my Father. I need this. I am in a tight."

Later on he told me that that was a great comfort and blessing to him.

Answers to prayer are not on a basis of our good deeds. On what basis are they, then? Living a good life? But the life I live is mighty sorry in His sight. No! On the basis of His loving mercy, He has it. He is able. He is not poor and He loves me. He wants you to be happy. His grace abounds. You have every right to ask it. Come on and ask that your joy may be full!

What a wicked thing not to pray or to pray only little prayers, to ask God for so little, when He loves us! But His grace abounds greater than sin and His grace is free. I have a right to come before Him and say, "Lord, I am yours." That is the way we are saved, and that is the way we are kept. We are in the red so bad now, we will never pay out. But let us pray for more blessings.

X. God Is Honored in Answering Prayer

David was a pretty sorry man, but the Lord did a lot for David. David said, "What shall I render unto the Lord for all his benefits toward me?" Do you know what he said? "I will take them every one and then go hollering for more." He said, "I will take the cup of salvation, and will call upon the name of the Lord."

God says, "I have grace. I would like the world to know how I love sinners. I would like for the saved to know how I love my children. I would like for the whole world to see how anxious I am to pour out my goodness."

I said, "Well, Lord, I am a good subject; why not try it out on me by answering my prayers and forgiving my sins?"

"Well," the Lord said, "I want somebody on whom I can show what great mercy I have, how abounding is My grace."

"I am a fit subject for that, Lord."

God said, "Where sin abounded, grace did much more abound." All of us would pass for big, bad sinners. Be glad to let God's abundant grace cover it and give you more than you can ask or think! The real basis for answered prayer is the marvelous, infinite, matchless grace of God, freely bestowed on all who believe. We can have our prayers answered because we are His and we have a God of grace who loves us freely. The mercy of God is poured out not for *our* goodness but *His* goodness, by *His* faithfulness and not by *our* faithfulness, not even by our love but by His love and on the basis of God's grace. Therefore, we can ask and receive that our joy may be full and that people may know that God answers prayer.

A man prays and God answers. The remarkable thing is not that man asks. Man does not get credit for asking. God takes the credit for giving. Ask and ye shall receive. The marvelous grace of God means that our prayers can be answered.

XI. Peace Follows Grace

And not only answered prayer, but peace. I am having a good time. I have touched on it before. Do you know peace? How does it come? It comes by grace. This same 5th chapter of Romans starts off: "Therefore being justified by faith, we have peace with God through our Lord Jesus Christ." I thought, that is a funny way to do. I will see about this business. So I looked up every place in the Bible that said anything about peace, and each time grace is stated ahead of peace. We can't have peace until we have grace. Where will I get peace?

Go out on a desert by yourself—that doesn't bring peace. An ancient man did it in Egypt. He built a column of stone thirty feet high and lived up there on that pile of stone for many years. There was nothing in that man's heart to give peace. Peace does not come from within.

Another man says, "I will dress myself in coarse sackcloth and tie a rope around my waist. I will put nails in my shoes to hurt my feet. I will whip and torment myself in order that I may earn the peace of God." Monks have done that many times.

Now, listen to me! There is nothing in the best of any of us to give peace. Peace cannot arise from the natural human heart. Sin was there first. And sin does not gender peace. All of us are sinners, and sin reigns in our mortal bodies; therefore, no peace can come from human goodness. *Peace comes from God.* It must come from the outside. It must come from the infinite God. Nobody can have real peace except the peace that is the gift of God. The Scripture says, "Therefore being justified by faith, we have peace with God through our Lord Jesus Christ." We are justified when God's grace is poured out. When God forgives our sins, peace comes in.

Not just once but numbers of times in the epistles and in the letters of Paul, Peter and John in the New Testament, peace follows grace. I want to show you how they begin. Paul wrote to the people at Rome:

> *Grace to you and peace from God our Father, and the Lord Jesus Christ.* —Vs. 7.

Grace is first, then peace. Peace comes after grace gets there.

Oh, sin in the heart! Sin abounds and reigns in the carnal heart. The soul that sins is the servant of sin. Sin brings heartache, trouble and anxiety. But just as soon as grace comes and abounds, it casts out the sin and a quiet peace comes in the heart where sin had brought trouble! Peace comes in. "Grace to you and peace."

Read I Corinthians 1:3: *"Grace be unto you, and peace, from God our Father, and from the Lord Jesus Christ."*

II Corinthians 1:2: *"Grace be to you and peace from God our Father, and from the Lord Jesus Christ."*

And in Galatians 1:3: *"Grace be to you and peace from God the Father, and from our Lord Jesus Christ."*

Ephesians 1:2: *"Grace be to you, and peace, from God our Father, and from the Lord Jesus Christ."*

Now Philippians 1:2: *"Grace be unto you, and peace, from God our Father, and from the Lord Jesus Christ."*

That is the way it goes. Now Colossians 1:2: *"Grace be unto you, and peace, from God our Father and the Lord Jesus Christ."*

I Thessalonians 1:1: *"Grace be unto you, and peace, from God our Father, and the Lord Jesus Christ."*

II Thessalonians 1:2: *"Grace unto you, and peace, from God our Father and the Lord Jesus Christ."*

It never did say, "Peace to you and grace." God's Word is verbally inspired, that is, inspired word for word and that is the order He gave. God always put the grace first. You had to have grace before you get peace.

Paul had been writing to the churches in those passages. Now when he writes to Timothy he adds an extra word! Preachers have to have a little more than other folks. Now notice a thing here. He writes to Timothy and says in I Timothy 1:2:

Unto Timothy, my own son in the faith: **Grace, mercy, and peace,** *from God our Father and Jesus Christ our Lord.*

And in II Timothy 1:2:

To Timothy, my dearly beloved son: **Grace, mercy, and peace,** *from God the Father and Christ Jesus our Lord.*

Now look at Titus 1:4:

To Titus, mine own son after the common faith: **Grace, mercy, and peace,** *from God the Father and the Lord Jesus Christ our Saviour.*

Isn't that interesting? "Grace and peace to you" when he writes to the churches; but when he writes to young preachers, Timothy and Titus, he says, "May grace be unto you"—then the mercy of God and then peace. Mercy and grace are very close kin. "Timothy, I want you to get it down here that the only peace is from the grace of God, and as God's continuing mercy abounds, you can have peace.

Until you get to be a preacher, you don't realize that then the Devil starts picking on you!

One of my girls has a temptation to say, "Mama, she hit me as hard as she could!" Every preacher needs to just try to tattle to God and say, "Father, the Devil picks on me and pesters me all the time!"

A preacher is tempted more. Paul said, "Listen, Timothy, if sin abounds, grace does much more abound, so I will put in another word. Grace and *mercy* and peace be unto you, from God our Father." And then when he wrote the second letter he said, "Grace, mercy, and peace, from God the Father and Christ Jesus our Lord." And to Titus, "Grace, mercy, and peace, from God the Father and the Lord Jesus Christ our Saviour." Isn't that interesting? Then to other people it is just "grace and peace." Now Philemon 3: *"Grace to you, and peace, from God our Father and the Lord Jesus Christ."*

Now I Peter 1:2: *"Grace unto you, and peace, be multiplied."*

And II Peter 1:2: *"Grace and peace be multiplied unto you through the knowledge of God, and of Jesus our Lord."*

Then II John verse 3 says: *"Grace be with you, mercy, and peace, from God the Father, and from the Lord Jesus Christ, the Son of the Father, in truth and love."*

John put mercy in there to that good woman's household of II John.

And then Revelation 1:4: *"Grace be unto you, and peace."*

Listen friends! If you want peace in your heart, the peace that passes all understanding, I will tell you how to get it. Brother Widner, you can try so hard to be good until you will be miserable. You can! And the harder you try, the more you see your faults. He wants you to try, yes, but listen! We ought to admit before we start, "I am not good. I am a failure."

Paul said, "I press toward the mark. I didn't count myself to have apprehended. So you had as well say, "I know I will fail, Lord, and I am going to fail, but Lord, I am going to plug along, trusting Your grace for peace. All my goodness is not enough." His mercy is enough. God is not going back on me. When I fail, when I sin, I will confess it and He will forgive me. God's mercy is enough to take care of anything that comes my way.

Seventh-Day Adventists are taught to keep the Sabbath, to try to keep more law, law, LAW! Some told me that it got heavier and heavier until they felt as if they couldn't make it.

Are you afraid you can't make it? Admit when you start, "I can't make it, Lord. That is the reason Jesus had to die for me. I will depend on the cross, on the blood. It has paid for everything. Lord, I have peace today in my heart because God loves me. My sins are all under the blood." Misunderstandings, failure, sin, ruin—all are under the blood and we have peace with God through our Lord Jesus Christ. Thank God for sweet peace!

You may wonder whether you are saved or not. Do you know

why? You are thinking about how you have acted. Look to the cross! Look to *Jesus*! He loves me. He died for me. He will never let me fall. I am fully trusting in Him. That is the way to have peace about your salvation.

Here is another word, then I will close. Whatever you need, if sin abounds, grace does much more abound. Everything we need is in the grace of God. Do you want victory? You can have it. Come every day and rattle the doorknob of Heaven. "Your mercy, Lord! Your grace, Lord!" He will give it. Where sin abounds, grace did much more abound. And as sin has reigned, grace must reign. Call for His grace. Use His grace. Magnify His grace. Tell about His grace. Believe in His grace. Depend on His grace. Magnify God and have sweet peace and victory in your own heart day by day.

> **"Marvelous, infinite, matchless grace,**
> **Freely bestowed on all who believe."**

Is there here a troubled, burdened soul? Lay it all on Jesus this morning. Come confessing your sin, your coldness and claim His abounding grace. The grace of God! Grace is sufficient! Leave it with Jesus Christ. Depend on the blood. Call to witness everybody, it is Jesus who must do it if it is done. He is able.

Will you call on Him? Depend on the grace of God? Grace will abound where sin abounds if you will let it. Whatever you need—salvation, keeping, cleansing, victory, peace—trust God and let grace abound!

AMAZING GRACE

> Amazing grace! how sweet the sound,
>   That saved a wretch like me!
> I once was lost, but now am found,
>   Was blind, but now I see.
>
> 'Twas grace that taught my heart to fear,
>   And grace my fears relieved;
> How precious did that grace appear
>   The hour I first believed!
>
> Thro' many dangers, toils and snares,
>   I have already come;
> 'Tis grace hath bro't me safe thus far,
>   And grace will lead me home.

When we've been there ten thousand years,
  Bright shining as the sun,
We've no less days to sing God's praise
  Than when we first begun.

IV. PRAYER LIFE

18—Prayer and Fasting

(Part of sermon preached in Dallas in 1936. Stenographically reported. Other Scriptures read were Esther 4:1-16; Ezra 8:21-23; Ezra 10:6; Nehemiah 1:4; Nehemiah 9:1-3; Daniel 9:3; and Jonah 3:5-10.)

Then came the disciples to Jesus apart, and said, Why could not we cast him out?

And Jesus said unto them, Because of your unbelief: for verily I say unto you, If ye have faith as a grain of mustard seed, ye shall say unto this mountain, Remove hence to yonder place; and it shall remove; and nothing shall be impossible unto you.

Howbeit this kind goeth not out but by prayer and fasting.—Matt. 17:19-21.

Again the Bible tells us that the disciples of John came to Jesus and said, "Why do we and the Pharisees fast oft, but thy disciples fast not?" They asked, "The disciples of John fast and the Pharisees fast; why is it Your disciples don't fast?" Jesus said, "The time is coming when the Bridegroom will be taken away and then shall My disciples fast."

When Jesus was taken away and the disciples were left and waiting for Pentecost, they did fast and pray. We are not told in the first chapter of Acts that they fasted then, but Jesus told ahead of time that they would, and we know they did fast before Pentecost.

Now turn to the second passage, Acts, chapter 13. Some may say that what I have been reading is in the Old Testament and that isn't for us today; that was all right in Bible times, but not now.

Let us see how New Testament Christians did about fasting and prayer. Acts, chapter 13: 1-4:

Now there were in the church that was at Antioch

certain prophets and teachers; as Barnabas, and Simeon that was called Niger, and Lucius of Cyrene, and Manaen, which had been brought up with Herod the tetrarch, and Saul [a group of Christian preachers and teachers].

As they ministered to the Lord, and fasted, the Holy Ghost said, Separate me Barnabas and Saul for the work whereunto I have called them.

And when they had fasted and prayed, and laid their hands on them, they sent them away.

So they, being sent forth by the Holy Ghost, departed unto Seleucia; and from thence they sailed to Cyprus.

Notice verse 2, ". . .they ministered and fasted," and verse 3, "And when they had fasted and prayed. . . ." Twice in that same chapter they fasted. They fasted and prayed to find the will of God, then God told them, "I want Barnabas and Saul to go work where I will send them." Then they fasted and prayed again—first for wisdom, then for power, and they got both. The Bible teaches fasting and prayer, and I would like to talk to you this morning about it.

The first thing: What fasting is not.

I. Fasting Is Not Merely a Form

The Pharisees set aside two days in every week to fast. I do not believe that pleased God. Even unsaved Pharisees followed that custom. People can fast and go without for religious rites and yet have hard hearts that do not seek God at all.

A form of fasting is not good. People may fast to gain the praise of man. The Pharisees evidently did that. But Jesus said, "When ye fast, be not, as the hypocrites, of a sad countenance: for they disfigure their faces, that they may appear unto men to fast." Jesus said when you fast, "Wash your face and go dress yourself up as usual and don't let anybody know you are fasting."

Fasting ought not be just for the public. Fasting can be done in public and people ought sometime to agree to fast together, as they did in Bible times, but fasting should not be done to impress men.

Notice this: Whether you are giving, or whether you are praying, or whether you are fasting, there is a particular warning in the Bible that it ought not be done to please men. You ought never do your giving to please men, yet you ought to give, and in Bible times they ofttimes gave publicly.

Jesus stood over by the treasury and watched as the people cast in their gifts. It is not only right to give; it is sometimes right to give publicly. But it is not right to give to be seen of men.

So in prayer, it is sometimes right to pray in public, if we pray to the Lord and for the glory of God. The publican prayed in the Temple publicly. The thief on the cross prayed publicly. Blind Bartimaeus on the roadside prayed in public and cried, "Jesus, thou son of David, have mercy on me."

Public prayer is all right. Solomon prayed in public when the Temple was dedicated. Jesus prayed in the Garden of Gethsemane before His disciples and taught them to pray public prayers. . .not necessarily long prayers. Prayer just to be heard of men is always wrong. To pray to men, to seek the favor of men or have the admiration of men, is always wrong.

Thus fasting ought never be to impress men. We may fast with people, but not to please people. Anybody who fasts and then boasts about it is likely not to get the real blessing. Whatever you do for the Lord ought to be done as unto the Lord. It ought never be made known to our own credit or our own glory.

Fasting as a form is not fasting. Fasting one day a week could be a very great blessing but it is so likely to get to be just a form. And one would go through the day and fast but not pray and with the shell but not the meat, not have the heart of the thing that would please God.

II. Fasting in Time of Special Need

But God's Word clearly teaches fasting. Fasting in the Bible by good men—the fasts I have read you about this morning—were times of special need. I believe it is right to pray, and it is right sometimes to pray all night when you are praying for something. And there are times when one ought to pray all day. Of course we ought to pray all the time, without ceasing, but there are times we should leave everything else to pray.

Fasting in the Bible comes from a sincere heart that must get hold of God in some great time of crisis when you want the victory, when you want to seek God and find Him.

Let me ask you this question: How many have ever had a time of fasting when it was not just especially public, but a time of seeking God, a time of so waiting on God, a time of so trying to get the blessing of God that you didn't eat? How many have had a time of fasting when it was from the heart sincerely? Many have. Those who haven't done that have missed one of the greatest blessings. Most of us are only children in the Lord. We drink milk, but we can't eat meat. We have not won great victories through the Lord. We haven't had great answers to prayer. Many have taken only the little first steps as children, and must be fed milk instead of meat.

I would like to have the blessed experience of great victories through fasting and prayer. In nearly every case I could win the victory over my own defeats, my own troubles, by fasting and prayer. Sometimes we could have victory in those things. God wants us sometimes to have them. But prayer and waiting on God, praying when you can't sleep and do not want to eat—*praying through* is the answer.

When you pray and don't get the answer at once, the remedy is to keep on praying. Pray with more earnestness, even as Jesus fell on His face and prayed and sweat great drops of blood and prayed the same words again, even the third time. So ought we to fast and pray.

I set myself up as no example in fasting and prayer, but I sometimes do, though not as often as I ought. "Howbeit this kind goeth not out but by prayer and fasting," Jesus said.

There are many problems that we will never get settled without fasting and prayer. There are many problems where prayer alone is not enough. "This kind goeth not out but by prayer and fasting."

.It takes sincere waiting, a certain amount of time for our prayer to be answered.

I want to lay on your heart these things. One thing made me feel I ought to preach on this subject. We have a need for revival in our church. We haven't had here a great revival in a good while. Brother Banta was in a good revival here in the winter while I was in Binghamton. We ought to have a great revival in the open air. We want to get our hearts close to God and we can do that by prayer and fasting! There are great things fasting can do for us. Remarkable things were noticeable in every case of fasting and prayer that I read you this morning.

III. Waiting on God, We See Ourselves Better

Fasting and prayer will help you get a sin question settled. There is a sad thing about our sins. Things can go on day by day and we see no harm in them. But when we spend time waiting before God and leave off food and sleep and get our mind on this business and really wait before God, then some things you didn't really believe were sins—things you had convinced yourself were all right—you get to see them as God sees them! Many habits, a critical tongue, a covetous heart, appear as sin while we fast and pray. I know from my own heart that is true. I know it is true with others. We have sinned and there is a hardness of heart. But as we wait before God, He reveals Himself to us and He reveals to us our sin.

Why doesn't God instantly answer back when we pray?

I preached on Friday night on Isaiah 59:1,2, "Behold, the Lord's hand is not shortened, that it cannot save; neither his ear heavy, that it cannot hear: But your iniquities have separated between you and your God, and your sins have hid his face from you, that he will not hear." There is only one reason prayer is not answered, and that is sin. Now when we wait before God, He shows the sin.

There are those who believe that praying is a hit-or-miss business like lightning—it may hit in the same place or it may not. That is not true about prayer. I know any Christian who waits before God can find why he doesn't get his prayers answered, why God isn't pleased with him, why he is not happy and can't win souls and doesn't prosper, why he is not healed of his sickness. As we wait before God, He reveals our sins.

Go back and notice the case of Nehemiah, who waited before God and fasted and prayed. A little further over all fasted and prayed and confessed, "Lord, we have married in with wicked people and have gotten heathen women for our wives." They saw their sins and put them away.

Everyone here needs to watch what you do. Fasting and prayer will show that we need to confess our sins.

Turn to the book of Daniel, 9:3,4. Daniel prayed and fasted. He set himself to seek God by prayer and fasting.

> *And I set my face unto the Lord God, to seek by prayer and supplications, with fasting, and sackcloth, and ashes;*
> *And I prayed unto the Lord my God, and made my confession.*

Time after time after time he mentions iniquities—the iniquities of his fathers, of their kings and their transgressions, breaking the law. And following are many, many, many words used, showing their sin.

There is something about getting close to God that reveals our sin. I want to confess that my life is poor and sorry. When I wait before God, I see it then. Otherwise, I think I am all right. I think I am a good man many times, don't you? But as I wait before God and get my mind off business and the paper and other details and wait before Him, my own sins begin to look mighty black.

This thing is true. You can measure your sins by somebody else's and they don't look so bad. But when you come to measure yourself by the Lord, you certainly look bad. You get a black man and put him by a coal pile and he doesn't look so black; but put him up beside a white-washed fence and he looks awfully black.

You put a sinner by another sinner, and he doesn't look so bad. Brother Arrant wouldn't look so bad by Brother Renz. But stand any Christian by the side of the Lord God for a half hour, or an hour, or a half-day, or a day and night, fasting and praying before God, and that Christian sees how black he is! The way to find your sin is to wait before God.

Fasting and prayer is a good deal like candling eggs. You sold bad eggs if you didn't candle them. The trouble with a lot of folks is when they come to pray, they do not "candle" their prayers. If they would use candling, they wouldn't bring a lot of prayers that God couldn't answer. You just say, "Lord, I am all right," but don't stop to check up. You turn on the light and put an egg over it and hold it so you can look through and see if it is all right.

You wait before God, and wait some more before Him and God will begin to let the light shine out and show things that are wrong in your life and heart.

So we need to wait. Fasting and prayer before God will show some things you need and show what is wrong and show why your prayers are not answered and why you are not happy and don't win souls and are not prospering. And many times fasting and prayer will show what is wrong with your family. It will show what is wrong with your business and your happiness. God will show when we wait before Him. There is something about waiting before God that reveals sin.

That is the reason Isaiah said, "In the year that King Uzziah died, I saw also the Lord sitting upon a throne, high and lifted up, and his train filled the temple." He saw the seraphims and they cried, "Holy, holy, holy is the Lord of hosts: the whole earth is full of his glory." And what is the next thing he began to cry: "Woe is me! for I am undone; because I am a man of unclean lips, and I dwell in the midst of a people of unclean lips; for mine eyes have seen the King, the Lord of hosts!" He didn't know that until he saw the Lord in the Temple. Waiting before God shows your sin.

IV. Waiting Before God Gives Grace to Confess Sin

You wait before God and He pays you no mind. When you ask and He does not give, then you know something is wrong. God will finally say, "Here is what's wrong." God keeps putting His finger on the sin as you wait. You say, "All right, Lord, I will

confess it. This is a sin, then." Heretofore you have just said,
"Lord, this doesn't matter. This is just a little habit of mine
which isn't so bad." You may feel that way about the habit, but
wait before God and fast and pray and talk to Him about it, and
you will say, "All right, Lord; I will confess that it is a wicked
sin and I ought to get rid of it. Hear me about this sin right here;
help me, Lord!"

When you confess it, you have it half whipped.

It may be grudge in your heart, or covetousness, or lust, or
picture shows, or indiscretion. Whatever it is, wait before God
and He will put His finger on it.

How many have had this experience? I have. I have been
checking up on myself. I come to pray, and every time I do, I
think about a certain thing—a certain thing I said or the way I
felt or a certain way I acted. Waiting and fasting before God
will cause us to finally break down and face this wrong. "It is
sin." Then you can forsake it.

The next thing is forsaking sin. Waiting before God will make
us willing and able to forsake sin. If we just pray, "Lord, give
me so and so," and go back home at once, we are turned down
and do not know why. But when we fast and pray and wait and
we ask Him, "Lord, give me so and so," He answers back, "I
can't do it till you unload your sin." Then we can say, "All right,
Lord, I will unload my wagon and get this out."

What happens now? After awhile when you have the wagon
unloaded, God pours it full of blessing, after you wait before
God! There is something in fasting and waiting before God that
makes you turn your back on sin, see it, confess it and forsake
it.

Listen to this. If you run in bad company, it will ruin you.
You run in good company and it will bless you. You become like
those you are with. If you stay with God, you become like
God—hating sin. The only way to get the best company is to
wait before God. Anybody can't wait with a whole heart before
God without getting so you hate sin and want to turn away
from sin and want God to forgive it and get it out of the way. If
you want that blessing, wait like Isaiah and Nehemiah did, like
New Testament Christians did.

I went to Chicago University in 1921 for graduate work. I left my teaching work at Wayland College to work on the M. A. degree in Chicago. I went to the University book store for a job to pay expenses. (I had worked in a book store at Baylor University.) I said to Mr. Fred Tracht, "I want a job in the book store here."

He answered, "We are already filled up and I have another fellow in mind when we need anybody."

But I said, "Well, you might need me. I will come back tomorrow."

He said I needn't come back. But I did—the next day. I said, "Mr. Tracht, anything open yet?"

"No, I guess not."

"Well, I just wanted to remind you that I have had experience in a book store. I love books. I am dependable and I want the job. I am going to work my way through here."

He answered, "Well, never mind. I have another fellow in mind if we need someone."

"That is all right," I said. "I will come back tomorrow."

He softened a bit and said, "Come back in a couple of weeks and we will see."

"I will be back tomorrow," I said.

I went back the next day. "I came by to see if anything had turned up."

"You say you worked in the Baylor University book store and you know books pretty well?"

"Yes, I think so—yes, I have."

"We will see about that," he said. "I might need you; I don't know. Give me your phone number and I will call you."

The next day I came back to ask if anything had turned up. Mr. Tracht said, "When can you go to work?"

I took off my hat and went right to work! That other fellow wasn't hanging around like I was, and I got the job.

When a man is persistent, don't you think God pays more attention? Don't you believe when one of His children comes and says, "Lord, I want so and so; I want to please You about it whether I get anything to eat or not, whether I sleep or not; and if anything needs changing, I want it changed to please You, Lord. I am going to wait until I get it"—the Lord is honor-bound to pay attention? If God says, "Ask, and it shall be given you; seek and ye shall find; knock, and it shall be opened unto you," then when someone comes with tears and earnestness and confession, waiting before God, wanting this more than something to eat, don't you know God is willing to hear a prayer like that? To be sure He is!

You ought to learn this blessed secret. There are certain kinds of demons that don't go out but by prayer and fasting. If we get hold on God, we will see some sin we didn't see before, we will confess sin that we didn't have grace to confess before, and forsake it. God is able and ready.

V. Waiting on God Helps Us Find and Do His Will

Another thing it will do for you: It will cause you to surrender to the will of God. One condition of prayer is that it be asked in Jesus' name. "If we ask anything according to his will he heareth us: And if we know that he hears us, whatsoever we ask, we know that we have the petitions that we desire of him." If we pray and ask according to His will, stay until we find His will, we will get it. Have you found it to be true that at times when you came to pray, you asked one way, then you changed your prayer a little to make it fit the plan of God? God says, "If you are going My way, I will give you the answer to your prayer."

Stay long enough to get on God's track. Find out what will please God. Do not simply say, "Lord, give me this," but wait till God shows whether the prayer is according to His will. Come and say, "Lord, I want You to see I am trying to find Your will and do it."

A friend of mine who was called to preach years ago told me this: "I was shocked to find I didn't want to preach. God saved me, Jesus died for me, yet I found rebellion in my heart. I was so ashamed of it. I went in my room and locked the door and prayed, 'Lord, I am ashamed to find rebellion in my heart, ashamed that I wasn't willing to do instantly anything You say.

I am not leaving here until I am willing to do whatever You say.' "

You will surrender to God if you stay at it in prayer and fasting. You will want to do the will of God.

I wanted to go to Africa if God called, but perhaps I would have to wait on God for grace first. You can't instantly make up your mind to that. I never said I wouldn't have any struggle about it. I would. Sure I would. I wouldn't want to go but think I would after waiting on God.

You ought to have it out with the Lord in fasting and prayer. You have sometimes found that true when God takes a loved one. You can't instantly say, "That is all right, Lord." Sometimes we should wait before God and let the Lord search out the heart. We should fast and pray before Him. Then, after awhile God will let His sweet peace come in and you will surrender and say, "All right, Thy will be done. I will be content." You get that only by waiting before God. A surrendered will comes from fasting and prayer.

How many here have lost loved ones, have lost a job, or your health, or some other precious thing, but only became reconciled to it after you waited before God? You couldn't do it instantly. That is a reason for fasting and prayer.

Sometimes people tell me, "I have a grudge I can't get out." It is not such a light matter, not like cutting down a weed. It is not that easy. Cutting it out is not enough. You have to get the roots. And one can't often do that in a minute or in a day.

But when anybody says, "Here is this wicked, vile plant in my heart"—it may be rebellion, hatred, grudge, unforgiveness. What you can do is hold it up in front of God until your heart finds itself in perfect accord with the will of God. "This kind cometh not out but by prayer and fasting."

Christian, any time you begin to pray and can't say at the beginning, "Have Thine own way, Lord, have Thine own way," and mean it, then wait on God. After you have waited awhile and let God do something for you and to you, you can then say, "Now, Lord, I am really willing and glad for You to have your way."

If God takes Mother, we wish He hadn't done it, but we won't fight God. It takes waiting before God to surrender so you can honestly say, "Lord, what You did was all right." May God give us hearts to wait before Him!

God wants you to work, to teach, to preach. Many times I haven't gotten the victory. Problems, problems, problems! Many of them will be solved only by fasting and prayer!

Take a bit of snow and put it in the sunlight. The sun shines down on it and after awhile it melts and runs away and is no more. Take the coldness of your own heart and your rebellious will that says, "Lord, I want my own way; I want to make money to provide well for my family"—put that poor, cold, rebellious heart before the Lord, and wait before Him and fast and let the light shine upon it, and the first thing you know the coldness has melted away!

Can you say, "I will preach, I will teach, I will fast and pray; where He leads me, I will follow"?

Fasting and prayer does something that all of us need. May God grant that we shall wait before God until our will is surrendered, until we can ask in Jesus' name. When you ask according to His will, you can get anything you want.

One reason for the time element in prayer, waiting in prayer and not eating anything, is that we may put first things first. That is seeking first the kingdom of God. Often it is more important to get somebody saved than to eat even when hungry. Say to God, "I am seeking Your will. I want to do what You want me to do." God will give you the blessing.

Every preacher knows if he eats all he wants, he can't preach like he wants to preach. If you have your mind and heart on preaching and leave off eating until you get through preaching, you find blessing and freedom and joy you didn't have.

God wants to be first—before your stomach. Put Him first in fasting and prayer and get a blessing of surrender to the will of God, knowing the will of God, asking according to His will, until you get the answer to your prayers!

19—Christ in Gethsemane

(Stenographically reported sermon preached Sunday night, September 24, 1939, Dallas, Texas.)

And being in an agony he prayed more earnestly: and his sweat was as it were great drops of blood falling down to the ground. —Luke 22:44.

Open your Bibles to Luke, chapter 22, beginning with verse 39 and reading to verse 46.

And he came out, and went, as he was wont [as accustomed], to the mount of Olives; and his disciples also followed him.

And when he was at the place, he said unto them, Pray that ye enter not into temptation.

And he was withdrawn from them about a stone's case, and kneeled down, and prayed,

Saying, Father, if thou be willing, remove this cup from me: nevertheless not my will, but thine, be done.

And there appeared an angel unto him from heaven, strengthening him.

And being in an agony he prayed more earnestly: and his sweat was as it were great drops of blood falling down to the ground.

And when he rose up from prayer, and was come to his disciples, he found them sleeping for sorrow,

And said unto them, Why sleep ye? rise and pray, lest ye enter into temptation.

A similar passage is in Hebrews 5:7 and it is necessary to a good understanding of this passage.

Who in the days of his flesh, when he had offered up

> *prayers and supplications with strong crying and tears*
> *unto him that was able to save him from death, and was*
> *heard in that he feared—*

referring, evidently, to Christ in the Garden of Gethsemane.
Now what is the meaning of this passage, especially verse 44?

> *And being in an agony he prayed more earnestly: and*
> *his sweat was as it were great drops of blood falling down*
> *to the ground.*

This is the most tragic prayer meeting the world ever saw but
it was not in vain. I say the most tragic because more things
hung on the outcome of this prayer meeting than on any prayer
meeting that was ever held in time or eternity.

Here Jesus came to pray. It is not generally understood for
what Jesus prayed. I remember that a young preacher said a
good many years ago that this is the only prayer Jesus ever
prayed that was not answered, but he was utterly wrong. This
prayer was answered. According to the Scripture just read in
Hebrews 5:7, "Who in the days of his flesh, when he had offered
up prayers and supplications with strong crying and tears unto
him that was able to save him from death, and was heard in
that he feared," this prayer was heard and this prayer was
answered. Jesus prayed through.

Now for what did Jesus pray? I was taught in my boyhood
and read this last week from G. Campbell Morgan that Jesus'
flesh shrank from the cross and that Jesus didn't want to go to
the cross when He said, "Father, if thou be willing, remove this
cup from me" and prayed the second time and the third time.
"Being in an agony he prayed more earnestly: and his sweat was
as it were great drops of blood falling down to the ground."

I. For What Did Jesus Pray in Gethsemane?

Now for what did He pray? He prayed that God would save
Him from death. He didn't mean, "Save Me from the cross." If
that was what Jesus was praying for, He was praying against
everything He ever said, He was praying against every
prophecy in the Word of God. If Jesus was praying for the
Father to keep Him from the cross, He was praying against the

thing He had planned to do before the world began, the thing He surrendered to do and had been announcing every day of His life that He would do.

And that isn't all. Suppose Jesus thought there was some other way to save sinners. If Jesus thought there were some other way to save sinners, He didn't know as much about the Bible as I know, for I know "without shedding of blood is no remission" (Heb. 9:22). And I know that every sacrifice, every type, every prophet down through the ages taught that without shedding of blood is no remission, and God's Passover Lamb must come and the blood must be shed and He must suffer the torments for us, and be mocked at and spit upon and He must die. He must utter the cry of the twenty-second Psalm. He must die, accused and taunted with the taunts that were foretold in the Bible.

Now I know that Jesus had to die to save sinners, and I am sure that He knew more than I know now. Jesus could not have been praying, "Father, I don't want to go to the cross. Please don't let Me die. Please save people some other way." I am certain in my mind that that could not have been the thing Jesus was praying for. No! No! If so, I remind you it is the only time in the life of Christ that He ever prayed against the will of God. If so, it is the only time in the Word of God where Jesus ever prayed and His prayer was not answered and that Jesus hung back and begged to get out of doing right and do what He promised to do and what the Father told Him to do. That cannot be. Jesus was not praying, "My Father, keep Me from dying on the cross!"

Then what was He praying for? That is the same old story that followed the life of Christ in relation to Satan, resisting the same thread of temptation all the way through. Jesus had been tempted to avoid the cross. Now Satan was trying to kill Christ in such a way as to miss the crucifixion. Self doesn't want to die, doesn't want to be mortified in the deeds of the flesh. Jesus was continually tempted to stay away from the cross. Now Satan would have killed Him before time, so that He would not die according to the Scriptures and save sinners.

When Jesus met the Devil in the wilderness, Satan said, "Do You see all the kingdoms of this world? You bow down and worship me and I will give You these kingdoms." Did Satan lie when he said that those kingdoms belonged to him? As far as rights are concerned, he lied, but as far as actual possession is concerned, in some sense he told the truth. It would have been no real temptation to Jesus otherwise.

No, I say the temptation was this. The Devil said, "Jesus, You want to reign, don't You?" If Jesus had answered him at all, He would have said, "Yes, and I am going to reign. I am the Seed of Abraham to whom was promised the land of Palestine, and I am the Seed of David to whom was promised the kingdom of David. I am the Son of God prophesied to die for sinners and prophesied to come the second time before I ever came the first time. Enoch the seventh from Adam prophesied that I would come the second time and that time I am coming to reign."

I am sure if Jesus answered him at all, He said, "I certainly do intend to reign over the kingdoms of this world," for Jesus had taught and afterwards taught His disciples to pray, "Thy kingdom come. Thy will be done in earth, as it is in heaven" (Matt. 6:10). And Christ is to reign on earth.

Now what was the temptation? The Devil said, "If You will fall down and serve me, You can have Your kingdom without a cross. You can have a crown without a crucifixion." And that was the temptation everywhere. That is the reason when Jesus told the disciples, 'The Son of man must be delivered into the hands of sinners and must be crucified and die and the third day arise from the dead,' and when Peter said, 'No, no. This shall not be unto Thee,' that Jesus turned and said to him, "Get thee behind me, Satan: thou art an offence unto me" (Matt. 16:23).

It is the same old thing that Satan brought to Jesus at every moment of His life, "You don't have to die, You don't have to die." Jesus must have said to Himself, "If I don't die, nobody will be saved! I could go and not die, but nobody could ever be saved!" That is the temptation Satan brought to Jesus Christ. Every time it was that thing.

Do you know why Jesus said to Peter, "Get thee behind me,

Satan"? Because Peter brought the message of Satan, though Peter knew it not. Peter had not planned it, but Peter that day was the chosen tool of Satan to tempt the Lord Jesus Christ to avoid the crucifixion.

You find later on when He came to the crucifixion, sitting down in front of Him was a great group of people. From three sources this temptation came again to the dying Saviour. The Pharisees said, "Come down from the cross and we will believe in You. Come on down. You said You were the Son of God—come on down and we will believe in You." The people said, "He saved others; let Him save Himself and we will believe on Him." And the thieves cast the same in his teeth. The temptation was to avoid the crucifixion, detour around the cross, take an easy way!

Now what was Jesus praying for in the garden? He was "exceeding sorrowful, even unto death." Jesus was about to die. The blood was already breaking from the veins. He was in such agony that He would have died had God the Father not answered His prayer. He was in the act of death then; "sorrowful, even unto death," because of grief and a breaking heart—this was literally killing His body out there. Jesus said, "If I die in the garden, with no cross, I cannot save anybody. If I die today before the passover lamb is killed instead of on the day it is to be killed, I cannot save anybody. If I die contrary to the Scripture, the Devil would win."

Satan tried to have the Jews stone Jesus (John 5:16,18; John 7:1, and especially John 8:59), so that His bones would be broken, when it had been written in the Scripture, "A bone of him shall not be broken" (John 19:36; Exod. 12:46). He tried to have the people of Nazareth throw Christ down a cliff where certainly He would have been killed and bones broken (Luke 4:29). Then He could not have been our Saviour.

And many other ways Satan tried to avoid Jesus' coming to the legitimate end and the fulfillment of every promise that He would die on a certain day in a certain way and following a certain pattern and say certain words on a cross, condemned outside the city of Jerusalem. So that night Jesus said, "Father,

oh, tonight the Devil wants to kill Me. Save Me from this
Satan's death that I may go tomorrow and die the divine death
and die for sinners."

And that night Jesus *prayed through!* He "prayed with strong
crying and with tears unto him that was able to save him from
death, *and was heard* in that he feared" (Heb. 5:7). And God
said, "I will send an angel to comfort Him and to strengthen
Him." And an angel from God came down and succored the Son
of God. He prayed, not to avoid the cross—no, NO!—but to
make it so He would live until tomorrow and tomorrow die as
God   had planned that He would die, as He came into the world
to die.

No, my friend, do not believe Jesus prayed, "My Father, don't
let Me go to the cross." Do not believe that. That is not what He
prayed for. He prayed, "Oh, My Father, if You do not intervene,
I will die here prematurely, for Satan has determined to kill Me
now, and I am dying now." And He prayed, "Oh, My Father,
take this cup and pass it on until tomorrow. Oh, if it is Your
will, all right, but, oh, My Father, if it is possible, then make
this cup pass from Me so I will live until tomorrow and die in
the way appointed and in the time appointed, between two
thieves and be buried in the rich man's grave and cry in the
agony of the 22nd Psalm."

He must be condemned to die by the Sanhedrin, then in
Pilate's judgment hall and have the lash of the cat-o'-nine-tails
on His back and have the soldiers cast lots for His garments;
and so He prayed, "My Father, let it be according to the
Scriptures. Let this death pass from Me tonight that I may meet
death tomorrow in the appointed way!"

We have too little understanding of the Gospel. "The Gospel
is that Christ died for our sins," somebody says. No, no. That is
not all of it. That is just part of it. Paul said, "This is the Gospel
(I Cor. 15:3,4), how that Christ died for our sins according to the
Scriptures," that is, Christ died on the day and at the place, in
the manner prescribed by the Bible, in the Old Testament.

Salvation depends on it being fulfilled to the letter. If Jesus
should die any other place or any other way or any other date,

then Jesus is not the Son of God and cannot save anybody. "Christ died for our sins *according to the scriptures*; and that he was buried, and that he rose again the third day *according to the scriptures.*" Twice in that short passage the Lord insists that "according to the scriptures" is the only way Christ can die and be raised to save anybody.

II. Jesus Prayed Through

I hope you will see Jesus there as He goes to pray. He said to His disciples, "Come and watch with Me. You need to watch and pray lest you fall into temptation."

You know, we have great temptation when weary, when discouraged. Discouragement is of the Devil. Don't you ever let the Devil get you down and make you think God has forgotten you. If you go by sight, scenes and circumstances, the Devil will whip you. I would say, "No, sir, I look beyond circumstances to the unseen Christ of God and to the intangible promises of God. I know God does what He says all right." But you need to watch and pray lest you enter into temptation. Discouragement—tiredness!

And the Scripture says 'they slept for sorrow.' They were so sad and discouraged and so disheartened that they gave up praying and went to sleep. The Saviour had picked out three particular ones of the disciples, Peter, James, and John, and said to them, "Watch with me." Later He returned and said to them, "Could ye not watch . . . one hour?" for they were asleep. Jesus prayed the prayer, "O my Father, if it be possible, let this cup pass from me: nevertheless not as I will, but as thou wilt" (Matt. 26:39). And He prayed the second time and came again, and he went the third time and prayed, and Matthew says, "saying the same words." The Lord Jesus prayed!

How suggestive that is! I believe public prayers ought to be short and to the point. Ask for what we want and then stop praying.

Our praying ought to be very much like William Jennings Bryan told a group of us. He went down into the Rio Grande Valley. He said a certain German farmer introduced him. This man was a prosperous, influential farmer, but he was not notorious as a public speaker. He said, "Vell, fellow citizens, they hafe asked me to introduce to you Mr. Bryan who vill speak to you. I hafe now done so, and he vill now do so." And he sat down.

I believe our praying ought to be as much to the point as that when in public. Public prayer ought to mean business, and ought to only touch those things that would be proper for all to pray about, such simple language that all of us in our hearts could say, "Amen," to it—fervent enough to include all of us, and no longer than all can gladly follow.

But when we are alone, God knows we ought to come and pray again the same words. Many times we ought to stay all night in prayer as did Jesus. Prayer is work. Intercessory prayer is work, hard work. Jesus sweat great drops of blood and He prayed and cried to God with tears and supplication and strong crying. The Lord Jesus Christ prayed through!

Now you have the setting of it. I call to your attention the first lesson for Christians, then if I can, the lesson for unsaved people.

III. How Much Was Paid for My Salvation!

There are two applications to which I call your attention. The first lesson is to Christians. It is, O my soul, how much was paid for my salvation! How much I owe to God! I wonder if the death of Christ becomes to you commonplace.

I preached the other night on the crucifixion of Christ. I said then as I meditated and planned and prayed about it, "O God, there is one thing I dread, and that is that I will preach so many times on the crucifixion and on the death of Christ until after awhile I can speak on the agony of Jesus on the cross and have no tears, after awhile I can talk about the dying breath of our Saviour as He prayed for sinners and have no broken heart." So I prayed that God would break my heart, and He did.

O God, forgive us preachers if we forget how much God paid for us!

Though I have perhaps some little gifts as a Bible teacher, and perhaps have less gifts as an evangelist—I have felt impressed more and more that we ought to turn our hearts back, not so much to teaching the letter of the Word, though that is important and I want to do it and know it ought to be done, but that more and more we enter into the passion that the Lord Jesus had and the burden and tears and the death and the sweating of blood! O God, help us! Do you remember how much was paid for you? You are not your own! You are bought with "the precious blood of Christ."

I had some thought, "If in some dramatic way I could portray the Saviour," and I recoiled in my heart. I sometimes act out some parts of my message, but I cannot picture the dying Saviour with the agony and sweating blood. Yet if some way the Spirit of God would show your heart how Jesus looked and how He felt and how He prayed and how He suffered when He was in the garden and when 'being in a great agony He prayed the more earnestly.' Oh, if we could but realize how much Christ paid for us, then we would love Him better.

Oh, I wish it could be so that I could say that I would never sin any more. I wish I would never grieve Him any more. I like this little chorus, "I ain't gonna' grieve my Lord any more." I like to sing it but every time I do, my heart rebukes me. I wish it were so, but it isn't.

But tonight for a Christian, I would like to lay on your heart how much you owe to the Lord Jesus Christ, how much you cost, and remember, you are dead. You went through Gethsemane; through Calvary; Christ died for you. You can go out tonight and say, "I belong to Christ. He paid for all my sins."

IV. Oh, That We May Enter Into Christ's Burden to Save!

There is another lesson for Christians and I hope you will get it. Oh, what manner of praying we ought to do! What manner of burdens ought we to have! That is laid on my heart now more and more. I feel that I need to have some of the burden Jesus had.

A preacher said to me the other day, "Don't you find it harder to win souls now than you used to?"

My friend, that is just an alibi. If we don't have a good many people saved, we say it is hard. Oh, we preachers are so hardhearted. We Christians are hardhearted. We Christians don't have a broken heart and tears. Oh, may we have the broken heart that Jesus had! We can have it and ought to have it. Jesus is our Example. The Lord Jesus died for us and the Scripture says, He "suffered for us, leaving us an example, that ye should follow his steps" (I Pet. 2:21). That was the pattern of Jesus. That is what He meant when He said, "If any man will come after me, let him deny himself, and take up his cross daily, and follow me" (Luke 9:23). So then we ought to follow after Jesus. He suffered for us, leaving that example.

Paul said, "I say the truth in Christ, I lie not, my conscience also bearing me witness in the Holy Ghost, That I have great heaviness and continual sorrow in my heart. For I could wish that myself were accursed from Christ for my brethren, my kinsmen according to the flesh" (Rom. 9:1-3). Oh, the pain in the heart!

Do you have any pain in your heart? Do you have any burden on your heart? Do you have any dying? Paul said on this matter, "I die daily. I am crucified with Christ."

We have used the term crucified until it now means nothing to us, when it ought to mean death. You are to die to self. You are to have your plans broken up, your ambition dead, your self laid on the altar.

We have so used the words *crucifixion* and *cross* as to steal their meaning. We make kind of a pretty symbol of the cross. To us it is a little bit of a gold thing that we hang on a chain, or a little bit of a pin that we stick in the lapel of our coats. It is a nice thing to sing about, a cross is. It is a sign on top of a church, a cross is. Or maybe it is some kind of a temptation. "My cross is that I had to do without a hat this winter." No! No! We have toned down the meaning of words and have violated every meaning in the world.

This thing the Lord is talking about is death-agony, bloody, terrible. We need to come back and see Jesus sweating the bloody sweat in an agony as He prayed and wept and cried and begged and cried and prayed before God and prayed through, lest we should all be damned; lest Satan should have killed Him that night before He went to the cross.

There is a lot of the Bible that we ignore. Amos the 6th chapter says, "Woe to them that are at ease in Zion." People ought not be at ease. We ought not be well satisfied.

One of the troubles with Christian people everywhere—preachers, Sunday school teachers—is that we are not burdened. "Woe to them that are at ease in Zion." Doesn't the Scripture say when Zion travailed, sons and daughters would be born? (Isa. 66:8). The reason we do not have more sinners saved is that we do not have more travail. We do not weep over people till we can't sleep or eat. We need the lesson of Gethsemane.

Fathers and mothers have brought a curse on their children. They have taught them to put school before revivals; they themselves put business before soul winning, pleasure before God. All over the country people have sold out like Lot. And they are going to reap the fruit of it.

What I started to say is, we cannot have revival unless somebody has travail, a breaking up of fallow ground, unless we have broken hearts and tears. We must have some sorrow or God cannot bless. "Break up your fallow ground [of your heart] and sow not among thorns" (Jer. 4:3; Hos. 10:12). It is time to sow in righteousness and reap in mercy. I tell you, we must have some broken hearts!

Oh, my Christian friends, the burdens on Jesus are our burdens, too. If He wept, we ought to weep. If He sweated, we ought to sweat. If He prayed, we ought to pray. If He was in an agony, we ought to be in an agony.

I say again, we ignore the plain meaning of so many Scriptures. Paul said in Romans the 12th chapter, "I beseech you therefore, brethren, by the mercies of God, that ye present your bodies a living sacrifice, holy, acceptable unto God, which is your reasonable service." And we have used the word *sacrifice* until it does not mean anything. We use the word *sacrifice* when we say, "I will give a dollar when I only meant to give fifty cents," or, "I will do without the ice cream I had planned for tomorrow."

A sacrifice means a lamb taken and slain and the blood poured out and the lamb burned on the altar. A sacrifice means Jesus nailed to the cross. We do not know what sacrifice means these days. We think it means a little self-denial or trouble. We have lost the meaning and have taken the heart out of the Word of God.

Yet back there Paul had the idea that it meant to die, not only a willingness to die in his heart, but he said, "I gave myself up to die." He gave up everything dear in this world. Paul said so. "I have suffered the loss of all things, and do count them but dung, that I may win Christ, And be found in him, not having mine own righteousness, which is of the law, but that which is through the faith of Christ, the righteousness which is of God by faith" (Phil. 3:8,9).

And he who was stoned and fought lions at Ephesus and was beaten with rods, in perils of the sea, in perils of his countrymen, despised, abused, imprisoned, that old saint of God said, "I die daily."

We try to use those words and live in nice houses with three square meals a day, ride in nice cars, have plenty of clothes. Nobody insults us. I dare say, nobody here has had a rotten egg thrown at you for Jesus Christ. No one has spit in your face. You have never had anybody curse you for Jesus' sake. You have never lost a good friend for Jesus Christ. Most of us have not. Yet we try to talk as if we have in some sense entered into the sorrows of the cross, or that we are the successors and heirs of the martyrs of the church. God forgive us!

We should realize, as Christians, the burden and agony of Jesus in the garden and that He was an Example that we should follow.

I will grant you, I know that something took place that night that I cannot re-enact. The same Scripture said, "He went a little farther." Brother Hoover, He went further than you and I will ever go. Yet there is a sense in which you and I enter into the soul agony of Jesus for sinners and the dying world and we ought to pray through. God help us to have some burden and sorrow and shame and agony and death of Jesus in the Garden of Gethsemane.

"And being in an agony he prayed more earnestly: and his sweat was as it were great drops of blood falling down to the ground." Jesus did that for a dying world.

V. We Are to Fill Up What Is Behind in Christ's Suffering

I do not wonder that Paul said, "I . . . fill up that which is behind of the afflictions of Christ in my flesh for his body's sake" (Col. 1:23,24).

That verse seems to mean a thing it can't mean. It seems to be contradictory. It seems that Paul enters into the atonement. It seems that Paul some way pays for man's sin, that there is priesthood, that there is substitution, that there is sacrifice, that there is atonement that a Christian has part in.

Well, if you make this distinction, that in one sense Christ alone paid for all our sins, I will admit that is true. I will say aside from that paying for the sins of the world on the cross, we should enter into Christ's suffering. If you mean in getting the Gospel to people, if you mean praying through for power and revival and victory and for a dying world, I know we ought to fill up what is lacking of the sufferings of Christ. To me that is past understanding.

That is one reason I feel preaching is such a holy calling. Like Paul, I feel I would like to say, "I magnify mine office." And God bless you, I am going to preach! I hope I may die if God ever makes it so I can't preach. For in some sense the Lord Jesus Christ saw fit to breathe on me, to put me in the stead of Christ that I may be an ambassador in Christ's stead. I pray that I may weep as He wept and suffer and agonize and wait with prayer and supplication and strong cryings and tears like Jesus did, and fill up in my body what is lacking of the sufferings of Christ.

You Christians, listen to our Saviour as He agonized and wept and sweated the bloody sweat and cried to God and prayed through in the Garden of Gethsemane. "And being in an agony"—"and being in an *agony,* he prayed the more earnestly," the Scripture says, "and his sweat was as it were great drops of blood falling down to the ground."

I wonder tonight how much you care. That is a strange thing.

What are Americans thinking about? War? A little, but not so much. Are they thinking about hospitals filled with the wounded and groaning ones? Are they thinking about unmarked graves? No. No! What are they thinking about? Widows and orphans weeping tonight in Romania, Poland, with maybe hundreds or even millions to die? No. No!

First, they are thinking about saving their own hides and getting rich if they can; sell all the guns they can, all the ammunition they can, make all the money they can, and to Hell with the rest of the world! That is what America is thinking about.

Do you have any sorrow for the sadness of the world today? I wonder how we can be happy with all the sin and burden in this world today; with all the sorrow that is in the world today.

Oh, the sorrows of the world and the troubles of the world! My dear friends, do you care about that? Do you care about that? I wonder.

I said something about being called to preach just awhile ago. I found in my pocket a bunch of notes—I suppose I have forty or fifty in my brief case. In Petersburg, Illinois, the pastor said, "We will pass these envelopes out, and if you want to put a note in telling Brother Rice how you have been blessed, do that." I guess maybe forty did. I was just looking over them—let's see one of these in my pocket, without any thought at all, let's see one of them. This one says: "Dear Brother Rice. I got a great blessing out of these meetings. I got saved Sunday night, and thank God for saving me. Pray for me."

And there are others like that.

VI. Why I Must Do the Work of an Evangelist

I have been torn very, very seriously between two pulling things in these last few weeks. Oh, how I have wanted to be with you! It seemed to me a tragedy not to help you with this tabernacle. I think you got along fine, and you built the tabernacle just as well as if I had been here. But it seemed to me a tragedy. I didn't get to drive a nail. You bought the lumber. You planned it. You put it up. I didn't get to shake hands or lead in prayer or win a soul around here while it was going on.

I have been torn between two loves. One is my people. I owe you something. I stick around and keep you from getting a good pastor! I owe you people something. But, my friends, I owe a dying world something, too. Like Paul, I must say, "I am debtor both to the Greeks, and to the Barbarians; both to the wise, and to the unwise. So, as much as in me is, I am ready to preach the gospel to you that are at Rome also" (Rom. 1:14, 15).

I have a call out to California. I know you think, "Brother Rice, I wish you would stay here." I know you do, and I would like to stay here. You say, "We would like to consult you about this and that, and have you visit our sick, and, Brother Rice, we wish you were here to push about the collection."

But, my friends, multitudes are dying. There are very few evangelists today. Many are starved out. Some were too money-minded. Some had sensations without doing much Bible preaching. Oh, I wish God would raise up some more Moodys.

I am for the pastors, but the place that lies barren is the field of evangelism in this country. Some preachers can go to a small church for a few days of meeting and with musical glasses and saws, can get a few people saved. That is good. But where is the man who can go to Atlanta, Georgia, or Kansas City, or even to Chicago or Philadelphia or Washington and, like Moody, Torrey, Chapman, Gipsy Smith in his heyday, win thousands to Christ? There are no more in America. Do you know any like that? The world is dying for lack of evangelists.

My people, the world is dying for lack of evangelistic preaching in the power of the Holy Ghost. (A lot of preachers have a true message, they are true to the Bible.) I cannot feel but that it is the call of God and I must go.

I want to lay on your heart, and I want you to feel the same way about it: Before you go to sleep tonight, will you pray with strong crying and tears for that missionary in Brazil, who for the pitiful little sum of $25.00 a month takes his family away into the interior, this cultured man, a man of ability? He rides in that little buggy because he can't afford a car on the money we pay him. He starts a Sunday school in his own home and now organizes a Baptist church and has begun to baptize new converts in the interior of Brazil. Tonight before you go to sleep, can't you pray, "O God, lay on me part of the burden that he has in Brazil. Give me a burdened and broken heart and travail of soul. Let me have part of the apostolic burden that preachers of old time and the apostles had for a dying world without Christ."

I don't need to threaten you—you are my people. You love me; I think you know my heart. God will bless you if you put souls first, if you get a burden for a dying world. If you don't, this church is going to die, and I hope we do. We ought to if we lose our burden; and we have already lost too much of it.

Some of you think I ought to stay here more. For the rest of my life I intend to spend a good deal of my time holding revival meetings.

"You can't be the best pastor this way," you say. But God called me to win souls. I begged Him for a broken heart and God knows I don't want to change it. I want a broken heart for sinners.

In one of these other letters a man said, "I came every night, and every night you hit me harder and harder. Finally" (he named the night, I don't remember), he said, "I had to settle it. I just had to settle it."

I don't know about the trouble in their home; I don't know about the drinking or whatever it was that had nearly broken their home—but his wife held on and cried and cried. "Now," she said, "now it is going to be all right at home, isn't it, Honey?"

And he bowed his head and said, "Yes, it is!"

And she kept saying, "It will be all right, now. It will be all right back at home, won't it?"

He went away just smiling and rejoicing and promising to begin prayer at the table instead of breaking his wife's heart, as he had done.

Oh, my friends, I look back on men such as he all over the country. Oh, if we had some young men who had a burden for the lost! We need preachers with broken hearts and part of the agony that Jesus had for sinners in the garden. Oh, may God give it!

I have been thinking much the last few days. I have in my study biographies of great men like D. L. Moody or George Mueller, who perhaps was next to Moody in blessing my life—that great English prayer man. Oh, if we could learn to pray like he prayed!

Then I think of the story of Spurgeon as told in *The Shadow of the Broad Brim* or the older biography. And the life of Hudson Taylor and of Robert Murray McCheyne, the great Scottish preacher. I think of Charles G. Finney. I think about a little handful of men who went under a haystack and prayed till God opened a mission field. I remember that Charles Wesley, John Wesley, Whitefield, after awhile Peter Boehler, got together and prayed and prayed and prayed for the Holy Spirit of God to come upon them in power. I think of Finney as he went up in a loft and wrapped himself in a buffalo robe and prayed nearly the night through for souls and power to win them.

I think of Moody who went two years burdened and in prayer. His heart couldn't get on anything else. Then the power of the Holy Spirit fell upon him on Wall Street in New York. And He came in such power that he said later, "If You don't withhold Your hand, Lord, I will die." Moody said, "I wouldn't give up what I got that night for all the wealth of the world. It would be only the small dust of the balance compared to what I got that night."

I think about David Brainerd, a missionary to the Indians who kneeled down in the snow and didn't think it cold for the passion of his heart as he prayed for the Indians of North America.

These men entered into the sufferings of Christ!

Oh, may God teach us to have a broken heart like Christ when being in an agony He prayed the more earnestly and His sweat was as it were great drops of blood falling to the ground.

VII. Sinner, It Was for You

And now, then, this message is for sinners, too. Oh, that message for sinners! Do you realize how tenderly our Saviour loved you? I preach hard against sin. But I love sinners, and I want you to come and see the love of the Lord Jesus as He wept over sinners that night and agonized for them. Don't you think if Jesus were thinking only of Himself, of His own ease, He would have been glad to have it over with that night? On the cross He died the next day and said, "It is finished," and gave up the ghost.

I want you to mark that—He gave up the ghost. That was His own intention, His own plan. That is the reason He said, "I lay down my life, that I might take it again. No man taketh it from me, but I lay it down of myself. I have power to lay it down, and I have power to take it again. This commandment have I received of my Father" (John 10:17,18). And He said to Pilate, "Thou couldest have no power at all against me, except it were given thee from above" (John 19:11).

When Jesus said, "It is finished," "It is finished," one could hear a triumphant ring in it. I can hear in the voice of the Saviour on the cross in that last cry, "Oh, thank God, it is done! The suffering is done, and I am glad to be done with it!" I think one could hear that in that cry.

Jesus was not thinking about Himself in the garden. He could have said, "Let it be done tonight. I will die and the agony will be over." If you think He was thinking only of Himself, you are mistaken. He was not. He was thinking of *you*. He was saying, "My God, don't let the Devil kill Me. Let this cup pass from Me and let Me live until tomorrow so I can die for sinners." Oh, Jesus died for *sinners*. He died for you and in the garden He prayed through and if He hadn't, He would have died prematurely and could not have saved any one.

I do not know how you people feel who plan to save yourself and keep yourself. You need not watch Jesus. You are not concerned with His agonies on the cross and in the garden.

Now what does the bloody sweat mean? His strong cries—what do they mean? You who are planning to save yourself don't need that. Romans the 4th chapter says, "If Abraham were justified by works, he hath whereof to glory; but not before God."

Go ahead and brag if you can save yourself, but don't be talking about Calvary. Call yourself a "Harrisite," Brother Harris, but not a Christian. You are not a Christian *if you are saving yourself.*

I got a letter and answered it this past week, from a man greatly bothered because I said that a born-again child of God had everlasting life, that he would never be lost. He wrote a letter rebuking me in strong terms for that "very dangerous doctrine," and sent me a booklet by a young Methodist preacher deriding as terribly dangerous and damnable that doctrine that one can be saved forever by the blood of Christ.

If you are here tonight and you are thinking in terms of saving yourself, then there is no use talking to you about Calvary and Gethsemane and the bloody sweat and the agony. That is nothing to you if you are saving yourself and keeping yourself. Go ahead!

But for sinners who need a Saviour, consider the sweetest picture that a mortal eye ever looked upon! Hear these words as the Saviour wept and prayed. It surely must have been the tenderest prayer that ever fell from mortal lips when Jesus prayed!

I know Jesus had a way of praying that fascinated His disciples, and as He prayed, as Luke the 11th chapter tells us, as He prayed so earnestly, with such anointing, so clearly with the presence and manifestation of the Spirit, He prayed with such compassion over sinners and out of His overwhelming love for sinners that a disciple said, "Lord, teach us to pray!"

I know what He was praying for! I know He would not have prayed without praying for sinners—that poor, dying, undone, wicked, guilty, Hell-deserving, Hell-bound sinners should be saved. That is what Heaven rejoices about now. He came to seek and to save that which was lost. And the scribes and Pharisees murmured, "This man receiveth sinners, and eateth with them." I know; I can tell what He was praying about. The Bible doesn't say, but I know what Jesus was praying about.

And one said, "Lord Jesus, teach us to pray." I think what He meant was, "O God, I thought I could pray until I heard Your

prayer. O Jesus, teach me to pray like that!" To have heard that
prayer of Jesus must have been the most enticing thing the
people ever heard.

But, O sinner, tonight if you could have heard Jesus pray in
the garden, then you would know how He loves sinners. And
then the next day He prayed the same way, saying, "Father,
forgive them, for they know not what they do." Oh, Jesus
prayed so that sinners might be saved. Thank God, He prayed
through until the morrow when He could go to the cross and pay
for our sins so that we might be saved.

You can be saved tonight: I wish you could realize, sinner,
that salvation is something that you can't pay for. You could not
pay for it if you wanted to. Jesus paid it all. So I think
Christians ought to pray through about things, but a lost sinner
does not have to pray through for salvation. He gives as many
as receive Him, the power to become the sons of God.
Whosoever calls upon the name of the Lord can be saved. He
died for sinners. Will you trust Him for salvation?

It doesn't take agony and waiting before you can be saved. If
you want to come trusting Jesus, He died for sinners. And when
you have Him, you have salvation. He prayed through so that
you might take it freely without agony. He suffered that you
might take it freely.

Do you want Christ tonight? Do you want peace and
forgiveness and salvation tonight? Then you may have Him,
and I hope you will.

20—"Have Faith in God"

(Sermon preached Sunday night, January 9, 1938, Dallas. Stenographically reported.)

PRAYER: Oh, Father, warm hearts. Teach us to pray. Lord, I pray like the man who brought his son, "Lord, I believe; help thou mine unbelief." Help us to obey Thy command to have faith in God. Make this a church of faith. For Jesus' sake. Amen.

I read in Mark the 11th chapter,

> *And on the morrow, when they were come from Bethany, he was hungry:*
>
> *And seeing a fig tree afar off having leaves, he came, if haply he might find any thing thereon: and when he came to it, he found nothing but leaves; for the time of figs was not yet.* —Vss. 12,13.

He found nothing but leaves. What a picture that is of many Christians—nothing but leaves! No fruit, only leaves withered.

> *And Jesus answered and said unto it, No man eat fruit of thee hereafter for ever. And his disciples heard it.* —Vs. 14.

Now begin with verse 19:

> *And when even was come, he went out of the city.*
>
> *And in the morning, as they passed by* [the next morning], *they saw the fig tree dried up from the roots.*
>
> *And Peter calling to remembrance saith unto him, Master, behold, the fig tree which thou cursedst is withered away.*
>
> *And Jesus answering saith unto them, Have faith in God.*

For verily I say unto you, That whosoever shall say unto this mountain, Be thou removed, and be thou cast into the sea; and shall not doubt in his heart, but shall believe that those things which he saith shall come to pass; he shall have whatsoever he saith.

Therefore I say unto you, What things soever ye desire, when ye pray, believe that ye receive them, and ye shall have them.

And when ye stand praying, forgive, if ye have ought against any: that your Father also which is in heaven may forgive you your trespasses.

But if ye do not forgive, neither will your Father which is in heaven forgive your trespasses.—Vss. 19-26.

Now I take the text from verse 22, "And Jesus answering saith unto them, Have faith in God."

Jesus had just passed by and His disciples said, "Look how the fig tree is withered away. Yesterday morning we passed this way and saw no fruit and now the fig tree is already withered away!" Jesus told them they could have the same faith. He told them they could have the same thing happen. He said, "I command you, have faith in God."

I remind you that the miracles that Jesus worked and the teaching that He did and the souls that He saved He did in His human ministry, in the weakness of His human body, filled with the Spirit of God. This Jesus who cursed the fig tree did it not as the Son of God who made it, but cursed it as the Son of Man, filled with the Spirit.

He came into this world and emptied Himself of His deity and glory and so then cursed this fig tree and Jesus said, "This is an example to you. If you have faith in God you can say to this mountain, Be thou removed, and be thou cast into the sea; and shall not doubt in his heart, but shall believe that those things which he saith shall come to pass; he shall have whatsoever he saith."

I. A Sin Not to Believe God

You are not to doubt in your heart. Now here is the command

of Jesus: "Have faith in God," and it is a plain command and there is no way to get around it. There is no doubt about His command. You are to have faith in God. Jesus said, "What I have, you ought to have also." It is your Christian duty. You can have faith in God. It is a plain command.

Jesus came down off the mountain, recorded in the 17th chapter of Matthew, and said to His disciples who had been unable to cast a demon out of a child, "O faithless and perverse generation, how long shall I be with you? how long shall I suffer you?"

The disciples said, "Why could not we cast him out?"

And Jesus said, "Because of your unbelief." And then He said, "Howbeit this kind goeth not out but by prayer and fasting."

Unbelief! Unbelief! Unbelief grieves Jesus. He said, "O ye of little faith." Another time, "Why is it that you have no faith?" Another time, "Where is your faith?" Many, many times the Saviour was grieved by the sin of unbelief. You and I believe that a lost sinner sins terribly when he does not accept Jesus as Saviour. It is a wicked, moral perversion in the heart when a sinner does not accept Christ. It is sin not to trust Christ for salvation. Then why would it not be a sin for a Christian not to have faith in God?

We are *commanded* to have faith in God. It is a command of Jesus that we have faith in God. He said, "Have faith in God." Now if it is a command, it must be a terrible sin not to have faith, for Hebrews 11:6 says, "Without faith it is impossible to please him." It is impossible to please God without faith. Without faith you cannot enjoy your prayers, God cannot give you what He wants to give you. You cannot please God without faith.

Lack of faith is sin. Unbelief blocks the hand of God, stops the mercy of God, turns away the face of God, keeps you from having power and joy and help when you need it. It keeps you from being a soul winner.

II. How to Get Faith: the Bible

It is a sin not to have faith in God! Now if it is a sin not to have faith in God, evidently there must be some way that you could get faith if you went after it. There is.

In the first place, you get faith by the use of the Bible. The Scripture says, "Faith cometh by hearing, and hearing by the word of God" (Rom. 10:17). If you do not have faith in God, you are not doing what you ought to do about this Scripture. There is something about the Scriptures that puts faith in you, helps you believe in God.

A man who does not believe that the Bible is true needs to read it with an open mind. That has convinced many a man. If one does not believe one is saved by faith, he needs to read the Bible. It proves salvation is wholly by grace. Faith will grow if you read the Bible.

The 1st Psalm says of the blessed man that does certain things, "his delight is in the law of the Lord; and in his law doth he meditate day and night. And he shall be like a tree planted by the rivers of water, that bringeth forth his fruit in his season; his leaf also shall not wither; and whatsoever he doeth shall prosper."

If you want to have faith that will prosper, that will get results and bear fruit, read the Word of God and meditate in it. You plow deep to make the ground bring forth food. When you dig in the Bible, it springs up faith in your heart. "Faith cometh by hearing, and hearing by the word of God."

If you will do what you ought to do about the Bible this year, reading it, meditating on the Bible, taking time for the Bible, letting it soak in, you will not sin about faith.

David said, "Thy word have I hid in mine heart, that I might not sin against thee" (Ps. 119:11). You won't sin about faith if you read the Bible as you ought. While making plans for the new year (the new year is not old yet, there is still plenty of time to make New Year's resolutions), why not resolve, "I am going to have faith in God. I am going to absorb, digest, meditate on the Scripture daily." Make it real in your life. Meditate day and night in the Scriptures. Believe God. Have faith to believe your prayers will be answered.

My heart was blessed last night when I came across the

phrase where Paul said, "You ought to support the ministry." He quoted Scripture from the Old Testament, "Thou shalt not muzzle the mouth of the ox that treadeth out the corn," then Paul said, "Doth God take care for oxen?" (I Cor. 9:9). And my heart leaped within me as I thought, God does not care mainly for oxen, but He cares for preachers who tread out corn for God. God says, "I want every preacher to have the muzzle taken off; I want you to see that he gets something to eat, and can go on with his work." God says, "I will see that the muzzle is taken off. I will give him something to eat." The Lord provided for oxen; thank God He can provide for preachers.

The Bible will grow your faith. Read the Bible. If you read about Pentecost you will have faith for revivals. If you read about the widow's cruse of oil (I Kings 17:8-16), you will have faith for daily bread. If you read about King Hezekiah's sickness and how the Lord gave him fifteen more years (Isa. 38), you will have faith to pray for healing for sickness.

Then you remember about King Hezekiah, when Sennacherib's army compassed the city to take it on the morrow. That night, after prayer, the death angel came and there were 185,000 corpses the next morning (Isa. 37:36-38). Read that and you will believe the Lord will take care of you if you will obey the command, "Have faith in God."

In reading the Bible you will find faith springing up to meet the promises of God. If it is all hearsay, all secondhand, you could not believe it much. But if you read here that God says He promises you this, and this, and see where He dealt so faithfully and mercifully with others, after awhile you have to begin to believe in God.

III. Grow Faith by Counting Blessings

Then if a man wants to have faith in God, what else will he do? Count his blessings! You are not going to have the faith you ought to have unless you count your blessings. Faith springs up from counting your blessings.

After the feeding of the five thousand and after the feeding of the four thousand, Jesus said, "Beware of the leaven of the Pharisees and of the Sadducees." The disciples thought it was because they did not bring any bread, and Jesus rebuked them and said, "How is it that ye do not understand that I spake it not to you concerning bread, that ye should beware of the leaven of the Pharisees and of the Sadducees? He said, "Do ye not yet understand, neither remember the five loaves of the five thousand, and how many baskets ye took up? Neither the seven loaves of the four thousand, and how many baskets ye took up?" (Matt. 16:9,10).

This is the point Jesus made there: "Come back and count your blessings, meditate on what I have done for you. Only believe I can do it now again and do not be worried about bread." If I would meditate on the way God cared for me last week, I would believe that next week He could do it again!

May I tell this little interesting personal thing. I had this week a sweet experience. Come Monday and we did not save out grocery money. I have no regular salary, just offerings, and Sunday's offerings designated for me, we usually spend in two or three days. Mary Lloys, my daughter (with Mrs. Rice away), phoned and wanted to know if she could have fried potatoes for supper. She phoned back in a little bit and said, "Daddy, I'm in trouble. I put on the grease and got it hot and peeled the potatoes and cut them up and fried some. I wanted to peel some more and there weren't any more potatoes!"

I said, "Go across to the New Deal grocery store and ask him to let us have some potatoes (ten pounds) and a can of spinach and I will come by and pay for it."

I don't remember what time that was. But they brought in the afternoon mail. I had not seen it, but I opened it and found fifty cents to use as I saw fit. What Mary Lloys got at the store cost forty-four cents. I went down there and paid them forty-four cents and had six cents left over!

We have had God give us fifty dollars in answer to prayer, thirty dollars a day for six months for radio bills in answer to prayer, and greater amounts, but that fifty cents was better than fifty dollars! It meant that God sent just what I needed, when I needed it. God says, "I am taking care of you and looking after your family."

Stop and count your blessings and see what God has done for you.

Have faith in God. Why do you not tell what God has done for you? That is what David meant when he said, "Because he hath inclined his ear unto me, therefore will I call upon him as long as I live" (Ps. 116:2). David said, "I go back and remember what He had done for me, the joy I had, the peace I had, the answers God gave, and am going to pray some more. I am going to ask Him for some more, He will hear me! I am going to ask God for some more."

Why do you not take a sheet of paper and write down your answers to prayer, times when the Lord heard you when you were in distress? Then you will say, "Lord, I'm going to ask you for some more!"

IV. Make God Some More Tracks

On the Pacific coast one winter a Chinaman was cook in a logging camp high in the mountains. One afternoon he was taking a walk in the snow. Hearing a shuffling sound behind him, he looked back and saw a giant grizzly bear sniffing at his tracks in the snow. Excited by the monster's appearance, the Chinaman said, "You likee my tracks? Velly well; I makee you some more!"

So when I go back into the past and count the times God has answered my prayers, I feel like making some more tracks to the place of prayer! Beloved, God does like our tracks of faith and encourages us to make some more! You look back and see what God has done for you, the prayers in the past God has answered, the prayers before that He has heard, then say, "I will give Him some more prayers to answer." That will help your faith. Count your blessings, and it will surprise you what the Lord has done. Have faith in God!

It is a sin not to have faith in God and it is a sin because it is not necessary to go on in unbelief. You can have faith if you will go back and count your blessings. Consider what God has done for you. Praise glorifies God partly because it impresses on your own mind the goodness of God and so builds faith. That is one reason you should praise Him.

V. Ask God for Faith

"Have faith in God." How? Have faith by asking for it, the Bible says.

Hebrews the 11th chapter says, "By faith Abel offered unto God a more excellent sacrifice than Cain." "By faith Enoch," "by faith Noah," "by faith Abraham," "by faith Isaac," and "by faith Jacob," "by faith David" did this, by faith the prophets did this. Then chapter 12 begins, still talking about faith, "Wherefore seeing we also are compassed about with so great a cloud of witnesses, let us lay aside every weight, and the sin which doth so easily beset us, and let us run with patience the race that is set before us."

Old Noah looks down here and says, "I wonder why John Rice doesn't have more faith." By faith righteous Abel brought a lamb for a sacrifice. Abel looks down and says, "I wonder why Thornton has trouble trusting God." Heavenly witnesses are looking down! Enoch looks down on Stark and says, "I wonder how Stark has trouble trusting God." Abraham who started to offer Isaac for a sacrifice (but God would not let Abraham kill him but provided a lamb instead)—Abraham looks down! There are heavenly witnesses around us! "Wherefore seeing we also are compassed about with so great a cloud of witnesses, let us lay aside every weight, and *the sin which doth so easily beset us*, and let us run with patience the race that is set before us.

What besetting sin is He talking about? The sin of unbelief! *Lay aside unbelief.* How? "Looking unto Jesus *the author and finisher of OUR FAITH!*" I look up to Jesus and say, "O Saviour, You are the Author of this faith I have. Then You give me the rest of the faith I need. You are the Finisher. Then, Lord, put the finishing touches on my faith!" Look to Jesus to bring you faith. That is what people did in Bible times.

Jesus said in Mark 9:23, "If thou canst believe, all things are possible to him that believeth." He said, "If you have faith, you can have anything." "And straightway the father of the child cried out, and said with tears, Lord, I believe; help thou mine unbelief."

If you want faith, you can have it. Ask for it. Say, "I do

believe. Lord, help my unbelief." You have a right to lay aside the weight and sin of unbelief and say, "Unbelief, I don't need you. I am going to have faith in God!"

In Luke the 17th chapter, beginning with verse 5, we find a prayer for faith: "And the apostles said unto the Lord, Increase our faith."

The apostles said, "Increase our faith." That man said, "Lord, I believe; help thou mine unbelief." Hebrews 12:2 says, "Looking unto Jesus the author and finisher of our faith." You can have more faith if you pray for faith!

VI. Faith Grows by Knowing and Proving God

The more experience you have with God, the easier it is to trust Him. If you knew the kind of God He is, you could not help having faith in Him.

There was a poor ignorant woman once to whom somebody said, "Well, you say you are saved for sure?"

She said, "I certainly am."

But this one argued with her that you have to wait until you get to Heaven before you can know, that if you fall into sins God may forsake you at any time.

She said, "Thank God, I take HIS word for it. I would be willing to be the second woman that God went back on, but I am determined I will not be the first! If He had gone back on a few others, I might have some fears, but I am determined I will not be the first one He forsakes."

He is not going back on me, because He never did on anybody else. The more you have to do with some folks, the more sure you are of them. The more you have to do with Jesus, the more you can risk Him. Faith grows by trying God out.

It is wonderful when people have confidence in you because they know you.

When I was a boy I remember one time going to a drug store owned by Neil Raborn at Dundee, Texas. I asked him if he would charge something to my dad. He said, "Yes, we will charge half the store to William H. Rice, or all of it, if he wants it." He knew my dad!

Is it not a wonderful thing about Jesus? The more you know Him, the more you can absolutely trust Him.

If somebody here is not a Christian, listen. One time a man was converted when D. L. Moody preached, and Moody told him, "Watch out or the Devil will hit you about tomorrow morning and tell you that you are not saved. You had better get a Scripture you can hang on to. Take John 3:16."

But the Devil did not wait until the next morning; he got after him that night. He could not sleep. The Devil kept saying, "You are not saved." But he said, "Yes, old Devil, I am. Here is John 3:16: 'For God so loved the world, that he gave his only begotten Son, that whosoever believeth in him should not perish, but have everlasting life.' So I am saved."

But the Devil came along again and said, "You don't know that the translators translated that right. You can't read Greek." The Devil had him in a tight place. "You don't know whether the promises are true or not." So far into the night he said, "I don't know whether it is translated right or not, but I am going to believe it, and when I come to die I am going to say, 'Lord, if I made a mistake it isn't my mistake, it is the translators.' " So he found peace and went to sleep.

Do not worry about the translation; just trust Christ. No translator could ever make the Bible promise more than Jesus promised Himself. Translators could not picture Jesus any better than He is, nor expect Him to answer prayer any more than He does.

I thank God that He is worthy of all trust. The more you know Him the more faith is going to grow. Get acquainted well with Jesus and so, "have faith in God!" I would use what faith I have. You can say, "God, I have got a little faith. I am going to use that. Help my unbelief." Faith will grow if you go like you are, trusting God the best you can. Try God out.

"Have faith in God."

V. APPLICATION OF SCRIPTURE TO CURRENT EVENTS

21—Lessons From East Texas School Tragedy

(Preached in 1937 at Fundamentalist Baptist Tabernacle, Dallas. Stenographically recorded.)

455 Dead in New London School Explosion. Why?

WARNING: "PREPARE TO MEET THY GOD!"

There were present at that season some that told him of the Galileans, whose blood Pilate had mingled with their sacrifices.

And Jesus answering said unto them, Suppose ye that these Galileans were sinners above all the Galileans, because they suffered such things?

I tell you, Nay: but, except ye repent, ye shall all likewise perish.

Or those eighteen, upon whom the tower in Siloam fell, and slew them, think ye that they were sinners above all men that dwelt in Jerusalem?

I tell you, Nay: but, except ye repent, ye shall all likewise perish.—Luke 13:1-5.

Our Saviour called the attention of the people to public calamities of His day and from them brought plain and searching lessons and warning of the judgment of God that must come on sin.

A group of Galileans had been caught in their sins and had been slaughtered by the Roman governor, Pilate. Their blood had been mingled with the blood of the animals they brought for sacrifices to the Temple. We do not know their crime, but

Jesus said, "Suppose ye that these Galileans were sinners above all the Galileans, because they suffered such things? I tell you, Nay: but, except ye repent, ye shall all likewise perish!"

The other public calamity was an "act of God." The tower of Siloam had fallen and killed eighteen citizens of Jerusalem, and Jesus warned the people saying, "Suppose ye that these Galileans were sinners above all the Galileans, because they suffered such things? I tell you, Nay: but, except ye repent, ye shall all likewise perish!"

I. A Terrible Calamity

So following the example of the Saviour, I call your attention to the terrible calamity which took place last Thursday, March 18, at New London Consolidated School in East Texas where fifteen minutes before closing time there was a great explosion, the walls of a $300,000 high school blew out, the roof lifted and then fell, killing 455 high school children and teachers and injuring many others.

This event shocked the world. Even the German Government for the time being left off its campaign of hate against the Jews and sent condolences to America over the sad death of so many young people. Newspapers were filled with scenes of disaster. Radio stations gave minute accounts. A wide section of our country poured aid into the district to clear the debris, rescue the wounded and recover and identify the bodies. Hospitals, morgues, Legion halls and churches were filled with the bodies of the dead and dying.

All who have tender hearts must be grieved at the calamity that has befallen so many homes. At our breakfast table we had a special prayer of thanksgiving that the dear Lord had in His mercy left our circle unbroken and all of our children were well while so many homes were stricken with grief over the loss of one or several children. We should all pray that God will comfort these fathers and mothers and through the tragedy will call them to love Him, trust Him and serve Him.

Last Saturday, with a preacher brother, I, along with Miss Viola Walden, drove the 126 miles from Dallas through Tyler,

Arp and Overton to New London where the tragedy occurred. We could sense a pall of sadness over all that territory. Funerals were in progress in every nearby town, and hospitals contained those injured by the explosion. We met or passed a half dozen funeral processions.

State Highway policemen, in front of a little Baptist church at 4:00 in the afternoon where a funeral was in progress, told us that since 12:00 funerals had continued one after another. The oil workers who made up most of the population of the little town of New London and the surrounding districts from whence came the pupils of this big consolidated high school, have not long lived in this territory. Most of them call other states or other sections of Texas their home; so bodies were being shipped far and near. Eight caskets were unloaded in Dallas from one car. A Dallas policeman saw an old model truck from East Texas which carried a coffin. It contained the body of a little girl killed in the explosion. Her father, driving the truck, said simply, "We are taking her home."

At New London we carefully examined the ruins of that great Consolidated High School building. The main part of the school had been built in 1933. I understand that later two wings were added. The first unit cost, I was told, $300,000. Other wings were added, an elementary building was erected. The building was the very finest. It was built out of expensive white brick backed up with hollow tile. The roof was of tile, the window openings had steel sashes, not wood. The guttering was of copper.

There had been no depression at New London. It was in the heart of what is claimed to be the richest oil belt in the world. In fact, on the school ground we saw the derricks rising over seven producing wells. The New London Consolidated School was known as the richest country school in the world. The equipment and faculty were all that was to be desired.

Yet all this was wiped out in a moment. The building was blown to bits. Only a small portion was left standing. Bricks shot in all directions, some falling one hundred yards away. I picked up out in the highway three or four bricks and pieces of tile which I have with me. Hundreds were killed in an instant and others were mangled. Only a few escaped unharmed. Four hundred fifty-five were known dead, including most of the teachers.

A barber told us he had only had six hours sleep in sixty hours. An undertaker came into the barber shop staggering as he walked. He had prepared five bodies in one night, had had no rest in many hours. He slumped into unconsciousness as he sat down. There were not enough preachers for the funerals. Some were brought from Beaumont. Doctors and nurses were sent from all over East Texas. A great many went from Dallas.

Some bodies were literally blown to pieces. Heads, arms and fingers were picked up in tubs and peach baskets. I saw a little torn jacket among the debris of broken brick and splintered wood, twisted iron and shattered concrete which had been removed from the building in the search for bodies. In the American Legion Hall one of our party saw the mangled form of a little girl twelve or fourteen years old who had not yet been identified. The body was bloody. Flies crawled on the sheet which covered it.

About the same time a man approached soldiers guarding the ruins and begged to be allowed to go into what was left of the gymnasium. His little girl had never been found, he said. The guard told me there were various estimates of from five to twenty-seven bodies that had not been accounted for or identified.

One family buried a child thinking it was their own and later discovered the little girl's body elsewhere and the heart-rending experience of another funeral. The first body was dug up and identified by another family. A thousand pathetic and heart-touching details occurred.

When the tower of Siloam fell on eighteen people and killed them, Jesus preached on that subject and said, "Think ye that they were sinners above all men that dwelt in Jerusalem? I tell you, Nay: but, except ye repent, ye shall all likewise perish." Certainly He would have taken notice of the terrible and sudden death of 455, and would have preached upon it.

II. You Cannot Rule God Out of This Calamity!

Many like to rule God out. Man in his boasted wisdom and culture and independence does not like to believe that he must give an account to God; that there is a God of judgment, a God of wrath, a God who rewards good and punishes evil. They do not like to acknowledge that God has His hands on all the affairs of this world. Men do not like to admit that God created the heavens and earth; naturally the same men do not like to believe He controls them.

The unbeliever, the worldly-minded describe such calamities as unavoidable "accidents." Such people naturally believe that this universe of God's came about by accident, or at least that the calamities and woes that beset the human race are mere unrelated happenings and not acts of an all-wise, righteous and personal God who controls the destinies of nations and planets and individual souls. BUT, MY FRIEND, YOU CANNOT RULE GOD OUT OF HIS UNIVERSE! YOU CANNOT IGNORE THE HAND OF GOD IN THIS CALAMITY!

The Bible has a thousand examples of the wrath of God expressed in such ruin. According to the Word of God, the whole race of men except Noah and his family were destroyed in the flood by the deliberate act of God and on account of their sins. According to the Bible, God sent ten plagues on Egypt, ending in the death of all the firstborn of every home where there was no blood on the door, and that because of their sin and unbelief. God says that He Himself destroyed Pharaoh and his armies in the Red Sea. The ground opened to swallow into eternal death Korah, Dathan and Abiram and their followers and families because of their sins. Numbers 16:31-35 says:

> *And it came to pass, as he had made an end of speaking all these words, that the ground clave asunder that was under them:*
> *And the earth opened her mouth, and swallowed them up, and their houses, and all the men that appertained unto Korah, and all their gods.*
> *They, and all that appertained to them, went down alive into the pit, and the earth closed upon them: and*

they perished from among the congregation.

And all Israel that were round about them fled at the cry of them: for they said, Lest the earth swallow us up also.

And there came out a fire from the Lord, and consumed the two hundred and fifty men that offered incense.

God expressly says that He Himself destroyed these sinners. When Nadab and Abihu carried strange fire into the tabernacle, they were killed with a flame from Heaven.

Again and again plagues came on the Israelites because of their sins, brought directly by the hand of God according to the plain statements of Scripture.

The 28th chapter of Deuteronomy expressly declares that drouths, plagues, pestilences, wars and famines come by the decree of God and because of man's sins. You cannot rule God out of His own world.

Lest some should say that God so dealt in the Old Testament but not in the New, that He thus judged Israel but not the Gentiles, or not Christians, let me remind you that the New Testament abounds with the same kind of illustrations. Jesus forewarned that the Temple at Jerusalem would be destroyed because Israel rejected their Messiah. And this destruction occurred forty years after His death in A. D. 70 and Jews were scattered to all parts of the world.

Ananias and Sapphira were struck dead for lying to the Holy Ghost (Acts 5:1-11).

King Herod in his pride sinned, "And immediately the angel of the Lord smote him, because he gave not God the glory: and he was eaten of worms, and gave up the ghost" (Acts 12:23).

The sorcerer Elymas was stricken blind because he hindered a man Paul sought to win to Christ (Acts 13:6-12).

Nor does the matter end there. The book of Revelation tells of case after case where God shall plague the earth again because of man's sins. We are plainly told that earthquakes, hail and disease will come as an expression of the wrath of God on cities, nations and individuals (Rev. 16).

In every age the God who made this world still controls it. There is a personal God. He is the center and sustainer of all things. Not one heart beats but by His deliberate choice. Every good gift is from God. Every calamity is by His consent.

III. "I Create Evil," God Says

In Isaiah 45:7 the Lord says, "I form the light, and create darkness: I make peace, and create evil. I the Lord do all these things." The word "evil" here means calamity, affliction, trouble. God is the one who brings trouble on sinners.

You cannot rule God out of the calamity that happened in New London, Texas, on Thursday, March 18th.

We are repeatedly told that chastening, bodily affliction, etc., are of God, and we are commanded, "My son, despise not thou the chastening of the Lord, nor faint when thou art rebuked of him: For whom the Lord loveth he chasteneth, and scourgeth every son whom he receiveth" (Heb. 12:5,6).

Did God know the gas was collecting in the basement and in the hollow tile walls of that Consolidated School building? Do you believe that God knew but could not interfere? No, if there is an all-seeing God, an all-wise God, He knew about it. If there is an all-powerful God, He could have prevented it. He could have delayed the explosion thirty minutes when probably every child and teacher would have been out of the building. He could have had some teacher, janitor, trustee or engineer check the heating system.

There is only one inescapable conclusion. God knew of the accumulation of gas, He knew about the spark that would set it off. He knew who would be present and who would be absent. God could have changed it but did not. Therefore, God Himself either permitted or brought about the calamity for His own purposes. THE EXPLOSION WAS THE JUDGMENT OF GOD.

Irreverent and self-righteous sinners join the infidels in accusing a God who would bring about a destruction of so many little children. But that is foolish, for everyone in the building would have died anyway, sooner or later. If you admit that God has permitted death for every individual of the human race except Enoch and Elijah and those now living, then it is silly to accuse God or attempt to judge Him as to when and how people must die.

"It is appointed unto men once to die, but after this the judgment," the Scripture says (Heb. 9:27). If the death of the race was brought by sin, then the death of every individual is brought by sin, too—either his own or some other's. Every death is a judgment of God against the sin of the race. If there was no sin, there would be no death. So it is not surprising if sometimes death is the judgment of God on the sins of individuals. Those who were saved are better off in Heaven. If any died unsaved, their death was no more terrible than if each died separately. Do not judge God!

IV. A Judgment, One of Many Judgments

These are terrible times we live in. In America we have had a great depression, the greatest in human history. We have had unemployment, bank failures, bankruptcy and human disaster on a national scale. Some shallow thinker may say the depression was brought on by manipulation of the stock market or by the policy of some national leaders. Well, then, how do you account for the fact that in the midst of that terrible time God sent a drouth greater than any that had been known heretofore, covering a territory 900 miles wide and 1,500 miles long? And how do you account for the increasing menace of floods so that the Ohio, the Mississippi and many other rivers have brought death, destruction of property, and human misery to uncounted multitudes?

Such events are classed even by the law of the land and legal terminology as "acts of God." And that is exactly what they are. The judgments of an angry God are upon America! Airliners crash into mountains or catch fire in the air and many die. On the Morro Castle steamer as people danced and drank, fire gutted the interior of the vessel and scores died in the fire or in the icy water. A hundred people die every day in America of automobile accidents, and murder stalks in our cities. Last week a famous hospital published the statement that within a few years one out of every five persons in America will die of cancer!

The curse of Almighty God, I say, is on America for our sins. The disaster that occurred in New London last week is only a part and parcel of a course of events that must alarm every thoughtful person.

V. Why New London Instead of Elsewhere?

We cannot always understand the acts of God. We do not have God's infinite wisdom. However, it may be helpful to suggest some reasons why the explosion occurred at this big Consolidated School in the thickly settled East Texas oil field.

In the first place, the wickedness of the East Texas oil fields is notorious. Many fine, devout Christian men and women are among the oil workers. On the other hand, there is an unusual proportion of wicked and godless people in the oil field. Usually the work is the same, seven days a week, so oil field workers generally are not a church-going people. The proportion of Sunday school and church attendance in the oil fields is usually less than the average.

Again, wages are high in the oil field and the ready money attracts great numbers of gamblers, beer parlors and dance halls. The people who follow oil booms, moving from one part of the country to another, are rather transient people. They do not have the settling influences of having homes in long-established communities.

The oil business itself is usually more or less of a speculation. Millions are made and millions are lost in the oil game. Fights are common. Profane language and blasphemy are sometimes unspeakably bitter. By nature oil field people are made out of the same clay as the rest of us, but their environment is even worse than the average.

In Texas there has been a constant war over the illegal running of oil. Thousands in East Texas have connived to defeat the enforcement of the law and to produce or refine or sell oil and its products in violation of state law. Perhaps these reasons may indicate why God brought a shocking warning in the heart of the East Texas oil fields.

The big Consolidated School had up toward 1,500 pupils enrolled. Nearby was a Baptist church. Baptists are stronger in Texas than any other denomination. Yet the announcement board said, "Sunday school attendance last Sunday, 78." Doubtless, many children over that wide area, cared for in that one school, attended Sunday school at various small churches in their respective communities. Many of their families were devout, God-fearing, church-going people.

But a community which would make so much of its schools, spending hundreds of thousands of dollars on building and equipment and having forty or fifty teachers, and yet having no large Sunday schools, would indicate that common schools were counted more important than Sunday schools, and education more important than religion.

But after all, oil-field workers did go to church. The families of the 455 dead and their friends and loved ones took time from work, took time to get a preacher and went to church. For once they left their work for religious services when they attended the funerals of their loved ones. In this terrible and lamentable tragedy, God came to the oil fields of East Texas. It was a judgment of God!

Perhaps in no other way could the warning have been sent to so many people. Cities in many states were represented . The destruction happened in a beautiful and expensive building. It was brought about by the explosion of gas, and so by the very wealth that built the building, that drew the people into that settlement; the wealth that is the god of so many!

On a blackboard in the ruins were found words like these, "Gas and oil, the greatest blessing of East Texas, made this school possible." That statement is not true. There are many things better than gas and oil. Even beloved children are better (if you forget Christ, and the Bible and salvation), and the "richest rural school district in the world" with seven producing oil wells on the school ground is today the poorest in the world, with 455 dead, with empty homes and aching hearts and with its little fresh mounds over which are withering wreaths of flowers! And it was the hand of God.

VI. God Means It to Be a Warning to Us as Well as to Them

But before any of us cast a single reflection upon the oil fields of East Texas let us remember the words of the Saviour about a like occurrence when the tower in Siloam fell and killed eighteen people. "Suppose ye that these Galileans were sinners above all the Galileans, because they suffered such things? I tell you, Nay: but, except ye repent, ye shall all likewise perish," He said.

The terrible calamity of New London is only one link in a chain of tragedy that stalks across this land. It is only one blow of the rod of God's wrath in the chastising of the wicked and godless people. It is an example that the rest of us need to heed. The mounting wrath of God makes it certain that disaster, death, pestilence and ruin are stalking every community in America.

I noticed the beer parlors in East Texas oil fields. In Tyler it was hard to find even a place to buy a sandwich that did not sell beer. But what about Dallas where I live? More and more the same condition exists. Liquor is sold in Dallas both legally and illegally. There are package stores on every hand selling whiskey and wine. Whiskey is sold by the drink in direct violation of the law.

During the Centennial the town was wide open with the connivance and consent of the city government. Lewdness, nakedness and indecency were flaunted before the public and advertised to the world. Newspapers joined in the nudeness for the "rake off" in advertising fees. Girls sold their bodies to public gaze and we know not to what private sin. Booky joints ran open. There was a well understood agreement not to enforce laws as long as the Centennial was open last year. And 1937 has the Pan-American Exposition coming on. A large percent of the politicians in the city are bent on preventing the enforcement of laws concerning liquor, gambling and lewdness. Exposition officials are already planning "strip" shows with which they will beguile the lewd and seduce the innocent.

Money is god in Dallas. For it, newspapers sell their honor. For it, politicians sell their city. For it, the citizenship sells its children. For it, women sell their bodies and multitudes sell their souls! God in Heaven, help us! How can we criticise the oil fields in East Texas! To us the Lord Jesus says, "Except ye repent, ye shall all likewise perish"!

East Texas may put education before religion and learning before God. The schools may teach that oil and gas are a greater blessing than salvation, peace of mind, forgiveness of sins. If they do, they only do what the schools do everywhere else. In Dallas our school buildings are used for dances, not only the high schools but also some of the grade schools. Dallas at one end of the chain arouses lust, stirs the passion and corrupts the morals of its youth in dance halls, sponsored by the schools, encouraged by most homes and ignored by most churches.

At the other end of the same chain Dallas establishes a free venereal clinic to take care of our over 30,000 cases of syphilis (health department figures)! If judgment comes on the New London oil field, how shall Dallas escape?

Yea, how shall all America escape? The government itself is in the liquor business. The President used all his influence to repeal the Eighteenth Amendment, to bring about the sale of beer. The administration violated its plain, emphatic covenant to protect dry territory. The White House itself serves liquor. And liquor drinking is followed all over America by a host of evils; drunken driving, crime, broken homes, mistreated children, heavier taxes and corrupt government. Divorce is on the increase. Liberty decreases while a corrupt government increases taxes, attacks the Supreme Court, violates the Constitution, pauperizes the poor and victimizes the rich!

Labor unions by common consent enter into lawlessness, seize and destroy property, sometimes even sanction murder in their strikes. Churches are busy about so-called "social gospel" and busy themselves more with wages, hours, legislation and reform than preaching the Gospel of Jesus Christ.

Churches have more ball games and parties than they do revival services. Church workers know more about suppers, plays, mock weddings and entertainments than they do about repentance, faith, the Holy Spirit, Heaven, Hell, judgment and the Second Coming of Christ!

The Lord Jesus Christ would say to us today, "Those 455 upon whom the New London schoolhouse fell and slew them, think ye that they were sinners above all them that dwelt in America? I tell you, Nay: But except YE repent, ye shall all likewise perish!" The curse of Almighty God is on America. How shall America escape?

As certain as there is a God in Heaven this *nation is due for strikes, riots, pestilences, drouth, floods, earthquakes, tornadoes, bloodshed, war, anarchy, dictatorship and national ruin if we do not repent!* The New London calamity was only a link in the chain of God's wrath, only one blow of His chastisement long overdue. I expect the hand of God to appear all over America, here in one way, there in another; in a trail of "accidents," disease and bloodshed across the continent. We have had a warning of the judgment of God on our country.

VII. The Folly of Loving Riches

May God help us by the sorrow of others to learn how precious are our children! If you have your children by you, well and strong, thank God! As I got up in the night recently to see if my little ones were well covered and warm, my heart went out to God in gratitude that He had given them to me—that they were mine, that they loved me, that they are healthy and well. Do not neglect your children! Take time to rear them carefully, to train them well, to discipline them strictly, to win them to Christ.

Many a man is too busy to appreciate his children and enjoy them, too busy to teach them the Bible. I am a poor example but I feel that the time we spend around the breakfast table daily, reading from two to four chapters in the Bible and having a circle of prayer and talking about God's blessings is about the most valuable time in the day.

Lot pitched his tent toward Sodom, then moved into Sodom, and it meant the ruin of his family. His wife was turned to a pillar of salt, two daughters reaped the fruit of drunken incest

PREACHING THAT BUILT A GREAT CHURCH

and others were burned and buried by the fire and brimstone in
Sodom.

I wonder how many men who followed the oil field into East
Texas this last week have been counting the cost to see whether
it was worth it, as they buried and mourned over their children!

My brother, in your insane rush for money, your greed for the
things of the world, you may lose your children too—lose them
to the dance hall, lose them to the beer garden, lose them to
drunkenness, prostitution and sin. Or they may grow up
respectable enough but be lost to God, lost to the church, and
lost at last to Heaven!

The poorest little home where godly, healthy, moral children
grow up is happier tonight than the richest home that has lost
its children, either by death or by sin. And if a broken family
circle here causes such sorrow, what will it be like in Heaven if
the family circle is broken there, too, if loved ones are missing
in Glory?

VIII. Make Friends With Death

Does the fear of death haunt you? Then from this monster
tragedy take warning while you can. Get ready to die. God's
Word says, "It is appointed unto men once to die, but after this
the judgment." Unless you are one of the Christians alive when
Jesus comes, you are born to die, appointed to die, and die you
must and will!

I know that people are offended if a preacher talks about
death, Hell and judgment. You are not ready to die, you say,
and you are not ready to talk about it either. But whether you
are ready or not, you are going to die. Some people do not like
"deathbed tales," they say. But if preachers are faithful they
will tell the truth about this, just as the Lord Jesus did when He
said, "The rich man also died, and was buried; And in hell he lift
up his eyes, being in torments" (Luke 16:22,23).

Oh, how I wish I could have preached to all that crowd who
went out suddenly to meet God, one day, one hour, before they
died and that God would have given me wisdom to warn them of
the certainty of death!

Those who do not like "deathbed tales" had better learn to like them for one of these days each one will have a deathbed scene of his own, all his own!

Isn't it strange that a lawyer can talk to a man about making a will in view of his coming death and the man is not offended? An insurance man tells him he should provide for the support of his family in case of his death and he believes he is sensible and provident if he takes out life insurance. Men think it only proper that hospitals and doctors, ambulances and undertakers should deal in death and cemeteries sell their lots in advance. But when a preacher warns of the certainty of death and of the certain judgment that follows death, men are offended! But a preacher who does not warn men to prepare for death is a coward and a traitor, and the man who will not listen to such warning is a fool.

My brother, death is just around the corner. This moment, this breath, this heartbeat is all you can be sure of. Not a person in the New London High School building dreamed of disaster. We picked up on the grounds arithmetic papers and language lessons still ungraded. To all of them alike—teachers and pupils—death seemed remote. It was out of their thinking, out of their plans. They thought only of life; their joys, their loves, their burdens, their problems, their plans, their ambitions.

Some, we trust, were prepared to die. Doubtless, many were not. Certainly none of them expected to die so soon. Just fifteen minutes before the school was to dismiss for the day there was the sudden rumbling roar of the explosion. Some were literally blown to pieces in a second, others hurtled through space to fall mangled and dying. Others in two or three seconds had life crushed out by the falling roof and walls!

What a warning that ought to be to all of us, that *death may come, yea, is likely to come at the most unthought of time and place and to the least prepared in heart!*

Sinner, if you are not prepared to die, you are not prepared to live. It may be with sudden heart failure you will go out to meet God. Or a drunken driver may crash into your car and you will die before the ambulance gets to the scene. Or explosion or fire or a bullet may end your life many years before you plan to die.

I remind you that every man expects to repent. Jesus warns that you are no better than those upon whom the tower of Siloam fell, no better than those who met sudden terror and grim death in the falling school building at New London. Millions are in Hell today because they died when they did not expect to die, died when they were not ready to die!

The shortest road to Hell is neglect. Most of the inhabitants of Hell, that place of the eternal damned, believed there was a God. Millions believed that the Bible was true. They believed that Christ died for sinners. They believed in their father's or their mother's God. Yea, they fully expected to repent after they made a little more money, or after they had a good time, or after they settled down. They expected to repent before they died—but they did not!

Let the school disaster last week be a solemn warning that men dare not trifle with God by postponing salvation. A jealous and a righteous God may call you to meet Him all unexpected any moment and that will mean the eternal ruin of your soul!

IX. Today Is the Day of Salvation

Christ died for you, sinner. Your debt was all paid on the cross. God loves you. Mercy is free. If you will come as a sinner to Christ, believe that He died for you, trust Him to forgive your sins, claim Him as your Saviour, He will forgive every one of your multitude of sins. "Come now, and let us reason together, saith the Lord: though your sins be as scarlet, they shall be as white as snow; though they be red like crimson, they shall be as wool" (Isa. 1:18).

You have only to turn with all your heart to Christ and put your trust in Him to be saved this moment. Turn from your sin, ask for forgiveness! Believe that Christ forgives you today! He will change your heart and give you a home in Heaven. The Scripture says, "Behold, now is the accepted time. . . To day if ye will hear his voice, Harden not your hearts, as in the provocation" (Heb. 3:7,8). If you want to be saved, do it now.

The other day a young married man in San Antonio, Texas,

signed the decision slip and sent it to me saying he was trusting Christ as his Saviour. On March 14th he was baptized. Yesterday I had a letter from him. It brims over with joy. He says He didn't know one could be so happy and be a Christian. He says his wicked companions laugh at him when he tells them he is done with the wild life. He says they simply do not know how grand it is to have such a wonderful Saviour!

Dear friend, won't you take Christ as yours today? Calamity may fall upon you any moment. Death is certain and often it is sudden. I beg you to turn to Christ with all your heart and be saved today. If you will, why not sign the following decision slip, clip it out and return it to me? I will greatly rejoice over it.

Here is the slip. May God give you grace to trust Him in your heart and sign it.

Dr. John R. Rice
Box 1099
Murfreesboro, Tennessee 37130

Dear Brother Rice:

I have read your sermon and I realize that I am a sinner. I know that death may come at any time. I believe that Christ died for my sins and here and now I trust Him to forgive all my sins, trust Him to change my heart and make me God's child. I trust Him to save my soul now and take me to Heaven at death. Today I depend on the mercy of God's dear Son who died for me and call Him my Saviour.

Name_____

Address_____

Date_____

22—Mattson Boy's Kidnaper and Murderer

Will the Kidnaper Be Caught? Should He Be Executed? What Has Happened to America?

(Sunday night sermon, January 17, 1937, at Fundamentalist Baptist Tabernacle, Dallas. Stenographically reported.)

Now will you pray with me?

PRAYER: Our Father, we pray that a solemn and serious hush may spread over this congregation as we come to face the eternal destinies of souls. Oh, we pray that this poor, unworthy preacher may have an enduement from Heaven; that I may speak for God, with the power of God, and that the Word of God may have free course tonight.

Lord, there are sinners here lost and undone. Convict them tonight. Let men know what sin will do to them, just as it did to others. Let men know their sins will find them out. Grant repentance and forgiveness to men here tonight. We pray that Thy Word may be rich, and quick, and powerful, and sharper than any two-edged sword and like a hammer that breaketh the rock in pieces. People have come from far and near, from all parts of Dallas and from beyond. You know how we need Thy presence. Send Thy blessing tonight. Let each one that is tempted find strength. Let the sad be comforted. Let the lost be saved. We pray, come in saving power and redeem people from Hell and from eternal judgment. For Christ's sake. Amen.

If you came here expecting some philosophical essay, you will be disappointed. I promised you a Bible sermon, giving the light of God's Word on modern sins; light for these dark days. You pray that God will help us.

Numbers 32:23:

> *Be sure your sin will find you out!*

Here is another one:

> *Be not deceived; God is not mocked: for whatsoever a man soweth, that shall he also reap.* —Gal. 6:7.

Some two or three weeks ago, a kidnaper came breaking into Dr. Mattson's home at Tacoma, Washington. He asked for money from the young people there and they said they didn't keep their money in the house. He said, as he seized a boy ten years old named Charles, the doctor's son, "You will do just as well," and he took the boy with him. He left a note demanding $28,000 ransom.

The father, of course, did all he could to get the child back. The newspapers helped somewhat. The federal G-men withheld pursuit for a time. The man broke into a filling station about one o'clock one morning and phoned in further instructions about the ransom. And still, though the money was ready, the boy was never brought home nor released.

Some ten days later, fifty miles away, near Everett, Washington, a young man was hunting rabbits. As he chased a rabbit through the snow, he came upon, in the bushes, the naked body of little Charles Mattson. Though he had been stabbed in the back, that was not enough to kill him. He had been abused by a sexual pervert, then bruised with beating, then his head had been crushed.

The blood of that ten-year-old boy is crying out to God tonight like the blood of Abel cried out against Cain. Would to God that every preacher in this country would preach what the Bible says about the results of crime and bloodshed.

I. Sin at First Appears Small

Before I give you some Scripture, think a bit of what is back of this kidnaping and murder of little Charles Mattson. I want to remind you that sin starts small. The Devil never comes to any man saying, "I will take you and make you a murderer and bring you to die in the electric chair and make you a public example of a fiend in human form that everybody despises in this world and in the world to come." The Devil never starts that way.

Sin always starts seemingly small. When Satan would ruin the whole world, the race, put them at enmity against God, land millions in Hell, he starts with a woman and a bit of fruit and says, "You will not surely die." He got Eve to eat of the forbidden fruit. Rebellion and disobedience are never small. Sin is never small.

When the Devil wants to take a man to Hell, he starts on him as a child and has him reject salvation for a time. He will say, "You are young. You have plenty of time." And little by little Satan leads him on, and the man burns in torment. One day he was a tenderhearted child, and it would have been so easy to be saved. "I will sometime, but not now," he said. Everyone who goes to Hell was one time so near salvation and Christ. Sin always starts small.

Back yonder before World War I, nobody expected it would start when a half-crazy student and anarchist shot dead the Archduke Francis Ferdinand at Sera Sevo, Austria, June 28, 1914. Nobody supposed that would embroil the world in war around the world, when thirty nations would be involved with war, millions would die and multiplied billions of treasure spent. Nobody believed that. But it happened. Sin always starts small.

I remind you that your destiny for Heaven or Hell may be balanced on a hair's breadth. Tonight you may say "yes" to Jesus Christ and be saved and spend eternity in Heaven. Or tonight you may say "no" to Christ and may do the thing that will make you worse than the murderer and kidnaper of the Mattson boy. Nobody intended to be that kind of a sinner. Sin always starts small.

II. The Murderer Was Once a Tender Boy

And now I want you to remember that the man who is the

object of the hunt, the No. 1 "Man   Wanted," the criminal hunted throughout the United States was once a mother's baby. She bore him under her heart and dreamed of the boy she would bring into this world. That mother went down into the valley of the shadow of death for him.

When her child was born, she nursed him at her bosom, parted his little hair, watched him day by day as he grew, taught him his first word. She saw his first tooth come! Little by little she saw him take the first step.

In her mother's pride, she saw him start one day off to school and wept a little, as mothers do, behind the door.

As the child grew, she hoped and prayed he would be a genius. She thought he would be the president of the United States, or dreamed he would be a great preacher. Every good mother (and most mothers are good) dreams her boy will be somebody.

Can you see that mother? There is a mother back there somewhere. Maybe she is still living. If so, that mother still thinks about him, and keeps the little baby shoes. When he is accused, she will say, "If they knew him like I do, they would know my boy wouldn't do a thing like that!"

That man had a mother. That man one time had a tender heart. That man, who took a hammer or hatchet and beat out the brains of that ten-year-old boy after violating his body, after sticking a knife in him, the man who tied the little fellow, naked, with a tire chain and beat in his head, and after a while left that little body out in the snow—that man was once a boy, a tenderhearted boy! If he had a pet rabbit that died, he wept over it, and couldn't bear the sight of blood. One time he didn't want to disturb a bird's nest, I dare say.

I don't want you to think that that man was always a fiend in human form, born different, reared different, made of different stuff from you. No, he was a man like you! He had a mother like you. Maybe he has a wife. God knows, maybe he has a baby! Even as the Lindbergh murderer and kidnaper had. He didn't start out to be what he is!

Oh, beware of sin that looks so small! It won't end up small!

I preach frequently down in the county jail and my heart

goes out to those men and I can hardly go in without weeping. Talk all you want to about hardened criminals—and they are hardened—but there is something compassionate about them that breaks my heart—shut up through the hours, days, weeks. Plans, dreams—everything broken. No hope of escape. Thinking always of some way to get outside. It breaks my heart and I weep when I preach to them. They listen to me, and we have multitudes saved at the jail.

Please don't think that this man is a different kind from you men here. Some of you here may turn out as he has, if you trifle with sin. You are made out of the same stuff that he is. He is now like a hunted beast. They will hunt him down with blood hounds if they can find the trail. Every newspaper tells of the reward offered for his capture. The President of the United States is helping. I am glad he is. Everybody is now trying to find him. Such a murderer ought to go to the electric chair. If we do right by him and by the nation and by our children and by God, he will.

But I want to remind you that that man was one time as clean and pure as your boy or as you were. Sin doesn't come to fruitage in a day. Stop tonight and think. Young people, if you are thinking about stepping over the line, doing wrong about anything, don't do it. If you take a dime, a ten-cent piece that isn't yours, you may be headed for the same kind of sin as this robber for $28,000 which he never got, who stole a child, then thought he had to murder him to get out of it. Perhaps he never intended to kill the boy. He thought, "Old Dr. Mattson has lots of money." He didn't really have much, he said, but the general impression was that he did.

A lot of you feel, "What if he does soak the rich? What does it matter?" Do you think a rich man has no love for his children? Do you think that a mother, because she lives in a nice house, has no care for her ten-year-old boy? This class hatred in America is a strange circumstance. If a man has money, people don't care what happens to him. That is not Christian. That is not humane. That is not Christlike. Something is bad wrong with me if I don't have a tender sentiment for that man tonight—if I lay my head on my pillow, my girls safe at home, I have sweet peace, and his boy is dead! Dr. Mattson is a Christian man, a prayerful man. I will read his statement in a moment perhaps. Ask God to bless his heart. He is my brother. Would to God I could comfort him. I might write him. I know he gets so many letters. I know I can pray for him and I will. Perhaps I will send him this sermon.

Do you care about that? We ought to. I want you to know that sin never did start big. It starts little in the sight of men. That man didn't intend to kill the boy. He thought, "This man is a doctor and has money. I will take some of his money. I need it." I am sure he had something in mind. He needed it, wanted it, and thought, "I will take the boy, then I can get the money."

So he took the boy but found it was a greater danger than he expected. He didn't feel safe. Maybe the little boy resisted him, learned his name, where he lived, who knew him. If the boy was turned loose, he would tell it and they would catch him, he thought. After a while he dared not show his head. And lest the child should talk, he took him out and beat in his head and left him.

That may happen to you. Sin comes in. It may be the seductive wiles of a beautiful woman. But after awhile that enchantress sin turns into a slave-driving sin that you can't free yourself of.

I beg you, my friend, don't deal with sin. Sin is terrible. Sin goes on and breaks the heart and brings you where you never thought you would go.

I have talked to criminals again and again and they wept as they said, "I never thought it would come to this."

Now beware of sin. That man never intended to end where he did. Sin is deceptive, misleading.

III. Loose, Evil, Public Sentiment Made the Crime Possible

Another thing was back of this kidnaping that made it so the Mattson boy could be stolen and murdered. There is widespread public sentiment that makes it possible. That isn't happening so often in England, and in other nations. Why not? There are several reasons why. In America there has been public sentiment that makes a class feeling, a class consciousness that is wrong and hateful and wicked and devilish. And God will not allow America long to stand if she doesn't have broken down this class hatred and war.

Labor unions are involved some. For instance, when a group of men in General Motors plant who don't own the things, moves in and takes possession. When men in a strike feel at liberty to tear up machinery or buildings they don't own, or tear up a business they didn't build, or murder because they don't want to work eight hours a day and a half-day Saturday. They want more money and think they can squeeze it out of them. You don't like that? I don't care. You can like it or lump it. That wicked sentiment is lawlessness. It makes it so that just because you have on overalls you have a right to swat a man who has more than you. That is murderous and wicked. That is criminal, I don't care who does it. That sentiment on the part of the public toward men with money is responsible for the kidnaping racket.

Out here at Parkland Hospital, spending my money and your money, taxpayers' money, the city put in conduits for lights in the new wing of a building. Some laboring people who didn't like the way it was done by contract stopped up the conduits with cement; now it is useless and $1,800 gone. If they have lights in the building they will have to be run inside the ceiling. Such class hate; such disregard of rights of others! That spirit is what made possible this kidnaping.

The plain truth is, no one man could go into another man's house in this country and take a struggling ten-year-old boy and walk away with him, and drive a car, and have a home, and buy groceries and gasoline, and mail letters and talk over the telephone, without somebody aiding him or shielding him, somebody taking his part.

I have been reading again my book on *The Electrocution of Raymond Hamilton.* When Raymond Hamilton had been sentenced to the electric chair after piling up some 395 years of penalty by jury after jury, after he had been condemned and put in jail and had broken out of jail and had been put back in and broken out again and killed somebody again, then this notorious, boasting murderer, hijacker, conscienceless criminal, moron, degenerate (when the only punishment they could give was the electric chair, laws of man and the laws of God demanded it), yet the *Dallas Journal* said that 35,000 people in Texas appealed to Governor Allred trying to get him to break his vow as a governor and break the law of the land and defy God and break the hearts of mothers of little children and everybody involved, to free that notorious man and to withhold him from the electric chair.

Those 35,000—some in Dallas, some likely were you who sit on these benches tonight, if so, God have mercy on your soul—you are the ones who make possible the Raymond Hamiltons and the Clyde Barrows and the murder and kidnaping of the Mattson child. And the way you mothers and fathers are rearing your children, the sentiment grown by preachers in the pulpit, in the schools, in moving picture shows, have brought about a sentiment in America not for obeying law, not for enforcing law, but have brought a sentiment to back up the kidnaper, back up the murderer; a sentiment against the government, against God, against the home. And you are to blame for the kidnaping and murder. Go   home and wash your hands! You still have blood on them—the blood of that boy! That wouldn't be possible if we didn't have in Dallas, in Texas, in America, a sentiment that is not for law enforcement.

Pick out twelve good men and true in this town, church men and church women, preachers, schoolteachers, a barber, a businessman, etc., put them on the jury—pick some out of this crowd—you are so far from God and have so little conscience about right, you have talked against the law, against the courts. Go on and put you   on the jury, and you would turn that thug, that murderer, that kidnaper loose, or put him in the pen for five years' time and in half that time petition the governor to get him out!

Yes, you, this crowd, tonight, are largely responsible for the kidnaping and murder and the crime and lawlessness of this country! That is one thing back of it.

Oh, my friends, this country is gone if we don't get some men and women with a conscience about right, with a conscience about obeying laws, with a conscience about discipline, with a concern about the Bible and God!

IV. Covetousness—You Are Guilty of the Same Sin; Every Liquor Seller Is a Murderer and for Covetousness

What else is back of this kidnaping? What caused it? Covetousness. That man wanted money. You are horrified tonight after I called it to your attention. You are horrified, but I remind you of two or three things. The same thing that made that man want $28,000 is exactly the same thing that faces thousands of people in Dallas. Every man in Dallas who gets a license to sell liquor, whether it is a drug store up here on the corner, or the Round Up, or the Brown Derby or the Nite Spot on Commerce where the man was shot down a while back, is guilty of the same sin!

Every man who gets a liquor license is exactly the same kind of murderer, the same kind of kidnaper, the same kind of blood is on him—the blood of covetousness! He would rather have money, blood-money, than be honest and decent and fair and temperate.

If you are in the liquor business, you have blood on your soul. You have blood on your soul, and you are a murderer. No man ever sold liquor but what he knew it would lead to drunken driving and accidents. He knew it would lead to quarrels and knife-fights or shootings. He knew it would break up homes. A man who sells liquor is a murderer. *Yes, sir, he is a murderer.*

I will say more than that. Very likely that man, that kidnaper of the little Mattson boy, would never have laid hands on him had he never been where they drank booze, never been with the crowd that drank and gambled. Every man who sells booze is a murderer, whether he sells it legitimately or illegitimately, whether with a beer license or with a package license, or whether he has a doctor's prescription. You are a bloody-handed murderer and you will meet God.

The Bible says, "Woe to him that giveth his neighbour drink" (Hab. 2:15). The woe of Almighty God is on every man, on every saloon-keeper, on every drug store operator who is in the liquor business, in any way, shape, fashion or form, and he is going to face the consequences. You are the same kind of dirty murderer as this man and you do it for the same reason—the love of money, covetousness.

You say, "Brother Rice, I have to make a living." That man probably said the same thing.

Here is another thing. You say, "Well, he is just one of a few." Oh, no, it is going on every day in Dallas. A man who rents a building for a saloon is the same kind of a sinner. What is the matter? Covetousness. He will rent his building to a man who sells booze and out of that will come broken homes, drunken driving, gunfights and murder. His sin is the same as that of this murderer who killed Charles Mattson—covetousness.

Why is it that every night spot, why is it that every Brown Derby, why is it that every beer joint in town keeps either a billy or a gun under the counter? Why? Do you know why? Because every man knows that the liquor business is bound to end in fights. A man comes in and drinks the booze you sell him, and that booze makes him so insane that you fear you will have to kill him before he kills you. That is the reason every man in the liquor business usually keeps a gun. He is in the murdering business anyway, and if the liquor doesn't kill a man he may have to do it with a gun. What for? For money, covetousness! He would rather have money than to have decency. Yes sir.

Now listen to me! As long as in Dallas this bloody liquor business can continue, you have all the makings of the murderers and the kidnapers. And you will reap it, too, in your own family and in your own life sooner or later, for as certain as God's Word is so, "Whatsoever a man soweth, that shall he also reap," "Be sure your sin will find you out"—as certain as that, one day they will catch up with you. If we didn't have a background in America of worshiping the dollar, of covetousness, of love for money, there wouldn't have been that mother lying weeping because her boy is dead and that father in heartbroken grief because his boy is gone.

Every businessman who puts money-making first is the same kind of criminal and sinner as that man. Man does not count it so, but one day you will meet God and God counts them the same. God sees the motives of your heart!

The *Times Herald* and the *Dallas News* and the *Dallas Dispatch* and the *Dallas Journal* and any other paper that takes a liquor advertisement are guilty of murder and kidnaping for the same reason—a love of money; exactly the same reason. They surely are. That is getting personal, isn't it? That is some of the background. That is what is back of it. That is what is wrong.

V. Once That Murderer Must Have Turned Down Christ

Do you know why that man became a murderer and a kidnaper? One day he heard the Gospel—I don't know where. I don't know whether he had gone to church and Sunday school much, probably not, but he either heard it on the radio or passed a street corner meeting of a group of Salvation Army workers preaching, or maybe he went to church or Sunday school, or maybe to some great evangelistic service to see what the preacher had to say. No doubt he heard the Gospel somewhere and turned it down, and tonight he is hunted like a beast. Maybe before I am through preaching someone will find him, and it won't be long, perhaps, before he will go to the electric chair—all of that because he turned his back on God sometime, somewhere; turned himself over to sin, and Satan took him until now despair must rule his heart. He turned down Christ, and now look where Satan led him!

My friends, after all there is just one safe thing in this world, and that is to be on the Lord's side and have your heart changed and get forgiveness and turn back to God. But for the mercy of God, the man you see here might be that hunted criminal, fleeing for his life. You might be the one who will die that kind of a criminal. We all have the weakness in our hearts, enough wrong in our nature, and only the mercy of God can keep us. I beg you, tonight, get on God's side and be saved. Repent of your sins and be born again. That is your only hope to get away from the terrible wages of sin.

VI. Death Penalty: God Requires It!

Now another thing. I promised you I would give you some Scriptures on this matter. Will that man be found? I think he will. I will talk to you about that in a moment. But after he is found, shall he be put to death? I answer without any doubt in the world. The Bible demands that he must be put to death. In the first place, the Bible commands either the murderer or the kidnaper must be killed. Another thing, if he is not, then the nation will be held accountable for it and blood will be paid for with blood. We must have it.

Sooner or later America will pay for that boy lying in the snow, that little abused body bruised and with his head crushed in. America will pay for it with the blood of the kidnaper-killer or with riot and blood and war. God's Word commands it and I will prove it to you from the Bible. I turn to Genesis the 9th chapter, verses 5 and 6. If you want to take these Scriptures down, all right.

> *And surely your blood of your lives will I require; at the hand of every beast will I require it, and at the hand of man; at the hand of every man's brother will I require the life of man.*
>
> *Whoso sheddeth man's blood, by man shall his blood be shed: for in the image of God made he man.*

I remind you that is the first chapter after the flood. That is the first message given to Noah after he came out of the ark and established himself and built an altar and worshiped God. From this time on, murderers must be punished by death. "And surely your blood of your lives will I require; at the hand of every beast will I require it, and at the hand of man; at the hand of every man's brother will I require the life of man. Whoso sheddeth man's blood, by man shall his blood be shed."

That is not in the Mosaic law. That was before any law of Moses. That was given to Noah, the father not only of the Jews but of all the Gentiles.

Turn next to Exodus the 21st chapter, the next chapter after the Ten Commandments. Begin with verse 12.

He that smiteth a man, so that he die, shall be surely put to death.

Now verse 15,

And he that smiteth his father, or his mother, shall be surely put to death.

Now for the kidnaper, verse 16,

And he that stealeth a man, and selleth him, or if he be found in his hand, he shall surely be put to death.

Now if the boy had not been dead and they found the kidnaper with the boy, yet he must be put to death, or if he returned him for ransom, he must be put to death, the Scripture says. That is in Exodus 21:16, so you will not forget it.

Here is more than that. I turn to Deuteronomy 24 and verse 7:

If a man be found stealing any of his brethren of the children of Israel, and maketh merchandise of him, or selleth him; then that thief shall die; and thou shalt put evil away from among you.

The kidnaper is to be put to death.

Now in Numbers 35:16-21:

And if he smite him with an instrument of iron, so that he die, [that is what that man did] *he is a murderer: the murderer shall surely be put to death.*

And if he smite him with throwing a stone, wherewith he may die, and he die, he is a murderer: the murderer shall surely be put to death.

Or if he smite him with an hand weapon of wood, wherewith he may die, and he die, he is a murderer: the murderer shall surely be put to death.

The revenger of blood himself shall slay the murderer: when he meeteth him, he shall slay him.

But if he thrust him of hatred, or hurl at him by laying of wait, that he die;

Or in enmity smite him with his hand, that he die: he

that smote him shall surely be put to death; for he is a murderer: the revenger of blood shall slay the murderer, when he meeteth him.

Now skip down to verse 30 through 33:

Whoso killeth any person, the murderer shall be put to death by the mouth of witnesses: but one witness shall not testify against any person to cause him to die.

Moreover ye shall take no satisfaction for the life of a murderer, which is guilty of death: but he shall be surely put to death.

And ye shall take no satisfaction for him that is fled to the city of his refuge, that he should come again to dwell in the land, until the death of the priest.

So ye shall not pollute the land wherein ye are: for blood it defileth the land: and the land cannot be cleansed of the blood that is shed therein, but by the blood of him that shed it.

Here is another one, Deuteronomy 19:11-13:

But if any man hate his neighbour, and lie in wait for him, and rise up against him, and smite him mortally that he die, and fleeth into one of these cities:

Then the elders of his city shall send and fetch him thence, and deliver him into the hand of the avenger of blood, that he may die.

Thine eye shall not pity him, but thou shalt put away the guilt of innocent blood from Israel, that it may go well with thee.

If that man be in jail, and they give him the death penalty and there be 25,000 or 50,000 people write the governor to pardon him and to get him out or commute the sentence to life imprisonment, listen to what the Scripture says about that: "Thine eye shall not pity him!" Put away the guilt of innocent blood that it may go well with the nation. It won't go well with this nation if we don't put away that guilt of innocent blood by executing that kidnaper-murderer.

Deuteronomy 21, verses 18 to 21, shows that even a stubborn

and rebellious son who won't obey his father and mother—the father and mother are to take him out to the elders of the city and say, "Here is our son. He is stubborn and rebellious," and they shall stone him that he die.

The trouble in America is there is no law, no enforcement in the home, not much in the school, not much in the government. Oh, my friends, make your boys mind! Make your children mind! Teach them discipline now. The Scripture says if you don't do it, later on, before he is grown, stone him, kill him or he will bring a curse on the nation and a curse on you. God wants law upheld. This chicken-hearted, mushy-mouthed sentimentality that does not want sin to be punished isn't how God would have it. God says He is a consuming fire. *God demands the death penalty for kidnaping and murder!*

You say, "Don't you think we ought to forgive people who do wrong?" Yes, if you do me wrong, I ought not carry vengeance in my heart. I ought to be glad to forgive any personal spite I have. But I still ought to want what God commanded to be done in the matter. There are a lot of other ten-year-old boys. I have a girl about that age. My girls are as precious as that boy. I don't have any money. Nevertheless, who knows, the time may come when someone might think I have, like they thought that man had, and take one of my girls for the sake of money; or your boy or girl.

Lest every mother's heart quake with dread when she hears a strange step, and for the sake of others it will keep from the sin, murder must be put down, kidnaping must be put down. If the American government can't stop kidnaping, the American government will fall. We can't enforce the law on anything else and this government is going to fall, if we can't do it. It must be done if we are not to have the curse of God on us for our sin.

Someone says, "But I think we ought to forgive them." Sure—but if that were my duty, I would turn the electric switch that would send him out to meet God. I would do it with a prayer after I had talked to him about his soul and tried to win him to Christ. I would do that with no guilty conscience.

This isn't a matter of personal responsibility. It is a matter where society as a whole is accountable to do what God said.

For this very reason we have government. God gives government and the government ought to do what God said to do. I do not believe that they do. I do not believe that they ought to call in the father that he might get some personal joy out of seeing the man die. I just think all of us together ought to thank God that justice and right are done. Law and good government do not encourage kidnaping and murder. That is what we ought to have. I would preach to the man. I would urge him to be saved. I would pray for him. But I would be grievously disappointed if the government didn't do what God commanded it to do.

VII. The Officers of Government Are Ministers of God Attending His Business

Someone will say, "Death is so bad. We ought not take what we can't give." The God who gave life is the same God who commanded to take it. It is God who demands it. The man, the electrocutioner, the man who pulls the switch or closes the door to the lethal chamber, acts as God Himself, as the agent of God. The Bible says, "The powers that be are ordained of God." God requires it of them.

Let me read it to you in Romans, the 13th chapter. I remind you this is in the New Testament, too, not only in the Old.

Let every soul be subject unto the higher powers. For there is no power but of God: the powers that be [sheriffs, governments, G-men] *are ordained of God.*

Whosoever therefore resisteth the power, resisteth the ordinance of God: and they that resist shall receive to themselves damnation.

For rulers are not a terror to good works, but to the evil. Wilt thou then not be afraid of the power? do that which is good, and thou shalt have praise of the same:

For he is the minister of God to thee for good. But if thou do that which is evil, be afraid; for he beareth not the sword in vain: for he is the minister of God, a re-

venger to execute wrath upon him that doeth evil.—Vss. 1-4.

The man who pulls the switch to execute that murderer and kidnaper will act as the agent of God, the minister of God, as definitely as I stand as a man of God to preach this sermon. The Scripture calls him "the minister of God to thee for good. But if thou do that which is evil, be afraid; for he beareth not the sword in vain: for he is the minister of God [it says that again], a revenger to execute wrath upon him that doeth evil."

Wherefore ye must needs be subject, not only for wrath, but also for conscience sake.

For this cause pay ye tribute also: for they are God's ministers, attending continually upon this very thing.

Render therefore to all their dues: tribute to whom tribute is due; custom to whom custom; fear to whom fear; honour to whom honour.—Vss. 5-7.

So the Scripture says. Now, my friends, God says if every man on the jury were a New Testament Christian, a spiritually-minded Christian, a loving, tenderhearted Christian, he ought to vote the death penalty to that man. In doing so he would be the minister of God.

Now what else? Turn to Numbers, chapter 35. Here is another word that shows we must answer to God and that God will see that blood is paid for. We dare not do anything but what God said. I read you a part of that chapter. Now let me turn to the last part, verses 30 through 34:

Whoso killeth any person, the murderer shall be put to death by the mouth of witnesses: but one witness shall not testify against any person to cause him to die [not one alone].

Moreover ye shall take no satisfaction for the life of a murderer, which is guilty of death: but he shall be surely put to death.

And ye shall take no satisfaction for him that is fled to the city of his refuge, that he should come again to dwell in the land, until the death of the priest.

So ye shall not pollute the land wherein ye are: for blood it defileth the land: and the land cannot be cleansed of the blood that is shed therein, but by the blood of him that shed it.

Defile not therefore the land which ye shall inhabit, wherein I dwell: for I the Lord dwell among the children of Israel.

Oh, there is no way to keep judgment for shed blood from coming on the land except that we shed the blood of the man who shed it. If that kidnaper and murderer be put to death in the electric chair, God will look down and say, "In that country they want justice, they want to keep down sin, and I will reward them accordingly." But if we let that man and others get by, God will say, "All right, they are storing up blood and blood they shall have, and war and riot." It is as certain as God in Heaven and as His Book. Yes, sir, that is certain. There is no way to cleanse the land but by the death penalty on murderers and kidnapers, and such like, the Scripture says.

Read in the 21st chapter of Deuteronomy how the first time in the world there was an inquest. When a man dies and no one is about, a coroner makes an inquest. If you didn't realize where that came from, we got it from the Bible. If they find a man who is killed in the country, what will they do? Find out which town is nearest, then the elders of that city shall come out, and if they find the murderer, they shall put him to death. But if they can't find the murderer, let them bring a heifer that has never been worked with, never been plowed with, and let her be brought out in the valley which is neither eared now sown and they shall strike off her neck and say as that sacrifice is burned, "O God, our hands have not done this. We do not know who did it. O God, cleanse our land from that blood. We don't know who did it and we don't want our city cursed." Then God will forgive the shedding of that blood.

If sin is not paid for, then that blood cries to God, like the blood of Abel.

VIII. Sin Is Certain to Be Punished

I have thought of that child, that cold little naked body in the snow, a great knife stroke in his back four or five inches long, and bruises over his body, and the back of his head caved in. I have thought that the God of mercy and tenderness who loves little children looked down on that child and said, "I will have to punish that. If I am to do right, I must see that that comes to punishment."

God Almighty will hold America accountable if we don't see that that criminal comes to justice. God has sworn that sin must be punished. "Be sure your sin will find you out." "Be not deceived; God is not mocked: for whatsoever a man soweth, that shall he also reap."

As certain as there is a God in Heaven, that must be punished. If we side with God and punish crime and turn to God, God will not let His wrath be on us. But if we fight against God and are for crime, the wrath of God will be on us. Punishment will be on us. Retribution and eternal judgment will be on us. May God warn you tonight as I try to speak plainly. You ought to like it, but if you don't it doesn't change it a bit in the world. God will do what He said He would do.

I mustn't spend much more time, yet my heart cries out against certain things. Here is Dr. Mattson's appeal. I read from the daily paper:

Tacoma, Wash., Jan. 16 (INS)—In a tragic statement to the press today, Dr. William W. Mattson, father of kidnaped and murdered Charles Mattson, today appealed for sterner preventive kidnaping laws and quicker and more certain punishment.

"Charles' passing is a heavy cross for us to bear, especially so in view of the gruesome circumstances under which he died. Yet we would not shirk our duty and wish it on someone else, for had not this fiend stopped at our door, he would surely have invited himself upon some other parent who possibly could not have borne the burden as well as we.

Urges Drastic Laws

"There undoubtedly is a fine act of providence which decrees what shall happen at a time like this, otherwise why should that rabbit have led the Morrow boy to little Charles' hidden body?

"This is unquestionably going to mean the eventual

identification of the culprit and that justice will be meted out as it always is in these cases. Is it possible that little Charles was sacrificed to further stimulate a previously enraged public to the enactment of even more drastic laws, both in the prevention of and in the punishment of this awful crime? If this is true, we shall feel that Charles did not die in vain.

"An undying faith in our Maker and a firm conviction that Charles' going was His will and desire will give us strength to carry on."

May God bless that good father tonight, that Christian father who had faith in his Maker when his boy is gone under such terrible circumstances.

You don't suppose I only intended to talk about that man I never saw, the man who may never be found. You don't suppose I brought you here to speak only on that, do you? Oh, I am far more concerned about *you*. The terrible thing is, Brother Thompson, that a man would sit here, with no fearful quaking in his heart because he is against God, that wicked man—same kind of heart—against God, therefore liable to any kind of sin. My friends, that man will die. If he doesn't die in the electric chair, he will die just the same. If judgment doesn't reach him through the courts of this land, it will reach him through the courts of God. That man cannot escape the effect of his crime. Maybe some technicality, maybe a plea of insanity, or some crooked, dirty lawyers may help defeat justice. That may be so. But "the mills of God grind slowly, but they grind exceeding fine." As a good queen once said to Cardinal Richelieu, "God does not always pay on Saturday night, my lord Cardinal, but He pays!"

"Be not deceived; God is not mocked: for whatsoever a man soweth, that shall he also reap."

IX. All Alike Are Sinners; All Need to Repent and Be Saved

I have talked to you about murderers, yet here in my audience tonight are murderers. I don't know which of you, but perhaps some one of you took a pistol and pulled the trigger. I don't know who of you stood trial for your life, or maybe it was never known who you killed. But there are in this audience tonight murderers of your unborn babies—bloody-handed murderers—and God Himself hears the cry of the innocent. That blood cries out to God and you will meet it. There are murderers here tonight. Your case is more important tonight than that other fellow. What about your case, poor sinner?

That isn't all. In John 3:15 we are told that "he that hateth his brother is a murderer." You have been guilty of the same sin. Maybe you didn't kill anybody, but your heart was black with hate. If it was, maybe more so than he, you are a murderer in your heart.

My friend, are you a murderer tonight? Over in Revelation we find that God doesn't make much difference between that man and you. There is a man here tonight not a Christian, a woman not a Christian. Be saved while you can.

This morning a woman hesitated at the door. I asked, "Are you right with God?" We went back to the cross this morning and saw again all Jesus bought for us—our salvation, security, safety, peace and fellowship. At the close I said to this woman, "Are you a Christian?"

She said, "I don't think so."

I said, "Oh, today is the time. Turn to Jesus," and she did, and trusted Him, thank God.

If you are unsaved, if you are away from God, you have the same kind of a heart as that murderer. You are lost, you are away from Christ and you are going to the same Hell. Everybody here—man, woman, child—who dies unsaved will go to the same Hell as that terrible murderer, that sinner. If you turn down Jesus Christ, you are the betrayer and murderer of Jesus.

A man stood in Olton, Texas, and said to me, "I have done all sorts of sins these other people mentioned, but the worst thing I ever did was that all my life, until three o'clock this morning, I turned down Jesus Christ." He was right. That is the meanest thing he could have done.

I beg you, turn and say, "Tonight I will repent of this wickedness, this rejecting Jesus and turn my heart to Christ and be saved while I can before I wake up in torment."

You are just like that other sinner. Don't try to make yourself think you are good. You are just like that other sinner. Don't let the Devil make you think you are better than that man.

I tell people in the jail that they are going to the same Hell as those on the outside, going to the same torment, if they don't trust Jesus.

I beg you to realize you are a sinner. You are lost if you are not born again. If you are not Heaven-bound you are Hell-bound. If you don't know you have been born again, I beg you, make sure while you can. One day you may wake up too late, condemned, doomed, lost, and be forever with the doomed in Hell, with all those who turned down Christ. Don't do it, my friend.

Over in Revelation, chapter 21, there is a word about Heaven. Listen, you who are on the outside:

But the fearful, and unbelieving, and the abominable, and murderers, and whoremongers, and sorcerers, and idolaters, and all liars, shall have their part in the lake which burneth with fire and brimstone: which is the second death.

These will be left out and all the murderers, whoremongers, idolaters and *unbelieving*, because they didn't take Christ, are on the outside. Listen now: "But the fearful, *and unbelieving*, and the abominable, and murderers, and whoremongers, and sorcerers, and idolaters, and all liars, shall have their part in the lake which burneth with fire and brimstone: which is the second death."

In there with all the murderers, with all the whoremongers; in there with all the abominable, will be those who don't trust Jesus as Saviour! The sin of all sins is unbelief and rejecting Christ. "He that believeth on him is not condemned: but he that believeth not is condemned already, because he hath not believed in the name of the only begotten Son of God" (John 3:18). Tonight you will turn, I hope, and be saved.

I don't know who that kidnaper is. I wish I knew. I would turn him in if I did, but that is not all. Oh, I would beg him to turn to

Jesus. Though his sin may be as vile as it can be, he could turn to Jesus Christ and be forgiven and saved. He might not escape the electric chair—I don't think he ought—but he could escape Hell.

The dying thief rejoiced to see
That fountain in his day,
And there may I, though vile as he
Wash all my sins away.

Don't you want to turn to Jesus?

A few years ago in Fort Worth a colored man killed a policeman. He was later found in Chicago. That poor colored man, after he had killed the policeman, fled away and for a long time they didn't find him.

He wrote me a letter. It gave no town, and we read the postmark. This poor Negro man wrote me a card and said, "Oh, pray for me, Brother Rice." I did pray for him. I prayed that God would save him. I don't know whether He did or not. If he wanted to be saved, he could be.

My dear friend, if you are lost, in Jesus' name, confess it to God, ask Him to forgive you. You say, "But I am good." No, we are all wicked. You say, "I try to do right," but you fail if you do try. We are all the same kind of sinners.

Do you know what you need? You need to be saved. You need your mother's God, your father's God. You need Him tonight. Don't you want salvation? I asked you to come and hear me preach tonight.

I am a good citizen and I want to make good citizens of you. I want to be true to my God in everything. I want you to do right; but that wasn't the main thing. I wanted to bring conviction, show you that men must suffer for what they do, that your sin will find you out. You can't do wrong and get by. Sooner or later sin will find you out. Chickens will come home to roost.

Oh, we are such sinners, but God loves us still, and God is willing to forgive. Tonight if you will turn to Jesus Christ, He will forgive and save you and you can go home happy. Don't you want to do it tonight? Don't you want to be saved tonight? I know God is ready and I hope you are.

(Eight held their hands for prayer. Several came forward. It was a great crowd.)

If you readers are unsaved, trust Christ today with all your heart and let me hear from you.

23—Lessons From the Abdication of King Edward of England

(Preached in 1937 in Dallas, Texas. Stenographically reported.)

Thou shalt not covet thy neighbour's wife.—Exod. 20:17.

It is not lawful for thee to have thy brother's wife.—John the Baptist to Herod; Mark 6:18.

Now let's pray.

PRAYER: Oh, Thou Lord Jesus, to be crowded out this Christmas time in the churches! Hearts on everything but Thee. Forgive us, Lord. We pray that our hearts may be prepared tonight. Oh, what hypocrisy to sing about Thee, yet put everything first at Christmas but Thee! We pray, move upon this congregation and convict before I shall say anything. And we pray men's hearts may feel smitten before God in His wrath and feel they need to repent and be saved.

Lord, arouse Thy people for the widespread sin everywhere. Bring us tonight to broken hearts, tears and conviction. Lord Jesus, Thou King of Glory, help us to love Thee tonight. For Jesus' sake, Amen.

In II Samuel, chapter 11, I read verses 1 through 17:

And it came to pass, after the year was expired, at the time when kings go forth to battle, that David sent Joab, and his servants with him, and all Israel; and they destroyed the children of Ammon, and besieged Rabbah. But David tarried still at Jerusalem.

And it came to pass in an eveningtide, that David arose

*from off his bed, and walked upon the roof of the king's
house: and from the roof he saw a woman washing
herself: and the woman was very beautiful to look upon.*

*And David sent and enquired after the woman. And
one said, Is not this Bath-sheba, the daughter of Eliam,
the wife of Uriah the Hittite?*

*And David sent messengers, and took her; and she
came in unto him, and he lay with her; for she was
purified from her uncleanness: and she returned unto her
house.*

*And the woman conceived, and sent and told David,
and said, I am with child.*

*And David sent to Joab, saying, Send me Uriah the
Hittite. And Joab sent Uriah to David.*

*And when Uriah was come unto him, David demanded
of him how Joab did, and how the people did, and how
the war prospered.*

*And David said to Uriah, Go down to thy house, and
wash thy feet. And Uriah departed out of the king's
house, and there followed him a mess of meat from the
king.*

*But Uriah slept at the door of the king's house with all
the servants of his lord, and went not down to his house.*

*And when they had told David, saying, Uriah went not
down unto his house, David said unto Uriah, Camest
thou not from thy journey? why then didst thou not go
down unto thine house?*

*And Uriah said unto David, The ark, and Israel, and
Judah, abide in tents; and my lord Joab, and the servants
of my lord, are encamped in the open fields; shall I then
go into mine house, to eat and to drink, and to lie with my
wife? as thou livest, and as thy soul liveth, I will not do
this thing.*

*And David said to Uriah, Tarry here to day also, and to
morrow I will let thee depart. So Uriah abode in
Jerusalem that day, and the morrow.*

And when David had called him, he did eat and drink

*before him; and he made him drunk: and at even he went
out to lie on his bed with the servants of his lord, but
went not down to his house.*

*And it came to pass in the morning, that David wrote a
letter to Joab, and sent it by the hand of Uriah.*

*And he wrote in the letter, saying, Set ye Uriah in the
forefront of the hottest battle, and retire ye from him,
that he may be smitten, and die.*

*And it came to pass, when Joab observed the city, that
he assigned Uriah unto a place where he knew that
valiant men were.*

*And the men of the city went out, and fought with
Joab: and there fell some of the people of the servants of
David; and Uriah the Hittite died also.*

It is no new thing for a king to take a faithful servant of his in
his army and steal that man's wife. David did that. So did King
Edward of England. I do not know how much of the cases are
parallel, but this much is certainly parallel: David saw a woman
that was not his, a woman who belonged to another man, and he
lusted after her, and broke up the marriage.

I do not know intimate details of the life of King Edward and
Mrs. Wally Warfield Simpson. But some ten days ago we saw
an alarming spectacle of a man who gave up his throne. He
ruled over 500 million people of England, Scotland, Wales,
Ireland, the Dominion of Canada, South Africa, Australia, New
Zealand, and parts of Africa and South America, and islands of
the sea besides. This king over 500 million people abdicated his
throne, which he had inherited by blood, for the love of a
woman who before had already proven untrue to two men.

The world wonders about that. What does it mean? The
British Empire on which the sun never sets was rocked to its
foundations. Who knows but that even yet as a result of such as
that, the British Empire will fall to pieces and Canada and
Australia and South Africa and India will become independent
nations. The world was shocked, the moral senses of the world
were shocked to find here was a man, a king, honored above any
other man on the face of the earth, who had for three years been

carrying on a clandestine love affair with a married woman, a wife of one of his guards.

She could not be queen because the moral sentiment of the English world wouldn't stand for that. That twice divorced woman, that untrue woman carrying on a scandalous and wicked course—untrue to her husband for a course of three years—England would never allow such a woman to be queen. The king of England finally had to take his choice, and he chose this woman instead of his kingdom.

I. Preachers, True to God, Must Rebuke Sin!

There are some lessons I want to call to your attention. When He was here, Jesus called attention to national and important affairs, then drew a lesson. He said in Luke 13:4 and 5:

> *Or those eighteen, upon whom the tower in Siloam fell, and slew them, think ye that they were sinners above all men that dwelt in Jerusalem?*
>
> *I tell you, Nay: but, except ye repent, ye shall all likewise perish.*

I have a right, then, to speak as Jesus did and call your attention to this great calamity of world-wide importance, the breakdown of moral fiber that will influence the race and people, and to draw some lessons therefrom.

I call your attention to the lesson in morals. Now, I know there are those who will criticise. Some will say, "I don't believe preachers should preach on sensational subjects." If newspapers have a right to speak on it, and if you in the home have a right to talk of it and follow after this wicked example, I have a right in the pulpit to warn people.

There are certain great moral questions involved that are taught in the Bible and I ought to speak about it, and I will. John the Baptist talked to the king himself and said, "Herod, it isn't right for you to have your brother's wife. It isn't right for a king to steal another man's wife just because he has the power to do it." So if John the Baptist did, John Rice ought to try to do it, and I am going to. If John the Baptist had a right to speak to the king as it is written down in the Bible, to make criticism of a king who got another man's wife because he was king, and if the Bible tells about David getting another man's wife because he was king, and suffering for it, I have a right to do so. I have not only a right but a duty to do it.

Do you know why I ought to? Because a lot of you sorry, good-for-nothing, Hell-raising, Hell-bound whoremongers in Dallas are about the same business, and you need to be warned. You are going to meet God. And because a lot of you women here would as quickly quit your husband for a title, or to carry on a clandestine affair, I need to warn you. You are held by the same kind of wicked ideals. For a little of the shallow tinsel of royalty, some of you would leave the husband of your youth and the father of your children and gad about to the end of the world with a man like Edward. It is important that preachers condemn such sin.

I was in the barber shop the other day (Brother Goldston has been so kind to me. He cuts my hair when I think to get it cut), and a woman came in and got to talking about this woman, Mrs. Wally Warfield Simpson. She said, "Well, I think she is a very sophisticated woman."

Maybe she is. These harlot women down here around the City Park are very sophisticated, too! That doesn't make it right for a married woman to be untrue to her husband and carry on a clandestine relationship with another man—even if he be king.

Many of you church members who claim to be Christians take up for that which is openly the breaking of marriage vows, a lie to God and man, and immorality on the face of it. Church people and sometimes preachers, take up for it. You ought to be sad about it.

Many of you are for that kind of life. I am against it. You have no business loving another man's wife. Adultery is not romance. Stealing is not romance. Breaking your vows is not romance. It is dishonoring God, and dishonoring God is not romance. Turning your back on a nation that trusted you is not romance. It is crooked, and sin. God calls men to account for sin. Something ought to be said and I am going to say it.

A moral lesson is involved here and preachers ought to speak out plain about it.

The Bible tells the case of David. Kings have a feeling that what a king does is all right, that uncensored action is the divine right of kings. David thought, "Here is a pretty woman down there." Now David was a good man as far as I know, and the king of England may have many admirable features. He loved poor people. I don't think it was all politics. You say, "Well, he was a great asset to England." Maybe—but he was a disgrace to England.

King David saw a woman bathing when he had gone out on top of the palace. Her husband, Uriah, was out fighting for King David.

II. Lust and Adultery and Broken Vows Are Not Proper Love

You say even if he was king, he had a right to love. Love is never honorable nor right when it means disloyalty, double-crossing a husband, violating a solemn vow, or breaking a marriage. It is not pure, God-given love, but it is lust, cheating, adulterous and inexcusably wicked. This man, Uriah, was one of David's main fighters in his army, a man who was glad to risk his life for his king, leave his wife and go and fight the king's battles. The lazy king stays home and lolls about and eats and drinks and thinks about women—and the man out yonder, risking his life and finally losing it for his king!

David thought, "But I am king. And a man can't help who he loves," says David—and King Edward. David saw a naked woman taking a bath. What he ought to have done was to go downstairs and to bed and behave himself and call the police or fire department if he must do something! But instead, David sent for the woman and violated his plain duty to God and betrayed his nation to whom he was upheld as a pattern. He was a traitor and a murderer of the man, his neighbor, who trusted him, his soldier who worked under him.

It was very similar to the case of Col. Simpson in England. Mrs. Wallis Simpson was the wife of an officer of King Edward's army—the Cold Stream Guards. We didn't know about it until recent months, but for three years—since

1933—King Edward, formerly the Prince of Wales, had been running around with this woman, the wife of one of the officers of his army. He went on a Mediterranean trip on his yacht, then to France, Switzerland, the play places of Europe, with this woman. English papers kept it a secret. Now for a year almost, his father, the former king of England, has been dead. Before the king died, he urged his son to be clean. And he was old enough to know better. He was forty-two years old—older than I am. Talk about him being a boy! He was an older man than I am and he ought to have as much sense as I have. If he had had, he wouldn't have done some things he did.

He ran around with this woman until finally the great king said to his son, who was then the Prince of Wales, "Son, for twenty-five years I have kept our name clean; now I will not see it dragged in the dust over this woman."

But Edward paid no attention. He was the prince of Wales. Later on the king commanded him, "Son, you will not do it." What did this man say to his aged and sick father, the king of England? "Sir, I will not be dictated to"—and he went on with his illegitimate and clandestine and underhanded love affair with this married woman!

III. Wallis Simpson, Untrue to Two Husbands, Not Worth the Sacrifice

David's case and this one is somewhat similar. Now what will happen? As certainly as there is a God in Heaven, that man will rue it. Do you suppose that this woman, who couldn't be true to another man, can be true to this one? She couldn't be true to an American army officer who married her and took her out of poverty and cared for her. Then she married another man, an Englishman, and could not be true to him. So she threw her love at the feet of a drinking, dancing, dissolute prince. She could be faithful to him, do you suppose? Does anybody here honestly believe that such a woman is worth King Edward's giving up an empire which rules over a fourth of the people of the earth? If so, you are certainly mistaken.

What is going to happen? I do not know. But as certain as God's Word is true, "Whatsoever a man soweth, that shall he also reap." And he will reap it, don't you doubt. So will you reap it.

A woman told me with tears and shame and with a broken heart, of her sin, then she said, "It is being visited on my own head. I am only reaping what I sowed. I am only getting what is coming to me." You, like David, will, too. It doesn't pay.

There are two or three sins here. One is coveting a neighbor's wife. The Lord very plainly says, in one of the Ten Commandments, "Thou shalt not covet thy neighbour's wife." This is important enough that the Lord said it. "Thou shalt not covet thy neighbour's wife." That is as clear as, "Thou shalt not kill." Edward broke a solemn command of God and he must give an account to God for it.

Another thing. If he did not commit adultery in the sense of the actual sin, he was responsible for the sin of adultery, for the Bible says, "He that putteth away his wife saving for fornication commits adultery." Honest people knew that was a framed matter on which Mrs. Simpson got her divorce. People don't go around in hotels committing adultery and calling in their folks to be witnesses, unless there is some reason for it. The fact of the business is that was a frame-up. A loyal soldier was trying to spare the name of his wife and save slander on the king. That kind of a faithful man, like Uriah, was betrayed by Edward and Wallis Simpson. Edward was guilty not only of covetousness, but of breaking up a marriage, which causes adultery, the Lord Jesus said.

That isn't all. He was untrue to a friend and servant. He betrayed the trust of a good man. At least he was good and loyal to his king and to his nation, and Edward betrayed that man. As surely as there is a God in Heaven, God will put that upon his own shoulders. God did on David, and God did on Herod, and God will on Edward, the Duke of Windsor! Your sin will find you out!

IV. Praise God for the Moral Sentiment in England That Would Not Allow Such a Woman to Be Queen!

England, perhaps, after all is not as snobbish as you might suppose. Mrs. Simpson was American-born, but she married an

Englishman and is now an English woman. Her citizenship is in England. English people did not rebel because she was an American. A number of American women have married into the nobility of England. The English papers did not object because she was an American, nor because she was a commoner. Since we have no titles of nobility in America, English people take our own value on that. If one is worthy, he is worthy whether he has a title or not. So it has always been, and it has been more so in this case.

English papers and English people, the prime minister and the chancellor, the English archdukes, did not object because this woman was an American or because she was a commoner. They objected because she was a character subject to slander and subject to talk, because she had broken her marriage vows twice over and was not to be trusted. She was evidently thought to be an unclean woman not fit to sit in the queen's chair, and I think the same thing. And we ought to honor the English people. The truth of the matter is, a few bold, strong men—Prime Minister Stanley Baldwin and some Bishops—that day may have saved England from the wrath of Almighty God.

My friends, immorality never pays, and the nation that endorses sin in its rulers and puts its seal on it will have the curse of God upon it, to face sooner or later. David did. War, bloodshed, division came out of it. Ruin, adultery followed with unceasing, heart-rending trend until David went to his grave.

Thank God, good men raised a protest! They have a better king now than they had a few weeks before. He is a cleaner man, a man more loyal to duty, more of a Christian man, and I thank God for that.

V. Beware! As Sin Enslaved Edward, It May Enslave You

There is another word I want to say. There is a lesson in prophecy and a lesson in morals. Now here is a lesson of the binding of sin. The lesson for sinners is this: If you go back three years or so, when that divorcee and wife of one of the Cold Stream Guards was presented at court and that night for the first time Edward set eyes upon her, and that night took her home in his own car, another man's wife the first time he ever saw her—he never dreamed, I am sure, of the end.

Do you suppose he would have trembled, would have been aghast, if he could have seen the infatuation that would so enslave him as to lose him the pride of his father, the honor of races, the throne of the greatest kingdom on earth? He did not see what sin would lead to. If he could have seen then in the future that little by little he will give way, his moral fiber will be decayed, he will be led on to break the heart of his old father, a good man, a Bible-reading Christian; if he could have foreseen, "I will break the heart of my old father and bring him down to the grave with scandal on his name," I think he wouldn't have gone home with that woman that night. I hope not.

No, my friends, sin starts out little, gets bigger and bigger and stronger and stronger until it binds you and binds you as it did Samson when it put out his eyes and brought ruin upon him. King Edward's moral senses were perverted, his eyes blinded, his character broken down little by little. Sin enslaved him. He never dreamed he would give up an empire of over a fourth of the world, never dreamed he would dishonor his kingdom and have to abdicate. Not only in England, but in Scotland, in Wales, in India, in South Africa, in Australia, in New Zealand, the sentiment compelled him to abdicate because of an unclean life. Surely he never dreamed this would come to pass. Never did he think one woman could wrap him, a man forty-two years old, around her finger until for the pleasure of living with her, he would give up the throne and bring disgrace on his name and family and the entire nation. And God knows he brought reproach on the name of religion! He was the head of the established church, the Anglican church. He didn't dream, I am sure, that he would bring disgrace on himself and break his mother's heart and send his father to his grave and break the hearts of multitudes of subjects. Sin—you never know where it will end!

Here a girl starts out. She says, "I will not go far. Just a little pleasure, just a little looseness in talk, just a little fun with the wild crowd, just a little time at the dance, just a sip of beer."

Never did she dream where she would land. Had she, she would never have taken the first step.

The man who starts out and says, "I will go to the Dallas Centennial and go through the 'Streets of Paris' and just look on a lewd, naked harlot woman, not indulge." (A lot of you church people have seen the same thing.) Just say he looks at that, and has just a little beer, a little night riding, just a bit of playing on the horses. And the first thing you know, money, then honor, then job, then family are gone. And God knows that is not all. Then the soul is gone! You didn't dream it, did you? Sin enslaves!

I have talked to a drunkard with a broken home. I have talked to the man whose health is gone. I have talked to the harlot with a hardened heart and damned soul. She has said to me, "Oh, I never dreamed it would come to this!"

I preached down at the jail. I felt God moving on the hearts of those men who stood and wept. Did you read about that man Adams who killed his wife the other day in South Dallas? That was the man today who stood and wept. His tears flowed down his face as he heard me speak and heard those songs. Do you suppose that man ever dreamed that sin would end this way? No!

My friends, you don't know where sin will end! Brother Cunningham, nobody is ever safe who takes one step on the road to sin. O people, turn your back on it! Flee to God for mercy.

As King Edward gave up home and throne and broke his mother's heart and gave up his kingdom, so many a man gives up his poor soul and gives up Heaven because of sin. You don't know what you will do. So don't take the first step.

Turn your back on sin. Turn to Jesus and be saved while you can. Go home saved and happy. That is the only way to be safe. Do it tonight, friend. What a lesson for sinners it is that a man raised to be a king, born to be a king, trained to be a king, with kingly blood and kingly training, supported at the cost of millions—but honor and character and self-restraint all went out the window at the sound of a woman's voice and the rustle of her skirts! He went too long that way.

You don't know! Sin will make you so blind you won't know it, like Samson—until you wake up with your hair gone, and your power gone, and your eyes put out, and you are grinding at the mill of Satan and cannot help yourself.

I beg you, beware of sin because if you sow it, you will reap it. If you sow to the wind, you will reap the whirlwind. If you have skeletons in the closet, they will one day come out. Your chickens will come home to roost one day. Your sins will find you out one day. That secret will be shouted from the housetops one day.

O sinner, today turn to Jesus Christ! He loves you even when you have played the fool, when you have broken every vow, when you have passed the last boundary of respect and human hope of reformation. Christ died for YOU! Trust Him today and be saved before it is too late. Christ, a greater King than England's prince, left Heaven to save you. Enthrone Him in your heart today. Trust Him. Repent of your sin before it drags you down! Christ is ready. Give Him your heart.

VI. TO THE UNSAVED

24—What's Wrong With the Dance?

Child of the Brothel, Sister of Drunkenness, Lewdness, Divorce and Murder, the Mother of Lust—a Road to Hell!

(Sermon preached in the Fundamentalist Baptist Tabernacle, Dallas, Texas, Sunday night, June 9, 1935. Stenographically reported.)

There are those who do not like plain preaching. That ought not to be true. Bible preachers preached plainly against sin. It is good for 1935 just as it was then, and I am going to do it whether you like it or not. I pray God will help the Gospel to take hold of your hearts tonight.

"The Dance! Child of the Brothel, Sister of Drunkenness, Lewdness, Divorce and Murder, the Mother of Lust—a Road to Hell!" That is a very plain subject, and I promised God, as I promised you in the announcement, that I am going to prove that before I leave here tonight.

If there ever was a time Christians ought to pray, it is now. I hope you members of this church, friends of this church, and friends of the Gospel will pray that God will have His way tonight.

Two passages of Scripture I want to use at this time. One is in Mark, the 6th chapter, verses 14 through 29:

And King Herod heard of him [heard of Jesus]; *(for his name was spread abroad:) and he said, That John the Baptist was risen from the dead, and therefore mighty works do shew forth themselves in him.*

Others said, That it is Elias. And others said, That it is a prophet, or as one of the prophets.

But when Herod heard thereof, he said, It is John, whom I beheaded: he is risen from the dead.

For Herod himself had sent forth and laid hold upon John, and bound him in prison for Herodias' sake, his brother Philip's wife: for he had married her.

For John had said unto Herod, It is not lawful for thee to have thy brother's wife.

Therefore Herodias [the woman in the case] *had a quarrel against him, and would have killed him; but she could not:*

For Herod feared John, knowing that he was a just man and an holy, and observed him; and when he heard him, he did many things, and heard him gladly.

And when a convenient day was come, that Herod on his birthday made a supper to his lords, high captains, and chief estates of Galilee;

And when the daughter of the said Herodias came in, and danced, and pleased Herod and them that sat with him, the king said unto the damsel, Ask of me whatsoever thou wilt, and I will give it thee.

And he sware unto her, Whatsoever thou shalt ask of me, I will give it thee, unto the half of my kingdom.

And she went forth, and said unto her mother, What shall I ask? And she said, The head of John the Baptist. [She said, "Get me that preacher's head on a platter, that is what I want!"]

And she came in straightway with haste unto the king, and asked, saying, I will that thou give me by and by in a charger the head of John the Baptist.

And the king was exceeding sorry; yet for his oath's sake, and for their sakes which sat with him, he would not reject her.

And immediately the king sent an executioner, and commanded his head to be brought: and he went and beheaded him in the prison,

And brought his head in a charger, and gave it to the damsel: and the damsel gave it to her mother.

And when his disciples heard of it, they came and took up his corpse, and laid it in a tomb.

From that time on preachers of John-the-Baptist type, honest preachers of the Gospel like John the Baptist, preachers true to the Bible and God, have been against the dance, and they ought to be.

ANOTHER BIBLE CASE OF DANCING

I read another case in Exodus, chapter 32. After a time of great blessing, when God led the children of Israel out of Egypt, they were in the wilderness; Moses went up on Mount Sinai to receive instructions from God. While up there, this terrible sin took place among the people on the plain below. They said they didn't know where their leader had gone. "Aaron, make us gods. We wot not what has become of this man Moses!" Aaron said, "Break off your golden earrings." He took their gold and molded it into a golden calf.

Now look at verse 6:

And they rose up early on the morrow, and offered burnt-offerings, and brought peace-offerings: and the people sat down to eat and to drink, and rose up to play.

Notice this. After they had dinner, they drank, then rose up to play—drinking, then play. And this play turned out to be naked dancing.

Now, let's read a little further in the same chapter.

And Moses turned, and went down from the mount, and the two tables of the testimony were in his hand: the tables were written on both their sides: on the one side and on the other were they written. [These are the Ten Commandments.]

And the tables were the work of God, and the writing was the writing of God, graven upon the tables.

And when Joshua heard the noise of the people as they shouted, he said unto Moses, There is a noise of war in the camp. [Joshua went up there with him.]

And he said, It is not the voice of them that shout for mastery, neither is it the voice of them that cry for being overcome: but the noise of them that sing do I hear.

And it came to pass, as soon as he came nigh unto the camp, that he saw the calf, and the dancing: [and the dancing! notice that] *and Moses' anger waxed hot, and he cast the tables out of his hands, and brake them beneath the mount.*

And he took the calf which they had made, and burnt it in the fire, and ground it to powder, and strawed it upon the water, and made the children of Israel drink of it.—Vss. 15-20.

Aaron began to make excuses for his sin. But now read verse 25:

And when Moses saw that the people were naked: (for Aaron had made them naked unto their shame among their enemies:)

Isn't it strange that even in the Old Testament drinking and nakedness and adultery went with dancing. Isn't that strange! Isn't that strange!

Now, read on:

And when Moses saw that the people were naked: (for Aaron had made them naked unto their shame among their enemies:)

Then Moses stood in the gate of the camp, and said, Who is on the Lord's side? let him come unto me. And all the sons of Levi gathered themselves together unto him.

And he said unto them, Thus saith the Lord God of Israel, Put every man his sword by his side and go in and out from gate to gate throughout the camp and slay every man his brother, and every man his companion, and every man his neighbour.

And the children of Levi did according to the word of Moses: and there fell of the people that day about three thousand men.

For Moses had said, Consecrate yourselves to day to the Lord, even every man upon his son, and upon his brother; that he may bestow upon you a blessing this day.—Vss. 25-29.

And then Moses prayed, "Oh, this people have sinned a great sin, and have made them gods of gold."

WILD PARTIES, ADULTERY, MURDER, IDOLATRY, DRUNKENNESS, NAKEDNESS ALL CONNECTED WITH THE DANCE

I have read these Bible passages which show the evil nature of the dance. The daughter of Herodias danced before Herod and other men, and on account of that dance the adulterous Herodias was able to make her husband Herod murder John the Baptist, one of the greatest men ever born of woman. Wild parties, adultery, irreligion and murder were connected with that dance.

In the other case, the children of Israel made a golden calf, ate, drank, pulled off their clothes, and had a big dance. In that case, idolatry, rebellion against God, drinking, nakedness and lewdness went with the dance.

"Dance" is used many times in the Bible but only a few times is it used in any sense that would compare with the modern dance. When David danced, he leaped and praised God. No embracing of the opposite sex. There was nothing to compare with the modern dance. David knew nothing about the "bunny hug," the "tango," "waltz," or "two-step."

In the Bible, ordinarily the dance mentioned was not like the modern dance. But there is one such case. Here the two sexes danced together, and they were naked, and when Moses saw their idolatry and nakedness, he said, "Who is on the Lord's side? let him come unto me. God will blot out the whole camp with His curse unless we bring vengeance on those wicked idolators, with their drinking, nakedness, and dancing."

Great numbers were killed. When the sin had been punished, God heard Moses' prayer, and the nation was spared.

These incidents from the Bible suggest certain evils that always go with the modern dance. The modern dance is wholly wrong. No good word can be said for it. It is as lewd as Hell. Every preacher ought to say some plain words about it, and I am going to do it. Pray while I speak tonight. It is a very, very serious matter. Other Scriptures I will refer to in a moment.

There are some things that ought to be said about it.

I. The Dancer Is Always in Bad Company

The kindest thing we could say about the dance is, it is bad company. Now, if that were all, that is plenty of reason why no child of God ought ever go to the dance. If only one reason, that would be enough. The nicest thing you can say about the dance is, it is bad company. Leave off temporarily the murder, drinking, divorce, lewdness and all the other wickedness that goes with it for a little time. The kindest thing you can say about it is, it is bad company.

As God is my witness, my five girls will not run with that crowd that dances, even if it be in the best homes in Dallas. If it is a dance, then it is as rotten as Hell. The Devil is in it. That has always been so. The Devil's crowd takes possession of the "nice, clean dance." As the farmer said the first time he saw a giraffe, "There ain't no sich animal!" There is no such thing as a nice, clean dance.

Somebody says, "Brother Rice, we just have a nice dance here in one of our nice homes." But it wouldn't stop at that. If it did, it is still as rotten as Hell. The Devil is still in it. The Devil's crowd will be attracted to it still. God wouldn't have anything to do with it. The curse of God is on it. Bad company flocks to the dance!

1. The Old Square Dance Was Bad; the Modern Dance
Is a Thousand Times Worse

When I was a boy back yonder in the country places, when the floors were rough, they had a fiddler or two or three in a corner and someone called out, "*Swing* your partner!" All there was about the dance that was anything like the modern dance was the company that you kept and the drinking that went on. As the fiddlers played, the man held out his hand and his girlfriend took his fingers and swung around a time or two, then took another man's fingers. There was not the hugging, the undressing, or the lewdness of the dance today. Those old dances, with the fiddlers in the corner and somebody stomping his feet, and swinging his partner, and somebody calling the sets, were nothing like the modern dance is. But some terribly wicked things went along with it even then.

I have seen the dance all the way from the country dance out yonder—or the square dance as it was called—to the modern dance. I have seen the time when they roped off the streets of Chicago and the elite there had a big celebration and danced. I have seen it in the dance halls. I have buried the victims of it. I have seen and wept and prayed over the victims of it when they were in jail; wept and prayed over homes broken by it. I have seen boys and girls go to Hell over it.

I know what I am talking about. I have a grudge against the modern dance. All of it is bad. One thing you can't get away from is that where there is a dance, there is always bad company. The Devil's crowd is there.

I preached one night about the dance, and a brother kept saying, "Amen!" "Amen!" "Amen!" After a time I said, "I have seen both kinds." This fellow said, "The old square dance is the only kind I was ever in." I said, "Then you don't know anything about the dance." He said, "The kind I knew was bad enough!" I said, "The kind you don't know anything about is ten thousand times as bad. It is as rotten as the poison of Hell!"

The kindest thing that you can say about the dance is that it is bad company. I knew the time at country dances when folks were nice folks on the whole, nice as the community average, when the dance didn't have the lewdness in it as it has now; girls didn't go to dances unchaperoned. They had lots more safeguards than they have now. But if there was any drunken blackguard in that community, he would be outside the window making remarks about the women folks. If there was any tough nut, any crack-brained bully in the community, he would be at the dance. If there was one in the whole community, he would be at the dance. If there was anybody drinking or carrying whiskey around, he would be drinking it out yonder in the dark, then he would set the bottle under the edge of the front porch. After taking a big swig, he would come in with red face and dance with some girl!

Say what you want to; but anybody that goes to the modern

478   PREACHING THAT BUILT A GREAT CHURCH

dances is with the Devil's crowd, with a crowd that will take you to Hell. If there ever was in a community some low-down, dirty rake who would seduce a girl and lead her to Hell, he went to the dance, no matter what kind it was. He got in his best licks at the dance. Nobody here will deny that.

Anybody who goes to a dance puts himself in with the Devil's crowd. That crowd knows it, too. No good church member has any business around there. It is bad company and no place for a Christian.

2. You Cannot Win Souls at the Dance

A preacher said to a girl, "You ought not to go; it is bad company. Your influence will be wrong. You will lose out."

She said, "I don't believe it."

The preacher said, "I can prove it. Listen, when you go to a dance, try to win somebody to Christ."

She said, "I believe I can do it."

So she went with her boyfriend to the dance. On the dance floor that night she asked, "Are you a Christian?"

"No, are you?"

"Yes."

"What are you doing here then?"

She didn't win him to Christ! And you won't win anybody to Christ in that crowd. The crowd is wrong, always has been wrong, the crowd that goes to the dance.

What is wrong about the dance? It is not good company. You are with the Devil's crowd, with the tough bunch turned loose. It is the reveling, drinking crowd, the adulterous crowd, not the Lord's crowd, not the praying crowd, the soul-winning crowd. You are not with the crowd going to Heaven when you go to the dance. It is as rotten as Hell. I say again, the kindest thing I could say about the dance is, it is bad company.

There are ten thousand reasons worse than that, but no man or woman in the world is safe in bad company. Lot wasn't! David wasn't! Peter wasn't! It caused Peter to curse and swear and deny that he ever knew Jesus. You are no better than these men, no stronger. No man or woman is safe in bad company. Nobody is in good company at the dance.

If there is a man here that is sixty or seventy years old, or one who knew the dance seventy years ago, if he is an honest man, he will stand up here and say it was the wrong crowd that hung around the dance. It always has been so. You know it is so, too. That is one thing about it.

II. Drinking and Dancing Always Go Together

Another thing: Drinking always goes with dancing. The Bible cases show it so plainly. Here we find a case where they jumped and danced around naked. First, they sat down to eat, *then to drink!* and then rose up to play and dance. If there is going to be any drinking going on, it will be at the dance. Folks who dance will drink. You may think you won't. You go to many dances and you are going to drink. They go together. The dance is a sister of drunkenness, lewdness, and divorce, the sister of wild life. Reveling will put you with the reveling crowd.

It turns out that folks who go to dances are folks who drink, gamble and curse. Sure. No girl need expect to keep the conversation right and herself modest and sober and safe who goes to dances. It is impossible for a young man to stay out of temptation to drink if he goes to the dance. The drinking crowd and the dancing crowd go together. In the Bible they went together. In Dallas they go together.

Go to a night club where dancing is, and that is where they are selling booze; there is where the bootlegger is. Every night club in this country is a bootlegging joint.

Who will deny that booze is sold in the Brown Derby? Who will deny that booze is sold and drunk at the Bagdad road house and night club? Who will deny that about the Melody Tavern, or about the Round Up here within three blocks of this church house? You won't! Where they dance, people drink. Any business that caters to the dancing crowd caters to the drinking crowd. Drunkenness goes with dancing. And most girls who ever took a drink took their first one when they went to a dance.

Again, I dare anybody to stand up and deny that at night clubs where they dance, that is where they drink, where someone will sell booze. They go together.

When Moses was on Mount Sinai, the people said, "We are tired of waiting for Moses. He is too old fogey anyway! He is too slow bringing us the Ten Commandments God is writing for him up there." They said, "First, let's get drunk, and then take off our clothes and have a nice dance!" And that is what they did! Moses came down and there saw the dancing and heard the noise. It was a terrible noise because that goes with it! You know drunken dancers always make a noise.

Brokenhearted Moses threw down the tables of stone on which were written the Ten Commandments, and broke them to pieces. Why break these tables of stone, Moses, just because of a nice dance? Because the dancers break every one of the Ten Commandments, break every commandment of God! Drunkenness, idolatry, nakedness, and other sins go with the dance now as they did in this 32nd chapter of Exodus. Turn and read it for yourself. Drinking goes with the dance.

Oak Cliff Young People in Fatal Accident Coming Home From a Dance

You read about that carload of Oak Cliff young people who were coming back from the Brown Derby night club a few nights ago in the small hours of the morning, and wrecked their car and scattered one young man's brains and blood on a sidewalk and steps, and put others at death's door. They were students of Oak Cliff schools. One boy told my wife, "They invited me to go. I came very near going. I am glad I didn't." How many of you knew one in that carload of young people? They were coming home in the wee small hours of the morning from Brown Derby dance hall; after dancing they started home, driving fast, of course, skidded, and one boy's brains were dashed out and scattered on the sidewalk!

I have no unkindness to say about them, but no honest person will deny that the drinking crowd is the dancing crowd. That is one reason why we have so many drunken accidents on the road home from the dance. I am just telling you right now, there are ten thousand reasons why no decent person ought to go around the modern dance. Drinking isn't safe, isn't right, and that goes with the dance.

Many of you remember about that Packard roadster coming in from Melody Tavern out yonder on the old Fort Worth-Dallas highway. That car hit a concrete abutment and dashed out the brains of that young man, coming in past the midnight hour. Now, what caused it? They had been to a dance, and drinking goes with it. I could remind you of case after case of such accidents. Often drinking, booze, drunkenness, and harlotry go with the dirty, rotten modern dance. That is so. Drinking goes with it.

That is charge number two against the dance! I dare anybody here to deny it! You know that is so. Drinking goes with it. I do not say that everybody who dances drinks. A lot of folks who get drunk are too decent to dance! I say that they are *too decent* to dance. But the fact of the business is, they are crimes of the same kind, the same kind of folks go together and you can't disassociate them.

III. Nudity and Lewdness Go With the Dance

Charge number three against the modern dance! I say that nakedness and the lewdness that goes with it, go with the dance.

Did you ever hear of Sally Rand, the fan dancer? She had at least a fan, had on that much clothes! Lewdness and nakedness go with dancing. You just turn over here in Exodus, 32nd chapter, where they started out in open idolatry. They started out by getting drunk and ended up by dancing naked.

Now, what is there about the dance that makes people want to pull off their clothes? There must be something! What is there about the dance that makes a man want the girl he has his arms around to have no clothes on? What about that?

What is there about the dance that changes the dress habits of women? Corset manufacturers agree that they have been practically put out of business by the influence of the rotten dance. Now, I don't care whether you wear them or not, but why is it they first had corset check rooms at dance halls in New York and then women began to go to dances without them, and now the dance has changed the dress habits of American women? What is there about the dance that leads people to discard clothes?

Tell me this—I see the ads in the papers and I see the shop windows—why is it that the thinnest, skimpiest little bit of feminine underwear, so little it would go in a coin purse—why is that called a "dance set" or a "dancette"? Almost no underwear at all! Why is that a dancette?

What is it about the dance that makes it so if a woman is to dress up in "evening clothes," dancing clothes, she has to show her breasts, has to have her dress open down the front? What is there about the dance that does that? There is something that does it, brother, and it is a straight-out appeal to lust.

Whether you like it or not, I dare you to stand up and deny it! Nakedness is a natural accompaniment of the dance. That is sad but so. I say, every woman who dances is tempted that way and most of them go that way.

As far as that is concerned, why should a woman who gives herself up to any man's arms cover up her body anyway? If her body is to be held tight against him, what should it matter whether she has any clothes on or not? The fact of the business is, it was impossible to get a nudist movement started until the modern dance got as rotten as Hell. We could have had no nudist camps except men and women were willing to go out together and pull off their clothes together. Charge that up to the modern dance.

Now, I am talking kindly and from the depths of my heart. I am trying to help people here tonight. Nakedness and lewdness and disregard for modesty go with it. When the dance comes in, modesty goes out.

1. Native, Maidenly Modesty Disappears in the Dance

A preacher named Jenkins some years ago preached in the First Baptist Church in Amarillo on the dance. The dance then was not nearly as bad as now. But Brother Jenkins said that a girl doesn't stay as modest after dancing as before; that a girl who has this man's arms about her and then that one's, and wears the evening clothes and all that sort of thing, doesn't stay modest, doesn't stay where she can blush, where she has the same virtuous reticence of character and mind. He said that she is not the same girl after she has had every man's hands on her; that such a girl doesn't stay the same.

A man got red in the face, as some of you are getting tonight. He got hot under the collar and said to himself, "This preacher is going to eat that. My girl Molly is as good a girl as any in this town, as good as she ever was, even if she does dance. That preacher is going to eat that. Dancing doesn't make any difference with her modesty."

He planted himself out at the front door of that Baptist church at Amarillo. But before the preacher got out to the front, Molly stopped him and said, "Brother Jenkins, you are right. I am not the Christian I used to be. I am not as spiritually-minded as I used to be. I am not the same girl I once was. Pray for me. The dance has done it."

Nearly everybody was gone. The preacher went on to the front, not knowing what was about to happen. Then the father said to Brother Jenkins, "I want you to know, you have got to take back what you said tonight. My girl is the same after dancing as before. Molly is as clean and modest and virtuous as she ever was. That is a reflection on my girl's character."

The preacher said, "Let's see what Molly has to say about it. Molly, come here."

The girl, with red eyes, came, and the preacher said to her, "Molly, I want you to tell your daddy what you told me."

She said, "Dad, I am not as modest as I used to be. I don't pray like I used to. I don't feel God's presence like I used to. The dance has been a curse to me."

The father said, "God help me! If I had known that, I wouldn't have let you go!"

I say now, there is something about the modern dance that breaks down conventionality, and makes a girl's virtue not safe and man's integrity not safe!

Charge number three against the modern dance is that it goes with nakedness and lewdness. Does anybody here want to deny it? If so, stand up and do it now!

There is more to it. Listen to me! You need not get up here and tear your hair because next year in that Fair Park in the

Centennial there will be a bunch of naked women on show for boys and girls at fifty cents a peep. Listen to me, you bunch of hens, you who have been carrying on these dances in your homes, don't open your chops. You have paved the way for lewdness, trained boys and girls for it. You put the dance on in the public school through the Parent-Teachers' Association. You are guilty in God Almighty's sight. You are responsible for it, and God will call you to account for it! The lewdness will curse Dallas in the Texas Centennial and you are partners in it, all you who give dances. You are as guilty as Hell! You are!

Now, my friend, you can't sow and not reap. You can't dance without paying the piper. It breaks down modesty, decency, and proprieties; it breaks down the conventions. Lewdness is brought on by the dirty, low-down, rotten dance. It goes with the modern dance. They are inseparable. Immodesty goes with the modern dance. Nobody will deny that. You get off and sweat all you want to. I dare you to stand on your hind feet right now and say it; I know this crowd knows that that goes with the dance. If you have anything to say, now is the time to say it!

IV. Dance and Divorce Go Together

Charge number four against the modern dance is divorce. Did you notice this thing in the Bible, in the account I read about the case of John the Baptist? The Lord Jesus Christ Himself said nobody greater was ever born of woman than John the Baptist. Jesus said he was the greatest preacher who ever lived. He is the one who walked up and said to Herod, "You are doing wrong. It isn't right for you to have taken your brother's wife. You are doing great wrong." And the woman hated him with undying hatred from that time on. But that honest preacher told the truth. That preacher had his head cut off because of a dancing girl, hated by one woman, a divorcee who wanted her girl to dance, and she didn't want the preacher to talk about it!

That bunch of women who run these P. T. A. dances for boys and girls in school—I know they don't like John Rice. I am telling you now, if God Almighty lets me live, later on you will not like me one-half as well as you do now! If God gives me grace and power, I hope to drive the dance out of the schools. I give you fair warning, you bunch of hens who would inflame the minds of the boys and girls, who would make prostitutes out of my daughters, who would ruin other folks' boys and girls, you P. T. A. women who go to that high school and have a dirty dance for high school boys and girls, and you who go on down here at James Bowie grade school with a bunch of boys and girls thirteen and fourteen years old and put on a dance for seventh grade pupils! Well, you parents and teachers who do that, I am going to give you something to talk about, if God lets me stay in Dallas!

If anybody doesn't like that, you can swell up and burst. If anybody in this church doesn't like that kind of preaching, we will give you a check-out anytime you say. You can check out now. If I hear any complaint about it, I think I will preach again on it next Sunday night. I will say right now; under God, I don't have to have your help. Nobody pays you to come to hear me preach. As God is my witness, no man is my boss. This Bible and the Lord Jesus Christ decide what I am going to preach, and I am going to preach it!

Some of you have a little bit of a high-stepping girl going to Hell by the dance road. I am trying to save your girl. And if you don't listen to me, you will reap it in bitter tears a thousandfold; you will reap if you go on with the sowing you are doing.

You men, hear me! You had better have an understanding when you get home! You had better have an understanding whether you are going to have a Christian home or not, a decent girl, or whether you are raising a prostitute. I am telling you, there is the poison of death in the rotten dance! I hate it for good reasons. I am trying to save people and keep people out of Hell. Multitudes are going to Hell on that road, the dance road, because they won't listen to the Gospel and turn to Jesus Christ and be saved. A dance-loving divorcee hated John the Baptist and had him murdered; so it will not be strange if the same kind, the dancing kind, hates other honest preachers.

Divorce goes with it. Here is the case of Herod. He liked his brother's wife. He got his brother's wife and married her and lived with her. That divorced woman was a dancing woman and taught her daughter to dance. I have no doubt that her daughter displayed her body in a half-naked condition to dance, for they liked it so well Herod said he would give her anything she wanted.

She said, "My mother taught me how to dance. Let me go and talk to my divorcee mother." Wicked Herodias, her mother, said, "Cut the head off that preacher! He wanted me to live moral and straight. He preached against sin! He didn't want me to leave one husband for another. Cut off his head!"

The Bible shows a connection between divorce and the dance.

1. Why Dancing Brings on Divorce

Now, my friends, I am just showing you that divorce goes with the modern dance. Why? Because you will not allow your wife to sleep in your bed and go out between times and hold against her body every man who wants to paw over her.

Honorable, good men are not going to sleep with that kind of a woman. I won't, and you don't want your wife doing that either. You just don't want that. I am telling you it breaks down confidence; it breaks down modesty, the only basis for true reverential, godly love. The modern dance does that. Every man here knows that is so. The immodesty, the promiscuity, the jealousy created by the dance, brings thousands of divorces.

How many men here tonight can say, "I don't care how many men put their arms around my wife when she doesn't have many clothes on; I don't care how many men look on my wife's breasts while she leans her head on another man's shoulder. I don't care who puts his leg between my wife's legs and dances"?

Note: After the sermon, I learned of a humorous incident that happened at this point. A man and his wife sat together hearing the sermon. He had gone to dances, insisted there was no harm in his dancing with other women. His wife was a Christian and did not dance. At this point she turned to her husband and said, "Now is your chance; stand up and say you don't think there is any harm in that. Go on, stand up. That's what you have been telling me all the time; now speak up!" She nudged him again and again with her elbow and spoke so that people around her heard her. His face turned fiery red, but he said not a word!—J. R. R.

2. Why Does Dallas Lead Texas, Texas Lead the Nation, and America Lead the World in Divorce?

The low-down, rotten modern dance brought about many divorces last year in Dallas County. There were 2,700 marriage licenses plus, and *over 2,400 divorces in Dallas County last year!* Any time the dance is a craze and the schools are turned over to it—LOOK OUT! Some of our church organizations are in the dancing business. Most preachers won't say anything though the whole town goes to Hell!

Divorces have mounted until Dallas is one of the most disgraceful cities in the world in that respect. Listen to me! America has more divorces than any civilized country in the world. Texas has more divorces than any state in the Union but there are not nearly as many people in Texas as there are in California, Ohio, etc. Texas had 18,065 divorces in the year, 1930—many more than Nevada, Illinois, Pennsylvania, New York, or California! And Dallas has nearly five times as many divorces per capita as the rest of the state of Texas! If anybody doubts that, go down to the County Clerk and find out. Divorce goes with the dirty, rotten modern dance.

You young women, listen to me! Young girls, if you want the love of a good man—I am not talking about passion alone and lust—if you want the respectful love and deep-seated love based on character, the kind of love that abides, lasts after you are old—if you want that from a good man who is to be the father of your children, who will love you still when your hair is gray, when youth is fled; love you still when your face is wrinkled—if you want a good man to love you like that, then God help you, my dear girl, live straight and leave the dirty, modern, low-down, rotten dance alone! [Amen! Amen! Applause.] That is charge number four against the modern dance. It leads to divorce. Divorce goes with it, just like it did in the case of Herodias.

V. Murder Goes With the Modern Dance

Now here is another charge. Murder goes with the modern dance. Deny it if you will! I could stand here and give you case after case. Bryan Roach, once the world's champion bronc rider, is now running a night club in Fort Worth. In that night club, in the last week, after the drinking, the dance went on and some strangers came in, drinking at the same place. Bryan Roach came out with a gun, the gun went off and killed a man. He was charged with murder, was put in the Tarrant County jail, but lawyers got him out on bail. What did that? Whiskey and the modern dance.

That is just one case. The world is full of cases like that. Why did that happen at a dance club?

How many remember the case of a man and a sixteen-year-old girl dancer in a night club between here and Fort Worth? At times they were dance partners and between times something else. This girl said or did something that angered him, so he beat her. She died. He said this girl took poison. She was rushed to Dallas. He was tried for murder. She came out of a divorced home. This sixteen-year-old girl was a professional dancer and living in adultery with these dirty crooks at the dance hall or night club. How many remember that case? Yes, you do. I am not making this up.

Murder goes with the modern dance. Why? Because a man who kills his wife is a man who doesn't trust her, despises her, believes her untrue. Remember, now, the breakdown of every instinct of morality and righteousness goes on when the modern dance goes on, and murder follows.

Husband Murders Wife as She Comes Out of Dance Hall at 2:00 A. M.

The saddest funeral I ever held was in Fort Worth at an undertaking parlor on Magnolia Street. The funeral was that of a young married woman stabbed by her husband as she came out of an upstairs dance hall at the corner of Hemphill and Magnolia Streets. She danced before she married, and then when she married she was never content to give it up.

God gave a little baby to the home, but this young mother would leave her baby in order to dance with other men until the wee small hours of the morning. Her husband pled with her. Her family begged her to take care of her baby and stay with her husband and to break with the wild crowd at the dance halls, but she would not.

One night her desperate husband waited at the stairway. At 2:00 a.m. she came down from the dance with another man, and the jealous husband stabbed her. That murder, like thousands of others, must be charged up to the dance.

I preached the funeral sermon. Many of the wild dancing crowd were there. Marks of dissipation showed on many faces. I preached a plain, tender Gospel sermon, telling them that God loves sinners. Seven or eight of them claimed Christ as Saviour as we stood beside that casket of a murdered woman, killed at a dance and because of a dance.

I will never forget the wail of the young woman's sister when she came by the coffin to say good-bye to the form of her beloved sister, once pure, sweet and good, but betrayed and misled and ruined by the modern dance. She cried, "O Brother Rice, she wasn't ready! She wasn't ready to go!"

And I warn you now, dancers, that dancing people are not ready to meet God!

I say that murder goes with the modern dance.

How many remember a shooting scrape and somebody killed at a country dance when you were a boy? I remember case after case of somebody cut with a knife, somebody shot with a shotgun at the dance; don't you? Murder goes with the modern dance—and all kinds of devilment. The curse of God is on it! The Devil is in it! There is terrible danger in it! God help you to leave it alone!

VI. The Dance, the Mother of Lust

Charge number six against the modern dance! What is wrong? The modern dance is the child of the brothel, sister of drunkenness, lewdness, and divorce, the mother of lust—a road to Hell. Not only the sister of murder but the mother of lust.

What is the attraction of the modern dance? Somebody says, "The reason I dance is for the music." You are a liar, and you know it! You say, "I dance for exercise." You are a liar, and you know it! "Well, I just dance for the company." That is not true either.

What is the trouble then? Why do men dance? Because of the inflammation of the sex passion! Why do women dance? For the same reason.

Somebody tells me this sometimes, "Brother Rice, I am living a clean life, and there is no temptation in the dance to me at all." No sensible man will believe that. God made all men with certain natural desires. God made woman a certain way on purpose. Sex functions are holy functions, holy and blessed, and they ought to be so regarded. They ought not to be perverted, misused, prostituted.

The natural attraction of husband and wife for each other is blessed of God. It makes marriage sweet and home a haven. It ought to be revered, controlled. This natural attraction ought not to be perverted, inflamed, and made to burn toward every lewd person near.

But that is what the dance does. To inflame the passion of sex toward other women is a sin against God. It leads to every kind of crime on earth.

Now, a man says to me who gets out here and dances, "All I am thinking about is just the exercise, the music, the entertainment, etc." But you get out and dance with one girl, your arm around her, her leg between your legs, she with not much clothes on, drawn close up against your body. You dance with her and then somebody else and then with somebody else hour after hour, with the closest possible contact, with no daylight between you. Yes, you dance so close together that the girl's dress works up above her knees. Often people at the dance kiss each other, put their cheeks against cheeks, with heated flush on their faces. They say things they wouldn't otherwise say, use language they otherwise do not use. That goes on. Men go on with that hour after hour, changing from one girl to another. Somebody says, "Brother Rice, I do not have bad thoughts when I dance." I say you are a dirty liar!

The best woman in this audience tonight, a woman true to her family, true to her husband, or a clean, modest girl, a Sunday school teacher, a praying Christian woman—take that woman and the best man here tonight, a clean man, true to his wife, an honorable Christian gentleman, a praying Christian, a soul-winning man—put the two together, not married to each other, put their arms around each other just the way people do every day in the modern dance—let the girl be dressed as they are at the dance—just let them go on with that an hour or two—and I don't care who they are, their natures will be inflamed with desire, with lust. That will happen with any normally developed man and woman.

There is one thing wrong with the modern dance. This is one thing that is terrible about it. *It is the breeder and mother of lust!* I think innocent people start out to dance; girls sometimes don't know what it is that makes it appeal to them. With women sometimes the sex nerves are not quite as definitely centralized as they are with men. God made man to be the pursuer—some way women don't understand quite as quickly about that, perhaps. But nobody here can deny that nobody goes long in the dance, nobody goes on and dances, no moral man, no moral woman can go on with the dance, without arousing the lustful passions. The dance can't go on long without that, and you know it. You say that is so with *some* kind of folks. No, that is true of *every* kind of folk who dance. It is terribly inflaming, and the dance is designed and intended for that, and on purpose.

That is why new dances are invented all the time. They call one the "bunny hug." Others are named after animal functions, after beastly functions and patterned after animals in the jungles. The dance is the mother of lust. No honest man or woman here will deny it.

That is the reason why again and again girls who danced, after awhile meet good men, get married, love their husbands, and *quit their dancing.* Married women know what is wrong with the dance, and good women don't want to inflame that passion toward some other man beside her husband. God knows you ought not. I do not fear denial. No honest preacher can fail to declare that the modern dance is the mother of lust.

1. A Scripture Against the Dance

What Scripture is there against the dance? Turn to Matthew

5:27,28. These words are from the mouth of the Lord Jesus
Christ Himself.

> Ye have heard that it was said by them of old time,
> Thou shalt not commit adultery:
> But I say unto you, That whosoever looketh on a
> woman to lust after her hath committed adultery with
> her already in his heart.

"Already in his heart." What's wrong with the modern dance?
If men go on, if women go on long in the modern dance, they will
commit adultery in their hearts. I do not say and I do not believe
that every woman who dances is indecent. But I do say that
every man who dances puts himself in terrible temptation.
Every woman who dances puts herself in a terribly
embarrassing and tempting position. If she goes long in that,
she will break down what moral fiber she has, what strength
she has. Every dancing woman endangers her virtue.

The Chicago Vice Commission a good many years ago started
out to find the cause of girls' going wrong. Jane Addams, who
died recently, was on that Vice Commission. The Chief of Police
was on it. A prominent preacher was on it.

They talked to three hundred prostitute girls in Chicago and
asked, "What led you wrong? What led you to become such a
sinner? What led you to become what you are today, a scarlet
woman?" Eighty-five percent of them (that would be all of the
three hundred except forty-five) said, "My first step wrong was
caused by the modern dance."

I tell you frankly, my friend, the dance itself is lustful and
lust-provoking and the mother of lust.

2. A Dying Girl of the Streets Asks, "Am I Any Worse Than Society Girls Who Dance?"

How well I remember when I preached one time on the street
in Fort Worth while attending the Seminary. We took that big
Nash truck and Seminary students and had a service on the
street at the corner of Tenth and Main. Either Brother
McMurray or I had some word to say about the dance. A young
nurse spoke to my wife. "I have a story to tell you. Perhaps you

will tell Brother Rice." She told my wife this story:

"I am a nurse in the City-County Hospital here in Fort Worth. A young woman there is dying with a venereal disease. She called me the other day and said, 'Nurse, you say I can't live long.' This girl dying in the City-County Hospital in Fort Worth, this seventeen-year-old girl with venereal disease brought on by sin, of course, said to me, 'Nurse, I know I have done wrong. I know I have sinned. I don't try to excuse myself. I have got to meet God pretty soon. Nurse, do you really believe I am so bad?'

"I said, 'Of course that is a terrible sin.'

"But this girl said, 'Nurse, do you think it is any worse for me? I went on and plied my trade to make a living. Nurse, do you think it is any worse for me than for these society girls who had their dances until after midnight and the latter part of the night men came down to see me?'

"I didn't know what to tell her. I didn't know what to say."

Yes, I think she was worse. That is, probably she knew she was doing more harm, but actually the women who danced and inflamed the men were guilty of the same sin, and every such night God booked them up as adulteresses and scarlet women, because Jesus Himself said that "whosoever looketh on a woman to lust after her hath committed adultery with her already in his heart." Certainly those who inspire the lust are equally guilty. Brother, put that down!

Some people are getting awfully excited about the increase of street women in Dallas. Sixty, the paper said this past week, sixty prostitute women were arrested who hadn't been in Dallas before. Sixty were arrested, but there may have been three hundred new ones who were not arrested whom the police didn't know about. Sixty new people come in here on the reports of the Centennial, making their living by prostitution roaming the streets of Dallas, infecting other people with venereal disease, etc.

The City Health Department is aroused by the 102 new cases of syphilis in Dallas, the 30,000 people who have syphilis today in Dallas, not counting gonorrhea. That is Dr. Bass's official health department report, his statement in the papers. That would mean approximately one out of every eight people in Dallas has that terrible disease now! That would mean eight thousand new cases every year in Dallas alone! One case now in every other home! Over the whole nation it is reported that about one in twenty have venereal disease, but in Dallas about one of every eight!

3. Three Deaths and 102 New Cases of Venereal Disease in Dallas Last Week

I remind you that in Dallas three people died in the last week with venereal disease. Of the total number of new cases of communicable diseases, 102 of them in the last week were venereal diseases. I have that report right here from daily papers; 102 cases of venereal disease, 90 cases of syphilis reported in one week, and 12 new cases of gonorrhea. *The Dallas Morning News* of June 9, 1935, says:

DALLAS PLANS WAR ON SYPHILIS AS DISEASE SPREADS—SEXUAL CASES OUTSTRIP OTHERS AMONG COMMUNICABLE ILLS IN WEEK

Mayor George Sergeant will take the lead in efforts to help Dr. J. W. Bass, City Health Officer, stem the tide of venereal disease in Dallas, he said Saturday when weekly reports showed that syphilis and gonorrhea far outstripped other communicable diseases in seriousness for the last seven days.

During the week the health department received reports on ninety new cases of syphilis and twelve cases of gonorrhea, as well as three deaths from syphilis and one from gonorrhea. Only nine cases of other types of communicable disease and two deaths were reported to the city for the week.

CALLS RECORDS TERRIBLE

"These records are terrible, and I will give Dr. Bass every bit of assistance I can in trying to protect our people," Mayor Sergeant said Saturday. He plans to call a meeting of city officials to discuss it within the next week.

Dr. Bass allayed fears of the people that Dallas is any worse than other cities over the country in venereal diseases by saying conditions are just as bad everywhere else but the people shun the facts.

"If every newspaper in the country would show the courage the 'Dallas News' has in bringing these facts before the people we would have much greater success in fighting venereal diseases," Dr. Bass said. When we say that Dallas has at least 30,000 cases of syphilis alone, based on a careful study of the situation, that looks bad, but every other city is in the same shape.

PROPHYLACTIC STATIONS FAVORED

Support for the plan of Dr. Bass to establish two downtown prophylactic stations was given Saturday by Dr. Arthur G. Schoch, one of the physicians who has been in charge of the Parkland antiluetic clinic for many months.

"These stations should be established and kept open day and night to help educate and protect the people," Dr. Schoch said, "One of the greatest moves the city and county could make, however, would be to give us more room at Parkland Hospital to give treatment to the poor for syphilis and we hope this will be done soon in the new building program."

In the last week, Dr. Bass has received messages from all over Texas offering assistance to any movement designed to stamp out venereal diseases, some of the people offering money to the cause.

The New Standard Encyclopedia says:

SYPHILIS, a contagious, infectious, and inoculable disease . . . It is commonly caused by impure sexual intercourse.

Again the same encyclopedia says:

The time of treatment should extend over at least two and one-half years after all visible signs of the disease have disappeared, and marriage should be prohibited during this interval!

This terrible disease brings ulcers, tumors, paralysis and insanity, and is often fatal. It is infectious for years after outward symptoms have disappeared, and many a wife with ruined health never knows why. Deformity, insanity and constitutional weakness follow sometimes for generations. And there are thirty thousand cases in Dallas, ninety new cases last week! May God have mercy on Dallas! And every dance that arouses lust and leads to adultery is to blame for that shocking condition in Dallas!

You complain all you want to, but as God is my witness, I want to cry out against that, and must cry out against that. Dallas is now in the very place of Sodom and Gomorrah. Only a merciful God keeps Dallas from being blotted off the map today.

The American home is gone, and when disease comes in, terrible disease that makes people unfit for marriage, and caused by sex impurity, until one of every eight persons in Dallas have it tonight, that is a terrible thing, and preachers of God ought to speak out. I must do it. If I am honest with God, honest with you, fair to my children, I have to warn sinners, and I will. That is a terrible thing, and we ought to be excited about it.

Dr. Bass has announced that every time a prostitute is arrested, she is examined for venereal disease and they keep her in jail and treat her until she cannot spread the disease any more temporarily. Actually the disease is contagious for years after all symptoms have disappeared. For my children, I am anxious about it. I don't want that to go loose on the streets. I am sorry about it. Frankly, we had as well put the men in jail as the women. And the dance is the mother of lust, a vital cause of adultery and the disease which it causes.

NOTE: After the service Dr. _____ of the Dallas Health Department met me at the door and shook hands. He said in effect, "For some years I have worked with the Health Department and examined the prisoners in the County Jail. Everything you said tonight about this business is so, and I am glad I heard your sermon."

4. The Connection Between P. T. A. Dance and Social Disease in Dallas High Schools

That isn't all. People get terribly excited about that. Why don't you get excited that in every high school in Dallas they have dances and teach these boys and girls to dance and to fill their minds with lust and inflame their passions? Then people wonder how it happens that hundreds of cases of venereal diseases are in Dallas high schools! Of course there would be!

Dancing arouses lust. Lust leads to sex impurity, and that spreads venereal disease. It is nothing short of the rankest hypocrisy to arrest prostitutes downtown and try to stop this wave of disease while you are feeding the hopper in every public school in Dallas.

Now, listen to me, you P. T. A. women! If you want to do something about this thing, you had better start where the business begins. It is a crime against God to have a dance in the public school building, to inflame boys and girls, then kick down every woman who has sold her soul, and her body is diseased, and she is despised by everybody, given up for Hell. You try to get that girl and put her in jail and stop venereal disease. That is not the place to stop it. The place to stop it is for preachers to speak out, teachers to speak out.

And you women—God bless these P. T. A. women! Most of you don't know what your sin is. You don't realize what a horrible crime you are committing in putting on these wicked dances in the schools! If you will begin in the homes, schools, churches, and bring back old-fashioned religion and modesty and respect for womanhood and make them start out to live a clean, decent life, and stop this dirty dancing in homes and high schools, you won't have this trouble. Stop the dances that are openly cultivating lust, and you won't hear of 102 new cases of syphilis and gonorrhea in one week in Dallas!

Dallas is in for one year of the same kind of sin that caused the destruction of Sodom and Gomorrah, with the Centennial and all the sin it will bring. And if the preachers don't cry out, God will bring some terrible calamity on this terrible and wicked city.

God, help us tonight. I have brought these charges, and I dare anybody to deny them. The dance causes lust and adultery, and that is a big reason why we have thirty thousand cases of syphilis in Dallas, some of it in the high schools.

I say that the dance is guilty and brings bad company, always bad company. Dancing fosters nakedness, brings about divorces, brings about murder, and the dance is the mother of lust and adultery!

Now, my friend, that isn't all. Loose living and gambling go with it. Gambling goes with dancing just as it goes with the dirty, rotten saloon. You say, "I don't think there is any harm in gambling. I don't think there is any harm in booze; no harm in dancing."

All right, I hope you don't come weeping, begging me to pray for your boy or girl, or to ask the Governor to pardon your boy to keep him from going to the electric chair! Many other mothers have. You are going to reap what you sow. Gambling is one thing that goes with the rotten dance. Why? They are twins. They are brought on by the same low standards of morals. The same crowd does it. Every kind of revelry and fast living go with the dance. They go together.

VII. The Dance, the Road to Hell

The next thing I bring to you is this word. According to the Bible, the dance is the road to Hell. I know there are other ways to Hell and only one road to Heaven. I remind you it is the broad way that leads to Hell, and many there be that go in thereat. There are lots of excuses as to why people go to Hell. There is only one way to Heaven, and that is by the blood of Christ.

Dancing leads people to Hell. Turn just a minute to Galatians. I hope you will be prayerful. I read to you here in Galatians 5:21:

> *Envyings, murders, drunkenness, revellings, and such like: of the which I tell you before, as I have also told you in time past, that they which do such things shall not inherit the kingdom of God.*

Turn also to I Peter 4:3:

> *For the time past of our life may suffice us to have wrought the will of the Gentiles, when we walked in lasciviousness, lusts, excess of wine, revellings, banquetings, and abominable idolatries.*

There are lots in there. The kindest word you can say about the dance is it is certainly reveling, and it is certainly in bad company. Don't you see how all this goes together—the revelings and lust, with other sins? The kindest words you can say about dancing are that it is a revel, and reveling in times past was enough for a child of God. Such reveling went with wine. God said it went with lust and banqueting.

Notice, the Scripture puts lasciviousness, lust, excess of wine, revellings, banquetings, and abominable idolatries all together in I Peter 4:3. Galatians 5:21 puts envying, murder, and drunkenness with reveling, and the dance is certainly reveling! Then we are plainly told "that they which do such things shall not inherit the kingdom of God!" The reveling of the dance and the sin that goes with it keeps people out of the kingdom of God. The dance is the road to Hell.

It is plain. I put them in the same class; God puts them in the same class; the Bible puts them in the same class.

The worst thing about the dance is that millions of souls go to Hell because they love the dance and will not repent; they love the dance and will not turn to Christ. One who holds to and loves lewdness and the results it brings on will not turn to Christ, will not turn for mercy and forgiveness. That is the worst thing about the dance.

You may say, "I am young; I can have a good time now; I have a long time to be old." My friend, all the time you are old, you will be reaping what you sowed while you were young. Eternity—LOST! is a long time!

1. Reformation Is Not Enough; Sinners Must Be Saved by the Blood of Christ

Oh, tonight I would be sorry if people went away just thinking I am talking on the moral subject alone. I have what the dancer needs. I have what the drinker needs. And if you are a murderer with hands dripping with human blood, I have just what you need.

Today we need, all of us together, to come and get under the blood. "The blood of Jesus Christ his Son cleanseth us from all sin." I must preach against sin. People won't repent unless I do. I must preach against sin. People won't turn for mercy and pardon unless they know it is a sin. But my principal object is to get you to Jesus Christ.

You might say, "I am going to quit my dancing." I hope you will. But you need more than that. You need salvation by the blood of Christ. You need to be born again, to have a change of heart. Quit your dancing, yes, but trust Christ today for salvation!

I have five girls. For their sake and yours, I beg you to leave off dancing. If there is a man here who dances, don't do it. It will put you in bad company. It will lead you to drink and lots of other things wrong. It will make you a prey to evil. It will lead you to where you thought you would never go. I hope you will quit the dance.

But, my friend, I don't want just to get people to reform, just to tell you the dance will take you to Hell. I come to offer you Jesus who died for sinners. He will save you, whoever you are, whether a dancer, a drinker—whatever you are.

May I say this word here? I don't want to put myself upon a pedestal and say, "I am holier than thou." We are made of the same clay. Christ died for me just as He died for you. I just trusted Jesus Christ, and He forgave me, gave me sweet peace in my heart. You can have it today. You need it today.

Is there a sinner away from God who needs peace? Dancing won't give it; drinking won't give it. Turn to Christ and get forgiveness and peace and joy tonight and go away happy. Don't you want that? Then take it today by trusting Jesus Christ for forgiveness.

2. Who Is on the Lord's Side?

Moses ended his appeal after the dancing, necking party by saying, "Who is on the Lord's side?" And I want to say the same thing tonight. Before we go away, who will say, "I am on the side of decency, on the side of good homes, morality, sobriety. I am on the side against the dance"?

That isn't enough. I want everybody here tonight to say, "I am going to be on Jesus' side." Who is on the Lord's side? Who is against dancing and drinking? I can't cast any rocks in this business. I do not dance. But I have sinned in many ways. We must all, you and I alike, come the same way, sinners trusting Christ for forgiveness. God loves you, Christ died for you, and Jesus is ready to save you tonight. Will you trust Him with all your heart?

I want to have prayer tonight. As God is my witness, I have been plain. I have taken time. I haven't tried to appeal to your emotions or your sympathy. I have tried to be honest, as I would want any man to be with my own children. I am going to ask

God to save sinners tonight. I don't care how much you reform, every woman might be as chaste and virtuous as she ever was, but unless you are born again, unless you let Jesus into your heart, you will go to Hell. Many say, "I am for good homes, against lust, dance," etc., and yet you might turn down Jesus and die and go to Hell.

How many want Jesus, will take Him, love Him, trust Him, let Him save you, and let Him make you His child and meet me in Heaven one of these days?

25—"Hast Thou Found Me, O Mine Enemy?"

(Sermon preached Sunday night, September 13, 1936. Stenographically reported.)

Ahab was king of Israel, with his capital at Samaria. He married the wicked Queen Jezebel. Ahab coveted the vineyard of Naboth for a garden of vegetables but could not buy it nor trade for it. So wicked Jezebel took the king's seal and sent orders to have Naboth stoned for blasphemy, then Ahab went down to take possession. Now read the rest of the story in I Kings, chapter 21, verses 17 to 29:

> *And the word of the Lord came to Elijah the Tishbite, saying,*
>
> *Arise, go down to meet Ahab king of Israel, which is in Samaria: behold, he is in the vineyard of Naboth, whither he is gone down to possess it.*
>
> *And thou shalt speak unto him, saying, Thus saith the Lord, Hast thou killed, and also taken possession? And thou shalt speak unto him saying, Thus saith the Lord, in the place where dogs licked the blood of Naboth shall dogs lick thy blood, even thine.*
>
> *And Ahab said to Elijah, Hast thou found me, O mine enemy? And he answered, I have found thee: because thou hast sold thyself to work evil in the sight of the Lord.*

Oh, how Ahab hated Elijah. And he feared him with a holy fear, and he said, 'Hast thou found me? I didn't know I would have to face you and face God. Oh, my enemy, have you found me?' Now the rest of verse 20 says:

> *And he answered, I have found thee: because thou hast*

sold thyself to work evil in the sight of the Lord.

Behold, I will bring evil upon thee, and will take away thy posterity, and will cut off from Ahab him that pisseth against the wall, and him that is shut up and left in Israel,

And will make thine house like the house of Jeroboam the son of Nebat, and like the house of Baasha the son of Ahijah, for the provocation wherewith thou hast provoked me to anger, and made Israel to sin.

And of Jezebel also spake the Lord, saying, The dogs shall eat Jezebel by the wall of Jezreel.

Him that dieth of Ahab in the city the dogs shall eat: and him that dieth in the field shall the fowls of the air eat.

But there was none like unto Ahab, which did sell himself to work wickedness in the sight of the Lord, whom Jezebel his wife stirred up.

And he did very abominably in following idols, according to all things as did the Amorites, whom the Lord cast out before the children of Israel.

And it came to pass, when Ahab heard those words, that he rent his clothes, and put sackcloth upon his flesh, and fasted, and lay in sackcloth, and went softly.

And the word of the Lord came to Elijah the Tishbite, saying,

Seest thou how Ahab humbleth himself before me? because he humbleth himself before me, I will not bring the evil in his days; but in his son's days will I bring the evil upon his house.

And now let us turn a little further over into the next chapter and begin reading at verse 34. Ahab and Jehoshaphat had gone out to war at Ramoth-gilead, against the king of Syria.

And a certain man drew a bow at a venture, and smote the king of Israel [Ahab] *between the joints of the harness:* [He had a coat of mail on—a great breastplate there and greaves over his legs, a plate over his back. He even had his feet covered up, and the only place where an arrow could get in is where the armor joined together. He couldn't be stiff all over. And there the arrow hit him between the joints of his harness.] *wherefore he said unto the driver of his chariot, Turn thine hand, and carry me out of the host* [out of the army]; *for I am wounded.*

And the battle increased that day: and the king was stayed up in his chariot against the Syrians, and died at even: and the blood ran out of the wound into the midst of the chariot.

God had said, 'Where the dogs licked the blood of Naboth when you stoned him there at Jezreel, there the same dogs will lick the blood of Ahab.' How can that happen when he was killed away over there at Ramoth-gilead?

And there went a proclamation throughout the host about the going down of the sun, saying, Every man to his city, and every man to his own country.

So the king died, and was brought to Samaria; and they buried the king in Samaria.

And one washed the chariot in the pool of Samaria; and the dogs licked up his blood; and they washed his armour; according unto the word of the Lord which he spake.

That is a remarkable story. I can't take time for the rest of it, but it came about that wicked Jezebel was killed too, and God appointed a man to do it.

Jehu said to two men about Jezebel as she looked out of a window, "Throw her down!" And they threw her down, and the dogs ate Jezebel, that wicked woman.

Listen, I want you to get this word of God. Here are blessed and eternal lessons that men must face. Prayerfully face them tonight as I speak.

I. Ahab Sold Himself to the Devil

Elijah, the prophet of God, said to Ahab, "I have found thee: because thou hast sold thyself to work evil in the sight of the Lord." Sin enslaves a man. If there is a man here tonight who is not in touch with God, a backslider or a lost sinner, that man

has sold himself to work evil. A man who is not right with God
has sold out.

Judas Iscariot sold out—sold his influence. Said he, "I know
where Jesus goes to pray, and for thirty pieces of silver I will
lead you out to the Garden of Gethsemane, and the One I kiss
will be the One." Judas sold himself, sold his eternal welfare, he
sold his testimony for the value of thirty pieces of silver.

Ahab also sold himself to work evil. A man who goes into sin
has sold out for a little bit of pleasure—for the wild, dirty crowd
that he runs with. He will break his wife's heart, lead his
children in sin, and make himself a slave for a little sinful
pleasure.

What do I mean by selling out to sin? I wish people would
realize the awful enormity of sin. When a man turns loose to
sin, he turns over control to demons. You may not realize it, but
this world is full of demons. The Devil goes around like a
roaring lion seeking whom he may devour. Some men are
possessed by devils now. Jesus said in the model prayer and
taught us to pray, "And deliver us from evil." In the original
Greek, He really taught us to pray, "Deliver us from the evil
one," from Satan and from the evil spirits around about us.

When you feel impressed to do so and so, and feel the
impression is from God, you had better try it and see. If you
have sold out, that may be a spirit of the Devil leading you
wrong. If anybody gets in a fight and commits some sin and
says, "Well, I felt led to"—look out! You may be led by evil
spirits.

Ahab sinned and sinned again and again and finally turned
himself over to devils and to evil spirits to do the wickedness
suggested by his wife. He sold himself out to work evil.

It is a bad thing to go on in sin. It is important that one not go
on in sin. Every boy and girl should be saved while young
because the older you get, the more the Devil binds you, takes a
mortgage on you. When you sell out to him, after awhile you
become a slave and can't control yourself. Your influence is not
your own, your temper is not your own, your thoughts are not

your own. A man who goes on in sin cannot think the thoughts he wants to.

A man who gambles says, "All right, I will go back to work and be the same man." But something has happened to that man. Work is not now very attractive. Working hard for a few dollars a day—that is too hard when you can take a lucky tip on a dog race or on "daily doubles" which might net a thousand to one, or a hundred to one—who knows! "I will try it," he says. Working is mighty slow going when you might get ten or fifteen dollars in a game of chance. Something happens to the man who gambles. He sells himself out to gambling. The Devil takes possession of his heart, soul and spirit.

Somebody gets angry and thinks it is a little matter. It never is a little matter to get mad. You sell yourself out when you get mad. You sow your wickedness, and a lot of bitterness springs up in your heart and controls you. You may think when you get mad it will be over in a minute. But poison is distilled there. You are never the same. Only God can take away the evil things when a man has sold himself to sin.

So about bitterness, malice, hate, unforgiveness. That is the reason the Bible said, "Let not the sun go down on your wrath." We ought to beware of the evil ones around us.

Ahab sold himself to sin.

If there is a girl here tonight who does not want to become a harlot and lose her virtue, who does not want to have heartache and heartbreak, who does not want to fall into ruin, don't open one little gap for the Devil. Don't drink the first glass of beer. Don't get on the dance floor. Don't run with the Devil's crowd. Don't go with an unsaved man or even a backslidden Christian. Don't let down the bars in one particular. That is one way sin takes possession, and you are a slave to sin.

Ahab was to be pitied. Yonder was a beautiful woman. The Bible says she was vain. Even when she was an older woman she was beautiful. When she heard that Jehu was coming, she went and "painted her face and tired her head." She was a beauty even then. She painted herself up. She didn't know she was painting herself and dressing herself to be trampled under feet by the horses and to be eaten by the dogs and have the dogs gnaw her bones. When Ahab married that woman and went with her to serve Baal—beware! He sold out to sin. Sold out to sin!

You know it is a sad business, Mr. Benavides. A lot of people come before your court—a narcotic case, or a drunk case. Many a man has good intentions, but he has a weakness, an appetite, a habit, a rut of character, a groove in his brain—something inside that has already sold out. He has a traitor in his own gate. He has sold out to sin!

It isn't that every man wants to be a sot drunkard who comes before your court, but if one sells out to sin, sin enslaves him and he is no more the man that he was.

It is said that a Greek tyrant, or king, of a certain Grecian city, was jealous of a certain great blacksmith in his town. Perhaps he was not loyal to the king. The blacksmith was brought before the king, and the king said, "I am told you can make a chain that no man can break." The man said he could. The king asked him to make one for him. So he made a chain so fine and welded every link so carefully—that was not so easy to do then—and when he got through, he brought it back and held it up before the king and said, "It is so strong that if it had an elephant on each end pulling, they couldn't break it."

The king said to one of his officers, "Bind *him* with it."

So it is. We make the chain that binds us and enslaves us as Ahab did when he let down the bars and gave way to sin and sold out.

Is there a lost man here? I wouldn't trifle with God. I talked to an unsaved woman down at the zoo today. She said, "I'm not ready yet." My friends, you trifle with that as if you thought you had forever to make a choice, as if you thought it didn't matter, that tomorrow would be just as good. If your baby were dying with diphtheria, tomorrow wouldn't be just as good for a serum. If you had a case of acute appendicitis, tomorrow would not be just as good to call the doctor. It might be too late then. The man who opens his heart to sin and sells out to sin, perhaps tomorrow will be too late for him ever to be saved. I wouldn't sell out to sin like Ahab did.

Sin is so hateful, so terrible, so enslaving, so pitiless, so merciless, that we should hate it and flee from it and run to the Lord for mercy. Ahab, Ahab, you sold out to sin! When Jezebel suggested a thing, conscience said, "Ahab, this will involve the murder of a good man, an innocent man." "Well, I am in it now. I have already married this woman and I am going her way." He sold out to it and went ahead and murdered Naboth for his vineyard. God booked up murder against him. God said, "All right, you will meet it. Your blood will be licked by the dogs. Your family will be cut off. Every male member will meet a violent death." "But I have already started out," Ahab said, "so I am going on."

Don't sell out to sin. I would hate it, avoid it, run from it. Is there a man here tonight who thinks, "What difference do a few drinks make?" My friend, it may mean the difference in ruin and success for your boy. A few drinks may mean the once happy home shattered and one day shame and disgrace and broken hearts. It may mean the difference between freedom and prison for something you will do when you are drinking and do not know anything about it. It means the difference between the wrath of God and His mercy. Don't sell out to sin!

But you think it is so cheap. You don't know all you buy when you sell out to the Devil. You buy trouble and certain judgment and punishment. Don't do it!

II. Ahab's Sin Found Him Out

What else about this man? He said when Elijah came and faced him, "Hast thou found me, O mine enemy?" Elijah answered, "I have found thee: because thou hast sold thyself to work evil in the sight of the Lord—I have found thee."

When we sin, we feel it is not such an important matter. The whole human race feels it is such a light matter when we sin. Oh, I know it isn't! Proverbs says the wicked woman commits adultery, then licks her lips and says, "I have done no evil."

Ahab said, "I want that vegetable garden. That vineyard of

Naboth's would make a fine place for early spring radishes, greens and onions. I could get everything fresh for the table down here. I will buy it or trade for it."

But Naboth said, "I can't sell it. It belonged to my father and my grandfather and my great-grandfather. I couldn't trade my vineyard and I couldn't sell it."

Ahab didn't like that. Then finally wife Jezebel said, "I will fix it for you," and Ahab let her do it. She said, "Take this man Naboth and set him on high and get two men to swear that he blasphemed God and the king and have him stoned."

They did what she said. Jezebel came to Ahab and said, "Now get up. Don't be turning your face to the wall. You have been missing your dinner. Eat, drink and be merry. I have everything fixed. They did what I told them to do. Naboth is dead. Go down now and take the vineyard."

"Go down and get the vineyard"—do you think that is all there is to this? He might have said, "To be sure it is. Why not? I am king, am I not? I didn't do it; the elders of the city did it."

Oh, yes, my friend, I know you didn't do it, but God knows your heart. The things you think are hidden from everybody will one day come out. Murder will out!

Ahab went down to take his vineyard, not thinking about the widow who was left, the little children, that innocent blood that cried out to God Almighty from that ground. That did not bother him. He had no conscience about that. He wasn't bothered about that.

But, my friend, God witnessed it. I wish you would realize there is an all-seeing eye that knows and sees and records. As the Negro people sing, "My God's a writin' all the time." God is writing down in His book. Don't think you will get by. There will be the man of God to point his finger in your face and say, "I have found you!"

When Ahab got down there and saw Elijah, he said, "Hast thou found me, O mine enemy?" Elijah answered, "I have found you."

My friend, hear me. As surely as there is a God, your sin will find you out. I know this to be true. I know God is merciful, and God is kind, but your sin will find you out.

Naboth is dead. His wife was ignorant of the whole plot. His children do not know about it. The elders of the city knew of the wicked plot but nobody will involve himself. But it will come out. Murder will out! It is coming out, brother, it is coming out! The Bible teaches that which was whispered in the corner shall be shouted from the housetops. Whatsoever a man soweth, that shall he also reap.

Let me press on your heart, as I have before, if one sin could get by unjudged, uncondemned, unpaid for; if one sin could get by God, that one sin would make a chaos out of God's universe and pull God from His throne and put out the glory of Heaven, ruin angels and take every soul out of God's hand. If one time Satan could make God a failure, if he could make God one time unjust and not able to take care of His own, not able to bring sin to judgment, Satan would have whipped God forever.

No, my friends, listen to me. As certain as there is a God, your sin finds you out.

If God had no witnesses but the dogs that licked the blood of Naboth, had had nobody to witness it but those dogs, those dogs would see that justice was done. Those same dogs, in the same place that licked the blood of Naboth, licked the blood of this wicked king. How could that be? That is not hard for God.

I know a man who has gone far in sin. I know a man who has deceived thousands. But just as certain as there is a God, this man will meet judgment. One time the cry of innocent Christians, misled by him, the cry of preachers he has abused and lied about and slandered, will be avenged. And as surely as there is a God in Heaven, his sin will come out. One day he will say, "Hast thou found me, O mine enemy?" and God will say, "I have found you."

My friend, listen to me. As certain as there is a God, sin must be paid for. I call on you today, hear me and take warning. Sin is a terrible thing, and what terrible things it brings! Sin, admitted and confessed and forsaken, will have God's mercy, but when one goes boldly on his way with a proud, haughty, scornful heart, hearing no reproof and turning his back on the preaching of the Gospel, one day he will come as did Ahab and face a man of God and say, "Hast thou found me, O mine enemy?" And he will say, "I have found thee! I have found thee! I HAVE FOUND THEE!"

My friends, God brings sin to judgment! And your sin will find you out. Your chickens will come home to roost. Ahab met his own doom. "Hast thou found me, O mine enemy? Hast thou found me?"

That is very much like the case of David when he committed the terrible sin with Uriah's wife. "That is in the past now," David thought. "I will not do that any more. That was bad."

But one day David's baby got sick. God's prophet Nathan came to David and said, "David, I know about a case down here, involving two fellows. One had a whole lot of sheep, and the other had one little ewe lamb. He petted it and treated it like a daughter, kept it in his bosom. . . .

"The rich man had a man come to see him one day and he grabbed his neighbor's lamb and roasted that. He took the poor man's lamb and roasted it for that visitor. The rich man had plenty for himself but he took his neighbor's pet lamb.

David said, "That man has to die. He is not fit to live. But before he is killed, he will have to restore fourfold. Take four lambs and give those to the other fellow."

And Nathan said, "David, you are the man! God says to you, 'I gave you your master's kingdom, Saul's kingdom. I gave thee thy master's wives unto thy bosom. And if that were not enough I would have done thus and so.' Here Uriah was a good man spending his life and willing to die for you and you take his wife and lead her into sin. Then you sent him down and got him killed! David, God hasn't forgotten."

"Hast thou found me, O mine enemy? Hast thou found me?"

"Yes," God says, "I have found you."

Your sin will find you out.

Ahab went to battle. So the Lord said (a prophet told him), "You are going to die." "Oh, is that so?" Ahab said! He got out among the other folks, took off his kingly robes and disguised himself. The Syrians said, "Don't smite anybody but the king of Israel."

Ahab thought he could cheat God. He dressed like a common soldier and got Jehoshaphat the king of Judah to wear his robes like a king. Nobody could tell he was a king. They chose Jehoshaphat the king of Judah to wear his robes like a king. Nobody could tell he was a king. They chose Jehoshaphat, thinking that he was Ahab, till he cried out, and someone said, "That is the king of Judah; let him alone."

One man saw from a distance Ahab disguised, and said, "Say, I believe I can hit that Israelite over yonder." So not knowing it was the king, he drew his bow at the fellow. He pulled back and turned loose. The arrow sped to its mark and hit the only place it could do any good. Underneath the common garments was a coat of mail, and the arrow hit between the joints of the armor.

Ahab said, "Get me to one side, I am wounded. Drive out to one side." So the driver drove the chariot and Ahab was out there, propped up in the chariot for awhile, but about sundown, he died and the blood formed a pool in the rich chariot of the king. The blood matted and coagulated on the floor of that chariot as the life blood flowed out of the wounded king. It was a just retribution for the blood of Naboth who was slain just because a wicked man wanted a vegetable garden.

So blood gathered in the chariot. After awhile a man blew a trumpet and said, "Every man to his own city and to his own house. The battle is over. The king is dead."

A man drove the chariot back to Samaria. A man drove down to a pool and washed out that clotted blood, washed off the king's armor, and out here where Naboth not long before has been killed and the blood run down from that innocent head as they knocked him in the head with stones to please a wicked king—those same dogs came as they washed the chariot and lapped up the blood of wicked Ahab! His sin found him out. And your sin will find you out.

Just an accident? It was not an accident with God. The man who shot the arrow didn't know he was aiming at the king, and he did not know he would hit him between the joints of his armor, but God did.

My friends, I have come to this conclusion. If a man is right with God, he need fear no man. Every arrow will fall short. If a man is not right with God, even if a man pull a bow at a venture, it will strike between the joints of his harness where he least expected it. No man is safe out of God's sweet will, in disobedience to God. Pleasing God, every man is perfectly safe. All may pull their bows in vain when God surrounds a man; but when God withdraws His hand, your blood will run out for the first man who draws a bow at a venture from   afar off.

My friend, sin finds you out. Don't let this slip out of your mind. Your sin, your sin, your sin will find you out just as certain as it did king Ahab. Your sin will find you out!

III. God's Prophets Are Not the Enemies of Sinners

Did you notice the king said, "Hast thou found me, O mine enemy?" There are those who believe preachers are their enemies. The people murmured against God and against Moses and said, "Why have you brought us out to die in the wilderness, to let our babies starve?"

Moses went to God and said, "O God, they are about to stone me thinking I am their enemy. They hate me. O God, what shall I do?" The people thought Moses was their enemy—a good man like Moses. Isn't that sad? Even Aaron and Miriam and others said, "Moses takes too much authority. Moses is our enemy." He wasn't their enemy.

One time when the people grumbled against God and against Moses, God sent fiery serpents among them that bit them and much people of Israel died. The people saw then their mistake when they began to die like flies. So you know what they did? They came to Moses and said, "Moses, pray for us."

A preacher is not your enemy if he is a good preacher and honest with God. The preacher stirs deep down in your heart. You are a sinner and you think he preaches too plain. He is not your enemy. I preach sometimes on the dance and kindred questions. Sometimes mothers say I talk too plain before young people. How little they know that their young people talk plainer among themselves than I do.

Somebody says, "That preacher gets after my sin. He is

against me. He is my enemy." If you only knew it, Ahab, the best friend you have is this old hairy prophet Elijah! This prophet would lead you back to God and lead the people out of sin and keep them from captivity and from the wrath of God which is upon them and upon you. "Hast thou found me, O mine enemy?" It is a sad thing for people to believe that a preacher is their enemy. But so often that is true.

And it is sad when people on the outside think preachers are their enemies.

Moses loved people so. He led them out of Egypt and wept before God to keep God from destroying them. Yet they thought he was their enemy.

Paul went before the Sanhedrin and preached Christ. One commanded another to slap him in the face. Everywhere Jews hated Paul, yet he said, "I could wish myself accursed from God for my brethren . . . according to the flesh." All that love—yet they hated him! Though they would have killed him, he loved them.

A preacher is not your enemy. I wish I was known as a friend of sinners. Jesus was. I wish I was known as one who loves people in trouble, loves people in sin.

I have been moved recently by several remarkable jail services we have held. My heart goes out to those men in jail. They are suspicious. They hear a good deal of preaching. Brother Grady, I have found in recent days that God has opened the hearts of these men. They say, "Let Brother Stroh sing so and so." They ask for certain numbers. What touched my heart was those seventeen and eighteen and nineteen and twenty-year-old boys lined up on the second floor. Some of them frankly let the tears run down their faces as they leaned on their elbows against the bars and listened as I preached.

A preacher is not your enemy. He is the friend of all sinners. O sinners, we ought to condemn sin. I must be against liquor, lewdness and wickedness in every form, and I ought to preach against it. But I ought to go out to weep over sinners. You can't be like Jesus unless you do that. I am not your enemy. I am your friend.

If any here tonight have a broken home, I hope you will come and ask me to pray. A woman asked me the other day to write her husband. She wanted to get things patched up. I did write him. I was glad to. I wanted to be a blessing. I have gone to them in heartbreak and trouble to tell them if there is anything I could do, I would like to.

My friend, the preacher is not your enemy.

"Hast thou found me, O mine enemy?" That wasn't what Ahab ought to have said to this preacher. He should have said, "Pray for me. I have sinned against God."

I wish you would run with preachers. Come to my house to see me. Come to my office to see me, sinner. Let me help you.

A girl came this morning, a grown young woman, and sat back there. When I went back to shake hands, she said, "I certainly enjoyed this service this morning."

I asked her if she were a Christian, and she said, "No."

"Did you ever make a start for the Lord?"

She said, "I have never been saved."

In a little bit she was saved and was glad to tell me.

Why run away from Christians? Don't you know that anybody who loves you and prays for you is not your enemy? A Christian is not your enemy. Tonight if I were not a Christian or if I had been saved but had gone a long ways off, I would look up anybody who loves God and ask him or her to pray for me. Do you want help and encouragement? I wish tonight you would seek me out and tell me you want my prayers. Oh, how glad I would be to help you!

I remember when I was twelve or thirteen years old. I had been converted when I was nine. My father had discouraged me and other people had. I didn't live for the Lord and I thought I was a lost sinner. I went those sad years with no joy, no peace. My father was busy, though a mighty good man.

One day old Brother Perry Harmonson preached. He said, "Anybody here who wants help come and shake hands and tell me you want me to pray for you." I did. I went when the service was over and said, "Brother Harmonson, pray for me."

That old country preacher said, "I will, John. Will you pray for yourself?" I agreed to do it.

When I got home I went out in the horse lot, and under the buggy shed and I prayed. Then beside my bed I prayed again. Then I thought, if Jesus died for me, why should I have to beg God? If Brother Harmonson wanted me saved, surely God does. Maybe God has already forgiven me. I will turn it over to Him and go to bed and to sleep. I found out that away back yonder I had gotten forgiveness. I took the whole thing up and went on my way rejoicing.

You ought not think a man of God is your enemy.

IV. Sinner, God Is Not Your Enemy

If I said that about preachers, how much more ought I to say it about God! "Hast thou found me, O mine enemy?" God is not your enemy. God loves men, and men think God is their enemy! Jesus died and poured out His blood for sinners. And sinners think He is their enemy! Some of you men never mention His name unless you do it with a dirty oath. Your enemy? No, He is the best Friend you ever had. He sought you and loved you and wept over you and died for you. He sent His Spirit to plead with you. No, He is not your enemy. He loves you. He is my Friend. He is not my enemy.

When Adam sinned he thought, "God will hate me." He couldn't face God but ran away and hid himself in the bushes. That wasn't the thing to do. He ought to have said, "God is the One who made me. He is the One who loves me. Everybody else might go against me but God loves me." He ought to have run to God, but instead, he ran from God and thought God was his enemy. Afraid of God!

Brother Cunningham, if I have sinned, I am not to say, "God is my enemy, I will get away, away from God." But I ought to say, "God loves me. He is the best Friend I have. He is my Father, and Jesus died for me. I will run to Him for help."

Do it. He will help you!

Ahab sinned. Ahab led Israel to sin. Ahab sold himself to sin. He and Jezebel killed preachers, murdered an innocent man. But Ahab, God is your friend!

Tell all sinners you meet God loves them though they have gone far in sin. Jesus died for them. You ought to know it. We don't have enough love and shed enough tears. We ought to let men know that God loves them.

Two men at Sherman, Texas, came to my door. I wasn't at home. They were underworld characters. My wife was afraid, because they wouldn't tell their names. When I came in the back way she told me two men were out front waiting for me. "Do you think you should go out there? I wouldn't get in the car with them." I had been preaching awfully hard against sin.

I said to one, "What is your name?"

"Never mind," he said, "we had rather not tell you now. Would you mind getting in the car?"

"No," I said, "I wouldn't mind."

"We are not here for any trouble," one of the men said. "I sat away back on the rocks where the old courthouse was torn down and heard you preach several nights. I saw people get saved. We didn't come to the front. We are not fit to do that. Decent people wouldn't come to the meeting if we were up there."

"You are welcome to sit on the front seat," I said.

But one of them said, "No, I couldn't. I just wanted to tell you I have gone so far in sin—is there any chance for me?"

One said, "My dad has spent $25,000 trying to break me from the dope habit."

The other said, "My mother's hair is white and her heart is broken over my sin. I have committed every sin under Heaven. But, oh, last night I saw So and So saved, and, we just wondered if there was any chance for anybody who has gone so far down as we have. Is there any chance?"

That broke my heart. I told them, "God loves you just like He loved me when I was a sinner. We are all in the same boat. God loves you, and He will save you if you trust Him."

I remember how the tears sprang in one man's eyes as he said, "That is not true. You don't understand how mean we are." Turning to the other, he said, "Did you hear this preacher putting himself in the same boat with us?" He was saved a few days later.

God is not an enemy of sinners. God must bring sin to punishment and condemnation, wrath and trouble on sinners, but, my friend, God is not your enemy. God loves you. Tell God, "O God, then I am a sinner, but if Jesus died for me, I will love Him and serve Him."

The woman taken in adultery, in the very act, might well have believed God was her enemy. She had broken the law, she had gone into sin. They brought this shamefaced woman with downcast eyes and bowed head before Jesus and said, "What do you say, Jesus?"

Jesus stooped and wrote on the ground. I have often wondered what He wrote in the sand. That day as the Pharisees said, "What will we do with her?" Jesus said, "All right, you want to stone her, don't you? If there is anybody here without sin, go ahead and cast the first stone. If you don't have any sin yourself, you can stone her." And Jesus stooped down again and wrote with His finger in the sand.

I wonder what He wrote. The oldest one must have said, "I can't do that." And their consciences began to smite them, and one by one they walked away.

But what about the poor woman? I wonder why she didn't leave? Because she knew this Man was not her enemy but her friend! He is a Friend of sinners. He said to the woman, "Woman, where are thine accusers? Hath no man condemned thee?" And she answered, "No man, Lord." "Neither do I condemn thee. Go and sin no more!" said Jesus.

One day, the saddest in the history of the world, there hung three men on three crosses on the brow of a hill outside Jerusalem. On the central cross was the Son of God, Jesus, my Saviour. On either side were two thieves, malefactors, criminals. They cursed and swore and railed at Jesus, these two, on this side and on that side, and said, "Get us down from here if you are the Son of God. Why don't you save yourself and save us?"

Those two cursed Him as He and they hung there. After awhile one turned—he had heard Him say, "Father, forgive them for they know not what they do"—and he said, "Lord, when thou comest into thy kingdom, remember me." Jesus said, "I will. Today shalt thou be with me in paradise."

Jesus is not the enemy of sinners. If you will repent, admit you are guilty, if you will turn to Jesus, if you want mercy, if you want forgiveness, then He is not your enemy but the best Friend any sinner ever had.

You think the friends of the wine cup are your friends. They are not. You may think wine, women and song are your friends. They are not. The prodigal boy, after he landed in the hogpen of sin, could bear witness that they are not your friends.

Many a man has had his heart broken when sinful friends left him. I will never forget when I preached in a country church near Decatur on how Judas betrayed Jesus and came back and threw the money down. When Judas said, "Take this money. It is the price of blood," they said, "We can't do it. . .see to that yourself. We did not do that." He threw the money down and went and hanged himself. I said then, "Your companions in sin never bring comfort in trouble. They are not your friends. They leave you alone in your shame."

I saw a hush go over that crowd. A young woman burst afresh into tears. Conviction was all over the congregation. I didn't know why then. But when the service was over, after profound conviction everywhere and people saved, I turned aside and the pastor said to me, "Did you know this? When you said your friends in sin are not your friends at all and they leave you, did you notice what happened? Did you see a certain young woman begin to weep? She just last Sunday came and made her confession. She is to have an illegitimate baby. But the young man who led her into sin has already ruined another girl in another community. He had promised to marry her, but has already gone on somewhere else now."

No, they are not your friends. Your best Friend is Jesus who died for sinners.

Tonight if there is a sinner here who has gone deep in sin, into black sin, bloody sin, terrible sin—if your sin is as black as Ahab's, don't call God your enemy. He is not your enemy. He is your Friend. He loves you. He longs for you. Jesus died for you. Come tonight and be saved.

I read a story Dr. H. A. Ironside related in his book, *Charge*

That to My Account. He said:

My eldest son taught me a lesson along this line when he was just a little fellow. There was nothing he liked to play more than bear. First, we had to put some chairs in one corner of the room, with an opening between them. That was the bear's den. Then I had to get down on all fours, with a big shaggy overcoat over me and be the bear. The little fellow would walk past the den, trying to look as if he had no idea that a bear was anywhere near, when suddenly the savage beast would take after him, and we would run through one room and into another. The little fellow was pretty fleet on his feet, but, of course, he would always be caught at last.

The last time we ever played bear, he had run right into the corner of the kitchen, but the corner didn't open. He had his face right in the corner, and was so excited, that he just screamed. Suddenly, you know, the bear was about to spring, when the little fellow wheeled right about face, caught his breath, and said, "I am not a bit afraid. You are not a bear; you are just my own dear papa," and he jumped right into my arms.

Then good Dr. Ironside said:

I got to my feet, held the little fellow close to me, and tried to quiet him. I said to myself as I walked up and down with him, "Blessed God, it was just like this with me once. I was running away from Thee. I was afraid of Thee. I thought You wanted to destroy me. I tried to find a hiding place from Thee, but Thou didst never give me up."

I remembered the time years before when God ran me into a corner, and I couldn't get away; and instead of trying to run, I turned to Him in repentance, in confession, and said, "I am not afraid of Thee. Thou art not my enemy. I throw myself into Thy loving arms. Thou art my refuge. In Thy tender care and loving mercy, I find a hiding place."

Maybe like Ahab you have gone to a vineyard to possess it and your sins face you. You may say, "I don't know what to do about my sins." I will tell you what to do. Think not that God is your enemy. I would say, "He is my Friend. He died for sinners. He loves me. I will cast myself into His arms. What He does about it—this loving Saviour—will be all right with me."

The prodigal boy had gone into a far country. He may have thought, "What will Dad say to me!" I imagine he thought, "I wasted money he labored a lifetime for—what will my father say about it? I couldn't face him." After a while, I imagine he thought, "I would like to go home but I can't. I have gone so far, I can't turn back. I've wasted my money and played the fool. I've gone with harlots; I've worn out my shoes, my robe is gone. I can't! I can't!"

But one time he got so far he couldn't do anything else. He couldn't run any farther down in the hogpen, so he said, "I will arise and go to my father." He wasn't afraid any more. His father ran to meet him and fell on his neck and kissed him!

God loves you, sinner. God loves you. I love you, too. I would like to help you. My heart goes out to you. God loves you. He is not your enemy. He is your Friend. Anybody in trouble, sorrow, heartbreak—any lost sinner or any child of God who has played the fool, missed the way, lost your joy, do come back to the best Friend any poor sinner ever had. Jesus died to save sinners—Paul never could forget it—"of whom I am chief." That is a faithful saying and worthy of all acceptation, isn't it? "This is a faithful saying and worthy of all acceptation, that Christ Jesus came into the world to save sinners; of whom I am chief" (I Tim. 1:15).

Are you a sinner? Have you done wrong? Have you played the fool? Then fall into the hands of Jesus who loves sinners like you and me.

Prayer: Our Father, tonight show us that our sins are on our trail. Teach us that Thou are not our enemy but our Friend. You love us. Show men that if in their hearts they will turn from sin, the enemy, You love them and You will bless and forgive.

Convict sinners. Give blessing to every Christian here, Lord. Bless saved people, church members, men who have drifted down, down, down. O Lord, I would not come to add this weight upon them but to say Thou dost love them. Oh, these men who drank, who cursed; these men who have sinned—let them see that You love them, that You are their Friend.

May they arise and come to the Father tonight. Let them do it. If there are boys or girls who have sinned and gone on lost, lost, lost, let them say, "I will not hide out and let Satan keep me away from God. I will run to Him and let Him kiss away my sins and my tears." Lord, tonight save!

(Several came.)

26—"Let Us Alone!"

(Sermon preached May 28, 1939, Galilean Baptist Church, Dallas, Texas. Stenographically recorded.)

And in the synagogue there was a man, which had a spirit of an unclean devil, and cried out with a loud voice,

Saying, Let us alone; what have we to do with thee, thou Jesus of Nazareth? art thou come to destroy us? I know thee who thou art; the Holy One of God.

And Jesus rebuked him, saying, Hold thy peace, and come out of him. And when the devil had thrown him in the midst, he came out of him, and hurt him not.—Luke 4:33-35.

Let me read verse 34 again. The devils said, "Let us alone; what have we to do with thee, thou Jesus of Nazareth? art thou come to destroy us? I know thee who thou art; the Holy One of God."

Let us alone! What a strange thing for anybody to say to God! Let us alone! Mankind has down through the years said to God, "Let us alone. Let us alone. What have we got to do with You? What business do You have interfering with our business? What business do You have with our daily lives? When we come to die, that is different. But about our work, our homes, our pleasures, let us alone, God. Let us alone!" Man cries out, "Are you come to destroy us? Do you want to take the good things away from us, and our pleasures? Do you want to take all our joy away? Let us alone; do not meddle with us, God!"

The sinner says, "Let me alone, God. Do not convict me with the Holy Spirit. I do not want people talking to me and reading the Bible to me. I will not read the Bible. I do not want You convicting me and calling me. Let me alone!"

Mankind cries out to God, mankind possessed of devils, misled, deceived, abused, and diseased by Satan, and says, "Let us alone!"

And on these tragic words, I will build the message tonight.

I. Christians May Be Let Alone

First, I will say that Christians may sometimes be let alone. Is that not a strange thing? I know it is true, of course, that the Holy Spirit will never depart from a child of God. Every one who has been born again has had the Holy Spirit move into his body, and the Holy Spirit has made him a child of God. Every Christian, then, has the Spirit of God. He cannot leave your body, because He dwells within you. And, too, Jesus said, "Lo, I am with you alway." Surely the Spirit of God in that sense will never wholly depart from the child of God.

A saved person has everlasting life. But in another sense, the Holy Spirit can depart, and God can depart from a Christian. I call your attention to some Scriptures on that matter. You remember the Lord said about Ephraim, "Ephraim is joined to idols: let him alone" (Hos. 4:17). I know that the Jews in the tribe of Ephraim were not all Christians, but some were, and God said to leave them to their idolatry and their sin.

And the book of Judges tells how Samson laid his head in Delilah's lap. Time and time again he joked and talked with her about where his strength lay—that strength that God had given him that made him the strongest man that ever lived. Finally, with her woman's wiles, she found the secret of his power; and he told her, "I have been a Nazarite from my mother's womb, and if my hair were cut off, I would be like any other man." And he did not know until she cut off his hair and cried, "The Philistines be upon thee," that his power was gone. He still thought, "I will arise as at other times and go out." But listen to these fatal words: "And he wist not that the Lord was departed from him!" God did leave Samson alone.

King Saul pitifully said, "God is departed from me!" (I Sam. 28:15).

If you read your Bible you will find that sad and tragic fact about many Christians. And if you read the lives of those near you who are Christians, you will find that tragic fact. Sometimes God does leave Christians alone as far as power is concerned. And as far as joy and assurance and rejoicing and the victory a Christian has a right to have are concerned, many a Christian is left alone.

If he meets temptation, he must meet it in his own power, for God is not manifestly there to help him. If there comes a time of sorrow, he does not have the comfort of the Holy Ghost but has only natural means to distract his mind. He does not have God consciously near.

Man need not deceive himself. He cannot have his own way and still feel the presence of God, and know divine guidance. When such a Christian comes to pray, he must pray alone, for the Holy Spirit does not help him pray. Many a Christian is left alone as far as the power and the manifest presence of God are concerned.

That is the reason David prayed in that wonderful fifty-first Psalm, "O God, cast me not away from thy presence; and take not thy holy spirit from me." I do not want to be left alone. Oh, every Christian here tonight should say, "I do not want to be left alone in any part of my business. Lord, take a hand in it all."

Those children of Israel in the desert sinned terribly. When Moses came from Mount Sinai he saw that the children of Israel had made an image of a golden calf and they were dancing around it naked, to their shame. "They sat down to eat and drink and rose up to play." Aaron had made them naked to their shame. So Moses came down, and God said, "Now Moses, get away, leave them alone. I am going to destroy them."

Moses pleaded to the Lord not to do that.

God said, "All right, I have heard your prayer and will not destroy them, but you will have to move the tabernacle outside the camp. I cannot stay in the midst of that group. I would have to destroy them."

So Moses moved the tabernacle outside the camp above which God's presence was seen to dwell at night in a pillar of fire and in the daytime in a cloud.

God said, "I will dwell outside the camp. I will send an angel along to lead you. I cannot go with that rebellious, stiffnecked and idolatrous people."

Moses said, "I do not want to go even to the land of Canaan if God does not go with me. I do not want to cross the River Jordan and see Jericho and the cities of all those countries or eat of the grapes of Eschol or live on the fat of the land that flows with milk and honey if God does not go." Moses said, "If thy presence go not with me, carry us not up hence."

God said, "All right, I have heard your prayer. Go ahead and move the tabernacle back in the center of the camp."

And every time they camped, they camped all around that holy tabernacle. That represents the joy and assurance and victory that a Christian may have. You may lose that and God may leave you alone. If God deals with you, I pray you will hear when God speaks. Do not grieve the Spirit of God. Do not have Him ever leave you alone.

II. Christian, Do Not Ask God to Let Anything of Yours Alone

How many of you today have something that is very precious to you, and you want God to leave it alone? I wonder? Is there something in your life you do not want to give up? I cannot know all your burdens in matters of business, but sometimes when you pray I think you say, "Don't touch my business. I am getting along fine."

But some of you pray, "Lord, bless my business, and guide it," and that is right. Did you say, "Lord, I would be willing tonight to take my hands off. I would be willing for You to do what You want to with my business"? Have you said, "Lord, I lay myself right on the altar tonight. Everything I have, You can have. Do what You want to do with it"? Be careful when you say that. God may take you at your word. This couple back here, if you had your little girl back, would you say, "O God, here is my little girl; if You want her, You can have her. You may have our dear little blond-haired girl if you want her"? Would you say that tonight?

I was thinking bit ago of dear Mrs. P. B. Chenault. She said to me when I went to see her in the hospital at McKinney, Texas, a few hours after her husband was killed, "Brother Rice, we were so happy! I was so proud to marry a preacher" (And Brother Chenault was such a good man, a good, clean man. He was a lovely Christian character.) "We were so happy, and I prayed, 'O God, let me have him a year. It seems too good to be true, Lord, but let me have him for a year.' "

And as she lay on that hospital bed in McKinney Saturday morning after Brother Chenault had been killed suddenly just a few hours before, I sat beside her bed and talked to her. She said, "Brother Rice, God was so good! I asked the Lord to let me have him for one year, and I had him seven! Praise the Lord! God does right."

Can you say, "If God wants my husband, my wife, my baby, He can have them"? Or I wonder if you would say, "Oh, no, God. Keep Your hands off. Let me alone. Let my babies alone. Let my wife, my business, my house alone. Let me alone!" Too many people are saying to God, "Hands off; let us alone!"

I talked to a man in San Antonio, Texas, who fifteen years before had prayed, "O God, spare my baby, my sick little girl. Don't take my baby." Finally he grew desperate and said, "If You take my baby, God, I will not pray to You any more. I will not serve You any more. I will not have anything to do with You any more."

God took the baby, and for fifteen sad, bitter, lonely, desolate years, years of drouth and famine and heartbreak, he was angry at God. He was one of the saddest men I ever saw. I went out and spent an afternoon with him. We leaned our chairs against the side of the house, and I said, "You told God to keep His hands off, and God did not do it. And you said to Him, 'I will keep my hands off God then, and I will not have anything more to do with Him.' Haven't you had enough of that? Aren't you tired of that?"

Finally he broke down. "Oh, yes, I have enough! But I don't suppose God would have me now." I showed him that God did love him and would forgive him. He came back to God.

Now won't you say, "O God, take me—all I have. All I have You can have"? Would you say that about your children?

I am becoming more and more concerned about missions. Would I say to my daughter Grace, "Grace, you may go and be a missionary"? I have wanted Grace to be my helper, to do my typing and my stenographic work. I have wanted her to play the piano for me. But would I say, "Grace, you go on to the mission field, even though we may never see you again, or only once in seven years, or you may never come back; you may be buried in Brazil"? Would I say, "Lord, don't take Your hands off. Don't leave us alone. If You want Grace, take her—or Mary Lloys, or my other girls"? I have been having Mary Lloys sing a little with me. If God wanted her to go to the ends of the world to win souls; with the many hardships and poverty involved, would I say, "All right, Lord, You may have her"? If God should lay His hand on any one of my children—if He said to me, "I want to break your heart," would I say, "O Lord, withhold Your hand; Lord, don't touch me; keep hands off my babies. O God, leave me alone"? Would I say that? Would you say that?

"Leave us alone! Leave us alone!" the demons in that poor lost man cried. I wonder what you would say tonight? Would you say to God, "Don't bother me. Take your hands off, Lord. I will watch out about my business"? Would you say, "God, don't meddle with it"?

My friends, that is not the way. Oh, say tonight, "I want God to have His way."

It is a sad thing for a Christian to be in a business that God cannot bless. Let us come again tonight and say, "Lord, You can have me, my family—all I have. Lord, I want You to have it." Let us give ourselves to the Lord Jesus Christ anew.

I am told that an Indian chief heard a preacher earnestly plead as he told the story of the Gospel. The Indian chief came and gave his blanket (and giving a blanket means something for an Indian).

That preacher said, "What is this?"

The Indian replied, "Me give it to the Lord; me give this blanket to the Lord."

The preacher went on talking. The Indian went off. After awhile he came back with his gun and laid it down and said, "Me give this the Lord. Me give it to Jesus."

The preacher took it, and went on preaching. The Indian went and brought his pony and gave it to the Lord.

The preacher kept pleading. Finally with tears streaming down his face, this Indian came and said, "No more got to give. Give myself to Him."

My friends, can you say tonight, "God, do not hold back Your hand. Take what You want—all I have, all I am"? It is a sad thing for a Christian to be left alone. Can you say, "Lord, have your way tonight"?

III. Satan's Lies—"What Have We to Do With Thee?" and "Art Thou Come to Destroy Us?"

The demons cried out, "Let us alone,. . .I know thee who thou art; the Holy One of God." It is a strange thing about the Devil. He does not mind your believing there is a God, but he says God is too far away to help you. The Devil says, "Sure, there is a God, but He doesn't answer prayer."

He tells us it is all right to have religion just so it does not interfere with our business. People say it is all right to be a Christian but one has to make a living. They say that a Christian has to attend to his business and offer a fellow a drink and be a member of the labor unions, and go the way the world goes. The Devil tells those lies.

The Devil tells young people that they cannot have a good time, that they will lose all their friends if they do not go to shows and other places of amusement. So young people say it is all right to be a Christian just so it does not interfere with pleasure.

The Devil says, "What have we to do with Thee? Now look here, Jesus, don't meddle in our business. Don't bother us."

The Devil tells you it is all right for the Lord to tell you what to do in spiritual matters and to talk about Heaven and a home up yonder after awhile, but he does not want you to let God have His way in your everyday life. Oh, my friends, the Devil has gained a great victory when he can get anybody to say, "I will give God a little time but this matter does not belong to God"; when he can get any Christian to say, "It is all right to give God one-tenth, but the nine-tenths are mine."

Don't you ever think the nine-tenths belong to you, and just one-tenth to God. To be sure, the tithe is the Lord's but the other nine-tenths are the Lord's, too.

Do you say to God, "When I give You a tenth, I have paid You off. So don't meddle with me any more. I will give You a dime out of a dollar; now take that and leave me alone"? You can't say that to God and get by. The rest belongs to God, too.

These devils said, "Why are You coming? Are You coming to destroy us before the time? It is not time for You to send the devils to Hell."

All the devils know their doom. But Satan tries to make you think, "What has God to do with the dinner I cook, or the job I hold?" The devils said to Jesus, "Let us alone! We are here in this man, and this is our own business. Let us alone! What have we to do with Thee?"

But God wants your whole business. Will you come and lay it down before Jesus and say, "Here I am, Lord. All I have, and all I hope to be, if God wants it all, He can have it"?

You cannot put a fence around a little lot and put God inside that fence. You cannot say, "Lord, you stay within that little part of my life." You cannot let God have just one little room or two in your heart. You cannot reserve part for yourself. You cannot invite God into your heart and life and say, "Here are all the keys but one little key."

F. B. Meyer tells us that in a vision he knelt in his room one night and gave Christ the ring of his will with the keys on it but kept back one little key, the key to a closet in his heart. The Lord said to him, "Are they all here?"

Dr. Meyer said, "All but one."

"What is that?"

"It is the key of a little cupboard," said Dr. Meyer, "in which I have something which Thou needest not interfere with; it is mine."

Then Dr. Meyer said the Lord put the keys back into his hand

and said, "My child, if you cannot trust Me with all, you cannot trust Me at all."

"I cried, 'Stop,' " he said, "and the Lord seemed to come back." Dr. Meyer held the little key in his hand and said, "I cannot give it, but if Thou wilt take it, Thou shalt have it."

Are you saying, "Lord, leave me alone; leave my job alone; leave this little room of my life alone; leave this secret pleasure alone; leave this joy alone"?

> **Is your all on the altar of sacrifice laid,**
> **Your heart does the Spirit control?**
> **You can only be blest, and have peace and sweet rest,**
> **As you yield Him your body and soul.**

Are you saying, "O God, here I am. Lord, I hold nothing back"?

The Devil says, "What have we to do with Thee?" and then said again, "Art thou come to destroy us?" That old liar the Devil! The Scripture says that "he is a liar from the beginning." The Devil comes, and these devils said, "Art thou come to destroy us? Leave us alone!" Jesus did not come to destroy.

I preached to you last Sunday night on the uncondemning Jesus: "For the Son of man is come to seek and to save that which was lost," and "God sent not his Son into the world to condemn the world, but that the world through him might be saved." The Devil says, "Are you come to destroy us?"

Oh, my friends, the Devil would have you think that it would ruin you if God ever took charge of you. The Devil would have you think you would be ruined if you gave up everything for the Lord.

Here is a young couple just starting out in the Christian life, or maybe they have not been converted at all. They say, "Yes, we want to be converted some day. We are going to live for God some day, but not now."

"Why not now?"

"Because while we are young, we want to have a good time. We are young but once, and we do not want to throw away our youth and life and love and happiness."

The old Devil makes young people believe that God wants to take away all the goodness, all the sweetness, destroy what is really worth having in life. But he is a liar from the beginning. His pleasures all deceive. God does not come to destroy. He does not come to take away the goodness and happiness, but He comes to make you happy. The Lord takes away only the things that burn and hurt.

I am so glad the Lord Jesus took charge of that situation and commanded the unclean devils to come out of the man and leave him alone. That man was happy and gloriously saved that day when the demons came out of him. I do not think the man was sad from that time on because the devils had been cast out.

The maniac of Gadara lived among the tombs, going from one tomb to another on the hillside, and at night sleeping by the bodies of the decaying dead. He would cry out and cut himself with stones, and no man could tame him, nor bind him. And when he saw Jesus, he cried, "What have I to do with thee, Jesus, thou Son of the most high God? I adjure thee by God, that thou torment me not." In the night he would cry out, and go naked. The people would tie him and try to put him in chains, but he would break the chains with the power of the demons.

Jesus came and said to him, "What is thy name?"

"My name is legion"—for he had a legion of devils in him. You remember that the demons said, "Do not send us away." They begged Him to let them go into the hogs. The hogs ran down a steep place into the sea and were drowned. When the devils were gone out, the man was sitting, clothed and in his right mind, at the feet of Jesus.

What joy do you think that man had in running naked and sleeping in the tombs and lying by decaying bodies? Oh, that was horrible! He was glad when the devils were cast out, and he said, "Thank God, I am saved!" And he got his clothes on and he was in his right mind and had joy in his heart.

The old Devil would make you think God wants to take away everything that is good, everything that would make you happy. But God does not want to do that. He wants you to be happy. If you will let Him have His way tonight, how happy He will make you!

Don't you believe the Devil. He wants to deceive you and tell you that God takes away the good things. But God means it for good and you can safely afford to trust Him.

IV. Sinners Say, "Let Us Alone"

Everywhere I go sinners say, "Leave me alone! Leave me alone!" Isn't it strange that when God wants to help sinners, they say, "Leave us alone"? I have seen a man desperately sick and when the doctor came he said to him, "Doctor, leave me alone."

I was called over to East Dallas several years ago to see a man who had an acute case of appendicitis. Some loved ones called the ambulance and he was taken to the hospital for an operation. When they got him to the hospital he wouldn't get on the operating table. He raised such an uproar they finally sent him home without an operation. But again he was in such misery and pain that they sent for the ambulance again. When they arrived the city doctor said to him, "This is the second trip. We are not coming after you any more. If you do not want us to take you to the hospital, all right, but we are not coming back if you change your mind."

Finally the man said, "If so and so will go with me, I will have an operation."

I have heard people say to the doctor, "Leave me alone," when the doctor probed and probed, and probed deeper yet. One can see there is immediate pain; a sensible person knows the doctor means good. That person does not say, "Leave me alone."

Is it not strange how a sinner will say to God, "Leave me alone"? If he were a sensible man, he would say, "I have to die and meet God. I know I cannot be here always. I must get ready."

It seems that every sensible man would turn in his heart and seek God. If people had any sense and were in their right mind, they would surely be getting ready to meet God. It looks that way; but instead a sinner says, "No, God, don't bother me! Let us alone!" It looks as if he would be running after God, but he is not.

If I go down and cry and sing and preach on the street corner, it seems people would crowd around to hear the message; but if you try to get them to stay, they will not. Rather, they say, "Leave me alone! I am not interested." And they do not want to get interested. "Leave us alone."

Often I have seen a sinner get concerned when a friend talked to him about his soul, or when he heard preaching. He would get so interested in his soul's welfare that he could not rest. I have seen this man go and get drunk to lose that conviction. Sinners try to fight off the Lord and conviction. They run with a wild crowd to try to get their mind off Christ and salvation. How foolish and how wicked that is!

It seems that every man who is unsaved would want to hear a preacher. It seems that he would want to find God, that he would read his Bible and pray. It seems that he would want to read Gospel literature. It seems every lost person would want to watch his step lest he be led away from conviction and from God. Any sensible man can find God right away. But you do not seek God.

Tonight somebody will leave this place unconverted. When I start to give the invitation tonight, somebody will get up and leave. Why? For more than one reason. They did not have a good rearing. Then they want to get away from that stirring, burning conviction of the Spirit of God who is talking to their hearts. If you get up and leave, you will be saying to God, "Leave me alone!"

Isn't it strange that a lost sinner will not read the Bible? Why? The Bible is sharper than a two-edged sword, piercing even to the dividing asunder of the bones and the marrow, and is a discerner of the thoughts and intents of the heart. The reason you do not read the Bible is because you do not want God talking to you. You say, "God, leave me alone!"

I talk to a sinner sometimes, and some Christian is offended when I talk to some sinner. He says, "You will run him away and do more harm than good."

No, my friend. Leaving sinners alone is of the Devil. God never says to leave them alone. If there were a man down in the surf at Galveston drowning, you would not say, "Let him alone." Then why would you say it about a lost sinner?

Sometimes a mother says about her boy, "Let him alone. You will run him away." That is of the Devil. The Devil says, "Let them alone."

I tell you now, one of these days I will give an account of all I do. I do not want it said that I let sinners alone until God lets them alone.

Let me tell you, my friends, if anybody ever comes to talk to you about your soul or to invite you to church, you ought to thank God that person is interested in you. You should say, "Somebody does not want me to go to Hell. Somebody cares about me." God loves you, and don't you say to God, "Leave me alone." Don't say that to any friend, of God, or yourself.

V. Christ Does Not Leave Sinners Alone

And here is another good point. Praise the Lord for this! The Lord Jesus did not leave him alone. He had devils in him and he cried out and said, "Leave me alone!" but God did not leave him alone. To me, this is a miracle of grace. God will not leave men alone. When they mock Him and run over Him, and fight off conviction, still the Spirit of God does not leave men alone. Isn't that wonderful? You were not saved the first time you heard the Gospel. You fought God off. You resisted conviction. You turned your heart away from God. Yet He sought you still!

Somebody asked a Scotchman to tell the story of his conversion. The Presbyterians used to be very rigid in this matter. One had to tell a pretty definite experience of grace to be admitted into membership in the Presbyterian church. So they said, "Tell us about your conversion."

"Well, I did all I could against being saved, and the Lord did all He could to get me saved, and the Lord won. That is the way I got saved."

The way you get saved, sinner, is that God loves you and pursues you. With His pleading voice He calls you.

Yet you say, "Leave me alone."

God will not leave you alone.

You say, "I have my business." But God says you have to die. And the Spirit of God talks to you and pleads with you again and again. A sinner says, "Leave me alone!" But God does not leave you alone. I am so glad God calls and calls and calls again and again when sinners do not want Him.

In this case the Devil says, "Let us alone. . .art thou come to destroy us? I know thee who thou art; the Holy One of God." Yet Jesus said, "Come out of him," and Jesus did not leave him alone.

Is there a sinner here tonight who has said to God, "Leave me alone"? Aren't you glad He did not do it? God has not left you alone. He still calls you, still loves you. Tonight turn to God and be saved. How tender is His mercy; how long-suffering is God. God wants you saved and He has not left you alone.

VI. But Christ Does Sometimes Leave Sinners Alone

There is another word I must say even yet. Sometimes God does leave men alone. In Matthew 15:14 some disciples came to Jesus and said, "Master, the Pharisees were offended at what You said."

Jesus turned to the disciples and said, "Let them alone, they are blind leaders of the blind. Let them alone."

It is a sad, sad thing when the Lord says about a sinner, "Let him alone. He is gone."

The Scripture says about some matters, "There is a sin that is unto death. I do not say that ye shall pray for it." It is a sad thing when God says to a Christian, as the Spirit does sometimes, "There is no use praying for that lost man. Let him alone. He is going to Hell, so let him alone." It is a sad thing when the Holy Spirit withdraws Himself from you and God says to the Holy Spirit, "He has been invited and invited, and You have been insulted, bemeaned and grieved and cast out all these long years. He has locked the door of his heart and You have been driven away, shut out and rejected. Now, Holy Spirit, come on home and leave him alone." And when that happens, a man is gone.

Oh, my dear friend, do not ever make it so God will leave you alone! Do not insult the Spirit so that He leaves you alone. That is the unpardonable sin. God loves you still and the Lord Jesus loves you still. You can go on and do all the mean things you can, and the Lord Jesus still cares for you in spite of it all. You may say mean things about Jesus; you may insult Him, blaspheme Him, yet you still can be saved. Infidels may be saved. People may spit on the Bible and burn it, but they still can be saved. You may hate every preacher and still be saved. I thank God some have been saved who hated me like poison.

But let me tell you, finally God may tell the Holy Spirit, "All right, leave him alone!" All preaching will be only like sounding brass and tinkling cymbals. He may never convict you and you may never be saved. If God ever tells the Holy Spirit to leave that man alone—as He said about the Pharisee, "Leave them alone, they be blind leaders of the blind"—brother, there is no more hope. It is a sad thing for a lost sinner to be left alone—with no conviction, no repentance, no change of heart and nothing but Hell for the future.

Tonight have you been fighting God and saying, "Leave me alone! Don't bother me"? Sometimes God lays His hand on a young man to preach, but he says, "Leave me alone, God. I have a good job. I do not want to give this up."

A preacher brother told me that he said to God about his career, "Lord, leave me alone. I want to be a lawyer, Lord. Leave me alone in my plans." But God said, "I want you to preach."

Have you said, "God, leave me alone. I do not want to give up my pleasure and die to myself. I do not want to be a Sunday school teacher and pay the price for soul winning. Lord, leave me alone"? Do not ever say that to God!

If you are a poor sinner tonight, do not ever any more say, "God, leave me alone." He might do it, then you would be lost forever. Do not go away tonight saying, "Leave me alone." Rather say, "I have a devil in me. Lord Jesus, do not leave me alone! Drive the devils out tonight and save me!" Tonight, tonight! Not some other time, but tonight. Oh, turn and let Jesus save you.

Do you want to be saved? You can be.

> **Almost I said, "Jesus save me,"**
> **Almost submitted my will;**
> **Almost persuaded to serve Him,**
> **But I rejected Him still.**

Now is the time to receive Him,
  Now is the time to be saved;
Now, while the Spirit is pleading,
  Now, Jesus waiteth to save.

27—Barriers Torn Down Between Man and God

(Sermon preached Sunday night, March 28, 1937, at Fundamentalist Baptist Tabernacle, Dallas, Texas. Stenographically reported.)

And, behold, the veil of the temple was rent in twain from the top to the bottom.—Matt. 27:51.

I open my Bible to the 27th chapter of Matthew and begin with verse 45 and read through verse 51. I ask you to join in a prayerful study of a few verses.

Now from the sixth hour there was darkness over all the land unto the ninth hour.

And about the ninth hour Jesus cried with a loud voice, saying, Eli, Eli, lama sabachthani? that is to say, My God, my God, why hast thou forsaken me?

Some of them that stood there, when they heard that, said, This man calleth for Elias.

And straightway one of them ran, and took a spunge, and filled it with vinegar, and put it on a reed, and gave him to drink.

The rest said, Let be, let us see whether Elias will come to save him.

Jesus, when he had cried again with a loud voice, yielded up the ghost.

And, behold, the veil of the temple was rent in twain from the top to the bottom; and the earth did quake, and the rocks rent;

And the graves were opened; and many bodies of the saints which slept arose,

And came out of the graves after his resurrection, and went into the holy city, and appeared unto many.

Now when the centurion, and they that were with him, watching Jesus, saw the earthquake, and those things that were done, they feared greatly, saying, Truly this was the Son of God.

And now again read verse 51:

And, behold, the veil of the temple was rent in twain from the top to the bottom; and the earth did quake, and the rocks rent.

I spoke this morning on Christ's resurrection. These two are the double theme of the Gospel. In I Corinthians, the 15th chapter, Paul said, "For the Gospel I preached unto you and by which you are saved is this: That Christ died for our sins, that He was buried and that He arose again the third day according to the Scriptures."

Now that is the Gospel I have preached. I preach on one phase of it this morning—the resurrection, and on the crucifixion of Christ tonight. I sometimes wish that in every sermon I could discuss the crucifixion of Christ, that which was foretold so many times in the Old Testament and the entire story repeated four times in the New and referred to again many times.

I want your hearts to be mellow. I want you to see the scene in your mind as Christ hung on the cross and there died for sinners, including you and me. Some of you are not Christians and you do not have any special reverence for church or for preachers or for Christians as a whole.

But when we come to preach on the death of Christ, even if you are an infidel, surely there is something so holy that it would inspire awe in your breast as it did in the breast of this centurion who said, "Surely this is the Son of God." Even Judas Iscariot must have been smitten to the very soul of his being. Even the Pharisees and scribes who had Jesus crucified, or Pontius Pilate who washed his hands and turned Him over to them, must have been stirred and trembled as the awful significance of the crucifixion of Jesus dawned on them.

I want you as seriously as possible to consider the crucifixion. I hope you have not come today with frivolous thoughts. Cast aside thoughts of making money, having pleasure, the doing of your business, family affairs, eating and drinking and such matters—forget them, and for a time look with me on the Saviour of the world as He hung on the cross and then see Him die.

No sooner had Jesus said, "It is finished," and gave up the ghost than the hand of God rent the veil of the Temple from the top to the bottom and the Holy of Holies lay open to the gaze of all the world who should come by that way. And the rocks rent, the graves were opened. God moved the hearts of multitudes, and the centurion said, "Surely that is the Son of God." There is a holy significance here.

I. An Earthquake When Jesus Died

Notice the earthquake. Earthquakes have a peculiar significance. Several times we are told that when God manifested Himself to men, there was an earthquake. Once was on Mount Sinai when God came down. Smoke covered the mount, the mountain trembled, and God said if so much as a beast touch the mount, he shall be shot through with a dart. No one was to touch it, for God was to speak and did speak with human voice from Mount Sinai to the assembled multitudes the words of the Ten Commandments. In the words of the psalmist, "The mountains skipped like rams, and the little hills like lambs" when God gave holy commandments from Mount Sinai.

Again we find when Jesus was crucified, when Christ died on the cross, the earth trembled and shook at the terrible wrath of God, at the awfulness of the death of the Creator, who was God. The universe of God itself was in travail when the Creator died. Jesus was the Creator of the heavens and the earth.

And again as I read you this morning, when He came out of the grave, the rock was rolled back and there was a great earthquake. That burial tomb could not hold Him. The angel rolled back the stone and sat upon it and there was a great earthquake at the resurrection of Christ.

One day Christ will come again to reign and His feet shall stand on the Mount of Olives. And when He does come, there will be an earthquake and the Mount of Olives will divide, and half will move eastward and half will move westward and there will be a great valley. In that earthquake, the cities of the nations will fall. Earthquakes have a peculiar significance.

In this time when Jesus died on the cross, the earth trembled and God reached down and tore the Temple's veil in two. The earthquake opened the graves and many saints came out after His resurrection and appeared unto many.

II. The Presence of God in That Holy of Holies Behind the Veil

Now about that veil. I read in Hebrews the 9th chapter something about the Tabernacle. And the Temple which followed it was similar. It was in two principal parts. First, the Holy of Holies—mentioned first, but it was really last. No one but the high priest was allowed to see in the very interior place, the Holy of Holies. The Temple was built out of cedars. The walls were plated with solid gold. Even the floor underneath was covered with solid gold.

It was furnished with very simple furniture. There was the Ark of the Covenant, a box about seven and a half or eight feet long, two and a half or three feet wide and of the same height, made of shittim wood and covered over with solid gold. Above that was the form of two cherubims, carved out of olive wood and plated with solid gold. The outspread wings of the two cherubims covered the width of the room—some twenty-two feet. The wing of one touched the wing of the other and the outer wing touched the wall. The two angelic figures hovered over the Mercy Seat which was on top of that golden Ark of the Covenant.

Inside of that box originally were certain things. There were two tables of stone on which God Himself wrote with His own finger the Ten Commandments. Besides that, there was Aaron's walking stick. It was an almond rod, a walking stick laid up before the Lord which blossomed and bore fruit. It was to prove the Levitical Priesthood of Aaron. That was in there.

And besides that, in the sacredness in the ark of God was a pot of manna from Heaven. It was gathered into a golden vessel. That which spoiled every day, when put in the Ark of the

Covenant, in that holy place, was divinely preserved through the years. This was in there.

Now over that box was the golden place called the Mercy Seat, and over that lid of the box there was the holy fire of the presence of God. That pillar of cloud by day and the fire by night that pointed the way and preserved them in the night as they came across the wilderness and wandered forty years, that literal presence of God was in the Temple. And over the Mercy Seat it was.

It was the divinely appointed custom that once every year the high priest would lift up the corner of the great veil that separated the Holy Place from the Holy of Holies. It was woven solid about six inches, and Josephus said if one had sixty yoke of oxen he couldn't tear it in two. The high priest lifted up the corner of that heavy veil, that shut out any light from the outside, and came in. He brought in first coals of fire in a golden censer and on these he sprinkled incense until the clouds covered the Mercy Seat. Then he brought in a basin with the blood of a bullock, the atoning blood brought once each year. He dipped his finger in this blood and sprinkled it upon the Mercy Seat and before that holy place.

On the high priest's garments were little bells, golden bells and golden pomegranates all around the skirt of his garment. The tinkling of the bells gave witness to the people outside of the high priest interceding to God for their sin.

Now that is the picture. I read you in the 9th chapter of Hebrews, verses 1-4:

Then verily the first covenant had also ordinances of divine service, and a worldly sanctuary.

For there was a tabernacle made; [later that was followed by the Temple, you remember] *the first,* [that is the first room] *wherein was the candlestick, and the table, and the shewbread; which is called the sanctuary* [that is the Holy Place].

Now that was the outside room. Then we come to the one I mentioned. It was in the Temple, very much like this in the Tabernacle but more elaborate.

*And after the second veil, the tabernacle which is
called the Holiest of all;*
*Which had the golden censer, and the ark of the
covenant overlaid round about with gold, wherein was
the golden pot that had manna, and Aaron's rod that
budded, and the tables of the covenant* [that is the tables
of the law, the Ten Commandments].

God said the high priest comes in and sprinkles the blood, but
when he returns, the veil is still there and shuts out the
inquiring eyes of other persons who wish to come in. The
common people never came in. And only the high priest once a
year. The Holy Spirit meant by this that the way is still closed
and that God has not yet revealed the way into the Holy of
Holies, how man may walk in and face God.

*And over it the cherubims of glory shadowing the
mercyseat; of which we cannot now speak particularly.*
*Now when these things were thus ordained, the priests
went always into the first tabernacle, accomplishing the
service of God.*
*But into the second went the high priest alone once
every year, not without blood, which he offered for
himself, and for the errors of the people:*
*The Holy Ghost this signifying, that the way into the
holiest of all was not yet made manifest, while as the
first tabernacle was yet standing:*
*Which was a figure for the time then present, in which
were offered both gifts and sacrifices, that could not
make him that did the service perfect, as pertaining to
the conscience;*
*Which stood only in meats and drinks, and divers
washings, and carnal ordinances, imposed on them until
the time of reformation.*
*But Christ being come an high priest of good things to
come, by a greater and more perfect tabernacle, not
made with hands, that is to say, not of this building;* [in
the temple of Heaven he is talking about].
Neither by the blood of goats and calves, but by his

own blood he entered in once into the holy place, having obtained eternal redemption for us.

For if the blood of bulls and of goats, and the ashes of an heifer sprinkling the unclean, sanctifieth to the purifying of the flesh:

How much more shall the blood of Christ, who through the eternal Spirit offered himself without spot to God, purge your conscience from dead works to serve the living God?

And for this cause he is the mediator of the new testament, that by means of death, for the redemption of the transgressions that were under the first testament [that is under Old Testament law], *they which are called might receive the promise of eternal inheritance.* —Vss. 5-15.

III. The Veil, Symbolizing Barriers Between God and Man, Now Torn Down

I want you to get the significance.

And now let's turn to Ephesians and bear with me a moment as I read you the Scriptures. Ephesians 2:11-18:

Wherefore remember, that ye being in time past Gentiles in the flesh, who are called Uncircumcision by that which is called the Circumcision in the flesh made by hands; [The Jews call you uncircumcised.]

That at that time ye were without Christ, being aliens from the commonwealth of Israel, and strangers from the covenants of promise, having no hope, and without God in the world:

But now in Christ Jesus ye who sometimes were far off are made nigh by the blood of Christ.

For he is our peace, who hath made both one, and hath broken down the middle wall of partition between us;

Having abolished in his flesh the enmity, even the law of commandments contained in ordinances; for to make in himself of twain [of Jew and of Gentile] *one new man, so making peace;*

> *And that he might reconcile both unto God in one body*
> *by the cross, having slain the enmity thereby:*
> *And came and preached peace to you which were afar*
> *off, and to them that were nigh.*
> *For through him we both have access by one Spirit*
> *unto the Father.*

In the second chapter of Colossians, verses 14 to 17:

> *Blotting out the handwriting of ordinances that was*
> *against us, which was contrary to us, and took it out of*
> *the way, nailing it to his cross;*
> *And having spoiled principalities and powers, he made*
> *a shew of them openly, triumphing over them in it.*
> *Let no man therefore judge you in meat, or in drink, or*
> *in respect of an holyday, or of the new moon, or of the*
> *sabbath days:*
> *Which are a shadow of things to come; but the body is*
> *of Christ.*

I wonder if your heart does not see already the thing I am starting to say tonight, that when the veil in the Temple was torn in twain from the top to the bottom, God was tearing down every barrier between man and God. And God said, "The way is open. Come in, sinners." That is, every barrier between man and God is taken down, and when Christ died on the cross and said, "It is finished," the way was open and God Himself tore the veil down. Now then, anybody who wants to may come in and be saved.

IV. The Barrier of Peace-Making Sacrifices Is Now Shown to Be Broken Down

Let me speak to you then on "Barriers Torn Down Between Man and God."

For that veil in the Temple pictured the body of Jesus. Jesus is the only Mediator, the only way between God and man. And when the body of Jesus was torn on the cross and the veil of the Temple torn in two by the hand of God, that meant the way into the Holiest of all was made manifest to every man who wants to enter and find peace and forgiveness and atonement and be at one with God—you who at one time were at enmity with Him. All of these barriers were torn down at the death of Christ, thank God, and there are no more peace-making sacrifices.

I remind you that blood is on every page in the Old Testament. Turn to the book of Genesis. There in the Garden of Eden Satan came in the sinister form of a serpent and caused Adam and Eve to sin. After that God killed animals, took their skins and clothed His erring children. Oh, my friends, Adam and Eve were saved by faith in the shed blood. There is blood there.

A little later we see righteous Abel offering the firstlings of his flock and God was pleased with that odor of burnt sacrifice that ascended to Him. The sacrifice of Cain had no blood in it and so did not please God.

A little later we see the children of Israel in Egypt and the passover lamb slain and the blood put on the lintels of the door after it had been caught in a basin. Then the people ate the passover lamb. What does the blood mean?

Over and over and over again Israel is never allowed to forget. And for fifteen hundred years, for a thousand and five hundred years and more, every Jewish family once every year must kill the passover lamb (or one lamb for two families, depending on the size of the family). Oh, they could not get away from blood, blood, blood! Morning sacrifice in the Temple, evening sacrifice in the Temple. There must be a lamb in the morning and a lamb in the evening. Besides this, they must bring a young bullock for a sin-offering, two scapegoats for the scapegoat offering, lambs, pigeons and turtledoves.

Those who are too poor to bring a lamb must bring two pigeons, or two turtledoves. They are a symbol of the coming Saviour. The two turtledoves picture Christ who is the Man of Sorrows and acquainted with grief. The young steer they brought pictures Christ as the suffering, burden-bearing Servant. The lamb pictures the innocent and pure Saviour. They were never allowed to forget that there must be shedding of blood.

Now through the years they brought their sacrifices to the

Temple but could not go into the Holy place. The Temple had a Holy place, and a Most Holy place, but nobody could go in but the high priest himself, and that only once every year. And he could never go without blood. A priest could not be a priest until he had had blood put on his right ear, and blood on the thumb of his right hand, and blood on the big toe of his right foot. He must be consecrated with blood. "Almost all things are by the law purged with blood; and without shedding of blood is no remission," the Scripture said.

Blood—the blood of goats, lambs, bullocks, pigeons and turtledoves—a river of blood through the years of the Old Testament!

It must have been to every Jew a haunting thing. God made so much of the blood. He said when you kill an animal, drain out the blood. Orthodox Jews will not eat meat unless the animal has been killed and dressed by particular plans. God had drilled in century after century, thousand years after thousand years, that a Jew must not taste blood. The blood must be poured out, for blood makes an atonement for the soul. They had been warned through the centuries. God must have blood before the veil is torn down.

My friends, I come tonight and tell you that the one Sacrifice they waited for those centuries has been made. All the peace-making sacrifices never made peace with God. Every time a lamb was killed, the blood of that innocent lamb only said, "This is not enough. I cannot pay for sin." And the smell of that fresh blood poured out always said, "This blood cannot cover man's sin. It only pictures that there must be One who will come and die for the sin of the world."

Men could not come and meet God except by faith that God had some other suffering Servant, not this bullock; some other Scapegoat, not these; some other pure white Pigeon of Heaven, not this one whose head was wrung off over running water; some other mourning Dove besides these two that the poorest brought. "We cannot pay for sin," they say. "We only point the way that God will have a Sacrifice to pay for every sin, every debt of mankind." When that time comes, the veil between God and man will be torn down, but not yet.

And now on the cross of Calvary, long foretold and sung of by psalmist, foretold by prophets, pictured by sacrifices these centuries, the Lamb of God has come to pay for sin. When Christ was on the cross He said, "It is finished," and He gave up the ghost. The rocks rent and the hills moved. The finger of God ripped down from Heaven and split that giant veil from the top—not beginning at the bottom but from the top down to the bottom. God tore it aside and said, "Sacrifices, peace-making sacrifices, are ended. There remaineth no more sacrifice for sin." God's Sacrifice has been made and the veil can be taken down now.

Man does not have to make peace with God. Peace has already been made. Praise His name, there remaineth no more sacrifice for sin! There is no more a barrier between God and man. The way has been paid for the debt has been paid for those who hear me tonight.

V. Peace With God Already Made: Will You Accept It Free?

Your sins may have been heavy. You may have been bent under the weight of your sins. Your conscience may have smitten you through these years on account of your sins. You people who are saved, people who are the children of God, may have felt yourselves far away from God on account of sin. You can come back tonight! Learn to walk up boldly! The way is open.

"But," you say, "I thought there was a veil between me and God. I thought I must pay my way back." The price has been paid! Peace has been made, the peace of the cross, by the blood of the cross. Now you can walk in boldly. You don't have to make peace with God. You don't have to buy salvation. You don't have to reform.

My friends, don't misunderstand. You ought to repent, you ought to turn your heart from sin and quit sin, but you can't do anything on the sin question to make peace with God. It has been done already! You can accept it, that is all. Thank God, the veil is torn down!

Oh, my sinner friend covered with sins of the years, walk in.

The blood of Jesus Christ has torn the veil down and we need no more lambs for sacrifices, need no more peace-making ceremonies, for peace has been made through the blood of His cross and you can come in.

Oh, I wish I could press it on your hearts! Everywhere I go I find men trying to be good in order to get to Heaven. They can't do it. Everywhere I go men say, "What must I do to be saved?" "What must I DO, DO, DO?" You can't do anything except believe on Christ and take salvation. It has already been done! The price has been paid. The blood has been spilled. When Jesus died, the Lord from Heaven said, "Now I can tear down the veil that stands between the Holy place and the outside, I can take it down now so that anyone who wants to may come and gaze in and walk into the Holy place." We may come in boldly.

Now that veil waited until peace had been made by blood; now it has been made. Your sins, then, though they be like scarlet, can be white as snow. And though they be red like crimson, they can be as wool. The veil is torn down, the veil of peace-making. Peace has been made. That barrier is torn down. God Himself tore it down when His Son died and said, "It is finished." The blood has been poured out. The price has been paid. When He said, "It is finished," God said, "Take the veil down, then, and let any poor, wicked, Hell-bound sinner who wants to, come boldly into the Holy of Holies and face God in peace."

Thank God, the veil is torn down! The veil is torn down! Barriers are torn down between God and man!

This is what we mean by free salvation. Christ has opened the way so that just by trusting in His shed blood, coming to God in your heart by faith you may have your sins forgiven and have peace with God. This is what we mean by salvation by grace. It is the unmerited grace and mercy of God which saves a sinner.

Poor, undone, Hell-deserving and Hell-bound sinner, there is no peace any other way. Flee to Jesus today! Come through the torn veil into the Holy of Holies.

In one second of a surrendered, penitent, trusting heart, you can enter into the peace of God through Jesus Christ, who tore down the partition between God and man. Do it today!

28—Lost—Your Soul!

(Sermon preached May 31, 1936. Stenographically reported.)

There are two or three Scriptures I will read. One is Luke 19:10:

> *For the Son of man is come to seek and to save that which was lost.*

Now we read Mark the 8th chapter.

> *And when he had called the people unto him with his disciples also, he said unto them, Whosoever will come after me, let him deny himself, and take up his cross, and follow me.*
>
> *For whosoever will save his life shall lose it; but whosoever shall lose his life for my sake and the gospel's, the same shall save it.*
>
> *For what shall it profit a man, if he shall gain the whole world, and lose his own soul?*
>
> *Or what shall a man give in exchange for his soul?—Vss. 34-37.*

And now turn to Luke the 15th chapter, verses 3 through 9:

> *And he spake this parable unto them, saying,*
>
> *What man of you, having an hundred sheep, if he lose one of them, doth not leave the ninety and nine in the wilderness, and go after that which is lost, until he find it?*
>
> *And when he hath found it, he layeth it on his shoulders, rejoicing.*
>
> *And when he cometh home, he calleth together his friends and neighbours, saying unto them, Rejoice with me; for I have found my sheep which was lost.*

Either what woman having ten pieces of silver, if she lose one piece, doth not light a candle, and sweep the house, and seek diligently till she find it?

And when she hath found it, she calleth her friends and her neighbours together, saying, Rejoice with me; for I have found the piece which I had lost.

And then comes the story of the Prodigal Son, beginning with verse 11.

The poor, wild boy went away from home like every sinner goes away from God. He came to the hogpen of want and hunger and came to himself and went home. Then we read:

But the father said to his servants, Bring forth the best robe, and put it on him: and put a ring on his hand, and shoes on his feet:

And bring hither the fatted calf, and kill it; and let us eat, and be merry:

For this my son was dead, and is alive again: he was lost, and is found. And they began to be merry.—Vss. 22-24.

The older brother wouldn't come in, and the father went out to meet him and said, "Son, thou art ever with me, and all that I have is thine." Now verse 32.

It was meet that we should make merry, and be glad: for this thy brother was dead, and is alive again; and was lost, and is found.

Lost!—What a terrible word it is! The Scriptures use it in two senses about lost people. Notice in Mark the 8th chapter the Lord said, "For whosoever will save his life shall lose it." A man can lose his life. Verses 35 and 36 say,

For whosoever will save his life shall lose it; but whosoever shall lose his life for my sake and the gospel's, the same shall save it.

For what shall it profit a man, if he shall gain the whole world, and lose his own soul?

Now a man may lose his life, and then a man may lose his

soul; so your life may be lost and then your soul may be lost.

Now you be prayerful as I speak on "Lost—Your Soul!" And let every one here consider, for what I have to say will be good for you, whether you are saved or lost.

First of all, if anybody here is trying to save his life, he will lose it. If there is anyone who sits out there and says, "I will live my own life and have my own way and have things of this world," then you will lose it. But you will say contrary to the song Brother Stroh sings:

> **This world is not my home, I'm just a passing thru.**
> **My treasures are laid up somewhere beyond the blue;**
> **The angels beckon me from Heaven's open door,**
> **And I can't feel at home in this world any more.**
>
> **O Lord, You know, I have no friend like You,**
> **If Heaven's not my home, O Lord what can I do?**
> **The angels beckon me from Heaven's open door,**
> **And I can't feel at home in this world any more.**

The Scripture says, "Whosoever shall save his life shall lose it." Whoever is here tonight who has your mind set on this world and your life set on this world, you are losing your life. You won't get what you think you will get. You will lose the very thing you are trying to save, and your life will be lost. The peace of mind, a happy, useful life—don't lose it.

I. Many Tonight Are Lost

What shall it profit a man, if he shall gain the whole world, and lose his own soul? Or what shall a man give in exchange for his soul?

My dear friends, you are in danger of losing your soul. I go further and tell you, you have already lost your soul. Your soul is now lost. If you tonight are not a Christian, if you haven't been born again, tonight you are doomed. Tonight you are lost, already lost. You are undone, you are condemned, and you are going to Hell. If you are not saved, you are lost.

He that believeth on him is not condemned: but he that believeth not is condemned already, because he hath not believed in the name of the only begotten Son of God.

Oh, if you are not saved, you are lost already, condemned

already, doomed already. That means that on God's record you are marked down as a lost soul. There is a cell on a corridor in Hell now that has your name on it. Tonight, dear friends, you are lost *now*.

You may say, "Brother Rice, I haven't done anything to get lost." You are lost to start with. You are lost before you do anything. You are a sinner born, and a sinner by nature, and tonight you are a sinner by choice, lost and condemned. You need to be saved.

Jesus gave the story of the lost sheep and said, "For the Son of man is come to save that which was lost." The Scripture says that, like the sheep lost out in the mountain, the shepherd leaves the ninety and nine in the wilderness and goes after that which is lost until he finds it.

The sheep was really lost, was really out in danger, really away from the fold, and out where the wolves will pull it down at any time. The sheep was lost and the shepherd went and got it and brought it in and then rejoiced and said, "Rejoice with me for I have found my sheep which was LOST."

The woman lost her silver. Somewhere in a crack in the floor it was really lost and in danger of being forever lost. But she took a candle and swept her house diligently until she found it.

The prodigal boy was lost, and twice the father said that "he was dead and is alive again. He was lost and is found."

My friend, God uses that word "lost" about every sinner here tonight who has not been born again. You are LOST. You are lost now, condemned now.

You should be considering that you have lost Heaven. You are missing Heaven. You do not have any claim to it at all. You do not have a deed to a home in Heaven. You do not have a place prepared for you. You haven't any clinch on it, no promise. You are undone. You have turned down God's only Saviour. Tonight you are lost and you are going to miss Heaven.

I would not want to miss Heaven. Brother Stroh sings about it sweetly. I do not want to miss my mother and miss seeing Jesus. I do not want to miss seeing David and hearing him sing and play on his harp. I do not want to miss the angel chorus and the streets of gold and the River of Life that flows out from under the throne of God and of the Lamb. I don't want to miss eating of the trees of life which bear twelve manner of fruit and bring forth their fruit every month and whose leaves are for the healing of the nations!

I want to be there when God kisses away all tears from our eyes! I want to be there! I would not want to miss Heaven. I am sorry for anybody who does not have a home in Heaven. I am sorry for anybody who does not have a place already prepared. I am sorry for anybody tonight who is condemned and lost. If you are lost, you are missing Heaven. I would not want to miss Heaven.

II. Death Is Coming for You!

You are lost! Lost! Lost! and yet death is coming! Death is a bad business for a sinner that is lost, isn't it? Death is a sad thing for the sinner. That is why people do not like cemeteries. Some people do not like deathbed stories in the pulpit because it gives them "the creeps." You know you are lost and condemned and you do not want to talk about death. You are afraid of death. You dare not face death. You know you are lost and it is a terrible thing to die, to die undone.

Did you ever know of anybody who died and said, "Can't you see them! Can't you hear the chains rattling! They are coming after me!" Yes, and there would be many more except in modern days when a man is about to die, particularly if he is not saved and not happy to die, the doctor will give him an opiate so people will not hear his screams. I tell you, there are countless millions who, when they die, know they must meet their doom. It is a terrible thing to die and face death when you are lost. Lost, condemned, and your sins piled high! Lost, and without mercy! Lost, and not under the blood. Lost, and no salvation!

It is terrible, my friends, for you loved ones to die lost, but you are going to die. So many people die who do not get ready. They do not intend to put it off too long; but they do. It is terrible to die when your chance is gone to be saved.

I think of that man who took a wrecker out on the road to

Waxahachie, Texas, and was struck by a bus. The car turned over on him and he died. He had heard me preach the night before.

And that man who worked at the Waxahachie Water Works heard me preach in that revival after such horrible things had shaken the town and two sudden deaths had occurred, and when I had said, "Somebody else will meet God before this time tomorrow night." They went down there at 5:15 and found him shot through the heart. I was called to preach the funeral.

I think of that young man in Roosevelt, Oklahoma, that twenty-year-old boy who heard me preach. He said to his companions, "Let's catch the train up to Hobart." He swung on the train and fell under it and was cut in two. He had no time to cry, "God have mercy!"

He had promised his mother that day at noon, "I will some day, but not now." And he died lost, lost!

Brother, it is a horrible thing to a man who is lost to face death. And it may pounce on you before you leave that door tonight!

It may be—I don't know—a fainting spell, a heart attack—who knows? Someone might say, "My head, my head!" and a clot of blood forms there, and in a little bit you are gone! You don't know what it is. There may be even now in your body the tumor, the cancerous growth that will take you to your grave in a short time. It may be that soreness in some part of your body—in the stomach or in the breast or in the kidneys or in the liver—may be a poison or a malignancy that will kill you in a few short days' time. Lots of men die suddenly these days. A terrible thing is death for the man who is lost.

What shall a man profit when he has his money, or what shall a man profit when he has houses and land? What shall a man profit if he has apartment houses bringing in rent every month? "Sitting pretty," aren't we? But what shall it profit a man if he has everything—only his soul is lost and he dies and goes to an eternal, awful Hell! When a man comes to die, what will those things matter? Good-by land! Good-by property! Good-by money in the bank! What will it matter if your soul is lost? Your soul is lost!

Oh, it is a terrible thing to die, unless you know you are saved. The Saviour told about a man who had a big plantation and made big crops. He built new barns and sat down and said to himself, "Soul, thou hast much goods laid up for many years; take thine ease, eat, drink, and be merry."

That night God came and said, "Thou fool, this night thy soul shall be required of thee; then whose shall all these things be which thou hast provided?"

Oh, when God comes and demands your soul, and it is lost! It is lost! My friends, you are facing death and you are lost!

III. Sinners Must Face Judgment

There is another thing, my friend. You are facing judgment. Judgment is coming! Judgment is waiting. "It is appointed unto men once to die, and after this the judgment." One of these days there is going to be a judgment away out in space, and a great white throne, and Jesus will sit on it and from His face the heaven and earth will flee away in that day. Oh, He is lowly and meek now, but He won't be then. He is now the humble Servant and the Man of Sorrows, but He won't be then! He is now the Lamb of God that taketh away the sin of the world, but He won't be that then!

The Lord Jesus Christ will be the Righteous Judge and the world will tremble before Him. The clouds will flee away. The earth will burst into flames. The heavens and the earth will flee from the face of Jesus when He sits on that judgment throne. Then He will be a Lion and not a Lamb. Then He will be a Judge, not the pleading lawyer, the defense attorney.

When He comes, then I remind you that the books will be opened. THE BOOKS—of your record, of your sin will be open and at that time you will kneel before Him and confess that He is Lord. You are facing that and you are lost! You are facing that and you have no advocate with the Father! Your sins are not covered and the record of your sins stands against you.

Brother White, it will be a terrible thing when a man stands before God and God begins to open up the book of his sins and he has no Saviour and no atoning blood and no salvation—nothing to answer except that he is lost and his soul is lost! But a lot of men go out that way—lost! And judgment is coming!

It comes, Brother, and you will face it. Your knees that won't bow to pray now, will bow then. Every knee is going to bow and that tongue of yours that won't call on God, that will not talk for Him—then God will have a way of making you talk. You will admit then that you are a sinner. You will admit that Christ is Lord, the Son of God. There will be no modernists then. No, sir.

But, my friends, let me remind you of this: You are going to face that and you are lost! Lost! LOST! You are a lost sinner if you haven't been born again; you are lost and facing judgment.

IV. Hell for Eternity for the Unconverted Sinner

That isn't all. You are lost and you are facing eternity. Do you believe in eternity? Someone says, "Brother Rice, do you know what I believe about Hell? I just believe that it is in this life, and all you are going to get, you will get it here."

First, you are lying. You believe nothing of the kind. You are trying to fool yourself. You do that to keep people from talking to you about your soul. There is in the breast of even the heathen savage in Africa some certainty that God put there that there is a Hell, that there is a hereafter, and that he must meet God. You know that is so. A man may bluster and blow if he wants to about no God and that he does not believe the Bible, but every man down in his soul has something that speaks to him that he can't down. That something is his inborn conscience. God put it there and it tells that man there is something besides this life, that there is a hereafter and he has a soul to be tormented in Hell or to rejoice in Glory.

Oh, my dear friend, you are going to face Hell if you are lost. You must face Hell, and Hell is reserved for those who reject Christ and go away lost. I am sorry to have to bring a message on Hell, but it is a fact and I must tell what is so. There is a Hell, and you have a never-dying soul to save and tonight some boy or girl who never studied about it and who thinks it doesn't matter but who thinks he has plenty of time, will say, "I must not go away, Mother, until I get it settled that I am not lost any more. I want to trust Jesus tonight so I won't have to face Hell and judgment."

Dear man or woman, whoever you are away from God tonight, I hope you will say, "I won't go away lost. I must face Hell and I must face God." I hope you will say, "I am not going away from here tonight lost and away from God." If you're lost, you're headed for Hell. If you are lost, *if you are lost*, IF YOU ARE LOST!

V. God Wants to Save You Now!

God wants to find you, and the Holy Spirit is seeking you tonight like the shepherd searched for the lost sheep, like the woman with the lamp searched for the coin. That is like taking the Word of God and turning on the light of the Spirit of God and sweeping for souls.

Tonight let the Lord find you. Let the Holy Spirit touch your heart. Don't go away lost. Be saved. What shall it profit a man if he shall gain the whole world and lose his own soul, or what would a man give in exchange for his soul? Don't do it! Don't go away lost.

Are you lost tonight? If you are not saved, you are lost. What can you do about it? Here is the good news: "The Son of man is come to save that which was lost."

The sheep is lost, but the shepherd loved that lost sheep. It is a strange thing that when a mother's boy breaks her heart, she loves that boy and may neglect the other children for that poor wicked soul. Here is the shepherd: he leaves the ninety-nine sheep that are all right in the wilderness—we say in the fold, but that is not what the Bible says—he leaves these in the wilderness. They are not lost. They are all right. He leaves them to the wilderness and goes after that which was lost until he finds it. Oh, the tender seeking of the Saviour for lost sheep!

I like that song which says,

> The shepherd went out to search for his sheep,
> And all thro' the night on the rocky steep
> He sought till he found him, with love-bands he bound him,
> And I was that one lost sheep.

I didn't find myself. The Shepherd came looking for me and found me, and I am not lost any longer! "The Son of man is come to seek and to save that which was lost."

And mankind has lost everything by sin. Adam lost the Garden of Eden by sin. Wouldn't it have been wonderful to live in a world with every animal tamed, to live in this world with no thorns on the roses, no mosquitoes to sting you, no smallpox germs nor any kind of disease germs, or any cockleburs to bother you? We lost that through sin. Oh, how much sin loses!

As I stood Thursday night in Pacific Garden Mission in Chicago, I could hardly keep back the tears. Some had been drinking, and some didn't have enough money to drink—these came and heard the Gospel.

One man who was converted said some would take a little fusel oil and some would take wood alcohol that blinds and kills people—that group that sat out there, the bums of Chicago on South State Street. God broke my heart as I preached to them. Five men were saved. They fell down on their knees and prayed and said they would trust Him and felt they were saved.

My friends, as I looked down on those people, they were so sad-looking, so untreated, so poor. Then when the services were over they went up to lay on bare cots and no bedding. They did the best they could. Then they would give them a cup of coffee in the morning before they left. Oh, I looked down on those men and thought, Sin did that! Sin lost this man his family. Sin lost this man his job. Sin took away the natural color on the men's faces and left there the pallor of disease and sin. Everything you lose, sin loses it for you.

Oh, my friends, sin has lost you enough; don't let it lose you your soul! The Lord Jesus comes to seek and to save that which was lost. And lost soul, He came to die on the cross—that is the only reason for a crucifixion. There is not any other explanation for the cross of Christ except that sinners are lost and Jesus came to find them.

It is a sad price He paid for lost sheep on the cross.

My dear friend, are you lost tonight? Don't go away lost. You can be saved and go home happy. Jesus died to save those who are lost. "He that believeth on him is not condemned, but he that believeth not is condemned already because he hath not believed in the name of the only begotten Son of God."

If tonight you will put your trust in Jesus Christ, you will not miss Heaven. You won't find Hell waiting for you if you put your trust in Jesus Christ. You won't have to face that judgment, for all the judgment was poured on Jesus and you can have peace through the blood of His cross.

All the remorse of a guilty conscience will fade away, and that burden of your sin that piles high on your shoulders will roll away.

Are you lost tonight? Don't go away lost. Go away saved, "For the Son of man is come to seek and to save that which was lost." Oh, my friends, it will be a sad day when men go to Hell. Can you imagine what will happen when a soul dies and goes to Hell?

VI. An Old Man Who Said He Didn't Need Christ, Died Begging for More Time

A man at Decatur, Texas, went through my revival. He died there. My sister told me about it. My sister had talked to him again and again for three or four years. He was over seventy years old. He had scoffed at religion and had laughed at it, and turned it down. He had had many friends talk to him about it, but he said he didn't need it.

But he died. And when he knew he was dying, he lay there on his bed and screamed, "O God, You ought to give me more time! Lord, give me time to repent! This isn't right, Lord. I haven't had a fair chance. Give me more time!" He died screaming out that God ought to give him more time! Those lips were soon stilled. But that wasn't the end. How do you suppose that man screamed in his spirit as he went on down to Hell? Oh, can you imagine that sinner who lay in his bed and screamed and cried and knew he was lost—can you imagine that man when his lips were closed and his eyelids down and there was no heartbeat and the doctors said, "He is gone"? But it isn't the end. It isn't all ended yet. His time is done, all right, but wait.

If we could open another world and hear the screams of that

soul as he went on down lost, lost, lost, lost, lost, forever, as that man goes on down to Hell. My friends, I wish we knew about a lost soul. I think we would care more if we could know the cries of the doomed in Hell. I wish sometimes God would have let me hear the cries of the rich man as he said, "Send Lazarus, O Abraham, send Lazarus!" He knew that he couldn't get a drink. He didn't expect a drink or even just a spoonful of water, but begged that Lazarus might just "dip the tip of his finger in water and cool my tongue, for I am tormented in this flame." Oh, if we knew the facts, the events after death of people who are lost and lost forever away from God, don't you think we would do something about it for those left?

VII. Christian, Do You Care That Many Are Lost?

Near our home in Dundee, Texas, eighteen miles north near Electra, when I was a lad, they started to dig an oil well and went down 180 feet with a twelve-inch bit, took out the big bit and put in another bit. While the hole was left uncovered and the men were busy about something else, a group of little children began playing about the hole. A five-year-old boy fell feet downward into the hole. Right on down he went. The hole was narrow enough to check his fall and the fall did not kill him. He fell down the 180 feet. People could hear his screams. The salt water was slowly rising, little by little, in the well.

Somebody told his father, and the father said, "Oh, don't tell his mother! We will get him out some way!" They got some ropes together and tried to catch the little fellow, tried to get the rope around the boy, but it was dark down 180 feet and they could not do it. The father said he would go down, so they put the rope around him, but his shoulders were too broad and he couldn't get down. And they couldn't get anybody small enough to go. They tried every way to get him out.

The crowds kept coming, driving in from Iowa Park, Wichita Falls, Holiday and all round. The paper said 5,000 people gathered around that hole while a few men worked frantically to get the little boy out. But the salt water continued to rise until it covered the little boy. Finally when all hope was gone and the child was dead, they let down grap hooks which caught in the little boy's clothes and the little body, and they pulled him out.

Now dear friends, people care about a child being lost. All are glad to go for help or take somebody to a doctor or to the hospital. You would do that. But oh, my friends, souls are lost away from God.

I wonder, Brother Stroh, if you would sing with me, "Souls Are Dying"? You are dying, my poor sinner friend. You face an eternity lost, eternally doomed, when you come to die.

But Jesus died to save you and you do not need to go away lost and be forever doomed. You can be saved, "For the Son of man is come to seek and to save that which was lost." Don't you want to be saved? Get this on your heart as we sing it. If you have neighbors, do something about them while you can. The time will soon come when you can't. If you haven't wept on that boy's shoulder, I would do my weeping now. You had better do that weeping now and your crying now or you will soon be crying at the grave when you can't do anything about it. It is a whole lot better than waiting until he is buried and lost and you have no chance. Don't do like that mother who wrote me, "Oh, do you suppose he was accountable?" Her boy died and she didn't know whether he was saved. Oh, why suppose about that? It would have been a whole lot better for that mother to have done her weeping before the boy died. Do what you can now; won't you do it?

> Souls are dying, Brother, do you care?
>   Souls undone away from God,
> My Brother, do you care?
>   Souls are dying, Brother, do you care?
> Souls are dying.

Lost sinner, hear me now, and this Word of God, "What shall it profit a man if he shall gain the whole world and lose his own soul." Take the money and all of it. Take the wealth and all of it. Take the fame, take all the railroad systems—make them all yours. Take the dividends that are coming in to you, then go and walk around every bank in town for it is all yours. Go in and say, "This money is all mine. I own it all."

Walk up and down the streets of Dallas or ride in the finest car you can find and say, "Every apartment house is mine. All the rent money is mine."

Then go to Washington and say, "This nation, this government, is all mine."

Take it all—the railroads, the mountains of wealth of the world and stack it all up and pile it up. Now then, listen! What are you going to do? Will you give that for your soul and eternity away from God in Hell and in torment? Nothing but pain forever, anguish forever, torment forever? What shall a man give in exchange for his soul?

O sinners, tonight, what fools you are if you go away lost. How foolish, how deceived and darkened and misled if you go away tonight lost. I hope you won't do it.

VIII. Saved! How Sweet the Word!

This has been a very simple message. God is speaking to your heart tonight. Are you lost? Well, I wouldn't go away lost. I would be saved tonight and go home saved and happy. Saved! Saved! Isn't that a good word—Saved!

> Saved!. . saved!. .
> My sins are all pardoned, my guilt is all gone!
> Saved!. . saved!. .
> I am saved by the blood of the Crucified One!

I am saved! Wouldn't it be fine if you could go home and say, "I am saved"?

We had a street meeting in Chicago and I had a chance to give a testimony. Here is an interesting thing. A boy—I guess he was eighteen—had just been saved. Somebody had won him to Christ that day. Someone said to him, "Don't you want to give a testimony?" That eighteen-year-old boy came up and with tears in his eyes said, "Thank God, I am saved!" Then he walked away from the microphone. That was a real testimony. Saved! Saved! Saved!

Brother, be saved while you can. Lost—that is terrible! Saved—how precious! You can be saved tonight. Be saved. Don't be almost saved. Don't tonight say, "I am going to be saved." Don't put it off and say, "I expect to be saved." But say, "I WILL be saved tonight. Tonight I trust Jesus. I am saved."

Don't you want to do that? All right, you can put your trust in Jesus tonight and be saved. We are going to pray.

I want every sinner to pray.

God hears sinners when they pray about this. Somebody who has never stopped to think before, some boy or girl who has become accountable, ask yourself, "Am I lost or saved? I must get saved tonight." Oh, boy or girl, don't be lost. Turn tonight and be saved. Some man said, "I am going to be saved, and I have been planning to be all this time. Tonight I will be. I will turn to Jesus. I won't be lost. I will be saved." Don't you want to?

How many will say, "Brother Rice, I have a boy or girl who is lost, or a husband lost, or some loved one lost, away from God"? Oh, what a terrible word, Lost! Lost! Lost! Lost! How many have some loved one who is lost, away from God? (Many hands raised.) That is terrible! God forgive you. Don't you care? What a revival we would have if people could get it on their hearts so they couldn't sleep!

You say, "My brother is lost." "My husband is lost!" If we could realize what that means, that would surely be a thing that would make it so you couldn't eat so much and couldn't sleep so well. He is LOST!

Now how many will say, "Brother Rice, I am lost but I want to be saved"? We are going to have a prayer right now that God will save you, and I am going to expect Him to do it right now, as you sit there in your seat.

Will you say, "Would you pray for me?" and you pray with me in your heart? God is willing to save you. "For the Son of man is come to seek and to save that which was lost."

(One young woman, a girl in the teens, held her hand high, then threw her arms around her mother and wept. The invitation was given, this young woman was saved, then others came, a backslider, a young man saved, then some to join the church.)

29—Paupers and Wicked May Come Free!

(Preached at Fundamentalist Baptist Tabernacle, Dallas, April 24, 1938. Stenographically reported.)

Turn to Isaiah 55. Let's read several verses.

Ho, every one that thirsteth, come ye to the waters, and he that hath no money; come ye, buy, and eat; yea, come, buy wine and milk without money and without price.

Wherefore do ye spend money for that which is not bread? and your labour for that which satisfieth not? hearken diligently unto me, and eat ye that which is good, and let your soul delight itself in fatness.

Incline your ear, and come unto me: hear, and your soul shall live; and I will make an everlasting covenant with you, even the sure mercies of David. —Vss. 1-3.

* * *

Seek ye the Lord while he may be found, call ye upon him while he is near:

Let the wicked forsake his way, and the unrighteous man his thoughts: and let him return unto the Lord, and he will have mercy upon him; and to our God, for he will abundantly pardon.

For my thoughts are not your thoughts, neither are your ways my ways, saith the Lord.

For as the heavens are higher than the earth, so are my ways higher than your ways, and my thoughts than your thoughts.

How true is God's Word! How sure it is!

For as the rain cometh down, and the snow from heaven, and returneth not thither, but watereth the earth, and maketh it bring forth and bud, that it may give seed to the sower, and bread to the eater:

So shall my word be that goeth forth out of my mouth: it shall not return unto me void, but it shall accomplish that which I please, and it shall prosper in the thing whereto I sent it.

God keeps His promises. God says, "If you will do what I have said here, I will give you the joy I have promised."

For ye shall go out with joy, and be led forth with peace: the mountains and the hills shall break forth before you into singing, and all the trees of the field shall clap their hands.

*Instead of the thorn shall come up the fir tree, and instead of the brier shall come up the myrtle tree: and it shall be to the Lord for a name, for an everlasting sign that shall not be cut off.—*Vss. 6-13.

Here is God's invitation to you. Though it was written for Jews primarily, and the message is to the people of David (as you see from verses 3 to 5), and the land of Palestine which will be restored; yet the message perfectly fits sinners who come to Christ for salvation, and God intended it to be so.

I. Thirsty May Come

First of all, who is to come?

Ho, every one that thirsteth, come ye to the waters, and he that hath no money; come ye, buy, and eat; yea, come, buy wine and milk without money and without price.

The Bible has many invitations, but the sweetest is, "Come, come, come!" When Adam and Eve sinned before they were cast outside the Garden of Eden, God ran after Adam and said, "Adam, where art thou?" From that time to this, God has been running after men, seeking men, calling, calling, calling!

Robert Harkness wrote a song,

> **I heard the Saviour calling**
> **In accents sweet and low,**
> **Forever calling, calling,**
> **And yet I would not go.**

Oh, it is wonderful that God calls and calls! So here He says, "Ho, every one that thirsteth, come ye to the waters." Here is good news for you. Anybody who is thirsty can come.

There are a good many homes where they don't want to hear me tell them about God. Sinners turn a cold shoulder. There are a good many who think they have no need, no hunger; they think they have plenty of time yet. But, thank God, some places I go know they need God.

I went to talk to a man the other day who had been drinking. "How are you getting along with God?"

"Well, that's my business," he replied.

I looked him square in the eye. "It is my business, too. I love you. I mean good, and it is my business, too."

He broke down and began to cry. "If anyone ever needed help, I do," he said.

"You can get help then. God loves you." I read Isaiah 1:18 to him, "Come now, and let us reason together, saith the Lord: though your sins be as scarlet, they shall be as white as snow; though they be red like crimson, they shall be as wool."

"That doesn't mean me," he said. "That is somebody else."

"Yes, it does mean you," I said.

"No, that is for somebody else. I don't mean to say you are telling a lie. But that just isn't for me."

I said, "Yes, it is for you." I told him I would pray for him. I urged him to get right with God.

"Not when I am full of beer," he said.

I went back two days later and asked him, "How is it with you and God?"

"I believe it is fixed up," he said.

When I went to see him this afternoon, his face was shining. We had prayer. His wife was happy, and so was he. They have started to church.

It is a wonderful thing that God calls every one who is thirsty. Are you thirsty? It is the call of God. Are you hungry? "Come, " God said; "Ho, every one that thirsteth, come ye to the waters."

I am glad God calls people. He is calling you. That is good news for you if your heart is hungry. If you are dissatisfied, that is a sign God is calling. He said, "Ho, every one that thirsteth, come ye to the waters, and he that hath no money; come ye, buy, and eat; yea, come, buy wine and milk without money and without price."

He that hath no money, let him come. You go down to a place where they have a big meal served at a dollar a plate. Or if you want a bed, they want money for it. The cheapest bed you can get, even if it be a cot, and where there are all kinds of people in one room, you have to pay something for it. But the Lord says, "If there is anybody who doesn't have money, I want you, I am calling for you." That is a wonderful invitation. God wants anybody. To a man who can't buy anything, God says, "Come on, I will give it to you free." That is right down my alley; isn't it down yours? He said,

> Ho, every one that thirsteth, come ye to the waters, and he that hath no money; come ye, buy, and eat; yea, come, buy wine and milk without money and without price.

Come without money and without price, and he that hath no money, let him come. The Bible says, "Wherefore do you spend money for that which is not bread? and your labour for that which satisfieth not? hearken diligently unto me, and eat ye that which is good, and let your soul delight itself in fatness."

Perhaps life has done something to you. You never are satisfied. You never get what you want. Did you try it all and it turned out bad?

Every now and then I meet people in sadness who tried marriage but love fled away. Oh, the bitterness and the ashes when love is gone!

> The night has a thousand eyes,
>   And the day but one,
> But the light of the whole world dies
>   With the setting sun.

The mind has a thousand eyes,
And the heart but one,
But the light of the whole life dies
When love is done.

Somebody cries that love has fled away and life isn't worth living. Many a man has talked to me, many friends have told me their problems, their burdens. They say, "Now I wish I were dead. There is nothing left to live for."

In San Antonio, a poor, harlot woman came weeping. Embittered, she told me, "I didn't have to go to the dogs! When my husband quit me and said he didn't love me any longer, I didn't care whether I lived or died." After she tried sin she found that didn't satisfy. And with a broken heart she asked if God would save a woman as far gone as she was. Thank God, I could tell her He would!

Are you dissatisfied with how you have spent your money? I see the prodigal boy leave his father's home. The old man says, "Son, won't you stay here?"

"No, I want to have a big time. Give me the portion of goods that falleth to me."

And sorrowfully his father divided his living. And not many days after—he didn't stay long when he had the money—the boy went into a far country and there wasted his substance in riotous living. But when he had spent all, there arose a mighty famine in that land, and he began to be in want.

You know, God has a Gospel that is good when a famine hits. Let depressions come, I have a Gospel good for depression times. Unemployment, poverty, distress, trouble are God's opportunity. Many find a Saviour when they lose everything. You had better lose your job and have God.

Brother Matthews told about a man the other day who had gone with his family to Arizona to pick cotton from January to March in the irrigated district. "Thank God, I got down!" he said. "He put me away out here where I would be saved."

If you are dissatisfied, if you have lost friends or money, if you have lost your health, and everything else, the Lord Jesus said, "Wherefore do you spend money for that which is not bread? and your labour for that which satisfieth not? hearken diligently unto me, and eat ye that which is good, and let your soul delight itself in fatness."

I am reminded of a woman who came to me in Chicago, one of seven women rum-runners in those days, at least seven who were known to international police. She ran liquor across the border—some at Detroit, some at other places along the Canadian border, some at Juarez, Mexico. This young woman heard me preach. I announced I would preach on "Whiskey-Prescribing Doctors and Druggists, Wet Politicians and Bootlegging Skunks." As I announced what I would do to that bunch, suddenly in the midst of the service, weeping, she got up and went away. But she came back to hear me later on, and waited to see me. "I went to Detroit in my car to get a load of booze. I got a load, but, every turn of the wheel, something kept saying to me, 'That man is right. You are nothing but a lousy bootlegging skunk.' "

She searched her heart, and God dealt with her. For hours she talked to me. She turned over that liquor, quit the business and came to God. But this is what she said: "That is right, that is all I am, nothing but a lousy bootlegging skunk. I haven't a friend but what I bought. If there came a time when I needed one, I wouldn't know anybody I could trust. I have worn my fur coats, have had nice cars, have bribed the police officers to get by, but I can't trust anybody. I haven't a friend I didn't buy, and friends you buy are not worth having! You don't have anything. You have spent your money for that which satisfieth not."

She went into a drugstore and timidly bought a fifty-cent Bible. Someway she found the sixteenth chapter of Acts and was saved.

You have gone out and been dissatisfied, deceived, disillusioned. If your heart is empty, if you tonight need something you don't have, something to bring joy, something to make life worth living, I have the message you need. You can have peace for your heart, forgiveness for your sins, bread that will satisfy.

Ho, every one that thirsteth, come ye to the waters, and he that hath no money; come ye, buy, and eat; yea, come, buy wine and milk without money and without price.

Come while you can.

II. The Woman Who Wished She Were Dead

A woman came to me at Shamrock, Texas. She had said to a friend, "I wish I were dead. I am not fit to live, and I am not having any peace. I wish I were dead."

Her friend said, "Don't say that. That is wicked."

"But it is so," the woman told her.

"Well," her friend said, "let's go see Brother Rice."

The woman broke down in my front room as she told me, "I am a member of a country club set. I attend the dance-and-card parties." Then she told how she had lived a life of pleasure; she had tried everything. Then she said, "If that is all there is to life, I wish it were done. It is a failure. I wish it were over. I wish I were dead. I have thought about committing suicide. If this is all there is to life, I have had too much of it."

"But that is not all there is to life," I told her.

"Is there any way for a person to have peace and joy and a life worth living?"

"Yes, there is."

"How can I get it?" she asked.

"Get down on your knees right here and tell God that your life has been a failure, that you are a sinner and want forgiveness, that you want peace. He has it for you."

She did, weeping as she prayed. I prayed, her friend prayed, and she found the peace she wanted.

Sin doesn't satisfy, but Jesus does!

A poor, fallen woman called my home one November night about eleven o'clock. We had already gone to bed. She and her friend wanted me to pray for them. They came just before midnight. After they came, we prayed. I said to her, "Turn your back on sin. It does not satisfy. It will only bring a burning memory, it will only bring heartache."

"Don't I know it!" she said. "Why do you think I get drunk? I am trying to drown it all, forget it all."

"If you are dissatisfied, if you have spent your money for that which is not bread and your labor for that which satisfies not, then hearken diligently to Me," the Lord said. Hear and your soul shall live. "Incline your ear," the Lord said, "and come unto me; hear, and your soul shall live."

God has a message for those who are dissatisfied and hungry. God has a message for those who have tried the world but found it wanting. God has a message for those who have tried the primrose path but found it thorny. God has a message for those who have drunk the cup of pleasure but found in the bottom dregs. God has a message for the folks who have tried Satan's way and have learned that the way of the transgressor is hard. God says, "Come on and buy it for nothing. It is free. You don't have to have money. You can't buy it, but I will give it free." Every one who is thirsty is urged to come. If you are thirsty tonight, hear God's message for you.

III. Sinners Must Hear to Be Saved

The first thing to do is to hear. Here it is: "Hearken diligently unto me." I hope you will listen tonight. I wish some way I could chain your attention so you would let these words sink down in your ears. I wish you would say, "I will remember every word that preacher says." I wish you would wake up and listen to God speak to your soul. "Hearken diligently," "incline your ear."

People have an idea that preachers ought to hold their attention, even Christian people, church people. No, you ought to come and listen so earnestly that any message out of God's Word would be sweet. It shouldn't have to be illustrated and made interesting to hold your attention. You ought to set your attention on God.

My sinner friend, if you are unsaved, you had better incline your ear and hear, turn your ear toward God. You had better seek God instead of waiting for God to seek you. He has been running after you a long time; now you had better run after Him. "Hearken diligently unto me."

Oh, of all the sins that send people to Hell, I think on this one thing more people go to Hell: You won't hear! You won't hear!

That is what the Saviour said, too. A sower went forth to sow, and some seed fell on hard ground and the birds picked it up and carried it away. Satan takes the Gospel out of people's hearts.

That is the reason Hebrews, chapter 2, said that "we ought to give the more earnest heed to the things which we have heard, lest at any time we should let them slip." Let me read that again. "We ought to give the more earnest heed to the things which we have heard, lest at any time we should let them slip." If you would give more earnest heed, you could be saved.

Preachers ought to demand attention and expect attention. That is the reason I so insist that nobody talk while I am talking, that there be no carelessness. It is a sin not to listen. You sin against God and against your own soul when you do not listen to God's message. God has a blessing for you if you will sit up and listen when you go to church. And you should have the children listen. You are lost and dying, you are going to Hell unless you turn your ear toward God. God has a message for you. He is calling you. He is pleading for you to turn back to Him and find Him while you can. "Hearken diligently unto me."

My friends, preaching is work for me, and listening ought to be work for you. Get the Scripture references and put them down. You won't remember them if you do not put them down in a notebook. Then feast on them; go back over them. God said to. You will learn something for your soul.

Oh, this preaching to people when the Gospel is shed off like water off a duck's back! I have sometimes wished I could go to Africa where they have never heard the Gospel, where they never knew that One loved them and died for them. I could tell them that God loved them, that Christ died for them and their eyes would burn and their hearts would be open.

Oh, you who are Gospel-hardened, you who have heard it so long! You had better learn to listen, for, "we ought to give the more earnest heed to the things which we have heard, lest at any time we should let them slip."

Is there somebody here tonight who doesn't want to go to Hell? Do you say, "I don't want to go to Hell. I don't want to burn in torment. I don't want to be forever away from God"?

Then turn and hear the Word of God. "Hearken diligently unto me," He said, "and eat ye that which is good, and let your soul delight itself in fatness. Incline your ear, and come unto me: hear, and your soul shall live." Turn your ear toward God!

There is a still, small voice tonight that calls. If you do not hear it, then your ear isn't turned toward God. The Holy Spirit speaks tonight. I feel His presence. Don't you?

If you will not hear God speak, it is because of a wicked heart. Your dull ear is turned away from God. You won't let God speak to your heart. God is calling all right. He is calling you today! He wants you today! You had better listen to Him. Poor sinner, hearken diligently. You can be saved today—now—if in your heart you will trust Him. If you will listen, He will speak and show you the rest of the way.

People are lost forever who will not listen to God. People who do not turn and hear the Word of God go to Hell. The first thing is to hear.

IV. "Seek Ye the Lord While He May Be Found"

What is next? "Seek ye the Lord," verse 6 says. Notice the Scripture says, "Seek God." When my father started out in revivals a good many years ago he had a "seeker's" seat, a bench for seekers. When he would start a revival meeting, he would say, "Those who would like to be saved in this revival, come and take this seat." And they would come and take the first or second seat as seekers. Folks who seek God can find Him. "Seek ye the Lord while he may be found, call ye upon him while he is near."

You hear me and you are not a Christian. If you go to Hell, it will not be God's fault. It is not God's move, it is not His turn. God hasn't wronged you. God hasn't sinned against you. He doesn't need to run you down. It is your move to seek God. You went against God, you ignored Him, you went headlong into sin. You wouldn't listen when God called. It is your move. If you do not seek God, you are going to Hell. You are doomed and lost. Oh, tonight I would seek God.

Seek ye the Lord while he may be found, call ye upon him while he is near.

There are two meanings in that verse. One is, He may be found. I am glad He is near. He is not far off. The prodigal boy went into a far country, and when he came to himself he said, "I will arise and go to my father." I used to preach that it was a long way home, until I found one day that that wasn't in the Bible. Just turn around and He is there. The Bible just says, "And he arose and came to his Father." It doesn't say how far it was. It wasn't far when he made up his mind, when his pride was buried, when he got hungry enough. And the Father ran to meet him.

Listen, my friend, God is near. He could be found today. Aren't you glad He is near? God isn't a long way off. He is near. He sent His Son to die for us. His Spirit is here now. The Holy Spirit is knocking at the door of your heart now. He says, "Behold, I stand at the door, and knock: if any man hear my voice, and open the door, I will come in to him, and will sup with him, and he with me."

Do you hear? You can find Him if you want to. He is near.

Seek ye the Lord while he may be found, call ye upon him while he is near.

I am so glad God has times of refreshing when God's Spirit moves. I want us to have a great revival here—a revival in the hearts and homes. Last Wednesday night about eight people got up to say they had had somebody saved in the few days before that. God has given us a moving of the Spirit for revival. Sinner, if you are hungry, you can seek the Lord and find Him, for He is right at your fingertips. Oh, call upon Him! Trust Him!

The next thing about seeking the Lord is this: There comes a time when you can't find Him. I know Satan will tell you, "Anytime will do," or, "Some other time is just as good," but that isn't true. There will come a time when you can't find God. Your heart will be too hardened or you will be too busy about something else.

I will never forget when a Methodist preacher came to hold a revival meeting in a town where I lived when I was a boy. He told about an old man who had gone far in sin, and after he was on his deathbed and about to die, he sent for the preacher. The preacher came to talk to him about his soul. When the preacher came in, they told him this man was out of his head, he was not conscious. This dying man was in a delirium, and he began to scream out, "Get out of my apple trees! Get out of my apple trees! I will have the police on you! Get out of my orchard!" He was delirious and he thought the boys were in his apple trees. The preacher tried to win him to Christ and said, "I am the Methodist pastor. I want to show you how to be saved." But the man cried out, "Get out of my apple trees!" The poor man died like that.

There is a time when it is too late to find God. There is a time when you can't find God. You may commit the unpardonable sin, or you may harden your heart, or you may go on until death saying, "There is always time enough to pray." There is not always time enough to pray, not time enough to repent, not time enough to find God, not time enough to read the Bible! You had better seek God while He may be found.

Someone says, "Brother Rice, the thief on the cross was saved at the dying hour." Yes, but that is only half true. You say the thief was saved at the dying hour, but which thief? There were two thieves there. One was not saved. He had the same opportunity as did the other. It is recorded that one thief was saved so that we might know that God has mercy. But it is also recorded that the other thief died and went to Hell so that we might not presume on that mercy. There will come a time when God can't be found. If you are not saved, then seek God today while He may be found.

I will give you this heartening word: If you want Him, you can find Him. If your heart reaches out toward God, He will reach out to you. The Father ran to meet His prodigal son.

Sinner, tonight if you will start out toward home, you can find Him.

Seek ye the Lord while he may be found.

V. "Call Ye Upon Him While He Is Near"

What else should sinners do? The next thing is to call on Him while He is near.

You say, "Can a sinner pray?" Yes, sinners can pray. "Will God hear a sinner pray?" Yes, a good many Scriptures tell us that God heard sinners pray. The poor, dying thief said, "Lord, remember me when thou comest into thy kingdom." And Jesus said, "To day shalt thou be with me in paradise." God did remember him.

The publican in the Temple prayed, "Lord, be merciful to me a sinner." And God did have mercy. Didn't Jesus tell us that he was justified? That sinner's prayer was heard.

I remember when my heart cried out to God and God forgave me and saved me. The 10th chapter of Romans says, "For whosoever shall call upon the name of the Lord shall be saved." I don't say you have to get down on your knees to be saved. I don't say you have to say words out loud to be saved. But God does say that anybody whose heart calls on God for mercy can get mercy.

Seek ye the Lord while he he may be found, call ye upon him while he is near.

Maybe you can't do it if you wait until some other time, but you can do it now. While He is near, call on the Lord. If I were a lost sinner, I would just say so: "O Lord, I am a sinner." Do you know what the prodigal boy said? "Father, I have sinned against heaven and in thy sight, and am no more worthy to be called thy son." Oh, you can turn now and call and God will hear. You can ask for mercy and get mercy. You can ask for forgiveness and get forgiveness.

An old song we used to sing says,

> **I will arise and go to Jesus,**
> **He will embrace me in His arms.**
> **In the arms of my dear Saviour**
> **Oh, there are ten thousand charms.**
>
> **Let not conscience make you linger,**
> **Nor of fitness fondly dream;**
> **All the fitness He requireth**
> **Is to feel your need of Him.**

Won't you call tonight while God is near? Won't you ask God to save you?

I will never forget one old man to whom I had said, "Are you a Christian?" and who answered, "I have been superintendent of a Sunday school."

"But that isn't what I asked. Have you been born again?"

"I haven't done anything wrong but curse a little."

"But that is not the question. You had as well say, 'I have just killed a few men now and then.' Have you really been converted and had a change of heart?"

Very seriously he said, "I guess I never did."

"Don't you think you had better get it then?"

"I guess I had."

He came down the aisle and kneeled at the front. That was in the first revival I ever held. He knelt on the straw and raised his old grisled face, lifted his hands and said, "O God, if You will save me, I will do anything You want me to do!" God did save him!

Call on the Lord. God is ready to save. He hears the cry of saints and He hears the cry of sinners who want forgiveness and mercy.

If you want it tonight, then come and get it. There is forgiveness and salvation for "whosoever shall call upon the name of the Lord shall be saved." It is for you, my brother. God has been calling you long enough. It is your time to call on God. If you call, He will forgive and save you. I hope you will trust Him now.

VI. "Let the Wicked Forsake His Way"

What else besides hear, and see, and call? Forsake your way. Turn your back on your sins.

> Let the wicked forsake his way, and the unrighteous man his thoughts: and let him return unto the Lord, and he will have mercy upon him; and to our God, for he will abundantly pardon.

He will! He will if you will but forsake your way. "Let the wicked forsake his way." I know God has terms that you don't like to meet, but those terms fit you. God's Word just says, "Let the *wicked* . . ."—you and me. But you say, "I am not wicked."

You are wicked enough to go to Hell. You are a sinner and you know it. You may be a nicely-dressed wicked person, but you are wicked. You may be moral, but you are wicked. You have a rotten heart inside. You are lost, condemned unless you get a change of heart. You need it now. "Let the wicked forsake his way."

Do you know what is taking you away from God? Why you are lost? Your own way—that is the trouble. "There is a way that seemeth right unto a man, but the end thereof are the ways of death."

Your own way. Do you know what sin is? Here is what sin is: "All we like sheep have gone astray; we have turned every one TO HIS OWN WAY"; that is what is wrong. Here is the sin and the condemnation. You have your own way, and therein is destruction and ruin. You need to say, "O Lord, take me. Let me not have my way, but Yours."

I said to a man this afternoon, the man I mentioned awhile ago, "You need to let Jesus have His way now."

"I have learned sure enough that my way doesn't bring anything but trouble," he said.

So it does bring trouble now, and it brings a smarting conscience and remorse and a wasted life. And it brings ruin after awhile. Your way will lead you to Hell. It is the broad way. If you are ever going to be saved, turn your back on your own way.

You say, "I can't ever be perfect."

I know, but turn your heart toward God and say, "Lord, I am sorry. I am a sinner." You can turn your heart toward God and away from your sin. That is what you will have to do in the heart. Every man must forsake his way and forsake his sins. If you do not do that, you are condemned, lost, away from God. You will never be saved without in your heart turning to God. That is repentance. Repent, repent, repent! Jesus said, "Except ye repent, ye shall all likewise perish" (Luke 13:3). God is "not willing that any should perish, but that all should come to repentance" (II Pet. 3:9). Paul said, "God . . . commandeth all men every where to repent" (Acts 17:30). To repent means to turn your heart to God, to change your mind about sin, about God, to forsake your way. I couldn't altogether agree with Sam Jones when he said, "Repentance means to quit your meanness." You might quit your meanness outwardly and still not be saved. Inwardly you must turn your heart from sin. It means you have to turn to God, and repenting of your sins would be trusting in Christ, and so you would be saved.

That isn't all. One must forsake his thoughts. "Let the wicked forsake his way, and the unrighteous man his thoughts."

Every man here has a way to be saved. Your thoughts are wrong. "I have not done anything so very bad," you say. What you mean is, "I have just about gotten myself saved" or "I am a pretty good fellow," or "I am a member of a lodge," or "I live up to my obligations," or "I take care of my family," or "I don't do anybody any harm," or "I do the best I know how," or "I live up to the Golden Rule."

Well, give up your way and your thoughts about salvation, because you are not going to be saved your way. Just say, "All right, Lord, any way You save me, I will take and be grateful. Lord, here I am. You save me Your way."

Many times people have said to me, "No, sir. If I don't feel a certain way, I will not do it."

One woman I tried to win at Allen, Texas, said, "If I do not shout like my mother shouted, I am not going to do it." I said, "If you set your heart on your own way, you will go to Hell." You can't lay down the law to God. If you are ever saved, you will have to say, "Lord, save me Your way, not mine."

Old Saul of Tarsus was on the road down to Damascus. There came a light from Heaven, and he fell on his face, and a voice said, "Saul, Saul, why persecutest thou me?" And he said, "Who art thou, Lord?" And the answer came back, "I am Jesus whom thou persecutest." Then old Saul gave up the whole thing and said, "Lord, what wilt Thou have me to do? I have been going my way; now what is Your way?"

And if you want to be saved and will turn your back on your way and take His way and trust Him, He will do the rest of it.

VII. "Return Unto the Lord"

One more word about it, and that is this?

Let the wicked forsake his way, and the unrighteous man his thoughts: and let him return unto the Lord, and he will have mercy upon him; and to our God, for he will abundantly pardon.

Doesn't that sound easy? It is when a man is seeking God, and has turned his ear toward God, and has called for God, and has forsaken his own way and given up all his plans, then let him return to the Lord, and the door will be open when he gets there. You don't have to argue with God after you turn your heart away from sin, when you have said, "Lord, not my way—my way is wrong—show me Your way. I haven't any plans left, I haven't any way of my own." Then just turn back to God.

Will you forsake your way?

"And the unrighteous man his thoughts." Are you willing to give up your plans and tell God so, and return to the Lord? He will abundantly pardon.

In your heart of hearts, will you say, "Lord, I am tired of sin. It doesn't satisfy. Just forgive me and save me"? If you trust it to Him, He will! He will! He will!

I remember one summer when I had just started out in soul winning. I was leading the singing in a revival. I didn't know much Scripture, but what I did know, I believed. I had found these two verses. So one summer I counted more than sixty people who trusted Christ as I held my finger on these verses. I said it about this way:

"The Bible says, 'Let the wicked forsake his way.' Will you turn your heart away from your sins and let Him show you how to be saved?"

"Yes."

"Well, that is repentance." (I don't divide it up that way now so much.)

"And the next thing is to return to the Lord. Are you willing to believe what He says and take Him up on His promises?"

"Yes, I am."

"All right, what does He say?"

"He says He will give mercy, and abundantly pardon."
"Do you believe He will do it?"
"Yes."
"Will you take Him up on that right now?"
"Yes."
"And will you turn from sin and trust Christ?"
"Yes, I will."

More than sixty people in one summer tried God out on that precious promise in those two verses.

VIII. The Joy That Follows Salvation

My friends, you can turn and get abundant pardon. Yes, *abundant* pardon. He will have mercy upon you, and He will *abundantly* pardon. That is what you need. I would look to Him and get it tonight. If you are thirsty, or dissatisfied, then incline your ear to God, forsake your way, seek Him, call on Him, forsake your thoughts and return to Him, and you will be saved.

"But I want joy," you say. I know, but you are ahead of the hounds. Look on down in the last of that chapter, at verse 12:

> *For ye shall go out with joy, and be led forth with peace: the mountains and the hills shall break forth before you into singing, and all the trees of the field shall clap their hands.*

You shall go out with joy! You are not supposed to get joy until you get salvation. You get the joy of salvation after you get the salvation. You can't expect to *feel* right until you *get* right. You can't expect to feel well until you call a doctor and turn your case over to him.

"For ye shall go out with joy, and be led forth with peace." Isn't that sweet? Salvation, then joy, and then settled peace that stays there! Then the mountains and hills shall break forth before you into singing, and all the trees of the field shall clap their hands. Isn't it fine that after you are saved the flowers smell sweeter, the birds sing louder, and all the trees seem like they are clapping their hands? That is because a sinner is saved.

What else? You will have joy and peace, and, "Instead of the thorn shall come up the fir tree, and instead of the brier shall come up the myrtle tree: and it shall be to the Lord for a name, for an everlasting sign that shall not be cut off."

Oh, it is sweet. That old barren life will begin to bring forth fruit after you are saved. It is sweet after you are saved. Instead of drunkenness will come soberness. Instead of quarreling will come peace. Instead of the Devil's works will come works of God and love for God, with the Holy Spirit dwelling within you. God brings peace. Peace like a river flows for you after you trust Him.

Friend, you take Him at His word. Seek Him today while He may be found. "Let the wicked forsake his way and the unrighteous man his thoughts, and let him return unto the Lord and he will have mercy upon him: and to our God, for he will abundantly pardon."

And more good news is promised. Like the rain comes down from Heaven and waters the earth and makes it bring forth fruit, so God's Word is just as truly from Heaven. If you believe it, it will bring forth the fruit of righteousness in your heart now. Won't you say, "Lord, I will take You up on that; I will do it now"? If you will, you will have peace.

Let us have an understanding. I am not talking about whether or not you join a church. If there is someone who doesn't know you are saved, I would make sure now and get it forever settled. You have inclined your ear, haven't you? Will you say in your heart, "Lord Jesus, I will turn my back on sin. I will give up my way. I will take Your way. I will come to You for that mercy and pardon, and take it and be saved. I want You to give me joy and bring up fruits of righteousness instead of the thorny tree. I will risk You for the peace and fruit, and here I come"?

In your heart trust Him. Will you take Christ now and turn your heart to God? Will you do that?

"Ho, everyone that thirsteth, come ye to the waters." Will you do it? Will you call on Him?

Do you want peace and forgiveness? Do you want to be on God's side? Do you want to be saved? If you do, then, you pray in your heart and forsake your way, ask God to save you and He will. Then won't you write and let me know?